DATE DUE			

OLD MEN DRUNK AND SOBER

OLD MEN DRUNK AND SOBER

HOWARD M. BAHR

Department of Sociology
Brigham Young University

THEODORE CAPLOW

Department of Sociology
University of Virginia

New York: NEW YORK UNIVERSITY PRESS 1973

Photographs by Jacob A. Riis are reproduced with the permission of the Jacob A. Riis Collection, Museum of the City of New York.

Photographs by Robert F. Crawford are reproduced with the permission of the photographer.

Library of Congress Catalog Card Number: 72-96370
ISBN: 0-8147-0965-6
Manufactured in the United States of America

PREFACE

This book reports the results obtained in the first six years of the Columbia Bowery Project, a study of homelessness and disaffiliation which is still underway, although both authors have left Columbia University and the focus of the study has widened to include disaffiliated women, old people in rest homes, and some other groups only indirectly related to the population we originally set out to study.

The Columbia Bowery Project began early in 1963 through the good offices of Dr. Lawrence R. Podell, then director of research for the New York City Welfare Department, who arranged a meeting between Theodore Caplow and Morris Chase, the experienced welfare administrator responsible for the organization of Operation Bowery within the Welfare Department. Operation Bowery was designed to improve and expand the services offered to homeless men by the Welfare Department and to explore the possibility of restoring some of them to health, full-time employment, and a normal place in the community. Chase was quick to see the opportuntiy offered to this enterprise by the research facilities of Columbia's Bureau of Applied Social Research and Caplow's experience in skid row studies. (It is pleasant to report that these expectations were largely fulfilled in the later successes of Operation Bowery.)

This meeting led to a contract whereby Columbia University, acting through its Bureau of Applied Social Research, agreed "to conduct a detailed study of the permanent and transient population in the Bowery area of the borough of Manhattan, City of New York, of their institutional arrangements, and of the current trends by which they are affected." The study was to be directed to a determination of the elements of a workable program for the rehabilitation of the homeless population of the Bowery area and was, according to the contract, to "make use of a variety of research methods including ecological analysis, direct enumeration, life history interviews, review of social agency records, participant observation, and situational experiment." As it turned out, all of these methods were actually used, but the life-history interviews became the major source of data.

The contract covered an appropriation of funds for a fifteen-month pilot study and explicitly provided that the execution of two later phases of the research would be contingent upon the success of an application for federal research funds to be prepared by the project staff. A three-year grant for the principal phase of the project, which was titled "Homelessness: Its Etiology, Patterns, and Consequences," was obtained from the Public Health Service in April 1965 and supported the Bowery Project until 1968, when another three-year grant from the National Institute of Mental Health for the study of disaffiliated urban women carried the investigation beyond the population with which this report is concerned.

Theodore Caplow acted as principal investigator throughout the study. Samuel E. Wallace was project director from November 1963 until January 1965, when he was succeeded by Howard M. Bahr, who directed the project for the entire duration of the two federal grants. The following men and women participated in the project as research associates: Michael A. Baker,* Martha L. Gershun,* Stanley K. Henshaw,* Stephen J. Langfur,* B. Luise Margolies,* George Nash,* Pat Nash,* Richard Riday,* Nan Markel Sigal,* and David Sternberg. Those whose names are starred in the foregoing list authored or coauthored one or more of the project's previously published reports. We have drawn heavily on some of these papers and monographs in the preparation of the present manuscript and acknowledge the courtesy of the following copyright holders in permitting the reproduction of excerpts from previous publications: University of Toronto Press, Journal of Studies on Alcohol, Inc., University of North Carolina Press, Southwestern Social Science Association, American Sociological Association, and the Society for the Study of Social Problems.

Interviewing and research assistance was given by Stewart Brownstein, Miguel DeTorres, George Eisen, Matthew Flickstein, Myron Freir, Howard Fuchs, Alan Furst, Abraham Geleibter, Larry Goldstein, Douglas Good, William B. Helmreich, Howard Honigman, Richard E. Kaplan, Elaine Klinker, Andrew J. Lewis, Joel Mason, Gerald Sachs, Julian Svedosh, and Martin Weiss. Coding and bibliographic assistance was given by Stephen Alicia, Harry E. Conklin,

N. Jefferson Garrett, J. Edward Hawco, Ran Hirsch, Joel A. Linsider, Manuel R. Llorca, Arthur Nealon, Vincent Pafumi, Orlando Rodriguez, Diane Villani, and Michael Wild.

The Bowery Project was fortunate in its secretarial and clerical corps. They were capable, cheerful, and hardworking beyond ordinary expectation, and we wish to express our sincere appreciation to Beverlee Bandell, Ann H. Calderwood, Sandra J. Hinkle, Nancy McCarthy, and Judith Price. We are especially indebted to Marcia J. Cebulski and Rita Aronow, who served both as research analysts and project secretaries.

The work reported here would have been quite impossible without the unceasing support and cooperation of Allen Barton, director of the Bureau of Applied Social Research, and of Clara Shapiro and Phyllis Sheridan, administrators of the same organization.

The final preparation of the manuscript was supported, in part, by Project 1960, Department of Rural Sociology, Agriculture Research Center, College of Agriculture, Washington State University.

The other persons who have borne a helpful hand, directly or indirectly with this work, are too numerous to mention, but we cannot close the list of those to whom we are obligated without expressing unstinted gratitude to the hundreds of homeless men and residents of the Park Slope and Park Avenue tracts who submitted to long and searching interviews with patience and good humor.

Howard M. Bahr
Theodore Caplow

CONTENTS

PART 2: The Lifetime Experience of Homeless and Settled Men

APPENDICES

PART I

A STUDY OF HOMELESS MEN IN NEW YORK CITY

CHAPTER 1

THE PROJECT AND ITS METHODS

This volume reports the principal findings of a sociological study carried out at Columbia University from 1963 to 1968. The drunk and sober old men who were the subjects of this study lived on the New York City Bowery, or if they belonged to one of our three control samples, they were inmates of Camp LaGuardia, lived in a decayed Brooklyn neighborhood called Park Slope, or enjoyed the luxury of Park Avenue apartments. The three control samples enabled us to compare the old men of the Bowery with other old men living in the same metropolis at the same time who resembled them in some ways and differed from them in others. The Camp LaGuardia men were homeless but temporarily sober. The Park Slope men were extremely poor and often drunk but not homeless. The Park Avenue men were not poor, homeless, or abstinent.

We made some use of nearly every research method known to modern sociology. Participant observation was particularly important in the early stages of the project when eager research assistants roamed the streets of lower Manhattan at all hours in various disguises. An annual census of the Bowery district was taken. Archival data, statistical analysis, case studies, detached observation, questionnaires, and sociometric instruments all figured in the repertory. But life-history interviews were our most important sources of information. The long interview form reproduced in Appendix III was the product of many months of experimentation and revision. We have considerable evidence, which will be submitted in due course, for its usefulness and reliability. Data from the life-history interview enabled us to trace the lifetime career of each individual in the four samples with respect to each major sector of social affiliation—family, school, work, religion, politics, and voluntary associations. Using this form, we interviewed 203 men on the Bowery, 199 in Camp LaGuardia, 125 in Park Slope, and 104 on Park Avenue. The interviews did not completely explain how each man came to be where he is now and what he is now, but they did illuminate some of the reasons for isolation and affiliation.

PURPOSE OF THE RESEARCH

The explicit purpose of the research was to extend knowledge of the causes and consequences of homelessness by analyzing the life histories of homeless men in the light of contemporary sociological theory. As thus defined, it had some relevance both to sociological theory and to practical policy. With respect to theory, we hoped to clarify the relationship between homelessness and affiliation on the one hand and between homelessness and other deviant life styles on the other. With respect to practical policy, we hoped to provide a body of information about homeless men that would be useful to the public and private agencies responsible for rehabilitating, supporting, repressing, and protecting them.

This rather broad purpose was translated into a list of objectives which, taken together, constituted the project's working assignment:

1. to enumerate and describe the Bowery population
2. to devise forms for obtaining life-history data from homeless men
3. to describe the process whereby men become homeless and evaluate previously proposed theoretical models of this process
4. to compare homeless men in various institutional settings
5. to evaluate the effect of these settings on their life situations
6. to compare the population of homeless men to one or more populations of settled men
7. to examine the part played by various types of social affiliation in the careers of homeless men
8. to ascertain the attitudes of homeless men toward their past and present careers and their expectations for the future

9. to evaluate the relationship between homelessness and parallel forms of deviance, particularly alcoholism, downward mobility, alienation, and anomie

THE CONCEPTS OF HOMELESSNESS AND DISAFFILIATION

As sociologists approaching a field of investigation, we did not, of course, come with blank minds but had certain preliminary ideas about how to organize our inquiry and arrange the information we would gather. These preliminary ideas included a tentative sequence of procedures something like this: (1) identify homelessness as the salient social characteristic of the men we would find and interview on the Bowery, (2) define homelessness in terms of disaffiliation, (3) identify the principal types of affiliation that ought to be taken into account in individual careers, (4) propose appropriate indicators for each type of affiliation. This sequence is more or less arbitrary since there is no way of demonstrating that homelessness and disaffiliation are the best of all possible concepts for describing these men and their situations. The initial choice of concepts can only be justified retroactively by showing how our understanding of what we have studied was augmented by the theoretical model we chose. This model may be briefly summarized as follows.[1]

Degrees of homelessness. Homelessness is a condition of detachment from society characterized by the absence or attenuation of the affiliative bonds that link settled persons to a network of interconnected social structures. Homelessness takes many forms, depending on the type of detachment involved and the local circumstances. Homeless men (as well as homeless women and homeless families) appear, so far as can be determined, in all large-scale societies.

Homeless men fall into many categories: single men in itinerant occupations, migratory laborers, vagrants and beggars, religious mendicants, outlaws and other fugitives, hoboes and derelicts. Homelessness seems to be a matter of degree, ranging from temporary to permanent and from the loss of a single affiliation to the absence of all affiliations. Itinerant workers, sailors and peddlers, for example, retain many of their affiliations; they are only as homeless as their mobility forces them to be. Religious mendicants, by contrast, give up multiple affiliations in favor of a single, predominant affiliation. At the end of the scale, the modern skid row man demonstrates the possibility of nearly total detachment from society.

Homelessness as a syndrome. In general, homeless persons are poor, anomic, inert, and irresponsible. They command no resources, enjoy no esteem, and assume no burden of reciprocal obligations. Social action, in the usual sense, is almost impossible for them. Lacking organizational status and roles, their sphere of activity extends no further than the provision of personal necessities on a meager scale. Their decisions have no implications for others. Only the simplest forms of concerted action are open to them since homelessness is incompatible with sustained involvement in a complex division of labor.

The observable behavior of the homeless person consists largely of activities that furnish subsistence or enjoyment without incurring responsibilities: mendicancy, petty crime, scavenging, casual conversation, and an incurious attention at spectacles. His social inertness renders him both innocuous and helpless. He is unlikely to engage in major crime or in a political movement or to protest forcefully on his own behalf. He is sometimes apathetic about self-preservation. Homeless persons in great cities and in refugee camps stand by and watch their companions assaulted by strangers without offering to interfere and without taking any measures to protect themselves. The combined effects of poor nutrition, exposure to the elements, neglect of injuries and illness, and insensitivity to emergencies lead to very high rates of morbidity and mortality in a homeless population compared to the settled population around them.

The homeless versus the settled. For reasons not entirely understood, the presence of a homeless population often arouses a degree of hostility in a settled population that seems entirely disproportionate. Ancient ballads preserve the image of the gypsy as rapist and kidnapper. Being homeless or vagrant became a felony in England in the fourteenth century and a capital crime under the Tudors; it is still treated as a criminal offense in many American and European cities. These reactions further separate the homeless man from his settled neighbor. Homeless populations often develop a special argot, secret signs, and a conventional distrust of outsiders; such habits have led imaginative observers to envision entire clandestine social systems, the Kingdom of Beggars or the Hobo Republic, but on closer view, these fantasies disappear and reveal the homeless population as an aggregate of unrelated individuals who share a common situation and some elements of a common culture.

A theory of homelessness. The term *home,* along with its special connotations of warmth, safety, and emotional dependence, expresses the idea of a fixed place of residence shared with a limited number of other persons. In current usage, a home does not imply a family (unrelated persons can make a home together), a household (a rest home may be much larger than a household), more than moderate fixity (in any given year, more than one in five U.S. families moves to a new home), or exclusivity (a special body of tax law covers taxpayers with two or more homes). Living outside a family and with no permanent address does not make a priest or a soldier homeless, but the man who occupies the same lodging on skid row for forty uninterrupted years is properly considered homeless. The essence of the concept goes beyond residential arrangements. Homelessness is best visualized as a relationship to society at large and best understood by examining the difference between the settled and the homeless.

A settled, active adult in any society participates simultaneously in several major types of organizations. This participation anchors him in the social structure by linkages with near and distant kin, neighbors, friends, compatriots, superiors and subordinates, colleagues, co-workers, departed ancestors, sacred and supernatural personages, people with the same interests, and even those who like to play the same games. Each of these memberships involves duties and privileges, restraints and rights, status and roles. Each requires sustained interaction with particular other persons who enter into the subject's life history and become part of the audience for his socially meaningful acts.

The pattern of such affiliations varies in detail from one time and place to another, but its general shape remains unchanged. In modernized countries of the twentieth century, the individual's attachment to society seems to involve six major types of affiliative bonds: family, school, work, religion, politics, and recreation. Taken together, these affiliations define who the settled person is, how he schedules his days and his years, the benefits he may claim from the social order and the duties he owes to it. Above all, they identify the other persons who are influenced by him and define the extent of their influence.

The fully homeless man is unaffiliated in all six sectors. He is not an active member of any organization and therefore has no enforceable responsibilities toward fellow members, no audience of persons influenced by his actions, no claim on social rewards beyond whatever minimum avoids the scandal of his starvation, and no duties to fulfill except those imposed as a condition of his remaining in a given territory. Clearly, this condition will be uncomfortable and sometimes dangerous. On the other hand, it may be attractive to those who reject both the goals of the larger society and the means of achieving them.

AN OVERVIEW OF SKID ROW

Skid row is the generic name of a type of district that appeared in all sizeable American cities about a hundred years ago and is now gradually disappearing from most of them.[2] The name seems to be derived from Skid Road in Seattle—a skidway which carried felled timber down to the water and attracted a settlement of itinerant lumberjacks and laborers—and apparently came into wider use because of its connotation of downward mobility. Several of the larger and more important skid rows, like the Bowery, have distinctive names of their own.

In midwestern and western cities, skid row almost invariably developed near the central cluster of railroad yards and freight terminals in obsolescent structures that had once been part of the central business district. The first lodging houses were open dormitories, sometimes with double or triple deck bunks, occasionally with hammocks, some providing no better beds than a wooden floor. In the wake of various reform movements these primitive facilities were considerably improved by the conversion of lofts into the cubicle type of lodging house and eventually by the construction of new buildings offering small single rooms.

Close to the lodging houses appeared the other characteristic establishments of skid row—cheap restaurants and bars, evangelical missions, soup kitchens, all-night theaters, barber colleges, second-hand stores, pawn shops, flea markets, public reading rooms, and various places of outdoor assembly. The number and scale of these institutions waxed and waned with the homeless population. The Bowery had more than a hundred lodging houses around 1900 compared to fewer than 30 today, and it no longer boasts a single all-night theater or barber college.

During the century of their existence,[3] skid row districts have sheltered a predominantly male, predominantly adult population made up of several distinct elements: (1) vagrants, wanderers, and seasonal laborers—hoboes, in the now-obsolete term; (2) chronic inebriates, some partly employed and others unemployable; (3) old men retired from manual employment and living on meager pensions or savings; (4) steadily employed men without family or community affiliations. These four types—the hobo, the bum, the old-timer, and the loner—make up the primary population of skid row, supplemented at various times by cripples, fugitives, temporarily unemployed workers, soldiers, petty criminals, and even a few women. The proportions of each type vary from time to time and from place to place. Today, the hoboes have nearly disappeared, and there are relatively more old-timers than ever before. About half of the homeless men interviewed in recent studies describe themselves as never married. The majority have no contact with relatives. Their job histories are characterized by low status, low pay, and brief tenure.

Skid row traditionally provided an oasis within the larger community where the subsistence cost of living was lower than anywhere else and where the ordinary norms of urban behavior were suspended. These protective features of the environment are not very well maintained under current conditions. The cost of a bed in a lodging house is often more than the rental of a furnished room elsewhere in the city. The prices in skid row restaurants are sometimes higher than in the cheap restaurants of other districts. A drunken man is much more likely to be arrested on a skid row street than if he makes a similar appearance in a residential district. The risk of being robbed or assaulted when drunk is very much greater in skid row than out of it. The environment does not offer the homeless man comfort or safety or even freedom from interference, but it does permit him to live in a certain style whose major components are isolation from women, wine-drinking, the free disposition of one's time, and the absence of compulsory obligations toward others.

Whether skid row is a specialized community or subculture, as some investigators believe, or an organizational vacuum, as others maintain, is a semantic question. Almost all observers agree that there are characteristic, acquired patterns of behavior on skid row, that considerable social interaction occurs among the homeless men in such districts, and that the system is sufficiently cohesive to entrap some of the men who come into it intending only a brief stay. On the other hand, there is no reliable report of skid row men engaging in collective action or even in mutual self-defense. Although some observers claim to see a status hierarchy among them, there is no corresponding structure of rights, duties, and relationships. Above all, there are no common goals.

Can refusal to act be considered a form of action? Skid row as a social system adapts to the external environment by not reacting to it, achieves its goals by having none, maintains its external adaptations by leaving them to chance, and screens its membership by accepting everyone who applies. It is perhaps unique among human communities in presenting no problem of entree for the sociologist. Like the policeman, the social worker, the evangelist, and the thug, he can enter and leave skid row as he pleases.

Whatever else he may be, the skid row man is not his brother's keeper. Nor his brother's opinion-leader, norm-enforcer, or action-initiator. That is to say, he is about as different from *Homo sociologus* as it is possible to to be while still remaining human. Therein lies skid row's fascination for the sociologist. For the price of a subway ride, he can enter a country where the accepted principles of social interaction do not seem to apply.

The same phenomenon can move the ordinary citizen to fury. Anyone who has worked on the problem of redeveloping a skid row district or relocating a population of homeless men can testify to the extraordinary hostility aroused by the prospect of a settlement of homeless men in a residential or business district. This sentiment was institutionalized until recently in what Pittman and Gordon [4] called "the revolving door"—the practice of arresting, convicting, and quickly releasing homeless men for intoxication, vagrancy, and other nominal offenses. When the Columbia Bowery Project began its work in 1963, this curious institution accounted for about one-fourth of all police arrests in New York City. Homeless men were arrested according to a quota system, not necessarily when intoxicated, to be released almost invariably the following morning. No one connected with the system, from the presiding judge down to the driver of the police van, had any clear idea of what it was intended to accomplish. In 1965, partly in reaction to the project's early findings, Operation Bowery's advisory committee, made up of representatives from a wide range of municipal departments and private agencies, proposed to replace the revolving door by a detoxification center located in the Bowery. Before this plan could be put into effect, two external developments put a stop to the practice. Beginning in January 1966 free legal representation in New York City courts was made available by the Legal Aid Society to homeless men charged with disorderly conduct; immediately thereafter the conviction rate in such cases dropped from 98 percent to 2 percent. During the same winter two separate decisions of the Federal Court of Appeals ruled, in effect, that public intoxication is not a crime. Following these decisions, the police department discontinued disorderly conduct arrests not involving an actual breach of the peace. With the sharp drop in arrests, the municipal jail ceased to be available to Bowery men for drying out and for cold weather shelter; pressure for a substitute facility built up rapidly and led to the opening of a detoxification center under the joint auspices of the Vera Institute and Operation Bowery. But even when the revolving door ceases to revolve, the settled community still perceives skid row as threatening although, curiously enough, the crime rate of homeless men with respect to outsiders is close to zero.

SKID ROW STUDIES

There is probably no other type of problem area in the United States about which we are as well informed as skid row. In what other area do we have solid empirical data going back nearly continuously for 80 years? Indeed, we must admit that the extent of our information is disproportionate to the number of persons involved or the urgency of the problems. The disproportion may be most charitably explained by the usefulness of homelessness studies for illuminating such broad social issues as the relationship between social status and personal satisfaction, or the mutual dependence of various types of affiliation. Studying a homeless population helps us to understand the situation of settled populations in the same society. This is particularly the case when, as in the present study, settled populations are actually studied at the same time.

The earliest American study of skid row we have been able to find is McCook's "Tramp Census" published in 1893.[5] It reported an enumeration of 1349 residents of municipal shelters in American cities with information on employment, age, health, length of vagrancy, reasons for vagrancy, nativity, marital status, alcohol consumption, criminality, and religion and compared these findings to those of a similar study of an English population. Jacob Riis's meticulous description of Bowery life-style and physical facilities dates from the same period.[6] He supported his observations by a variety of quantitative data and by an extraordinary group of documentary photographs, some of which we will reproduce in a later chapter. Nascher's study of the Bowery *The Wretches of Povertyville,*[7] written between 1903 and 1906, was less sophisticated than its predecessors but was followed soon after by three studies of extraordinary quality: Solenberger's analysis of social and demographic data from the case records of 1000 homeless men who applied for public assistance in Chicago between 1901 and 1903, supplemented by life-history and institutional material; [8] Laubach's interview study of 100 homeless men in New York City, prepared as a Columbia dissertation in 1916; [9] and Rice's sophisticated typology of homelessness, based on his participant observation in the Bowery from 1916 to 1917 and his later experience administering a public shelter there.[10]

The landmark study of skid row is Nels Anderson's *The Hobo: The Sociology of the Homeless Man,*[11] based upon participant observation in Chicago and other cities from 1918 to 1920 and supplemented by 400 interviews, numerous case histories, and extensive institutional material. The Anderson study was one of the great series of works describing various aspects of urban life that were produced by the Chicago school of urban ecologists in the 1920s and 1930s. It should be read in conjunction with two later and less well known works by Anderson, his *Men on the Move,*[12] published in 1940, in which he partly rejects what he calls the romanticism of his earlier treatment of the hobo, and his nearly forgotten monograph on the Bowery from 1932 to 1934, which includes a wealth of quantitative data and descriptive material.[13] A notable study that belongs to the same period as *The Hobo* but which has received less attention than it deserves is the Heller Committee's survey of 846 dependent aged persons and of 18 institutions and relief agencies in San Francisco in 1925. It includes an interesting chapter based on 100 interviews with homeless men in San Francisco.[14]

The Great Depression vastly increased the number of homeless men and added to their ranks an unprecedented wave of homeless women and children. The most impressive of the depression studies was Sutherland and Locke's *Twenty Thousand Homeless Men,*[15] the report of a sociological team who studied by participant observation the emergency shelters established for homeless men in Chicago and also developed significant policy recommendations.[16] Culver's interview study of employed transients in California,[17] Potter's review of the two censuses of homeless men undertaken by the Committee on the Care of the Transient and Homeless in 1933,[18] Bassett's bibliography of transiency and homelessness,[19] Schubert's analysis of case records of transients in Buffalo, New York,[20] and McKinsey's analysis of similar records in Missouri belonged to this same period,[21] as does Caplow's participant-observer study of homeless transients conducted in 1939 [22] and Weinberg's study of isolation among Chicago homeless men based on life-history data.[23]

In the 1950s and 1960s a new wave of skid row studies was stimulated by the federal urban renewal program, as one skid row district after another was considered for clearance and urban renewal. Many of these studies remained unpublished in the files of local housing authorities, but a number of them were brought into the public domain, including large action-oriented surveys of skid row districts in Sacramento, Chicago, Minneapolis, and Philadelphia.

The Sacramento studies are described in a series of reports published by the Redevelopment Agency of the City of Sacramento.[24] Several successive surveys of the skid row population, including interviews with a 10 percent sample of hotel and dormitory residents in 1957, provided the factual basis for an extensive redevelopment plan of that city's labor market area.

The major research effort of the Chicago program was the interviewing of a random sample of more than 600 residents in four major skid row areas of the city in 1958. Interviews averaged two and a half hours; most of the questions referred to the current situation of the respondents, although some life-history information was obtained. The survey was conducted by the National Opinion Research Center in connection with the Chicago Community Inventory under the direction of Donald J. Bogue.[25]

The Minneapolis study was prepared by the University of Minnesota in conjunction with the Minneapolis Housing and Redevelopment Authority. Theodore Caplow was the principal investigator. A special census of the Minneapolis skid row was undertaken with the assistance of the U.S. Bureau of the Census. Intensive interviews were then conducted with a random sample of 280 homeless men. The final report described the institutions of skid row and the demographic characteristics of the population, discussed problems connected with health, drinking patterns, and housing; analyzed the availability of housing for relocation purposes, and made recommendations for action.[26] Much of the participant-observation data is included in a later work by one of the investigators describing "skid row from the inside." [27]

The Philadelphia study was conducted by the Department of Psychiatry of the Temple University School of Medicine, under authorization of the Greater Philadelphia Movement (a businessman's organization) and the Redevelopment Authority of the City of Philadelphia. In some respects it was more intensive than any previous study: during a weekend in February 1960 two hundred medical students interviewed nearly 80 percent of the residents of Philadelphia's skid row; 2249 of the area's 2857 residents were interviewed using a short form with 80 percent of the respondents and a long form with the other 20 percent. Most of the data obtained had to do with the men's current drinking patterns, living accommodations, health, and their perceptions of themselves and their neighborhood, although some information about personal and family experience, work history, and education was also obtained.[28]

From these major studies, and some others of smaller scale, there emerged a fairly consistent description of skid row and its men. Skid row men were found to be impoverished, aged, socially isolated, subject to high morbidity and mortality, and afflicted by a high incidence of alcoholism. Fewer of them were transients than had been supposed.

The typical skid row of 1960 consisted of a complex of cheap bars and restaurants, cubicle hotels or lodging houses, missions and shelters, barber colleges, second-hand stores, pawnshops, and spot-job employment agencies that hired and paid by the day. Associated with these were tattoo parlors, all-night movies and burlesque shows, and the revolving door of police court and workhouse.

THE BOWERY IN PARTICULAR

The Bowery is the most famous skid row in the United States. It is not the largest—Chicago, San Francisco, Los Angeles, and Detroit have larger skid rows—but it is one of the oldest. It was fully developed within a decade or so after the Civil War, and the Bowery Mission was founded in 1879.

The research reported in this book is the first large-scale study of the Bowery in many years. Most of the previous Bowery studies have dealt selectively with the client population of some particular institution.[29] Before the present study the most extensive investigation of the Bowery was Anderson's study, completed nearly forty years ago,[30] of 1000 clients of the Municipal Men's Shelter.

Our study came about in this way. In the fall of 1963 at the direction of Mayor Robert F. Wagner, the New York City Department of Welfare established Operation Bowery to develop a program for dealing effectively with the problem of the homeless population concentrated in the Bowery. The health, employment, alcohol, housing, and other problems of the Bowery population were to be examined, with the long range objective of restoring as many men as possible to useful and productive lives and providing supportive care for the rest.

Operation Bowery was administratively related to the Department of Welfare but was outside the usual machinery of that department. Its policy body, the Interdepartmental Project Committee, included representatives at the deputy-commissioner level from all of the municipal agencies concerned with the problems of homeless men. The commissioner of welfare served as chairman.

The contract establishing the Columbia Bowery Project was executed in October 1963 between the Department of Welfare and the Bureau of Applied Social Research. It stated that:

> . . . the Bowery area in the City of New York is inhabited by a large number of men who present problems of homelessness, excessive use of alcohol and other anti-social behavior patterns, the precise nature, causes and magnitude of which are not known, and which adversely affect the welfare of the Bowery area and the City of New York as a whole; and . . . in order to aid the City of New York in its efforts to remedy these conditions and to rehabilitate these men, it is necessary that a comprehensive study be made to determine the nature, causes and magnitude of the problem as well as to determine the type of program required for the rehabilitation of said homeless population and of the Bowery in which it lives. . . .[31]

Operating under a one-year grant from the City of New York, the Bowery Project estimated the number of homeless men throughout Manhattan and on the Bowery, began a series of annual enumerations of the Bowery population, located habitats of homeless men outside the Bowery area, described procedures and determined the frequency of arrest and arraignment of homeless men, calculated death and hospitalization rates for Bowery men, investigated illness and causes of death among the men, analyzed particular aspects of Bowery life (for instance, bars, spot-job employment agencies, and land values), and completed a bibliographic survey of previous works about skid row and homelessness.

Among the findings of this first year's research were the following:

1. The population of the Bowery was decreasing: between February 1949 and February 1964 it declined from an estimated 14,000 to 7611.

2. Arrests of homeless men for disorderly conduct and related offenses in 1963 totaled at least 50,000—approximately one-quarter of all arrests in the city on all counts.[32]

3. Not all homeless men were skid row men. Manhattan had at least 30,000 non-Bowery homeless men.

4. Mortality and hospitalization rates among Bowery men were

very high, with mortality rates at every age three to five times the national rates.

5. Skid row men did not turn out to be more difficult to interview than other lower-class respondents.

In 1964 the U.S. Public Health Service approved a proposal entitled "Homelessness: Etiology and Consequences" which extended the duration of the Columbia Bowery Project from 1965 to 1968. This phase of the research was to include the preparation of a life-history interview form and the interviewing of a random sample of the Bowery population. The proposal stated that homelessness would be viewed within the context of an individual's total experiences, using the life-history data to analyze the development of the homeless condition, the impact of skid row upon individuals, the social consequences of homelessness, and its relationship to alienation and anomie.

It seems likely that the Bowery in its present form will cease to exist in the near future, just as skid rows in other cities are disappearing. The present population of the Bowery is a relatively small proportion of the homeless population of Manhattan, and it is decreasing by about five hundred men a year. The eventual redevelopment of the area between Cooper and Chatham Squares will probably disperse the problem rather than solve it; at the time we began our work, the redevelopment of the Cooper Square end of the Bowery was thought to be imminent. It has since been repeatedly delayed. The impending dispersal of skid row men lent a certain urgency to the research; it seemed important to assemble meaningful data about the problem while the population of homeless men was still concentrated and readily accessible.

It is not necessary to recite the history of the first road built by the Dutch settlers in Fort Amsterdam (now Wall Street) to their farms (*boweries*) upcountry.[33] The Bowery has evolved through at least five distinct periods, beginning as the only highway into the city, gradually changing into a street of small shops, and then experiencing two periods of illumination, first as a white-light district with promenades, beer gardens, cheap theaters, and street auctioneers; later as a red-light district of saloons, whorehouses, gambling halls, burlesque shows, and shooting galleries. In 1934, Anderson described the Bowery as "a street distinctive only for its past," remarking that it had entered a period of obsolescence and that no new buildings had been erected for more than a decade. The street was then the city's largest concentration of homeless men, the main stem of Manhattan.[34] Since the thirties the Bowery has become an increasingly pure skid row; the wandering hoboes, the migratory workers, and the temporarily unemployed have all but disappeared, leaving the street to the home guard who have come there to stay. The Bowery became "drunk and prim and quiet. . . . Up the tile stairways of the flophouses sit the most retired men in the world." [35]

The commercial lodging houses and the bars located on or just off the Bowery are central features in the lives of most of the Bowery's residents. There are also restaurants, employment agencies, liquor stores, secondhand stores, missions, and the Municipal Men's Shelter. Homeless men on the Bowery are in a highly visible majority, and a man serviced by the institutions there cannot be unaware that he is "on the Bowery."

The Bowery and its adjacent side streets may be divided into four segments from north to south: Cooper Square to Houston Street, Houston to Delancey Street, Delancey to Canal Street, and Canal to Chatham Square. In 1964 the Columbia Bowery Project's observers described these segments as follows.

Cooper Union (a college of art and architecture) and several old commercial buildings surround Cooper Square. Between Cooper Square and Houston Street most of the buildings fronting on the Bowery are small and old. Seven commercial lodging houses there dominate the scene; there are few other large buildings. Some of the structures are in very poor repair and are partly or entirely empty. Between Houston and Delancey, the buildings are more substantial, but lodging houses and bars for homeless men still predominate. However, there are more businesses not catering to homeless men than in the northern segment, particularly wholesale restaurant suppliers. Many of the wholesale establishments look busy and fairly prosperous.

Below Delancey Street there are fewer skid row facilities. The area is predominantly commercial; in addition to dish and restaurant suppliers there are store fixture and furniture makers and lamp dealers who sell to the general public. There is one massive granite concentration which includes three respectable banks. The intersection of the Bowery and Canal Street is an important center for Manhattan's jewelry trade and attracts many jewelers, jewelry salesmen, and customers. There are many commercial lodging houses in this quarter of the Bowery but fewer bars and other skid row facilities.

Below Canal Street is Chinatown. Although many of its structures are old, the area is bustling and in good condition. There is a large, imposing bank and the only new building on the entire Bowery, a block-long apartment house for middle-income families. Four lodging houses and several bars serve homeless men in this quarter, but they are not obvious. Casual visitors to Chinatown are not aware of being on skid row.

It is easy to identify dirty and disheveled "Bowery bums," but not all homeless men can be distinguished by appearance. Some of the working men and pensioners who live on the Bowery dress neatly, but the majority are shabby, and many are obviously intoxicated. A considerable number are disabled or bear the marks of recent injury or violence. Some are on crutches. Some have long beards and wild hair. In the winter men may be seen wearing several suits of clothes and even two overcoats.

Homeless men on the Bowery stand around because they have nothing else to do. They stand silently on the sidewalks or lean against a wall or shuffle slowly along, alone or in groups. Most of the lodging houses require their guests to spend their days out of their living quarters; only the infirm are allowed inside during the day.

In 1966 the Department of Welfare instituted a Day Center Program at the Men's Shelter. Its purpose was to provide the men with a "wholesome alternative" to lounging on the streets. Facilities were available for reading, television, and table games. During the first six months of the program as many as 160 men per day used the center.

Many Bowery men sleep in the street. They lie in doorways, on street corners, and they may be seen sprawled side by side next to several of the bars. At night some of the men sleep on the sidewalk in groups, and other crawl into boxes on the sidewalk to sleep.

Many outsiders may be seen on the Bowery. Some of them work for wholesalers in the area and may patronize Bowery facilities during weekdays. At night or on weekends they are not in evidence. Some tourists visit the Bowery; occasionally a group is led through by a guide, and tour buses make it a regular feature.

A sizable residential or family population lives just off the Bowery. Jewish, Puerto Rican, Chinese, and Italian families live in adjoining neighborhoods; they do not differ visibly from families of similar economic level who live elsewhere in the city.

The family population has to adapt to the problems presented by homeless men. Children playing on the side streets learn to step over Bowery men asleep on the sidewalks. One building superintendent calls the police whenever Bowery men sit in front of his building, and women in another building throw water at them out of upper story windows.

Most of the women seen on the Bowery are members of the family population or customers and employees of the stores. Disheveled or intoxicated women are occasionally seen, usually connected with the Women's Shelter program of the Department of Social Services' Bureau of Shelter Services for Adults, which at the time of our study was located on the Bowery and sometimes housed as many as 50 women.

The Bowery day starts early. Many homeless men are on the streets at 5:30 A.M. Some of them make their way to the Men's Shelter, which serves breakfast beginning at six o'clock. The bars do not open until eight, and so more men are on the street in the early morning than during the rest of the day. Automobile traffic is especially heavy between eight and ten in the morning. At noon, workers can be seen on their way to and from restaurants, especially in the southern half of the Bowery.

In the late afternoon the wholesalers and tradespeople are gone, and the homeless men take over the Bowery. As it gets dark, the men may be seen standing in small groups in front of lodging houses and bars. After nightfall most of the homeless men are off the streets, except for those sleeping outside.

Late at night the Bowery is very quiet; there is no revelry. The only entertainment outside of the bars is provided by two movie theaters. Both are Chinese and are closed by midnight. From midnight until five in the morning there is very little activity; a few men lie on sidewalks and in doorways; an occasional pedestrian shuffles slowly by.

For outsiders the Bowery is not particularly dangerous even at night. Relatively few arrests for major crimes are made in the Bowery. For the aged pensioners who make up a large proportion of the Bowery's population the situation is quite different. They are exposed to theft and robbery, especially on the days when pension and welfare checks are delivered.

Old men, drunk or sober, are easy to rob. Managers and clerks do not encourage the older men to leave the lodging houses at night. When a robbery occurs, it is extremely difficult to find a sober complainant who will go to court. The first rule of Bowery life is to mind one's own business and to stay out of other people's troubles. Many of the older men prefer to accept a monetary loss rather than risk retaliation. The "rolling" of drunks or sleepers occurs frequently, day and night. If a man lies down on the street or in a doorway to sleep, his pockets may be searched ten or twenty times before he wakes up.

THE HABITATS OF THE CONTROL SAMPLES

The following pages contain descriptions of the habitats of our three control samples: Camp LaGuardia, Park Slope, and Park Avenue. A word of preliminary explanation may be in order.

The New York City Department of Welfare operates an institution for homeless men known as Camp LaGuardia. Many of the inmates were formerly Bowery men; in fact, men are assigned to the camp through the Municipal Men's Shelter on the Bowery. They go voluntarily and may leave voluntarily, but while at the camp they must adjust to an institutional setting. We thought that much could be learned about the consequences of homelessness by observing the adjustment of skid row men to a total institution. Accordingly, a random sample of the population of the camp was interviewed, using the same life-history form designed for the "free" skid row men on the Bowery.

The original research proposal called for interviews only with homeless men; but as the research proceeded, various findings suggested an improvement in procedure—the inclusion of a control group of settled low-income individuals for comparison, with the expectation that the etiology of homelessness might be thrown into much sharper relief by comparing homeless men with a settled population. Consequently, we interviewed a sample of male residents in a Brooklyn slum neighborhood called Park Slope.

Fairly late in the research program it began to seem advantageous to find and interview a sample of high-income men in order to separate the concomitants of disaffiliation from those of poverty. An upper-income neighborhood along Park Avenue in Manhattan was selected as the research site.

Camp LaGuardia.[36] Camp LaGuardia, an institution for the custody and rehabilitation of homeless men, which is supported by the Department of Social Services of the City of New York, is located in a rural area near Chester, New York, about 60 miles from Manhattan. At the time of the study it had a maximum capacity of 1050 men and operated nearly at capacity. The camp was established in 1934 when the Welfare Department acquired the site from the city's Department of Corrections, which had used it as a women's prison. Several of the buildings, including the main building, were built as prison structures and have not been extensively altered since.

One of the ideologies supporting the operation of the camp is the alleged therapeutic value of rural life. Men in various states of debilitation are sent to the camp on the assumption that a few months of healthy rural life will get them "cleaned up" and better able to cope with the urban world when they leave. When a man has reached this state of renewed mental and physical health, the camp staff may help him find a job. Aside from the therapeutic value of the rural setting the camp provides light work, adequate medical care, and limited drinking. The staff have come to believe that the regimen is only temporarily beneficial because most of the men resume their old patterns when they leave. The camp does not have resources for individual treatment, although there have been attempts to add a psychiatrist or a psychologist to its staff.

The ideology of the staff is that the camp is a good place for the men to be and that the outside world is a bad place for them because, among other things, they cannot handle money responsibly, they drink too much, and they are prey for thieves. Many of the inmates are old men who are not completely incapacitated but who cannot work much. The staff encourages the Men's Shelter to send them old men, many of whom will remain for years.

It is less expensive for the city to support a man at Camp LaGuardia than on the Bowery. In 1965 the average daily cost per man at the camp was between $2.00 and $2.50; it was more than $3.00 on the Bowery.

The camp has 267 acres of land, some farmed and the rest rented out to local farmers. The main building was the original prison, and it houses the administrative offices, cafeteria, recreation room, library, infirmary, canteen, and some of the sleeping quarters. The old building has dark stained woodwork and small windows but is nevertheless informal and comfortable. The dormitory rooms originally were prison cells; they are extremely cramped and had barred windows until the spring of 1966. Most of the men sleep in barracks which were built during the Great Depression. Other utility buildings, including a garage and a food warehouse, are scattered around the property.

In 1965 the camp had a paid staff of fifty, including three part-time chaplains, a part-time dentist, and a part-time physician. Most of the staff live on the grounds or in nearby communities; there was relatively little staff turnover.

The primary qualifications for admittance are age, income, physical condition, and, for returnees, camp record. Few men under age 30 are ever admitted. In the winter when there is more demand for places, the age limit is raised to 55, but frequent exceptions are made. Potential residents must meet the Men's Shelter income requirements. Furthermore, men who have a record of misbehavior at the camp are not allowed to return. Men who need hospitalization or are nonambulatory are not admitted, but other men in poor health are given preference.

Four out of every five of those admitted have been at the camp before. It is not uncommon for a man to be admitted every winter and to leave every summer. There is also a substantial home guard of about three hundred permanent inmates. Some of these men have responsible jobs and are important to the smooth functioning of the camp.

Each man is assigned a job around the camp, even if he is not capable of doing much. Some tasks, such as policing the grounds, are recognized as make-work. The published description of the camp says that some men "do the lightest of work, expressly for the purpose of keeping them interested and occupied." Most jobs are unpaid, but a few of the more important ones pay ten or twenty dollars a month. The work is not strenuous; the workday ends between 2:00 and 2:30 P.M., and many men share every task.

A man may leave the camp whenever he wishes without affecting his chances of returning. When he leaves, he has a closing interview with a caseworker and is given a bus ticket back to New York City and subway fare. Most of the men who leave do so ostensibly to take a job. For August 1965, 10 to 15 percent of those leaving were recorded as self-separated, that is, without jobs. Slightly less than 10 percent of the separations were for medical reasons, and about 5 percent were for other reasons. Of 349 separations only four were disciplinary measures.

Several kinds of recreation are available. On warm days a great many men may be seen walking or sitting around the grounds. However, other types of recreation are available and used: a recreation room with TV sets, checkers, and two pool tables, a library with current magazines and four thousand books, and a tap room that serves beer at seven cents a glass. The tap room is open from 5 to 9 P.M. every day and on Saturday and Sunday afternoons. Each man is allowed to walk into the nearby town of Chester six times a month.

Social interaction at the camp is not intensive. According to staff members, most of the men are loners. Many appear to have acquaintances but not close friends or established cliques.

Each man is given $2.00 every other week to buy personal items or to spend as he wishes. On the other hand, all men with outside income, such as Social Security benefits, retirement pensions, or Railroad Retirement Act payments, must turn it over to the camp. They may keep any excess over their cost to the camp, calculated in 1965 to be $2.32 per man per day. The camp helps the men to apply for Social Security benefits, and often a man will get a check for over $1000 to cover back payments. At this point he has a choice of leaving the camp with his check intact or paying the camp for his past stay. Needless to say, most men choose the former, but a fair number, perhaps a third, prefer to pay the large sum rather than leave. Some men say they would not know what to do if they left the camp.

Park Slope. Brooklyn was arbitrarily designated as the borough where a lower-income census tract would be selected for sampling. There were two criteria involved in the selection of the specific tract:

it had to be a "poor" tract (with the median income of all families and unrelated individuals in 1959 at $4000 or less), and its ethnic composition had to be somewhat similar to that of the Bowery population. Most of the tracts which met the first criterion were predominantly Black or Puerto Rican. The one tract which met the low-income criterion and had an ethnic composition even remotely like that of the Bowery was Tract 161, which was accordingly designated as the universe from which the lower-income control sample would be drawn.

In 1960, 4200 people lived in Tract 161, occupying 1511 of the 1578 housing units there. Many units were in poor condition: census enumerators classified 6 percent of them as dilapidated and 42 percent as deteriorating. The comparable proportions for the borough of Brooklyn as a whole were 3 percent and 13 percent respectively.[37]

The ethnic composition of the tract in 1960 was 20 percent Irish, 20 percent Negro, 17 percent Puerto Rican, and 9 percent Italian, with smaller proportions of Germans, British, Poles, Scandinavians, and Russians.

The Park Slope area, which includes Tract 161, was an upper-class residential area in the late nineteenth century. Obsolescence set in around the turn of the century; many of the old mansions were replaced by apartment buildings, and the brownstone row houses began to be subdivided into furnished rooms. As early as 1922 a Brooklyn newspaper noted that isolated pockets of urban blight were appearing in Park Slope. Since the Second World War there has been little new construction in the area; the postwar housing shortage accelerated the conversion of brownstones into rooming houses. The area's socioeconomic level has continued to decline, although there are a few moderately prosperous sections remaining. Tract 161 is one of the poorest in Park Slope.

Park Avenue. Data from the 1960 census reports were used to compare the characteristics of the three Manhattan census tracts having the *highest* median incomes. None of the three tracts had many Blacks or Puerto Ricans, so racial composition was not a relevant criterion. An attempt was made to find a tract that would give a fairly wide range of occupations and a high proportion of elderly rich men. The tract with the highest median income (0060) had a very high concentration of professional and technical workers (44 percent compared to 26 percent in Tract 0082) and a relatively young male population (the median age of males was 45, compared to 55 in Tract 0082).

Tract 0082 was finally chosen as the least unsuitable. It embraces fourteen blocks on the east side of midtown Manhattan, bounded by Park Avenue, Fifth Avenue, Thirty-fifth Street, and Forty-second Street. It is that part of the Murray Hill section closest to the business district centered on Fifth Avenue and Forty-second Street, and it has the highest rents in its immediate area. Housing is in high-rise luxury apartment buildings and older brownstone houses. We have called the sample drawn from this tract the Park Avenue sample.

The characteristics of respondents in the Bowery sample and in each of the three control samples are discussed in the following chapter. For details about the problems of data gathering in each neighborhood, the reader is referred to the appendix on research procedures.

NOTES

1. This summary is adapted from a more extended discussion in Theodore Caplow, Howard M. Bahr, and David Sternberg, "Homelessness," *International Encyclopedia of the Social Sciences,* Vol. 6 (1968), 494-499.

2. For a more extended history of American skid rows, see Samuel E. Wallace, *Skid Row as a Way of Life* (Totowa, N.J.: The Bedminster Press, 1965), Chapters 1 and 2.

3. Some of the material in the following pages is adapted from Theodore Caplow, "The Sociologist and the Homeless Man," *Disaffiliated Man: Essays and Bibliography on Skid Row, Vagrancy, and Outsiders,* ed. Howard M. Bahr (Toronto: Univ. of Toronto Press, 1970).

4. David J. Pittman and T. Wayne Gordon, *Revolving Door: A Study of the Chronic Police Case Inebriate* (Glencoe, Ill.: The Free Press, 1958).

5. John J. McCook, "A Tramp Census and Its Revelations," *Forum,* 15 (August 1893), pp. 753-766.

6. Jacob A. Riis, *How the Other Half Lives* (1890; rpt. New York: Hill and Wang, 1957).

7. I. L. Nascher, *The Wretches of Povertyville: A Sociological Study of the Bowery* (Chicago: Joseph J. Lanzit, 1909).

8. Alice Willard Solenberger, *One Thousand Homeless Men: A Study of Original Records* (New York: Russell Sage Foundation, 1911).

9. Frank Charles Laubach, "Why there are Vagrants: A Study Based Upon an Examination of One Hundred Men," Diss. Columbia Univ., 1916.

10. Stuart A. Rice, "The Homeless," *Annals of the American Academy of Political Science,* 77 (May 1918), pp. 140-153.

11. Nels Anderson, *The Hobo: The Sociology of the Homeless Man* (Chicago: Univ. of Chicago Press, 1923), p. 302.

12. Nels Anderson, *Men on the Move* (Chicago: Univ. of Chicago Press, 1940).

13. Nels Anderson, *Homeless in New York City* (New York: Board of Charity, 1934).

14. Heller Committee for Research in Social Economics, *The Dependent Aged in San Francisco,* Univ. of California Publications in Economics, 5, No. 1 (1926).

15. Edwin H. Sutherland and Harvey J. Locke, *Twenty Thousand Homeless Men* (Chicago: J. B. Lippincott, 1936).

16. Harvey J. Locke, "Unemployed Men in Chicago Shelters," *Sociology and Social Research,* 19 (May-June 1935), pp. 420-428.

17. Benjamin F. Culver, "Transient Unemployed Men," *Sociology and Social Researsch,* 17 (July-August 1933), pp. 519-535.

18. Ellen C. Potter, "The Problem of the Transient," *Annals of the American Academy of Political and Social Science,* 176 (November 1934), pp. 66-73.

19. Lucy A. Bassett, *Transient and Homeless Persons: A Bibliography* (Jacksonville: Florida Emergency Relief Administration, 1934).

20. Herman J. P. Schubert, *Twenty Thousand Transients: A One Year's Sample of Those Who Apply for Aid in a Northern City* (Buffalo: Emergency Relief Bureau, 1935).

21. John Paul McKinsey, "Transient Men in Missouri," Diss. Univ. of Missouri, 1940.

22. Theodore Caplow, "Transiency as a Cultural Pattern," *American Sociological Review,* 5 (October 1940), pp. 731-739.

23. Samuael Kirson Weinberg, "A Study of Isolation Among Chicago Shelter-Home Men," master's thesis, Univ. of Chicago, 1935.

24. See Davis McEntire, *Population and Employment Survey of Sacramento's West End* (Sacramento: Redevelopment Agency of the City of Sacramento, 1952); Catherine Bauer and Davis McEntire, *Relocation Study: Single Male Population* (Sacramento: Redevelopment Agency

of the City of Sacramento, 1933); Davis McEntire, *Relocation Plan: Slum Area Labor Market, Sacramento* (Sacramento: Redevelopment Agency of the City of Sacramento, 1959).

25. Donald J. Bogue, *Skid Row in American Cities* (Chicago: Community and Family Study Center, Univ. of Chicago, 1963); *The Homeless Man on Skid Row* (Chicago: Tenants Relocation Bureau, City of Chicago, 1961).

26. Theodore Caplow, Keith A. Lovald, and Samuel E. Wallace, *A General Report on the Problem of Relocating the Population of the Lower Loop Redevelopment Area* (Minneapolis: Minneapolis Housing and Redevelopment Authority, 1958).

27. Wallace, *Skid Row as a Way of Life.*

28. Leonard Blumberg *et al., The Men on Skid Row* (Philadelphia: Temple Univ. School of Medicine, Department of Psychiatry, 1960); *What To Do About the Men on Skid Row: Report of the Greater Philadelphia Movement to the Redevelopment Authority of the City of Philadelphia* (Philadelphia: Greater Philadelphia Movement, 1961).

29. For example: Robert Straus and Raymond G. McCarthy, "Nonaddictive Pathological Drinking Patterns of Homeless Men," *Quarterly Journal of Studies on Alcohol,* 12 (December 1951), pp. 601-611; Boris M. Levinson, "The Socioeconomic Status, Intelligence and Psychometric Pattern of Native-Born White Homeless Men," *Journal of Genetic Psychology,* 91 (December 1957), pp. 205-211; Aaron D. Chaves, Arthur B. Robins, and Hans Abeles, "Tuberculosis Case Finding Among Homeless Men in New York City," *American Review of Respiratory Diseases,* 74 (December 1961), pp. 900-901.

30. Anderson, *The Homeless in New York City.*

31. Bowery Project Staff, *Summary Report of a Study Undertaken Under Contract Approved by the Board of Estimate, Calendar No. 14, December 19, 1963* (New York: Bureau of Applied Social Research, Columbia Univ., 1965), pp. 1-2.

32. The arrest procedures changed several times after 1963. In 1964 arrest rates were higher than usual; allegedly the increase reflected the city's efforts to clean up for the World's Fair. In 1965 rates dropped back to their normal level. In 1966 the policemen stopped making arrests on the disorderly conduct statute that had previously been the most common charge and substituted certain park and traffic regulations. In 1967 a new state public intoxication law went into effect, but fewer arrests were made than previously. Under current procedures, arrests are made on specific complaints in which public intoxication is combined with other illegal behavior, such as panhandling, committing a public nuisance, or violation of park regulations. In addition, facilities

for providing inebriated men with medical attention rather than incarceration have been established.

33. The reader interested in the conversion of that road into today's Bowery is referred to Elmer Bendiner, *The Bowery Man* (New York: Thomas Nelson and Sons, 1961) and Alvin F. Harlow, *Old Bowery Days* (New York: Appleton-Century-Crofts, 1931).

34. Anderson, *The Homeless in New York City,* pp. 41-44.

35. Bendiner, *op. cit.,* p. 90.

36. The description of Camp LaGuardia is adapted from a project memorandum by Stanley K. Henshaw.

37, U.S. Bureau of the Census, *U.S. Census of Housing: 1960, Vol. III, City Blocks, Series HC (3), No. 274* (Washington, D.C.: U.S. Government Printing Office, 1961), Table 2.

CHAPTER 2

HOMELESS MEN AND SETTLED MEN

We shall begin by identifying certain characteristics of skid row men, using results of several skid row surveys to establish the incidence of each characteristic. Then these incidences will be compared with the incidences of the same characteristics in our Park Slope and Park Avenue samples and in the national population.

BOWERY MEN COMPARED TO OTHER SKID ROW MEN

Comparative data were drawn from sample surveys of four skid rows (Sacramento, Chicago, Minneapolis, Philadelphia) and of an institutionalized skid row population (the alcoholic inmates of the Monroe County Penitentiary in New York).[1] Adding the Bowery and Camp LaGuardia samples, we have findings from seven skid row populations. However, for some variables we do not have information from all seven samples. For example, the Sacramento report does not include information on nativity, vocational attainment, religion, or marital status. For any particular characteristic, data from one or more of the seven populations may be missing.

Even when the data were available, there were often inconsistencies in the way the findings were presented. Sometimes categories were not comparable. An attempt was made to maximize the comparability of the published data by recomputing percentages to exclude all "no answer" and "don't know" responses. Thus some of the entries in the tables which follow differ slightly from those reported in the source publications. Furthermore, some categories were combined to increase the congruency between studies.

The questions eliciting the data on a given variable often vary from study to study. Personal income is an example. In the Chicago study, the respondent was given a printed income distribution and asked to choose the category that most closely matched his annual income; then the interviewer checked his response by asking about estimated income from specific sources (wages, pensions, interest, rents, investments, and gifts of money). In the Bowery study, the interviewer asked, "About how much is your present monthly income?" and the respondent provided his own figure. Then the interviewer inquired about the sources of that income and the contribution from each source. We do not know how much such differences in wording affected the results. For almost every item to be discussed here the findings from different cities are based on responses to questions that were worded differently. Accordingly, small differences cannot be taken as meaningful.

Finally, there were time lags among these studies. The earliest of the seven surveys, the study of incarcerated inebriates at the Monroe County Penitentiary, was completed in 1954; the Sacramento, Chicago, Minneapolis, and Philadelphia surveys were carried out during the period 1957 to 1959. The Bowery and Camp LaGuardia surveys were made in 1966. Some differences between the New York findings and those from other skid rows may result from this time lag. For example, if Bowery men had higher annual incomes than residents of other skid rows (they don't), the difference might reflect inflationary trends and not increased buying power. Keeping these limitations in mind, the seven skid row populations will now be compared with respect to age, race, nativity, education, religious preference, marital status, occupation, and income.

Age. Age distributions for residents of the five skid rows and the two institutionalized skid row populations are given in Table 2-1. Minneapolis skid row men were older than any other group. Only Camp LaGuardia, an institution catering specifically to elderly men, had more men at the upper ages, and for the oldest group, men aged 65 or over, even Camp LaGuardia did not approach the proportion of aged men on the Minneapolis skid row. Next to Minneapolis, Sacramento and Camp LaGuardia had the largest proportions of men 65 and over, but only one of every four of their residents were that old, compared to one-third of the Minneapolis skid row men. Men under 45 were most numerous in Sacramento, followed by Chicago and Rochester. The two East Coast skid rows, New York and Philadelphia, were most alike in age distribution.

Race. The Sacramento skid row contained a sizable number of Latin Americans, mostly of Mexican descent. These men made up

Table 2-1

CHARACTERISTICS OF RESIDENTS OF FIVE SKID ROWS AND TWO INSTITUTIONALIZED SKID ROW POPULATIONS (IN PERCENTAGES)

	Sacramento[a] 1957	Chicago[b] 1958	Minneapolis[c] 1958	Philadelphia[d] 1959	Bowery 1966	Rochester[e] 1954	Camp LaGuardia 1966
Age							
Under 35	13	10	4	7	7	10	1
35-44	15	24	12	20	21	27	6
45-54	22	29	24	29	26	36	22
55-64	26	19	24	27	25	}27	48
65+	25	18	35	17	21		24
Total	101	100	99	100	100	100	101
Race							
Whites	84	88	95	84	70	82	75
Blacks	14	9	3	15	29	18	25
Others	3	2	2	2	1	—	1
Total	101	99	100	101	100	100	101
Nativity							
Native-born	76	85	76	90	77	91	79
Foreign-born	24	15	24	10	23	9	21
Total	100	100	100	100	100	100	100
Educational Attainment							
Grade School							
0-4 years	—	18	14	13	15	41	8
5-7 years	—	22	21	23	16	41	23
8 years	—	20	26	24	19	32	26
High School							
1-3 years	—	21	22	22	24	13	24
4 years	—	14	12	12	19	10	15
College							
1+ years	—	6	6	7	8	4	4
Total	—	101	101	101	101	100	100

Table 2-1 (Continued)

	Sacramento[a] 1957	Chicago[b] 1958	Minneapolis[c] 1958	Philadelphia[d] 1959	Bowery 1966	Rochester[e] 1954	Camp LaGuardia 1966
Religious Membership or Preference							
Catholic	—	39	—	42	53	40	53
Protestant	—	35	—	39	37	42	42
Jewish	—	1	—	1	1	—	2
Other	—	7	—	3	2	—	1
None	—	18	—	16	5	18	2
Total	—	100	—	101	99	100	100
Marital Status							
Never married	51	44	52	48	55	41	53
Married	4	—	4	—	2	2	—
Widowed	7	11	14	13	7	6	10
Separated	—	16	9	21	28	32	27
Divorced	36	29	21	18	9	19	10
Total	98	100	100	100	101	100	100
Annual Income[f]							
$0-499	15	25	13	21	29	—	—
500-749			40	9	5	—	—
750-999	4	22		15	6	—	—
1000-1499	24	17	13	17	18	—	—
1500-2499	26	19	20	17	28	—	—
2500-3499	12	14	7	12	7	—	—
3500-4499	18		5	3	3	—	—
4500+		3	2	6	4	—	—
Total	99	100	100	100	100	—	—
Occupation							
Professional, technical, and kindred workers	—	—	2	1	—	—	—
Managers, officials, and proprietors except farm	3	1	7	1	1	3	2
Clerical, sales, and kindred workers	2	14	13	3	7	2	8

Table 2-1 (Continued)

	Sacra-mento[a] 1957	Chicago[b] 1958	Minne-apolis[c] 1958	Phila-delphia[d] 1959	Bowery 1966	Rochester[e] 1954	Camp LaGuardia 1966
Craftsmen, foremen, and kindred workers	3	8	7	7	6	23	7
Operatives and kindred workers	4	10	14	8	4		8
Private household workers	—	—	—	—	—		—
Service workers, except private household	36	39	28	23	54	72	61
Farm laborers and foremen	31	—	—	2	2		2
Laborers, except farm and mine	21	28	29	55	27		12
Total	100	100	100	100	101	100	100

a. Western Real Estate Research, *Analysis of the Sacramento Labor Market Area* (Sacramento: Redevelopment Agency of the City of Sacramento, 1957), Table P-2, P-3, P-5; and Davis McEntire, "Population and Employment Survey of Sacramento's West End" (Sacramento: Redevelopment Agency of the City of Sacramento, 1952), pp. 6 and 23, unpublished. Available figures on nativity did not include Negroes and other races. The former were considered natives, and the latter were not included in computing the above percentages.

b. Donald J. Bogue, *Skid Row in American Cities* (Chicago: Community and Family Study Center, Univ. of Chicago, 1963), pp. 91, 108, 110, 262, 102; and Theodore Caplow, Keith A. Lovald, and Samuel E. Wallace, *A General Report on the Problem of Relocating the Population of the Lower Loop Redevelopment Area* (Minneapolis: Minneapolis Housing and Redevelopment Authority, 1958), p. 93.

c. Caplow *et al.*, pp. 22, 60, 71, 25, 74, and 93. Figures on income are from an unpublished table in the files of the Minneapolis Project.

d. Leonard Blumberg *et al.*, *The Men on Skid Row* (Philadelphia: Department of Psychiatry, Temple Univ. School of Medicine, 1960), pp. 3, 6, 11, 8, 12, 35, 75, and 62.

e. David J. Pittman and C. Wayne Gordon, *Revolving Door* (New York: The Free Press, 1958), pp. 18, 21, 28, 34, 36, 30, and 35. Figures refer to employment at the time of interview, or, in the case of Rochester, to "primary occupational skills, regardless of whether they were currently being utilized."

f. Figures for the Bowery sample are based on reported monthly income. In converting these to annual income, slight modifications in category limits were necessary. Thus, for the Bowery sample only, the lowest income category includes mean earning up to $540 a year, rather than $500; the upper limits for the other categories are, respectively, $780, $1020, $1500, $2460, $3540, and $4500.

about 15 percent of its total population. They are included in the White category in Table 2-1. None of the other skid row samples had more than a handful of Latin Americans.

The Minneapolis skid row was the "whitest" of the populations represented. In part, this may explain why it had more elderly men, since skid row Blacks tend to be younger than skid row Whites and all of the other populations represented had a substantial proportion of Blacks, ranging from 9 percent in Chicago to 29 percent on the Bowery. In any event, it is clear that the Bowery in 1966 had twice as many Blacks as any of the other skid rows at the time they were studied. There is some evidence that the proportion of Blacks on the Bowery increased during the decade 1956 to 1966, and it may be that if the data on the other skid rows were more current, they would show higher proportions of Blacks. Nevertheless, the size of the difference suggests that even at present the Bowery is probably "darker" than most skid rows in northern cities.

Nativity. Inspection of Table 2-1 shows that immigrants were most numerous on the Minneapolis and Sacramento skid rows and on the Bowery. Since there were many Blacks on the Bowery, almost all of them natives, the proportion of foreign-born Whites on the Bowery was somewhat higher than in Minneapolis. That foreign-born skid row men were more numerous on the Bowery than in any of the other cities under consideration might be expected, given New York's large foreign-born population. The high proportion of immigrants on the Minneapolis skid row is somewhat surprising. Also unexpected is the comparatively low representation of immigrants on Philadelphia's skid row. Philadelphia had the lowest proportion of immigrants (10 percent) of any of the skid rows under consideration.

The dominant country of origin for foreign-born skid row men varied from city to city. A foreign-born resident of the Bowery was most likely to be Irish; 4 percent of the entire Bowery population (and 9 percent of the Camp LaGuardia population) were born in Ireland; these immigrant Irishment constituted 20 percent of the Bowery immigrants (43 percent of the foreign-born Camp LaGuardia men). Similarly, about 20 percent of the foreign-born residents of the Philadelphia skid row were Irish. In Minneapolis, on the other hand, the overwhelming majority of the foreign-born on skid row were

Scandinavians, and the Irish were scarcely represented: 54 percent of the foreign-born skid row men were Scandinavians, and all the remainder of Western Europe accounted for only an additional 14 percent of the foreign-born.

Education. The frequency distributions of Table 2-1 reveal only slight differences in educational attainment. Bowery residents appear slightly better educated: 27 percent of them completed four years of high school, compared to between 18 and 20 percent of the other skid row populations. At the other end of the scale, a smaller proportion of Bowery men than any of the other populations had fewer than eight years of schooling: 31 percent of the Bowery and Camp LaGuardia men had little schooling, compared to between 35 and 41 percent of the other samples. Again, however, the time lag may be the critical factor. The apparent differences in education may be attributed to the fact that men in the Bowery sample grew up somewhat later than the men represented in the surveys of the other skid rows.

Religion. The Bowery and Camp LaGuardia samples were more heavily Catholic than the other samples. They also had fewer men reporting no religion. In part, this is a consequence of differences in the question about religion. The Rochester study asked about religious affiliation, and the Philadelphia and Chicago studies asked if respondents had ever been members of churches or religious groups. The Bowery and Camp LaGuardia men responded to questions about their religious preference, which resulted in the reporting of preferences by men never affiliated with a church.

However, if we can draw no conclusions from the differences among the skid row populations in proportion of men reporting no religion, it is possible to generalize from the ratio of Catholics to Protestants in the various samples. In Chicago, Philadelphia, and among chronic alcoholic inmates of the Monroe County Penitentiary, Catholics and Protestants were about equally represented. In the Bowery and Park Slope samples Catholics outnumbered Protestants in a ratio of about five to four. The relatively high proportion of Catholics in the New York samples reflects the high proportion of Irishmen among them.

Marital status. The proportion of men who had never married varies from 41 percent among imprisoned chronic alcoholics in Rochester to 55 percent of the Bowery men. In addition, divorced men appeared about twice as frequently among the other populations as in the Bowery and Camp LaGuardia samples, and the proportion of separations and desertions was much higher for the Bowery, Camp LaGuardia, and Rochester samples than for the other skid rows. The relatively high proportion of separations and desertions in the New York samples may reflect the difficulty (until recently) of obtaining divorces in New York State. It may also be a consequence of the relatively high proportion of Catholics in the Bowery and Camp LaGuardia samples.

Widowers and divorced men were much more numerous in the other skid rows than in New York. They made up about one-third of the Chicago, Minneapolis, and Philadelphia skid rows, but only one-sixth of the Bowery population, and one-fifth of the Camp LaGuardia population.

Annual income. The most striking results of comparing personal incomes among residents of the various skid rows was the high proportion of Bowery men in the lowest income bracket (Camp LaGuardia men, of course, were not employed in the usual sense, and income figures for them would not be meaningful). In 1966 the proportion of Bowery men making $500 or less per year was larger than it was seven to nine years earlier on the other skid rows. In other words, Bowery men in 1966 had *lower* incomes than men living on other skid rows some years earlier. Given the intervening inflation, it follows that the difference in actual buying power was even greater. Apparently there were more destitute men on the Bowery than on any of the other skid rows for which data were obtained. The Philadelphia skid row also had a fairly high percentage of men with less than $500 annual income.

Although the Philadelphia and Bowery skid rows had the larger proportions of men at the extremely low end of the income scale, Minneapolis had the lowest median income. The median income for the Minneapolis sample was below $1000; for the Chicago, Philadelphia, and Bowery samples it was between $1000 and $1500. The "richest" skid row men were in Sacramento, where their median income in 1957 was between $1500 and $2500 and almost one-fifth reported incomes of more than $3500 a year. Less than 10 percent of the residents of other skid rows had incomes that high.

Occupation. The distribution of skid row men by current or last occupation is given in Table 2-1. The Bowery distribution was not very different from that of other skid rows. The proportion of white-collar workers (the top three categories in the occupational hierarchy, including professionals, managers, clerical and sales workers) on skid row ranged from 5 percent in the Philadelphia and Rochester samples to 22 percent in the Minneapolis skid row. The Bowery and Camp LaGuardia samples were approximately in the middle of this range, with 8 and 10 percent in white-collar occupations.

Skilled and semiskilled workers (craftsmen and operatives) were also a minority on skid row. The proportion ranged from 7 percent in Sacramento to 23 percent in the Rochester sample. Again the Bowery and Camp LaGuardia samples occupied an intermediate position, with 10 percent and 15 percent, respectively.

It is apparent in the occupational distributions that most skid row men are either service workers or laborers. On some skid rows, such as Sacramento's, farm labor was an important occupation. But in most cities, laborers worked in the construction, transportation (usually railroad), or manufacturing industries. In Sacramento 88 percent of the skid row men were laborers or service workers. In the other samples the proportions were smaller, but only one skid row—Minneapolis—had fewer than two-thirds of its men employed in unskilled labor or service work. One difference between the Bowery and Camp LaGuardia samples and the other skid rows is that the proportion of service workers was higher (and of laborers correspondingly lower) in the New York samples than in the others. Over half of the Bowery men were service workers, most frequently dishwashers, cooks, porters, countermen, or busboys, and at Camp LaGuardia the proportion was 61 percent.

The proportion of men at the upper part of the occupational hierarchy—white-collar workers, craftsmen, and operatives—might be used as an index of the heterogeneity of skid row. By this standard the Bowery and Philadelphia and the Sacramento skid rows manifested the least occupational diversity and prestige, while the Chicago and Minneapolis skid rows appeared much more heterogeneous. The fact that 41 percent of the employed residents of the Minneapolis skid row held jobs other than service work or unskilled labor suggests that it was an attractive skid row in terms of its capacity to attract different types of workingmen.

Reasons for living on skid row. When skid row men were questioned about their reasons for living on skid row the most frequent response was that it did not cost very much to live there. One-third of the residents in Sacramento's labor market area gave cheap living as their major reason for living there, one-fifth of the residents of the Philadelphia skid row said that inexpensive living was what they liked about skid row, and more than half of the Chicago skid row men gave similar reasons for liking skid row as a place to live.[2]

Two questions about reasons for living on the Bowery were included in one of our pilot studies: What made you decide to stay in a lodging house rather than somewhere else? and Why did you pick a place on the Bowery to stay? Judging from the responses to these questions, cheap lodging is a dominant incentive drawing men to the Bowery. Almost two-thirds of the men mentioned cheap lodging and eating facilities as reasons for living on the Bowery.

Another frequently offered explanation for living on the Bowery was that the respondent had been given a ticket to one of the Bowery lodging houses by the Municipal Men's Shelter. One-fourth of the respondents said they were on the Bowery because the Men's Shelter tickets permitted them to live there.

Only one-sixth of the respondents reported any positive liking for the Bowery. Some of these men stated that they liked the neighborhood or found nothing wrong with it, others remarked that they were tired of sleeping on sidewalks, or "had to get a room somewhere, with at least a little respect." Finally, over one-sixth of the men indicated that they had come to the Bowery because they were seeking escape and anonymity, because of their chronic drinking, or for personal or family reasons.

In contrast with studies of other skid rows, relatively few Bowery men mentioned the congeniality of the area or the proximity to friends and social opportunities it afforded. One-fourth of the Chicago respondents said they liked the people on skid row, 14 percent of the Philadelphia respondents liked the congeniality and social life on skid row, and approximately the same proportion of Sacramento respondents gave proximity to friends, availability of amusements, or other social reasons for living where they were.[3] In contrast, only 5 percent of the Bowery respondents gave such sociability reasons.

The Bowery seemed much less attractive than the other skid rows as a labor market. One-third of the Sacramento sample and one-fourth of the Chicago sample said they lived in the skid row area because it was easy to find work there or because it was convenient to work, but only 11 percent of the Bowery men reported that they had come there seeking work or that they were working nearby and found it convenient to live on the Bowery.

One conclusion that may be drawn from these findings is that the Bowery is a fairly inefficient skid row. If the social function of skid row is to provide relative anonymity, cheap lodging and food, employment opportunities, recreation, and sociability, the Bowery does not seem to be competitive with other skid rows, particularly in the latter respects. The other skid rows discussed in this chapter seem to provide more entertainment and sociability and to be more active as employment centers. In contrast, Bowery life is dominated by the elements of skid row existence that are associated with social inertia. If the essence of skid row life is social withdrawal, the Bowery represents the skid row life style in its purest form.

HOMELESS MEN COMPARED TO SETTLED MEN

Having compared Bowery men with residents of other skid rows, let us now contrast them with three other populations: the lower-income, settled population of Park Slope, the upper-income men in the Park Avenue sample, and the adult male population of urbanized areas in the United States. We shall not consider the Camp La-Guardia men specifically in these comparisons; in most respects they are similar to the Bowery men, and the addition of a second skid row population would complicate the comparisons needlessly.

Age. The Park Slope and Park Avenue samples were designed to yield age distributions comparable to those of skid row men. As it turned out, the Park Slope respondents were slightly younger than the Bowery men, and the age distribution of Park Avenue men was very close to that of the Bowery men (see Table 2-2).

Table 2-2

CHARACTERISTICS OF BOWERY, PARK SLOPE, AND PARK AVENUE RESPONDENTS COMPARED TO ALL ADULT MALES IN U.S. URBANIZED AREAS (IN PERCENTAGES)

	Bowery 1966	Park Slope 1966	Park Avenue 1967	U.S. Urbanized Areas[a] 1960
Age				
Under 35	7	—	—	58
35-44	21	33	23	13
45-54	26	30	21	11
55-64	25	19	26	9
65+	21	18	30	8
Total	100	100	100	99
Race				
Whites	70	62	100	88
Blacks	29	37	—	11
Others	1	2	—	1
Total	100	101	100	100
Nativity				
Native-born	77	50	84	93
Foreign-born	23	50	16	7
Total	100	100	100	100
Educational Attainment				
Grade School				
0-4 years	15	11	2	7
5-7 years	16	23	—	13
8 years	19	19	3	16
High School				
1-3 years	24	22	8	20
4 years	19	17	16	22
College				
1+ years	8	8	71	22
Total	101	100	100	100
Religious Membership or Preference				
Catholic	53	55	10	22
Protestant	37	32	36	72
Jewish	2	2	48	3

Table 2-2 (Continued)

	Bowery 1966	Park Slope 1966	Park Avenue 1967	U.S. Urbanized Areas[a] 1960
Other	2	2	5	1
None	5	9	1	2
Total	99	100	100	100
Marital Status				
Never married	55	32	23	10
Married	2	51	66	81
Widowed	7	5	3	4
Separated	28	7	1	2
Divorced	9	5	7	3
Total	101	100	100	100
Annual Income				
Less than $499	29	8	—	3
$500–$999	11	2	—	6
$1000–$1499	18	11	—	
$1500–$2499	28	11	—	16[b]
$2500–$3499	7	18	2	
$3500–$4499	3	17	1	23[c]
$4500–$6999	3	23	3	27[d]
$7000–$9999	1	8	7	15
$10,000–$19,999	—	2	20	10
$20,000 and over	—	—	66	
Total	100	100	99	100
Occupation				
Professional, technical, kindred workers	—	4	35	13
Farmers and farm managers	—	—	—	—
Managers, officials, and proprietors, excepting farm	1	4	56	12
Clerical and kindred workers	6	10	1	9
Sales workers	1	1	6	9
Craftsmen	6	21	1	21
Operatives and kindred workers	4	26	—	20

Table 2-2 (Continued)

	Bowery 1966	Park Slope 1966	Park Avenue 1967	U.S. Urbanized Areas[a] 1960
Private household workers	–	–	–	–
Service workers, excepting private household	54	30	2	8
Farm laborers and foremen	2	–	–	–
Laborers, excepting farm and mine	27	4	–	7
Total	101	100	101	99

a. Sources, respectively, are U.S. Bureau of the Census, *U.S. Census of Population: 1960. Selected Area Reports. Type of Place,* Final Report PC (3)–1E (Washington, D.C., U.S. Government Printing Office, 1964), Table 1, Table 5; U.S. Bureau of the Census, *U.S. Census of Population: 1960. Subject Reports. Marital Status,* Final Report PC (2)–4E (Washington, D.C.: U.S. Government Printing Office, 1966), Table 4; Bernard Lazerwitz, "Religiouns and Social Structure in the United States," in Louis Schneider, ed., *Religion, Culture, and Society,* (New York: John Wiley, & Sons, 1964), p. 427; U.S. Bureau of the Census, *Marital Status, op. cit.,* Table 4; *ibid.*, Table 6; *ibid.*, Table 5; *ibid.*, Table 6; *ibid.*, Table 5. Figures for age, race, and nativity are for all males in urbanized areas. Those for educational attainment, marital status, and income are for males 25 and over; those for religion are for a sample of the U.S. population (both sexes) 21 and over; and those for occupation are for males 14 years of age and over. Income figures are for 1959.

b. $1000-$2999

c. $3000-$4999

d. $5000-$6999

Bowery men are old men. Almost three-fourths of the national population were under 45 years of age, but only 28 percent of the Bowery men were that young. Half of the Bowery men were between 45 and 65, compared to only one-fifth of the national population. Finally, men over 65 were about three times as numerous on skid row as proportionately in the national population.

Race. One of the criteria guiding our selection of a low-income census tract for a control sample was that its ethnic composition be comparable to that of the Bowery. In New York City there are few low-income tracts with predominantly White populations. Accordingly, the similarity of racial composition between the Bowery and the Park Slope sample does not mean that the racial composition of the Bowery is not unusual. Almost all other tracts in the city at comparable income levels are populated by Blacks or Puerto Ricans. Thus, one important difference between the Bowery men and other impoverished city populations is that the latter are predominately non-White.

No racial criteria guided the selection of the Park Avenue sample, but we were somewhat surprised to find that all of the respondents there were white. The ethnic composition of the Bowery was approximately the same as that of New York City as a whole. Both had higher proportions of Blacks than did the combined urbanized areas of the country.

Nativity. Almost one-fourth of the Bowery men were foreign-born, but in other sections of the city, such as the Park Slope census tract, the proportion of foreign-born men was much higher. All three of the New York City samples had higher proportions of foreign stock than did urbanized areas in the country as a whole.

Education. The Bowery and Park Slope samples are very well matched with respect to educational attainment, and with the exception of slightly higher proportions of men with zero to four years schooling and substantially lower proportions of men with college experience, their educational distributions are like those of the national population of males age 25 and over living in urbanized areas. The most striking contrast in education is that between the Park Avenue men and the other populations. Seventy-one percent of the Park Avenue respondents attended at least one year of college. That figure is more than three times as high as the national proportion and nine times higher than the proportion of college men in the Bowery or Park Slope samples.

Religion. The Bowery and Park Slope samples have remarkably similar religious compositions; slightly over half are Catholic, and about one-third Protestant. The predominance of Catholics was not characteristic of males in the country as a whole, but it was not particularly deviant for New York City. As with race and education, the Park Avenue sample was the most deviant in religious composition; almost half of the men living there were Jewish, and even by national standards Catholics were severely underrepresented.

Marital status. This variable is the first characteristic in which skid row men were clearly distinct from settled men. Only 2 percent of the Bowery men were married at the time of the interview, compared to over half of the males in all other populations. In urbanized areas in the entire United States, over 80 percent of the men over 25 were married. The New York City samples had lower proportions married; among the Park Avenue men the proportion was two-thirds. The fact that over half of the Bowery men had *never* been married marks them as atypical. Furthermore, even though most of the Bowery men had never married, the incidence of separation, divorce, and widowhood among them was higher than for any of the other populations.

Income. The figures on annual income in Table 2-2 reveal sharp differences among all populations represented in the table. The Bowery men are the poorest: in 1966, 86 percent of them had annual incomes of less than $2500. Next are the Park Slope men, with a median income of approximately $3500. In the national population over half of the men made more than $5000 in 1959, but these incomes pale beside those of the Park Avenue men. One out of every 10 males aged 25 and over in the national sample had an income of $10,000 or more, but 86 percent of the Park Avenue men had incomes that high, and two-thirds of them reported annual incomes of $20,000 or more.

None of the populations represented in Table 2-2 had an income distribution congruent with any of the others. Each group seems to represent a different point on a continuum, ranging from the abject poverty of the Bowery men to the great affluence of the Park Avenue men.

Occupation. The occupational distributions which conclude Table 2-2 parallel the income distributions in that four distinct patterns are apparent. The Bowery men again stand at the lower end of the continuum. They are concentrated in two occupational categories, service workers and laborers, and these two categories account for the present or last occupations of more than four-fifths of the Bowery residents.

Service workers were also common in the Park Slope sample, but so were operatives, craftsmen, foremen, and kindred workers, and 19 percent of the Park Slope men were white-collar workers. The most common categories in the national population of employed males aged 14 years and over were craftsmen, foremen, and kindred workers (21 percent) and operatives and kindred workers (20 percent). In addition, almost half of the national population (43 percent) were white-collar workers, with professionals (13 percent) and managers, officials, and proprietors (12 percent) represented about equally.

Finally, there is the Park Avenue sample. Managers and officials were relatively more numerous there than were service workers among Bowery men. One-third of the Park Avenue men were professional or technical workers, and well over half were managers, officials, and proprietors. In fact, 98 percent of the Park Avenue respondents held or had formerly held white-collar jobs.

In summary, we have four distinct occupational distributions: a predominantly blue-collar population, mostly temporary workers employed as laborers or service workers on the Bowery; a higher status blue-collar group, in which steadily employed craftsmen, operatives, and service workers make up more than three-fourths of the total in Park Slope; a nearly equal division between white-collar and blue-collar occupations in the national sample; and the totally white-collar Park Avenue population.

THE DECLINE OF SKID ROW *

For several years expert observers of the Bowery noted a continuing decline in its homeless population,[4] but until 1964 no fully substantiated data were available. In that year the Bowery Project began a series of annual enumerations. Four annual enumerations

* This section draws upon a previously published paper by Howard M. Bahr, "The Gradual Disappearance of Skid Row," *Social Problems,* 15 (Summer 1967), pp. 41-45, with the permission of the Society for the Study of Social Problems.

were conducted under the auspices of the research project,[5] and we made estimates of the Bowery populations in 1949 and 1963.[6] After 1967 the annual censuses of the area begun by the Bowery Project were continued by the Bureau of Shelter Services for Adults of the Department of Social Services.[7]

Comparisons of these estimates and enumerations reveals a steady and fairly rapid decline in the Bowery population between 1949 and 1969, followed by a leveling off and very slight decline between 1969 and 1972 (see Table 2-3). Between 1949 and 1968 the population declined from 13,675 to 4354, a total decline of 68 percent. Note that between 1963 and 1968 the annual decline ranged from 6 to 11 percent.

In an attempt to determine whether the declining Bowery population represented part of the national trend or was limited to New York City, inquiries were sent in August 1966 to commissioners of welfare in 40 United States cities having sizable skid row areas.[8] The

Table 2-3

WINTER POPULATION OF THE BOWERY, 1949 TO 1972[a]

Year	Bowery Population (homeless men)	Decline from Previous Census	
		Absolute	Percentage
1949	13675	—	—
1963	6938	6737	49.37
1964	6477	461	6.6
1965	6093	384	5.9
1966	5406	687	11.3
1967	4851	555	10.3
1968	4354	497	10.2
1969	4344	10	0.2
1970	4284	60	1.4
1971	4325	-41	-1.0
1972	4152	173	4.0

a. The 1963 estimate is for a day in January. The other figures are for February. Date of enumeration for the 1964 to 1967 period was the last Friday in February. The 1968 to 1972 enumerations have continued the pattern of making the count late in the last week of February; the 1972 enumeration was for February 24, the last Thursday in the month.

letter requested information about recent population trends in each city's skid row(s) and asked if the city sponsored redevelopment or rehabilitation programs that impinged on skid row and its men. In all, correspondents in 28 cities[9] provided information about population trends affecting their skid rows. Sometimes the commissioners themselves replied, and sometimes the inquiries were referred to local experts on the staffs of agencies dealing more directly with skid row.

Data from the 28 cities are summarized in Table 2-4. They demonstrate a consistent national trend: The skid row population seems to be gradually disappearing. However, the apparent trend should be interpreted in the light of some qualifications about the data.

First, the quality of the data varies from city to city. In some cases census statistics or administrative caseloads provided an empirical basis for judgment, but in others we have only the opinions of local experts. A second qualification concerns the extent of population

Table 2-4

CURRENT POPULATION TRENDS IN SKID ROWS IN SELECTED AMERICAN CITIES, 1966

Skid Row Population				No Information
Increasing	Stable	Decreasing		
Tacoma	Birmingham	Chattanooga	Omaha	Akron
	Boston	Chicago	Philadelphia	Baltimore
	Richmond	Cincinnati	Pittsburgh	Buffalo
		Cleveland	Portland	Columbus
		Detroit	Providence	Denver
		Fort Worth	Rochester	Indianapolis
		Houston	Sacramento	Kansas City
		Milwaukee	St. Louis	Los Angeles
		Minneapolis	St. Paul	Oakland
		Nashville	Toledo	Norfolk
		New Orleans	Seattle	San Jose
		Oklahoma City	San Francisco	Syracuse

decline. Some of the reported declines are very large, involving 50 percent or more of the total skid row population; others are relatively small.

To what can the decline be attributed? Does it represent a real decrease in the number of homeless men, or is it due merely to their dispersion from the skid rows to other urban areas?

Most observers on the Bowery attributed the local decline to one of three factors: (1) national prosperity, (2) changes in the composition of the population, and (3) changing policies of the Department of Welfare.

According to the national-prosperity view, skid rows are barometers of the level of the economy. When unemployment is down and business booming, skid rows are almost empty; when business falters and jobs are hard to get, skid rows fill up. As one hotel manager put it, "The lodging houses are barometers of business; business down, you're up." This explanation would seem to be supported by the slowed rate of decline in the period 1968 to 1972, a period of national economic recession in comparison with the previous decade.

Changes in the composition of skid row populations also are partly due to the state of the economy. When jobs are easy to find, most of the men who want to work are employed. Then only the hard-core derelicts and unemployables are left on skid row, and they are easy prey for muggers and thieves. It is widely believed on the Bowery that there has been a recent influx of Black hoodlums, and that consequently many older men are afraid to come to the Bowery. According to one informant:

> The backbone of the Bowery, the old pensioner, is going the way of all flesh, death or a home; and this leaves the worst element, which tends to chase others. Hence a vicious circle. Medicare should hasten this decline and thus we have left only the rotten core—the wino-derelict.

The changing character of the Bowery was also attributed to a Department of Welfare policy of placing unattached men in off-Bowery rooming houses rather than skid row lodging houses. Naturally the lodging house owners were unhappy about this policy. In the words of one of them:

> . . . the whole city instead of the Bowery then gets ruined. . . . They [homeless men] belong down here. We're not losing them; they're taking them out. It's not that the men want off the Bowery—they're forced; they [Department of Welfare] won't give them tickets if they stay here; they'd rather be here.

It is probable that the factors mentioned above, or similar ones, have influenced population changes on skid rows elsewhere than in New York City. One important factor operating in many cities which has yet to exert much direct effect on the Bowery is urban renewal. In many cities, urban redevelopment programs have dispersed skid row populations, replacing skid row institutions with more respectable facilities such as concert halls and civic centers. At the present time urban renewal for the Bowery area is still in the planning stages.

Neither in New York nor in the other cities is it possible to assert that the homeless population is disappearing. In fact, several of the officials who corresponded with us stressed that the population decline on skid row was due to dispersion and did not represent any diminution of the homeless population. Note, for example, the following comments by informants in Houston, Rochester, St. Louis, and San Francisco:

> Many buildings previously housing homeless men have been demolished . . . resulting in some rather undefined spread of our skid row area in numerous directions.

> . . . our traditional Skid Row, has been recently removed by an urban redevelopment project . . . making regrouping in other parts of the downtown area a strong possibility, if not an absolute necessity.

> The situation hasn't been alleviated, it's merely been displaced. Instead of one big Skid Row we now have a lot of little ones around the city.[10]

> It is our impression that . . . smaller "skid rows" are proliferating in various areas of the city. . . . It is also our impression that the number of "unattached" men of low economic status residing out-

> side of institutions has in nowise diminished over the past 15 years in San Francisco.

These remarks may not reflect conditions in other cities: in some places declines of skid row populations may represent real attrition of the homeless population. In general, however, there is little evidence that the absolute number of homeless men is declining.

To some extent, the dispersion of skid row men will obscure the problem of homelessness. If they no longer have an ecological base, homeless men may receive less attention from the public and from social agencies. On the other hand, an increase in the number of homeless men in a particular neighborhood makes them more visible in that area and may provoke hostile reactions among other residents.[11]

With the dispersion of skid row men and the transformation of the skid row area to other patterns of land use, homeless men will no longer have to bear the stigma of skid row residence. The absence of this stigma should facilitate their rehabilitation. For example, the homeless man living off skid row may be less likely to consider himself a failure and to be perceived as a failure by others. But the passing of skid row does not obviate the need for continued attention to homelessness in other social settings.

NOTES

1. David J. Pittman and C. Wayne Gordon, *Revolving Door* (New York: The Free Press, 1958); Western Real Estate Research Corporation, *Analysis of the Sacramento Labor Market Area* (Sacramento: Redevelopment Agency of the City of Sacramento, California, 1957); Davis McEntire, *Population and Employment Survey of Sacramento's West End* (Sacramento: Redevelopment Agency of the City of Sacramento, California, 1952); Donald J. Bogue, *Skid Row in American Cities* (Chicago: Univ. of Chicago, Community and Family Study Center, 1963); Theodore Caplow, Keith A. Lovald, and Samuel E. Wallace, *A General Report on the Problem of Relocating the Population of the Lower Loop Redevelopment Area* (Minneapolis: Minneapolis Housing and Rede-

velopment Authority, 1958); Leonard Blumberg *et al., The Men on Skid Row* (Philadelphia: Temple Univ. School of Medicine, Department of Psychiatry, 1960).

2. Western Real Estate Research Corporation, *op. cit.,* Table P-7; Blumberg *et al., op. cit.,* p. 157; Bogue, *op. cit.,* p. 135.

3. Bogue, *op. cit.,* p. 135; Blumberg *et al.,* p. 157; Western Real Estate Corporation, *op. cit.,* Table P-7.

4. The Bowery reached its peak population during the depression, when the number of homeless men there on any given day varied from about 15,000 in April 1930 to over 20,000 in March 1935. See Nels Anderson, *The Homeless in New York City* (New York: Welfare Council of New York City, 1934), pp. 46-47 and 413; and Welfare Council of New York City, *Homeless Men in New York City* (New York: Welfare Council, 1949), pp. 1 and 23.

5. The methods and findings of these enumerations are reported in George Nash and Patricia Nash, *A Preliminary Estimate of the Population and Housing of the Bowery in New York City* (New York: Bureau of Applied Social Research, Columbia Univ., 1964); and Michael A. Baker, *An Estimate of the Population of Homeless Men in the Bowery Area, New York City, February 26, 1965* (New York: Bureau of Applied Social Research, Columbia Univ., 1965).

6. Nash and Nash, *op. cit.,* p. 15; and George Nash, *The Habitats of Homeless Men in Manhattan* (New York: Bureau of Applied Social Research, Columbia Univ., 1964), p. C-5. See also a discussion of past enumerations of the Bowery in Baker, *op. cit.,* pp. 23-28.

7. Results of Bowery censuses for the years 1968 through 1972 were obtained in correspondence from G. E. Walsh, Deputy Assistant Commissioner of the Bureau of Institutional Services for Adults, City of New York Department of Social Services.

8. The list of cities was taken from Donald J. Bogue, *Skid Row in American Cities,* p. 6.

9. After three mailings, we had replies from 36 cities. However, correspondents in eight cities were unable to give us any information about recent changes in the population of their skid rows. The "No Information" column of Table 2-4 includes those eight.

10. Dickson Terry, "Old Skid Row is on the Skids," *St. Louis Post-Dispatch,* March 14, 1965, p. 1F.

11. See, for example, Joan Shapiro, "Single-Room Occupancy; Community of the Alone," *Social Work,* 11 (October 1966), p. 25; Martin Arnold, "West Side Asks Aid with Misfits," *New York Times,* March 16, 1965, p. 41; and Jon Lowell, "City Faces Skid Row Cluster, Council Told," *Detroit News,* February 24, 1967, p. 4B.

CHAPTER 3

HOMELESSNESS AND DISAFFILIATION *

Most research about homelessness has focused on residents of skid row. Previous investigators have recognized that some homeless persons live elsewhere, but there are few empirical studies of the homeless man outside of skid row. As a result, there is a dearth of information about the homeless population as a whole.

Levinson has compared the homeless men on skid row to the visible part of an iceberg of homelessness.[1] The dimensions of the submerged bulk of the homeless population in one area may be inferred from Nash's estimate (1964) that in Manhattan alone there were 30,000 homeless men in addition to the 7500 residents of the Bowery.[2]

DEFINITIONS OF HOMELESSNESS

The definitions of homelessness underlying most studies can be roughly grouped into two classes. One of these is the spatial, or ecological, view, in which residents of a particular urban area are defined as homeless. In the other perspective, homeless men are the unattached and isolated, regardless of their economic status or area of residence. Sometimes both orientations are blended in a single work which defines homelessness in the latter sense but limits research to homelessness as spatially defined.

In one of the earliest large-scale studies of homelessness, Solenberger recognized that not all homeless men visit charitable institutions and live on skid rows. She pointed out that the term homeless applied to men who had left one family group and had not yet identified themselves with another, and stressed that her work did

* Portions of this chapter are adapted from "Homelessness, Disaffiliation and Retreatism," in Howard M. Bahr, ed., *Disaffiliated Man: Essays and Bibliography on Skid Row, Vagrancy and Outsiders* (Toronto: Univ. of Toronto Press, 1970), pp. 39-50, and are used by permission of the University of Toronto Press.

not apply to the entire population of homeless men, but merely to those "who live in cheap lodging houses in the congested part of any large city." Her sample consisted of men who applied for assistance at the Chicago Bureau of Charities between 1900 and 1903.[3]

The homeless man described in Anderson's *The Hobo* is the "migratory casual worker." Neither his description of homeless men as "the men who inhabit Hobohemia" nor his classification of types of homelessness alluded to the existence of homeless men outside the ranks of lower-class casual workers and nonworkers.[4] The focus of Sutherland and Locke was even more limited: throughout their work homeless man was synonymous with shelter man.[5]

Dunham was among those who identified homeless men in terms of their skid row habitat while defining them in terms of personal characteristics or "situational factors." He approached a formal definition of homelessness by characterizing the homeless as those who have a high probability of being incompletely socialized and who are socially isolated to a high degree.[6]

Clients of skid row agencies were the subjects of Levinson's studies of homelessness, but his definition of homelessness includes not only skid row men but all persons who have learned a "fundamental detachment from life" and a "nonacceptance of the values of our society." [7]

The title of one of the reports of Bogue's Chicago study, *The Homeless Man on Skid Row,* implied that there may be homeless men elsewhere, but the reports gave exclusive attention to the skid row man. Bogue recognized a broad category of homeless individuals, "civilian persons living outside of regular households but not in institutions," but was concerned only with the portion of this population that resided on skid row.[8]

Wallace documented the diversity in researchers' definitions of homeless and skid row men, listing five attributes by which the unattached have been identified in the past: transience, residence on skid row, chronic inebriation, extreme poverty, and separation from kin.[9] He combined these characteristics in a classification scheme subsuming them all under the term skid-rower. His choice of the latter term was somewhat unfortunate because half of the cells in his table referred to persons who did not live on skid row, and several of the works he cited (such as Pittman and Gordon; Minehan) to support the contention that researchers differ in their definitions of skid-rower were not defining skid row men at all but, rather, chronic police-case inebriates or transients.[10]

What the five characteristics have in common is that they all are related to what Caplow, Bahr, and Sternberg have called "detachment from society characterized by the absence or attenuation of the affiliative bonds that link settled persons to a network of interconnected social structures." [11] Thus, transience tends to prevent one from establishing stable social bonds, while residence on skid row and involvement in its institutions place one in a stigmatized minority. Chronic inebriation disrupts social bonds as well as physiological balance, extreme poverty prevents one from performing customary roles in society, and living without kin removes one from the principal social context of interpersonal responsibility. In short, the elements utilized by various writers to describe the homeless or skid row population all have to do with the weakening or absence of affiliations.

Social affiliation, the unifying element in the diverse definitions of homeless or skid row persons, also provides a link to one of the major theoretical perspectives of modern sociology, Merton's anomie theory. According to this theory one responds to the strains generated by disjuncture between societally prescribed goals and available means for achieving those goals by rebellion, innovation, ritualism, or retreatism. Merton identifies tramps and vagrants as retreatists,[12] but there has been a notable lack of research on the dimensions and consequences of retreatism. A clarification of the relation between retreatism and disaffiliation seems in order.

RETREATISM AND DISAFFILIATION

The terms withdrawal and retreatism are closely linked, and perhaps an attempt at delimiting retreatism may begin with a consideration of their dictionary meanings. As a transitive verb, to *withdraw* means to take something back or away; as an intransitive verb, it means to retire, to retreat, or to go away. In either sense, there is motion from one place or state to another.

Retreat may be defined as retirement or withdrawal from what is difficult, dangerous, or disagreeable, and may also denote a place of seclusion, privacy, safety, or refuge. The term focuses on the act of leaving the difficult or disagreeable situation, but retreat *from* something necessarily is retreat *to* something. Like the fleeing general who is merely "advancing in a different direction," one moves from one place or state to another. On the other hand, retreat connotes a coming out of circulation, a step from activity into inactivity or from active into passive service.

The parallel between spatial and social withdrawal makes it apparent that there are absolute and relative degrees of retreat and that one cannot retreat from where he has never been. Thus, certain inert segments of the population do not manifest much retreat. They may be outsiders, but they have never been affiliated to any great extent.

It is difficult to separate retreatist behavior from the normal processes of making choices between more or less agreeable alternatives. All men are retreatists in the sense that they tend to retire from what is disagreeable and embrace the agreeable. When is withdrawal retreat, and when is it merely change? Just as all members of society may engage in illegal behavior without thereby being considered criminal, so may they all manifest some degree of withdrawal from social involvement without thereby qualifying for the label retreatist. As with the term criminal, the term retreatist might be reserved for those who manifest a high degree of retreatist behavior.

If retreatism is conceptualized as a type of disaffiliation, the problem of measuring it is greatly simplified. Any measure of social involvement may serve, and the concept is culture-free. Whatever local form social affiliation happens to take, retreatism denotes withdrawal from that involvement.

Now that retreatists have been identified as a subclass of the population of disaffiliates, the relation of retreatism to other forms of disaffiliation may be considered briefly. In this connection we must give some attention to the process of becoming homeless or disaffiliated.

At least three major paths to disaffiliation may be distinguished. First, external changes may leave an individual with few affiliations. For example, his family and friends may die, his occupation may become obsolete, or biological changes (disease or senility) may make him incapable of forming or maintaining new organizational ties; at the same time social change or natural accidents may remove his old affiliations. In these cases society may be seen as withdrawing from the individual: his world disappears, and he remains alone and unattached, a stranger from another time or place.

A second possibility is that the individual withdraws from society. That is, he may estrange himself from organizations to which he formerly belonged; for numerous reasons he may voluntarily cut himself adrift. The man without a country is a classic example of this type of withdrawal. In some cases society may expel the individual, or the cost of his remaining in society may be so great that he feels constrained to leave. Exiles and outlaws are examples of this type.

A third avenue to unattachment is lifetime isolation. Some perons are outsiders from their youth and have never been affiliated to any degree. Such persons may be considered undersocialized in the sense that for one reason or another they have not had the experience and opportunities which serve to provide most people with ties to several kinds of communities and organizations.

Disaffiliation is one of the fundamental processes of social life. Organizational ties are continuously formed and dissolved. From the standpoint of a particular group, a disaffiliate is one who terminates his membership in the group. Factors contributing to that termination and the disaffiliate's subsequent career may or may not be of interest to the remaining members of the organization. It is possible that his disaffiliation from the one organization precedes more intense and extensive affiliations. Nevertheless, from the standpoint of the original organization, disaffiliation has occurred. Thus, what is retreatist behavior from one point of view may be interpretable as affiliative from another.

Since formation, cessation, and attenuation of ties is a predictable aspect of ongoing social life, organizations establish norms for recruiting, reactivating, and replacing role-incumbents. Not only do organizations have established procedures for dealing with the disaffected and marginal members, but they have modes of interorganizational sanction whereby to some degree even a former member is available for sanction, provided he is a participant in another organization that is part of the same societal system.

The stability of the larger system is threatened not by the continual forming and dissolution of bonds, but by the dissolution of bonds without the formation of new ones. The disaffiliate who does not reaffiliate moves beyond the power of particular organizations and ultimately beyond the reach of organized society. He poses a threat because he has moved out of the reward system; he is a man out of control. Being functionally, if not actually, devoid of significant others, property, and substantial responsibility, he is not subject to the usual social constraints. It is no threat to the fully disaffiliated man to threaten him with the forfeiture of his property, the imprisonment of his family, or the loss of his job. He has none of these. Perhaps the only sanction remaining is corporal punishment, and in a system where the use of such punishments is minimized there is no predictable way to control the retreatist. He may go along with the rules, but there is no guarantee that he will do so, and because he is not part of the system, he has no important stake in its continuity. Hence, he cannot be trusted.

Although total disaffiliation puts one beyond the power of the society, in another sense the retreatist is the most powerless of men. Where ordinary men have multiple channels through which they can invite the support of others, he has only himself to call upon.

A SOCIAL-PSYCHOLOGICAL APPROACH

The conception of retreatism outlined above permits the researcher to identify the retreatist in terms of his behavior (the number of his memberships, for instance) but does not take into account his perceptions or expectations. An alternative approach based upon the individual's conceptions of what is normal or socially expected will be considered briefly.

If the essence of retreatism is social withdrawal, a measure involving the subject's perception of the extent of his own withdrawal would seem justified. The advantage of a social-psychological definition of this kind is that it requires no assumption that all retreatists have the same opportunities for affiliation or the same understanding of social expectations. In effect, each man provides his own standard, and the extent of his retreat is measured against that standard.[13]

By this definition, a person who did not measure up to society's expectations as he perceived them might be a retreatist in his own eyes and yet elicit no societal sanctions. In contrast, the definition of retreatism as overt disaffiliation involves behavior of higher visibility and a greater likelihood of sanctions. The degree to which retreatists in the latter sense (extreme disaffiliates) also perceive themselves as having withdrawn from those activities expected of them is an open question.

Skid row, like any other area of the city, may include affiliated men as well as disaffiliates. Among the population of disaffiliates some may be identified as retreatists, depending on the extent of their current and former affiliations. In the framework offered, all retreatists are disaffiliates, but not all disaffiliates are retreatists. In the remainder of this chapter we shall look at the affiliations of our sample of skid row men and attempt to determine how disaffiliated they are in comparison with our control samples.

INTERSAMPLE CONTRASTS IN AFFILIATION

In the exploratory phase of the Bowery Project, we defined a homeless man as (1) living apart from kin of any sort, (2) over 21 years of age, (3) paying subsistence rent or no rent, and (4) not holding responsible employment. Artists, students, and inmates of hospitals, nursing homes, and prisons were specifically excluded, even if they met the four criteria.[14] This definition included almost all the people ordinarily identified as homeless; it was a combination of conspicuous characteristics of homeless persons but lacked an explicit unifying concept.

We moved in time to the position outlined above, that homelessness is a condition of general disaffiliation from social organizations. Traditionally, the homeless man has been viewed as unattached, and to describe homelessness in terms of disaffiliation is not an extreme departure from earlier definitions; but it does extend the phenomenon from the skid row population to all persons characterized by the absence or attenuation of affiliative ties.

The designation of minimally affiliated individuals as homeless was hypothetical. Before the extent of organizational affiliation could be used to measure homelessness, it had to be shown that persons considered homeless by traditional criteria such as skid row residence were in fact characterized by minimal affiliation. A comparison of the organizational affiliations of skid row men and the control samples was a useful first step. If the definition of homelessness in terms of

Table 3-1

PERCENTAGE OF RESPONDENTS AFFILIATED, FOR VARIOUS MEASURES OF LIFETIME AND CURRENT AFFILIATION

Measures of Affiliation	Bowery		Camp LaGuardia		Park Slope		Park Avenue	
	Percentage Affiliated	Total (N)	Percentage Affiliated	Total (N)	Percentage Affiliated	Total (N)	Percentage Affiliated	Total (N)
Lifetime measures								
Ever married	47	200	47	199	71	123	77	104
Ever voted	65	203	71	199	71	125	96	104
Over 8 years education	51	198	43	195	47	118	94	103
Organizational affiliations(s) in youth[a]	54	200	53	198	42	122	74	103
Current measures								
Currently employed	39	203	—	—	74	125	91	104
Saw family member within past year[b]	35	195	20	194	67	117	90	103
Attends church at least twice a month	25	201	31	194	39	122	22	103
Belongs to informal group[c]	31	203	35	199	35	124	72	104
Has organizational affiliation(s)[d]	23	202	17	199	52	122	63	103
Has close friend(s) in New York City	33	201	20	199	50	123	80	104
Knows names of more than 5 neighbors	49	200	58	198	45	123	61	104

Table 3-1 (Continued)

Measures of Affiliation	Bowery		Camp LaGuardia		Park Slope		Park Avenue	
	Percentage Affiliated	Total (N)	Percentage Affiliated	Total (N)	Percentage Affiliated	Total (N)	Percentage Affiliated	Total (N)
Would like to know more neighbors	22	196	24	191	29	120	34	98
Would join a neighborhood organization	65	197	50	186	66	120	51	83
Conversed with 6+ people yesterday	53	202	57	197	54	124	71	103

a. Refers primarily to membership in voluntary organizations; jobs, church membership, family affiliation, and school attendance are excluded. Youth is defined as before age twenty.

b. Family member living with respondents is excluded.

c. Men responding affirmatively to the question, Are there certain men you often hang around with? were considered as belonging to an informal group.

d. Refers primarily to voluntary organizations (see note a).

disaffiliation is valid, skid row men should be found to be less affiliated than men in the other samples.

In Table 3-1 the four samples are compared with reference to 14 measures of lifetime and current affiliation. For the present we will not discuss the inconsequential differences between the Bowery and Camp LaGuardia samples. References to skid row men apply to both samples, and as a rule, statements about Bowery men also apply to Camp LaGuardia men. These 14 measures will be used throughout this book as indicators of affiliation. The Park Avenue men are more affiliated than the other respondents on all but two of these measures. The exceptions are the expressed willingness to join an organization devoted to improving conditions and services in their own neighborhood and regular church attendance. Several of the Park Avenue men indicated that conditions and services in their neighborhood were already adequate, and the greater willingness expressed by Bowery and Park Slope men to join such an organization probably reflects the relative inadequacy of conditions and services in their neighborhoods rather than any marked affiliative tendency. Church attendance is most frequent among the Park Slope men. The Park Avenue respondents are the least likely to attend church services.

Let us examine the data of Table 3-1 from another perspective. First, note those indicators which reveal extreme disaffiliation linked to skid row residence, that is, those items where there are sharp contrasts between the Bowery men and the Park Slope men. One lifetime measure (ever married) and four measures of current affiliation show such contrasts. We have discussed the atypical marital experience of skid row men in Chapter 2. As for the current affiliations, we see that the Park Slope men are about twice as likely to be employed, twice as likely to have seen a relative within the past year, more than twice as likely to maintain one or more memberships in formal organizations, and slightly less than twice as likely to have at least one close friend in the city. To summarize, the skid row man has few jobs, contacts with kin, formal memberships, or close friends.

In several other respects, however, he is very much like his low-income counterpart from a settled neighborhood. The Bowery man was just as apt as the Park Slope man to have voted, to be educated, or to have participated in organizations in his youth. The Bowery man is somewhat less likely to attend church frequently, but he considers himself part of an informal group of men just as often as does the Park Slope man, and he is just as likely to know the names of his neighbors and to talk to them.

Now let us consider the differentials between the three low-income samples and the Park Avenue men. Almost all (96 percent) of the Park Avenue men have voted at some time in life, but fully one-third of the Bowery men and more than one-fourth of the Park Slope men have never voted. Ninety-four percent of the high-income men completed more than eight years of formal schooling, compared to only half that proportion in the low-income samples. In addition, the Park Avenue men are twice as likely to belong to an informal group of friends or to have friends at all. Eighty percent of them have at least one close friend in New York City, compared to half of the Park Slope men and one-third of the Bowery men. Although the Park Avenue respondents are only slightly more likely to have married than the Park Slope men, they see their relatives much more frequently than the men in the other samples. They talk to more people on an average day and know the names of more of their neighbors. In youth they were more affiliated with voluntary associations and they continue so throughout life.

It is plain that disaffiliation is a relative thing. The skid row man is disaffiliated in some ways, but in other ways he is just as bound in the social network as is the lower-income settled man. All of the lower-income samples manifest substantial disaffiliation when compared to the higher-income sample. The social and affiliative distance between Park Slope and the Bowery is no greater than that between Park Avenue and Park Slope.

NOTES

1. Boris M. Levinson, "The Homeless Man: A Psychological Enigma," *Mental Hygiene,* 47 (October 1963), pp. 590-601.

2. George Nash, *The Habitats of Homeless Men in Manhattan* (New York: Columbia Univ., Bureau of Applied Social Research, 1964).

3. Alice Willard Solenberger, *One Thousand Homeless Men: A Study of Original Records* (New York: Russell Sage Foundation, 1911), pp. 3-4.

4. Nels Anderson, *The Hobo: The Sociology of the Homeless Man* (Chicago: Univ. of Chicago Press, 1923), pp. ix, 87, 89.

5. Edwin H. Sutherland and Harvey J. Locke, *Twenty Thousand Homeless Men* (Chicago: J. B. Lippincott, 1936).

6. H. Warren Dunham, *Homeless Men and Their Habitats: A Research Planning Report* (Detroit: Wayne Univ., 1953), p. 14.

7. See the following studies by Boris M. Levinson: "The Socioeconomic Status, Intelligence, and Psychometric Pattern of Native-Born White Homeless Men," *Journal of Genetic Psychology,* 91 (December 1957), pp. 205-211; "Some Aspects of the Personality of the Native-Born White Homeless Man as Revealed by the Rorschach," *Psychiatric Quarterly Supplement,* 32, Part 2 (1958), pp. 278-286; "Subcultural Studies of Homeless Men," *Transactions of the New York Academy of Sciences,* 29 (December 1966), pp. 165-182; and "The Homeless Men: A Psychological Enigma," pp. 596-597.

8. Tenants' Relocation Bureau, *The Homeless Man on Skid Row* (Chicago: Tenants' Relocation Bureau, 1961); Donald J. Bogue, *Skid Row in American Cities* (Chicago: Community and Family Study Center, Univ. of Chicago, 1963), p. 5.

9. Samuel E. Wallace, "The Road to Skid Row," *Social Problems,* 16 (Summer 1968), pp. 92-105.

10. David J. Pittman and Wayne T. Gordon, *Revolving Door: A Study of the Chronic Police Case Inebriate* (New York: The Free Press, 1958); Thomas Minehan, *Boy and Girl Tramps of America* (New York: Farrar, Straus & Giroux, 1934).

11. Theodore Caplow, Howard M. Bahr, and David Sternberg, "Homelessness," *International Encyclopedia of the Social Sciences,* Vol. 6 (1968), 494-499.

12. Robert K. Merton, *Social Theory and Social Structure* (New York: The Free Press, 1957), p. 153.

13. We have profited from an unpublished paper by John R. Dugan in which he proposes a social-psychological definition of retreatism and a procedure for operationalizing the elements of the "retreatist equation."

14. Nash, *op. cit.,* pp. A-1, A-2.

CHAPTER 4

TESTING OTHER EXPLANATIONS OF HOMELESSNESS *

Other perspectives on the etiology of skid row living and disaffiliation include the hypotheses of institutional living, of generational retreat, of social or economic marginality, and several multiple-factor explanations of homelessness. Several of these approaches will be taken up in this chapter.

According to the institutional-living hypothesis, prolonged association with total institutions or other environments that provide the necessities of life with a minimum of individual initiative may incapacitate inmates for life in more demanding contexts. They may establish patterns of behavior incompatible with the outside, and the necessary adjustment may be so difficult or painful that they choose, explicitly or by default, to continue as institutional men. The basic notion of generational retreat is that lonely men rear lonely sons; the social withdrawal of the fathers continues in their offspring.

As for marginality, there is the economic marginality of the poor: for persons at the very bottom of the status hierarchy there are neither inducements nor pressures to affiliate. The hypothesis is that poverty and disaffiliation go together; people on the bottom never have had many affiliations or have withdrawn from those that proved unrewarding or irrelevant.

Related to economic marginality but conceptually distinct is social or cultural marginality. Rapid social change as well as normal biological processes dislodge people from the systems in which they were socialized. Consequently, they find themselves deserted—aliens in an unfamiliar world. Examples of such persons are immigrants who have never been assimilated, workers whose occupations have become obsolete, transient men who have never been domiciled in a stable community, and elderly people whose friends and relatives have all died or moved away.

* Portions of this chapter were adapted from Howard M. Bahr, "Institutional Life, Drinking, and Disaffiliation," *Social Problems,* 16 (Winter 1969), pp. 365-375, with the permission of the Society for the Study of Social Problems.

The multiple-factor approach builds on the assumption that no single factor or group of factors provides an adequate explanation of disaffiliation and homelessness. The researcher attempts to identify the various elements which combine to explain disaffiliation or other social pathologies. We shall consider each of these perspectives in turn.

INSTITUTIONAL HABITUATION

One of the dominant hypotheses about the development of chronic inebriety is that the dependency needs of undersocialized individuals are met in institutional patterns of living and that prolonged exposure to institutional life enhances the probability of excessive drinking.[1] An undersocialized person is by definition disaffiliated, having a life history characterized by limited participation in family, peer group, or community activities.[2] However, most of the relevant studies have not included control samples, and it has not been demonstrated that institutional experience is more common among disaffiliates and heavy drinkers than among more normal populations.

Several writers have described the role of institutional experience in the life histories of homeless men. Pittman and Gordon found that almost all of their respondents had lengthy institutional experience; only one-fifth of the men they studied had no experience with these types of facilities. They consider the institutional setting as an artificial social context which places a minimum of demands on the individual, aside from his specific occupational assignments. The institution provides the basic necessities (food, shelter, and clothing) and a well-ordered routine for structuring time. An institutionalized pattern of heavy drinking is part of the same subculture.[3] Pittman and Gordon's description of the drinking culture that permeates institutional living will illustrate this point.

> The Army, the Navy, the work camp, the railroad gang, and the lake steamer, all are rich in drinking culture. In these groups the harsh, the monotonous and the protective but controlled routines are broken by the nights, weekends and layoffs which offer opportunities to drink. Drinking is a preoccupation and conversations at work are filled with talk of drink. The imagery and love of

> drinking are built up through these talks and stories. Fantasy around future drinking episodes serves the function of reducing the impact of heavy jobs in heat and cold, and of alleviating dull routines, sexual deprivation, and the loneliness of the all-male group. Drinking becomes a symbol of manliness and group interaction.[4]

Noting a high proportion of railroad workers among Chicago skid row men, especially among heavy drinkers and alcoholic derelicts, Bogue suggested that either the railroad was a major benefactor of chronic alcoholics, employing them when no one else would, or else the railroad maintenance gang perpetuates a drinking culture that substitutes for normal family life.

> By the first view, the railroad serves a laudable welfare service. By the second view, the maintenance gang perpetuates a social institution that was characteristic of frontier America in mining, logging, cattle herding, and many other occupations; all these groups of males who worked in prolonged isolation from average community contacts developed and maintained a tradition of heavy drinking.[5]

Straus has suggested that institutional experience at a crucial age period, perhaps between the ages of 17 and 24, makes it difficult for men to adjust to normal community life later on. "Having spent a number of years in a protected environment they . . . failed to learn many of the simple amenities for getting along in a normal society." Consequently, homeless men never accept "civilian" life. Instead, their histories show a progression of types of institutional experience such as railroad and lumber camps, seasonal agricultural employment, work as attendants in public hospitals, and casual laboring jobs in resort areas. Most of these situations provide food, clothing, and shelter but demand little initiative. Moreover, drinking is a common form of recreation in each of these settings. As the men grow older, their health and incentives deteriorate; and missions, shelters, and jails come to play a larger role in their lives, first between jobs and later on a semipermanent basis. Thus, "the homeless man has been caught in a spiral of ever-increasing dependency in which alcoholism of a non-addictive plateau variety is a form of functional adjustment to his routine and low level of existence." Straus reported that 93 percent of a sample of homeless men had lived in institutions and that for at least 70 percent of the group the institutional pattern was dominant.[6]

Similarly, Gordon described the skid row alcoholic as one who had an ill-adjusted career in which alcohol use was a primary means of adaptation, following a serious deprivation in childhood and youth which limited his chances for successful life adjustment. In addition to drinking, institutional experience in semiprotected environments such as CCC camps, the Army, railroad gangs, lake steamers, jails, lumber and fruit camps, hospitals, missions, and shelters habituates the men to dependent living and prevents them from achieving independence in early adulthood. Withdrawal from family or jobs is also adaptive in the sense that it protects the withdrawee from failure to meet family expectations. The lifelong pattern of occupational drifting and unemployment permits homeless men to adapt to social expectations with a minimum of effort and competence.[7]

The connection between disaffiliation and employment in occupations which limit normal social activity was also noted by Wood, who included sailors, peacetime soldiers, miners, loggers, cowboys, hoboes, hired men, and bunkhouse men in her list of isolated types.[8]

These observations suggested that (1) institutional experience is more common among skid row men than among other populations, (2) there is a positive association between the duration of institutional experience and disaffiliation, and (3) there is a positive association between the duration of institutional experience and drinking.

Institutional experience. Part of our life-history interview included a detailed migration history, and in conjunction with this history there were questions about persons, if any, with whom the respondent lived during each year of his life. The answers provided the data for an analysis of institutional experience, although respondents' occupational histories were also consulted.

A basic feature of institutional life is that one eats, sleeps, and works with other men. Usually this pattern is associated with specific occupations, but only for certain strata within these occupations. For example, the peacetime military officer may live with his wife and family and maintain a style of life that is essentially civilian, but his men are more likely to live and eat with other soldiers. The same considerations apply to the railroad fireman as compared with a track worker. Whether or not a given pattern is institutional depends on whom the respondent lives with, rather than on the nature of his occupation. If he lived with other men in group quarters of some kind during a given period, he was considered as engaged in institutional living. If he lived alone or with a family, he was not so classified, even though he worked at an occupation characterized by institutional patterns.[9]

In all the samples the most important source of institutional experience was military service. Among the skid row men other frequently mentioned experiences were as hospital patients and as seamen. Prisons, orphanages, and railroad camps were also mentioned frequently. Other contexts for institutional experience included farms, CCC and WPA camps, the circus, construction projects, hotel kitchens, logging camps, and police units. Students in dormitories and fraternity houses were classified as living in an institutional context, as were reform school inmates, a seminarian, and a man who lived in a monastery. In the Park Avenue sample the only major form of institutional experience, other than military service, was in student dormitories.

Institutional experience and skid row residence. As anticipated, more institutional experience was reported by Bowery men than by Park Slope men (see Table 4-1). Between one-third and one-half of the Bowery men [10] had never lived in an institutional setting, but almost two-thirds of the Park Slope men could claim that distinction. The differences between the skid row and Park Slope samples are particularly striking at the other end of the continuum: between one-quarter and one-third of the Bowery respondents had lived in institutional settings for five or more years, but only 13 percent of the Park Slope men reported that much institutional experience. However, the differences between the Bowery men and the upper-income men were mainly in type rather than extent of institutional experience. Only at the extreme upper end of the continuum (10 or more years lived in group quarters) were the Bowery men clearly overrepresented. At other points the distributions were quite similar. Thus we have equivocal support for the first hypothesis: institutional experience is more common among skid row men than among other

Table 4-1

DISTRIBUTION OF RESPONDENTS BY NUMBER OF YEARS LIVED IN GROUP QUARTERS (IN PERCENTAGES)

Years in Group Quarters	Bowery	Camp LaGuardia	Park Slope	Park Avenue
0	38	48	62	47
1-2	14	12	5	13
3-4	17	15	20	16
5-9	16	14	8	18
10-14	6	2	2	3
15 or more	8	9	3	2
Total	99	100	100	99
N	203	199	125	104

poor men, but it is also more common in the histories of well-to-do men than among poor men.

Institutional experience and disaffiliation. Having shown that institutional experience is more common among Bowery men than Park Slope men, the related question of the effect of institutional experience on affiliation may be considered.

Most Bowery and Park Avenue men had lived at least a year with other men in some institutional setting. To distinguish the men who experienced a "normal" pattern of institutional experience, two or three years in the military service, for example, from those for whom it occupied a more significant part of the life history, respondents were divided into three groups by length of time spent living in group quarters: (1) men with less than one year, (2) men with one to four years, and (3) men with five or more years in group quarters. For brevity, respondents in the last category are identified as institutional men.

On most of the variables listed in Table 4-2 institutional men do not differ from other men. When they do, the difference is often in the unexpected direction, that is, they manifest *more* affiliation than noninstitutional men. For example, in the skid row samples institutional men are more likely than other men to have belonged to youth organizations, and among Camp LaGuardia men they presently belong to more voluntary associations. The institutional men in Park Slope are more apt to have voted, and on the Bowery they are better educated than noninstitutional men. In the Park Avenue sample the men with some institutional experience are more likely than other men to have close friends in New York City.

The hypothesized relation between institutional experience and disaffiliation does not appear in any of the samples. The only differences which support the hypothesis that institutional experience fosters disaffiliation are these: (1) only one-fourth of the institutional men on the Bowery have seen members of their families within the past year, compared to almost half of the noninstitutional men; however, in the other samples institutional men are somewhat more likely to have had recent contact with their relatives; (2) in the Camp LaGuardia and Park Slope samples the institutional men are less likely than other men to be regular church attenders.

Institutional experience and drinking. According to the third hypothesis there is a direct association between heavy drinking and institutional experience. Given the positive evaluation of drinking supposedly fostered by institutional living, it was anticipated that regardless of the extent of their drinking, men with long institutional experience would be more apt to consider themselves heavy drinkers than men who had not spent much time in institutional contexts. Secondly, irrespective of their self-conceptions, it was expected that the institutional men would report greater consumption of alcohol than their fellows.

Some association between drinking and institutional experience appears in three of the four samples (see Table 4-3). The association is strongest for the qualitative index—the rating—which suggests that conceiving of oneself as a heavy drinker is less difficult if one has been exposed to cultures where heavy drinking is positively sanctioned.

The association between drinking and institutional experience is strongest in the Park Slope sample, moderate in the Camp LaGuardia and Park Avenue samples, and not evident at all in the Bowery sample. Apparently there is an association between drinking

Table 4-2

PERCENTAGE OF RESPONDENTS THAT ARE AFFILIATED, BY NUMBER OF YEARS LIVED IN GROUP QUARTERS, FOR TWELVE MEASURES OF LIFETIME AND CURRENT AFFILIATION*

Measures of Affiliation	Years in Group Quarters											
	Bowery			Camp LaGuardia			Park Slope			Park Avenue		
	None	1-4	5+	None	1-4	5+	None	1-4	5+	None	1-4	5+
Lifetime measures												
Ever married	53	36	51	45	48	50	72	71	65	82	74	67
Ever voted	68	64	63	74	67	70	62	84	88[a]	98	97	92
Over 8 years education[b]	34	59	63	42	43	46	41	61	41	76	97	96
Organizational affiliation(s) in youth[c]	48	56	60	48	45	68	34	55	53	76	68	75
Current measures												
Currently employed	40	39	37	—	—	—	73	71	82	92	87	96
Saw family member within past year	45	35	23	17	21	24	63	74	73	90	90	88
Attends church at least twice a month	26	19	30	37	35	18	46	23	40	18	32	17
Belongs to informal group[d]	29	31	34	36	30	40	36	36	31	69	74	75
Has organizational affiliations[e]	23	22	23	17	9	26	49	57	53	59	65	67
Has close friend(s) in New York City	35	34	31	24	11	20	49	58	41	69	90	88

Table 4-2 (Continued)

Measures of Affiliation	Years in Group Quarters											
	Bowery			Camp LaGuardia			Park Slope			Park Avenue		
	None	1-4	5+	None	1-4	5+	None	1-4	5+	None	1-4	5+
Knows names of more than 5 neighbors	47	52	48	52	57	69	44	42	53	57	71	54
Would like to know more neighbors	16	31	21	27	18	25	34	24	27	37	28	35
Would join a neighborhood organization	66	67	66	54	39	53	70	63	69	52	48	50
Conversed with 6+ people yesterday[f]	54	50	56	57	47	66	54	48	65	67	74	71
Lowest N[g]	73	60	56	90	49	47	70	29	15	46	29	23

*Underscoring denotes differences significant at the .05 level.

a. For the Park Slope sample measures of significance are based on 2 x 2 rather than 2 x 3 tables; the 5+ category was combined with the 1-4 category to meet the assumptions of X^2.

b. For Park Avenue men, the cutting point was set somewhat higher, at 12 years or more.

c. Refers primarily to membership in voluntary organizations; jobs, church membership, family affiliation, and school attendance are excluded. Youth is defined as before age 20.

d. Men responding affirmatively to the question, Are there certain men you often hang around with? were considered as belonging to an informal group.

e. Refers primarily to voluntary organizations.

f. For Park Avenue men, 7+ people.

g. Number of cases varies slightly due to incomplete information.

Table 4-3

EXTENT OF CURRENT DRINKING, BY NUMBER OF YEARS LIVED IN GROUP QUARTERS (IN PERCENTAGES)

	Years in Group Quarters											
	Bowery			Camp LaGuardia			Park Slope			Park Avenue		
Extent of Current Drinking	0	1-4	5+	0	1-4	5+	0	1-4	5+	0	1-4	5+
	Percent of Samples											
None or Light	35	34	33	31	30	16	61	58	35	41	33	29
Moderate	29	29	32	29	24	22	26	29	47	59	67	71
Heavy or Spree	36	37	35	40	45	61	12	13	18		**	
N	72	62	60	94	53	49	72	31	17	49	30	24
	gamma = .00, n.s.*			gamma = .22, n.s.			gamma = .20, n.s.			gamma = .18, n.s.		

* To meet the assumption of X^2, it was necessary to combine 1-4 and "5+" into a single category; n. s. means not statistically significant.

** There were only two cases in this category; n.s. means not statistically significant.

and institutional experience, but it is not as strong as has been suggested. In contexts such as skid row, where other powerful factors encourage excessive drinking, the relative importance of institutional life as an antecedent to heavy drinking is diminished.

In his classification of "routes to homelessness," Wallace asserted that the majority of skid row men are "drawn from the ranks of those occupations which by their very nature separated men from their fixed places in established society—migratory workers, lumberjacks, soldiers, seamen. . . ." [11] The present study supports this position, although with some reservations. Over half of the skid row men had three or more years of institutional experience, but so did two-fifths of the Park Avenue and a third of the Park Slope men. As a group skid row men clearly have more exposure to itinerant occupations and institutional experience than the control samples, but a sizable proportion of the skid row men have had little or no institutional experience, and a like proportion of the control sample respondents had been exposed to institutional life without being routed toward homelessness. That institutional experience is only moderately predisposing to homelessness is evident if the findings are stated another way: at least 40 percent of the skid row men had no institutional experience at all. This proportion may be contrasted with Pittman and Gordon's finding that only one-fifth of their respondents had no institutional experience, and Straus's observation that only 7 percent of another sample of homeless men had not lived in institutional settings.[12] The lower frequency of institutional experience among the present samples of skid row men is attributable, in part, to the fact that they are random samples of the entire population of two areas, whereas the earlier findings refer to more homogeneous populations, such as arrested inebriates or clinic patients. It is likely that these select populations of arrested inebriates or clinic patients are more deviant than the skid row population in general, and that the more deviant a male population is in terms of dependency or drinking behavior, the higher its proportion of men with extensive institutional experience is likely to be.

However, if the form of deviance considered is merely disaffiliation, institutional men are not more deviant than noninstitutional men. One explanation for this unexpected finding is that institutional experience is itself a form of affiliation and fosters certain derivative affiliations. It often involves occupational ties, close bonds with fellow workers, and involvement in voluntary associations. Hence, when men who have worked in institutional settings are compared to other relatively unaffiliated populations, they do not appear disaffiliated.

It may be argued that the relation between institutional experience and disaffiliation holds only for those men who have spent most or all of their worklives in institutions. But such men are rare, even on skid row. Respondents in the skid row samples had an average worklife of more than 30 years, yet less than 10 percent of them lived in institutional settings for even half that long. Therefore one source of confusion may be in regarding institutional experience as a lifelong pattern, when most often it is only a phase or series of phases in a diverse work history punctuated by periods of living alone or with relatives and friends.

Finally, with reference to drinking and institutional experience, the relation is not as obvious as the literature would suggest. The expected association between drinking and institutional experience appeared in three of the four samples, and so tentative support is claimed for the hypothesis. The absence of the expected association among the Bowery men suggests that while arrested inebriates may have extensive institutional experience, men with institutional experience do not necessarily become inebriates. Among the many factors associated with the drinking behavior of skid row men, institutional experience plays a modest role.

In conclusion, it should be stressed that these findings about the place of institutional experience in the etiology of drinking and disaffiliation are based on a definition of institutional experience as residence in group quarters. Conceivably the results might have been different if institutional experience had been defined differently, in terms, say, of employment in occupations that isolate workers from the wider society. Furthermore, whether institutional experience leads to disaffiliation depends on how disaffiliation is defined. Institutional life may insulate one from the larger society, but it may also foster more intense ties among the men living and working together. Thus the same forces that lead to alienation from the wider society may strengthen group solidarity within the institution.

We have demonstrated that the assumed relation between institutionalized experience and disaffiliation is questionable, and that the link between institutional experience and drinking is not direct and obvious. The path from institutional residence to excessive drinking and, perhaps, to disaffiliation appears to be an extremely complicated one, not at all the highway some of the literature would suggest. The most difficult research problem, specification of the conditions under which institutional experience fosters heavy drinking, remains unsolved. Future research should focus on men with extensive institutional histories who are neither heavy drinkers nor disaffiliates as well as on the population of inebriates, isolates, and other deviants with such backgrounds.

GENERATIONAL RETREAT

The basic hypothesis in the generational-retreat model of disaffiliation is that the skills, attitudes, and values acquired in the family of orientation determine whether one initiates and maintains affiliations in a normal manner. One of the more distinguished proponents of this position is George Homans. He suggests that men whose groups have been destroyed or those who have withdrawn from their initial social groups and have not established new affiliations will rear children of "lowered social capacity."

> The cycle is vicious; loss of group membership in one generation may make men less capable of group membership in the next. The civilization that, by its very process of growth, shatters small group life will leave men and women lonely and unhappy.[13]

In other words, the social withdrawal of the fathers is visited on their sons.

The focus of the interview was on the affiliative history of the respondent rather than on that of his parents, but some data relevant to the generational-retreat hypothesis were obtained. Specifically, four variables—presence of both parents in the home, parental interaction with friends, parental activity in church, and parental involvement in other community organizations—were used in constructing a typology of parental-affiliation patterns. Each variable was dichotomized into categories of high and low affiliation. Thus, with respect to the first variable, homes in which both parents were present until the respondent reached age 16 were classified as highly affiliated, and all other situations were grouped in the category of low affiliation. If friends visited the parental home at least once a month, the family was defined as high on the variable of parental interaction with friends. If the respondent reported that his parents were active in any organizations or that they attended church frequently, his family was classed as highly affiliated on these variables. Combining the four variables yielded 16 types of parental affiliation (see Table 4-4).

Table 4-4

INCIDENCE OF THE SIXTEEN TYPES OF PARENTAL AFFILIATION IN OUR SAMPLES (IN PERCENTAGES)

Types	Both Present in Home	Visited by Friends	Active in Church	Active in Organi- zations	Bowery	Camp LaGuardia	Park Slope	Park Avenue
1	+	+	+	+	19	15	10	32
2	+	+	+	0	36	37	43	17
3	+	+	0	+	1	2	2	14
4	+	+	0	0	2	5	8	15
5	+	0	+	+	2	1	0	0
6	+	0	+	0	3	8	6	2
7	+	0	0	+	0	1	0	0
8	+	0	0	0	3	1	4	2
9	0	+	+	+	4	6	3	4
10	0	+	+	0	19	15	18	6
11	0	+	0	+	0	1	0	3
12	0	+	0	0	2	2	1	2
13	0	0	+	+	0	0	0	0
14	0	0	+	0	6	5	4	2
15	0	0	0	+	1	1	0	0
16	0	0	0	0	2	2	3	1
Total					100	102	102	100
N					172	170	113	100

In the lower-income samples three of the types account for more than two-thirds of the respondents.[14] The largest single group of men—about 40 percent of each sample—are those whose parents were present in the home, were visited by friends at least once a month, were active in church, but did not participate in other organizations. Two other groups, approximately equal in size, account for an additional 30 to 40 percent of the samples. These are the respondents whose parents were highly affiliated (affiliated on all four variables) and the men whose parents were visited by friends and were active in church, but did not belong to any other organizations and suffered a family breakup (divorce, desertion, or the death of at least one parent) before the respondent was 16.

Among the upper-income men the most frequent report of parental affiliation was that the parents were highly affiliated on all four variables. Other common patterns were that the parents lived together and were visited by friends but were not active in either church or voluntary organizations or both. These four types accounted for more than three-fourths of the families of Park Avenue men.

Clearly the parents of the highly affiliated Park Avenue men had more affiliations than the parents of the lower-income respondents, but among the low-income samples there were few differences in parental affiliation. The largest difference was nine percentage points between the Park Slope and the Bowery sample in the proportion of highly affiliated (+ + + +) families of orientation, and contrary to expectations, the Bowery men were *more* likely than the Park Slope men to manifest that pattern. These findings do not support the idea that retreat to skid row is a consequence of having been reared by parents who were themselves disaffiliated.

In testing the association between social affiliations of respondents and those of their parents, the sixteen parental-affiliation types were divided into two categories: a high parental-affiliation group that included respondents whose parents were affiliated on at least three of the four variables and a low parental-affiliation category consisting of respondents whose parents were less affiliated. Then these two categories of respondents were compared with respect to several measures of current lifetime affiliation. The results of the comparison are given in Table 4-5.

The evidence is not compelling, but there are indications of a

Table 4-5

PERCENTAGE OF RESPONDENTS AFFILIATED BY EXTENT OF PARENTAL AFFILIATION, FOR VARIOUS MEASURES OF LIFETIME AND CURRENT AFFILIATION*

Measures of Affiliation	Bowery		Camp LaGuardia		Park Slope		Park Ave.	
Parental Affiliation:	High[a]	Low	High	Low	High	Low	High	Low
Lifetime measures								
Ever married	51	43	52	45	77	69	79	71
Ever voted	69	65	77	61	74	67	98	94
Over 8 years education[b]	56	45	41	48	53	42	97	69
Organizational affiliation(s) in youth[c]	58	45	61	48	52	31	71	77
Current measures								
Currently employed	39	44	—	—	78	69	92	89
Saw family member within past year	38	28	20	20	68	60	94	80
Attends church at least twice a month	27	22	31	33	54	26	26	17
Belongs to informal group[d]	36	24	41	31	44	25	68	83
Has organizational affiliations[e]	28	21	23	13	52	50	65	57
Has close friend(s) in New York City	39	26	26	13	55	50	79	83
Knows names of more than 5 neighbors	54	44	62	55	46	40	71	43
Would like to know more neighbors	24	18	24	18	34	22	25	47
Would join a neighborhood organization	74	61	53	48	72	64	45	60
Conversed with 7+ people yesterday	48	41	48	48	58	29	69	77
Lowest N[f]	102	62	98	63	61	45	60	32

*Underscoring denotes differences significant at the .05 level.

a. High affiliation denotes in all four samples at least three of the four kinds of affiliation: both parents present in home, friends visited parental home at least once a month, active in organizations, attended church frequently.

Table 4-5 (Continued)

b. For Park Avenue men, the cutting point was set somewhat higher, at 12 years or more.

c. Refers primarily to membership in voluntary organizations; jobs, church membership, family affiliation, and school attendance are excluded. Youth is defined as before age 20.

d. Men responding affirmatively to the question, Are there certain men you often hang around with? were considered as belonging to an informal group.

e. Refers primarily to voluntary organizations.

f. Number of cases varies slightly due to incomplete information. In the Park Avenue sample, the Ns were 51 and 24 respectively for the statement, Would join a neighborhood organization.

moderate association between the extent of a respondent's affiliations and that of his parents. In most cases the differences are small, but the pattern is consistent. In the Park Slope sample, for each of the 14 measures of affiliation men with backgrounds of low parental affiliation were less affiliated than men from high-affiliation backgrounds. The same pattern prevailed among Bowery men, with the single exception that slightly more men from families of low parental affiliation were currently employed than men from high-affiliation backgrounds. Among the Camp LaGuardia and Park Avenue men the pattern is less convincing, with 9 of 13 differences in the expected direction among Camp LaGuardia men and only 8 of 14 differences among Park Avenue respondents. In summary, 44 of the 53 relationships reported in Table 4-5 are in the expected direction, and 7 of them are statistically significant at the .05 level. Another significant relationship (Park Avenue men on the variable of Would like to know more neighbors) is in the opposite direction. Thus, there is only tentative support for the proposition that the disaffiliation of their parents is partly responsible for the disaffiliation of men in these four samples. The relationships are not strong enough to justify acceptance of parental affiliation as an important element in the etiology of homelessness.

MARGINALITY—THE CASE OF THE IMMIGRANT

Immigrants are likely candidates for homelessness. The immigrant is one who leaves his parent culture, relinquishes his organizational ties in one country, and attempts to establish himself in another. The probabilities of isolation and retreat would seem to be enhanced among newcomers who do not immigrate in company with friends or relatives.

Being newcomers and strangers, most immigrants find employment in low-status occuaptions, and they may experience difficulties in establishing other affiliative ties because of their low status, foreign ways, or language difficulties. Persons once detached from the social fabric are likely to remain somewhat detached. Consequently we expected disaffiliation to be more prevalent among immigrants than in the general population. In testing these ideas, two questions were considered: (1) Are immigrants overrepresented among skid row men, and (2) are immigrants on skid row less affiliated than native-born skid row men?

Immigrants on skid row. As we noted in Chapter 2, the proportions of foreign-born men were 23 percent on the Bowery, 21 percent in Camp LaGuardia, 50 percent in Park Slope, and 16 percent on Park Avenue. On this basis immigrants are clearly not overrepresented on skid row. An alternative procedure is to compare the proportion of immigrants in these samples with census figures on the foreign-born population of New York City. In 1960, 17 percent of the population of the New York Standard Metropolitan Statistical Area were foreign-born. In Brookly and Manhattan the proportions were slightly higher (20 percent and 22 percent, respectively), almost exactly the same as for Bowery men. On this basis also, the proportion of immigrants on skid row seems surprisingly low since immigrants tend to enter the labor force at the bottom of the occupational hierarchy and ought to be overrepresented in low-income areas.

Affiliation of immigrants. It was anticipated that within samples immigrants would be less affiliated than natives, and in the skid row samples this expectation was supported for lifetime measures of affiliation (see Table 4-6). Compared to the immigrants, the native skid row men were much more likely to have married, to have voted, to be relatively well-educated, and to have belonged to voluntary organizations during youth. Among Bowery men, natives were more affiliated than immigrants on all of the lifetime-affiliation indicators and on most of the measures of current affiliations. But at Camp LaGuardia there were fewer differences between natives and immigrants in current affiliation. Immigrants were more likely to attend church, and natives more often knew the names of their neighbors and engaged in more conversations. In all four samples natives were better educated, had belonged to more organizations in youth, and were more apt to have voted. Current church attendance was the only measure of current affiliation on which the immigrants consistently surpassed the native-born.

Native respondents in the Park Slope and Park Avenue samples were not clearly more affiliated than the foreign-born. In both of these samples the immigrants were more likely to have been married and more likely to know the names of their neighbors. Most of the intersample differences were small; in the Park Avenue sample none of the differences between immigrants and natives were statistically significant. We conclude that the marginality associated with immigrant status is not an important antecedent of either skid row residence or disaffiliation.

ECONOMIC MARGINALITY

Our analysis of economic marginality is based on two measures: the economic status of the respondent's father and that of the respondent himself. In both cases the measure of occupational status is the Duncan Socioeconomic Index (see Chapter 8). With reference to paternal status, we attempted to determine whether men with low-status fathers were more numerous on skid row than in the control samples, and whether they were more numerous among the disaffiliates than among other men. Similar questions were posed with respect to the respondent's own occupational status.

Paternal socioeconomic status and skid row residence. The low-income samples do not differ in paternal occupational status. About

Table 4-6

PERCENTAGE OF IMMIGRANTS AND NATIVES AFFILIATED, FOR VARIOUS MEASURES OF LIFETIME AND CURRENT AFFILIATION*

Measures of Affiliation	Bowery		Camp LaGuardia		Park Slope		Park Avenue	
	Immigrant	Native	Immigrant	Native	Immigrant	Native	Immigrant	Native
Lifetime measures								
Ever married	<u>30</u>	<u>51</u>	38	50	76	66	82	75
Ever voted	<u>41</u>	<u>72</u>	<u>48</u>	<u>77</u>	64	79	82	99
Over 8 years education[a]	<u>31</u>	<u>57</u>	32	46	<u>33</u>	<u>60</u>	71	90
Organizational affiliation(s) in youth[b]	<u>35</u>	<u>59</u>	48	54	36	48	65	76
Current measures								
Currently employed	26	43	—	—	70	77	94	91
Saw family member within past year	24	38	20	20	66	69	88	90
Attends church at least twice a month	36	22	<u>46</u>	<u>27</u>	<u>54</u>	<u>25</u>	24	22
Belongs to informal group[c]	26	33	31	36	32	39	59	75
Has organizational affiliation(s)[d]	17	25	17	17	56	48	53	64
Has close friend(s) in New York City	37	32	19	20	56	44	76	80
Knows names of more than 5 neighbors	41	52	<u>43</u>	<u>62</u>	45	44	71	59
Would like to know more neighbors	21	23	25	24	<u>40</u>	<u>21</u>	31	34
Would join a neighborhood organization	<u>51</u>	<u>71</u>	54	44	74	63	53	50
Conversed with 7+ people yesterday	38	47	32	50	47	48	71	70
Lowest N[e]	42	147	40	145	57	57	16	82

*Underscoring denotes differences significant at the .05 level.

a. For Park Avenue men, the cutting point was set somewhat higher, at 12 years or more.

Table 4-6 (Continued)

b. Refers primarily to membership in voluntary organizations; jobs, church membership, family affiliation and school attendance are excluded. Youth is defined as before age 20.

c. Men responding affirmatively to the question, Are there certain men you often hang around with? were considered as belonging to an informal group.

d. Refers primarily to voluntary organizations.

e. Number of cases varies slightly due to incomplete information. In the Park Avenue sample, the Ns for Would join a neighborhood organization were 68 and 15, respectively.

two-fifths of the respondents' fathers (Bowery, 43 percent; Camp LaGuardia, 38 percent; Park Slope, 42 percent) followed occupations with status scores of 15 or less, and approximately one-third had status scores higher than 30. Since the paternal status distributions of the low-income samples are so much alike, the answer to the first inquiry is clearly negative: men with low-status fathers are not proportionately more numerous on skid row than in other settled, low-income neighborhoods.

Of course, the Park Avenue men had high-status backgrounds; only one of them had a father whose occupational status was 15 or less, and two-thirds of their fathers' status scores were over 50. Poor men's sons are more likely than rich men's sons to end up on skid row.

Paternal socioeconomic status and affiliation. The influence of paternal occupational status on patterns of current affiliation was not marked; only one of the 39 intrasample differences was statistically significant, and in several cases the direction was not as anticipated, that is, the men with the lowest paternal status were the most highly affiliated. Accordingly, we have not taken space to present the table showing proportions of respondents affiliated by paternal status for the 14 measures of affiliation.

However, some effects of paternal status were apparent in the measures of lifetime affiliation. In every sample there was a significant direct relationship between paternal status and filial education, and in the low-income samples paternal status was positively related to membership in youth organizations and voting. However, there was no consistent relation between paternal status and respondents' marital history. On balance, paternal status is not a very successful predictor of either the current or the lifetime level of affiliation in this sample.

Lifetime occupational status and skid row residence. Lifetime occupational status is the mean status score of all the occupations a man has followed, weighted for the length of time he held each of them. Men with low lifetime status have held low-status occupations all of their lives; men with higher status have held higher positions for at least part of their lives. It was presumed that skid row men would have had lower lifetime occupational status than the men in the control group. The data confirmed this expectation, as may be seen in Figure 8-2, which shows lifetime profiles for occupational status by sample (see Chapter 8). Here we will merely state that from early adulthood on, Park Slope men have had higher occupational status than skid row men, and the intersample differences increase with age. The contrast between Park Slope men and Park Avenue men is similar and even more striking. We may conclude that skid row men have distinctive mobility histories.

Lifetime occupational status and affiliation. Examination of the relationship between lifetime occupational status and each of the fourteen indicators of affiliation previously introduced led us to two major findings. First, there was a consistent positive relationship between affiliation and lifetime status in all four samples. In other words, men with high lifetime status were more likely than men with low lifetime status to have married, to have voted, to have achieved high levels of formal education, and (with the exception of the Park Avenue sample) to have participated in youth organizations. This finding is consistent with much previous research showing a direct relationship between social status and affiliation.

The second finding separates the two skid row samples from the two control samples. Among skid row men measures of current affiliation did not show any consistent relationship to lifetime status. For example, the skid row men with the highest lifetime status were least likely to report contact with their families during the previous year. Given the stigma attached to skid row residence, it is conceivable that the men who have fallen the furthest, that is, those who previously held jobs with fairly high status, are most isolated from their families. They were also less likely to be currently employed or to attend church frequently. However, the skid row men with the lowest lifetime status belonged to fewer informal groups and reported fewer close friendships than the men of higher status.

In the control samples, the expected relationship between current affiliation and lifetime status did appear. With the exception of the two items which reflected valence toward affiliations rather than artual affiliation (Would like to know more neighbors, Would join a neighborhood organization), the respondents with the highest status were more affiliated than the other respondents on every item.

For example, 41 percent of the Park Slope men with high lifetime status scores (31 and above) had seen a relative other than those living with them during the past year, but only 26 percent of those with low-status scores (15 and under) had that much contact with their relatives. Two-thirds of the high-status men maintained voluntary affiliations at the time of the interview, but only 29 percent of the low-status men had such memberships. The same pattern appeared in Park Avenue; three-fourths of the men with high lifetime status (70 and over) had voluntary affiliations, compared to 55 percent of the men in the low-status category (less than 60). The majority of the intrasample differences in the control samples were not statistically significant.

MULTIPLE-FACTOR EXPLANATIONS

Among the researchers who have identified the multiple symptoms, or conditions, in the life history which predispose an individual to homelessness are Lee Robins and Donald Bogue. We will briefly review their multiple-factor approaches and then compare the incidence of the factors they identify as significantly related to homelessness in our three lower-income samples (Bowery, Camp LaGuardia, and Park Slope.) We shall not include the Park Avenue sample in these comparisons because most of the conditions identified by Robins and Bogue are much more common among poor families than middle- or upper-class families.

Robins suggests that sociopathic personality is a psychiatric disease, and that its symptoms include poor work history, marital instability, social isolation, excessive drinking, vagrancy, dependence on social agencies, and alienation from and hostility toward one's family and acquaintances. She reports that the disease shows both inter- and intragenerational continuity: fathers of sociopaths tend to be sociopaths or alcoholics, and juvenile antisocial behavior is a precursor of adult sociopathic personality.[15]

Diagnosis of personality disorders among Robins's subjects was by two or more psychiatrists who evaluated a standardized life-history interview and assigned subjects to one of several diagnostic categories, including "sociopathic personality," "alcoholism," "schizophrenia," "anxiety neurosis," and "well." Persons designated as sociopaths had to manifest during their adult lives at least five of nineteen "criteria for the diagnosis of sociopathic personality."[16]

A similar list of factors was published by Bogue in *Skid Row in American Cities*. He enumerated 20 different conditions that might contribute to the development of homelessness, and reported that one or more of these factors appeared in the histories of all but 3 percent of his respondents. On the basis of the distribution of these factors among his respondents, Bogue generalized that the skid row man is either a victim of economic circumstances, physical handicap, or psychological or sociological abnormality (poor mental health or poor social adjustment). Like Robins, he stressed the continuity of the deviant career and consequently rejected the undersocialization hypothesis, arguing that many homeless men are not immature or incompletely socialized but rather follow a deviant course of socialization from early boyhood.[17]

In the first two columns of Table 4-7, Bogue's factors associated with the development of homelessness are contrasted with Robins's criteria for diagnosis of sociopathic personality. Under each factor's title is given the percentage of respondents having that characteristic. The last three columns show the proportions of respondents in the low-income samples of the current study whose histories manifest that particular factor.

The proportions of respondents in the Bogue and Robins samples are listed for reference purposes, but comparisons between these proportions and those reported for the Bowery, Camp LaGuardia, and Park Slope samples should be made with great caution: usually the operational definition used by Bogue or Robins differs from that of the present study.

Operational definitions of the 18 variables for which there are findings from the current study are found in Table 4-7b. A description of the specific criteria used in the other two studies is too

Table 4-7

THE INCIDENCE IN BOWERY, CAMP LAGUARDIA, AND PARK SLOPE SAMPLES OF FACTORS ASSOCIATED WITH SOCIOPATHY AND SKID ROW RESIDENCE

	Factors associated with:		Incidence in Sample[a]		
	Sociopathy (Robins's List)[b]	Skid Row Residence (Bogue's List)	Bowery	Camp LaGuardia	Park Slope
1	Poor work history (82%)	Irregular employment or unemployment (42%)	79%	86%	45%
2	Heavy drinking (74%)	Problem drinking (38%)	53	56	26
3	Poor marital history (71%)	Marital discord (28%)	17	16	11
4	—	Low standard (level) of living (27%)	86	100	44
5	—	Poverty as a child (8%)	41	37	47
6	Public financial care (80%)	—	80	100	24
7	—	Social maladjustment (26%)	25	16	27

Table 4-7 (Continued)

	Factors associated with:		Incidence in Sample[a]		
	Sociopathy (Robins's List)[b]	Skid Row Residence (Bogue's List)	Bowery	Camp LaGuardia	Park Slope
8	Lack of friends (55%)	–	11	12	9
9	Vagrancy (65%)	Wanderlust, restlessness (25%)	(a) Lived in many (6+) places		
			37	44	10
			(b) Many (10+) moves		
			16	21	5
10	Reckless youth (60%)	–	20	34	2
11	–	Discontinuance of family (death of wife or parent) (16%)	35	35	31
12	Many somatic symptoms (30%)	Poor health (10%)	44	27	18
13	–	Physical handicaps (7%)	51	47	25
14	–	Failure in realizing ambitions (6%)	49	43	52

Table 4-7 (Continued)

	Factors associated with:		Incidence in Sample[a]		
	Sociopathy (Robins's List)[b]	Skid Row Residence (Bogue's List)	Bowery	Camp LaGuardia	Park Slope
15	Repeated arrests (81%)	(5%)	(a) Two or more arrests for drinking offenses		
			40	50	3
			(b) Other arrests		
			27	20	10
16	—	Borderline intelligence (3%)	8	5	7
17	School problems and truancy (79%)	—	11	10	12
18	—	Cultural conflict because of ethnic, religious background (10%)	16	11	42
19	Impulsive behavior (66%)	Emotional instability (20%)	—		—
20	Excessive drugs (15%)	—	—	—	—
21	Physical aggression (61%)	—	—	—	—

(Table 4-7 Continued)

	Factors associated with:		Incidence in Sample[a]		
	Sociopathy (Robins's List)[b]	Skid Row Residence (Bogue's List)	Bowery	Camp LaGuardia	Park Slope
22	Sexual promiscuity or perversion (59%)	—	—	—	—
23	Pathological lying (16%)	—	—	—	—
24	Suicide (attempts) (9%)	—	—	—	—
25	—	Conflict with relatives other than wife (8%)	—	—	—
26	—	Extreme egocentricity (6%)	—	—	—
27	—	Laziness (2%)	—	—	—
28	—	Orphanhood (2%)	—	—	—
29	Use of aliases (31%)	—	—	—	—
30	Poor armed services record (28%)	—	—	—	—

(Table 4-7 Continued)

Factors associated with:		Incidence in Sample[a]		
Sociopathy (Robins's List)	Skid Row Residence (Bogue's List)	Bowery	Camp LaGuardia	Park Slope
31 Lack of guilt about sexual exploits and crimes (36%)	—	—	—	—

a. Numerical bases for percentages in Table 4-7 appear in Table 4-7a. Operational definitions for attributing the presence of the 31 factors are given in Table 4-7b.

b. Parenthesized percentages refer to the proportion of respondents in the Bogue or Robins studies whose histories manifested that particular factor.

TABLE 4-7a

NUMERICAL BASES FOR PERCENTAGES IN TABLE 4-7, BY FACTOR NUMBER

Factor Number	Bowery	Camp LaGuardia	Park Slope
1	185	188	112
2	200	198	125
3	199	199	123
4	190	199	120
5	182	183	119
6	192	199	118
7	194	196	111
8	200	196	122
9[a]	196	197	124
9[b]	198	189	124
10	178	174	109
11	197	196	123
12	203	198	125
13	203	198	125
14	112	103	73
15[a]	196	195	121
15[b]	192	197	121
16	194	194	121
17	193	194	119
18	202	199	125

lengthy to be included here, and the reader is referred to the sections of those works already cited.

Only about half of the 18 variables for which there are relevant findings differentiate between the skid row men and the Park Slope respondents. Those factors that do not seem any more important in the backgrounds of skid row men than among men in the Park Slope sample will be noted first.

Poverty in childhood characterizes a larger proportion of Park

Table 4-7b

STANDARDS FOR ATTRIBUTING THE PRESENCE OF FACTORS ASSOCIATED WITH SKID ROW RESIDENCE AND SOCIOPATHY TO BOWERY, CAMP LAGUARDIA, AND PARK SLOPE MEN

In the present study, respondents were defined as manifesting the various factors associated with skid row residence and sociopathy if they met the following criteria.

1 Poor work history	Any *two* of these: (a) worked more than three years at day-to-day jobs (b) worked more than five years at short-term (less than six months duration) jobs (c) unemployed for six or more consecutive months, *or* during more than one-third of entire work-life did not work a full year (d) history of downward mobility (fifteen points or more on the Duncan Socioeconomic Index)
2 Heavy drinking	At some time in life respondent was a heavy drinker by the count criteria outlined in Chapter 13.
3 Poor marital history	More than one marriage, or else listed at least three areas that were often a problem in his marriage.
4 Low standard of living	Current monthly income is $150 or less, or else his mean lifetime occupational status is 15 or less on the Duncan Socioeconomic Index.
5 Poverty as a child	Any *two* of these: (a) father was unemployed a year or more while respondent was growing up

Table 4-7b (Continued)

	(b) mother worked outside the home (c) left school because he had to work, wanted to help out, or similar reason indicating family economic difficulties (d) occupational status of father was 15 or less on Duncan Socioeconomic Index
6 Public financial care	Any *one* of these: (a) ever on welfare or other community aid (b) ever received meals or lodging from Municipal Men's Shelter or other shelters or missions (c) ever a resident at Camp LaGuardia (d) ever received unemployment insurance or other public financial assistance
7 Social maladjustment	Defined in terms of present attitude as indicated in responses to attitude scales. At least *three* of these: (a) high anomie (b) high self-estrangement (c) low self-esteem (d) high misanthropy
8 Lack of friends	*All* of these: (a) does not belong to an informal group of friends (i.e., answered no to question, Are there certain men you often hang around with?) (b) has no close friends in neighborhood (c) knows five or less neighbors by name (d) had less than five conversations on day preceding interview

Table 4-7b (Continued)

	(e) agreed with the statement: These days a person doesn't know whom he can count on.
9 Restlessness, wanderlust	(a) lived in at least six different places (b) moved at least ten times
10 Reckless youth	Any *one* of these: (a) ever arrested before age twenty (b) expelled from school (c) started drinking heavily before age twenty
11 Discontinuance of family (broken home)	Parents stopped living together (either death, separation, or divorce) before respondent was sixteen years old.
12 Poor health	*Either* of these: (a) perception of health as poor, or (b) report of disability which has interfered with his working
13 Physical handicaps	Had a physical disability at some time in life.
14 Failure in realizing ambitions	The discrepancy between status of occupations aspired to in youth and highest occupational status achieved is 20 or more points on the Duncan Socioeconomic Index.
15 Repeated arrests	(a) arrested at least twice for drunkenness or disorderly conduct (b) ever arrested for other offenses
16 Borderline intelligence	*Both* of these: (a) completed less than eight grades of formal schooling

Table 4-7b (Continued)

	(b) perceived self in lower third of class academically
17 School problems and truancy	Left school because he did not like it.
18 Cultural conflict	Born in a non-English-speaking country.

Slope men than skid row men. Many skid row men are from poor families, but so are almost half of the low-income men who do not end up on skid row, judging from the control sample.

Another relatively unimportant factor is social maladjustment as indicated by current attitudes. If social maladjustment is reflected by expressions of anomie, misanthropy, self-estrangement and low self-esteem, the control sample appears as maladjusted as the skid row samples.

Another factor that does not seem particularly important is lack of friends. It may be that the friendships reported by Park Slope men are more stable than those claimed by the skid row men; but in terms of the number of men who are totally without friends, skid row is not different from Park Slope.

As Bogue defines discontinuance of family, it includes the death of a wife as well as the death of a parent. Given the age of the skid row men he studied, it is probable that most of them had lost at least one parent. In the present analysis the family-discontinuance variable was limited to family breakup occurring before the respondent reached maturity, that is, the broken-home variable of Chapter 7. As noted there, skid row men are no more likely to come from broken homes than Park Slope men.

Another relatively unimportant factor in the etiology of skid row life is cultural conflict. Lacking a direct measure of cultural conflict, we assumed that men born in countries where English was not the primary language would be more liable to cultural conflict than men from English-speaking lands. That culture conflict may be a relatively minor factor in the development of homelessness is apparent in the fact that men from non-English-speaking countries are approximately three times as numerous in the control sample as on skid row. Furthermore, the White ethnic group most represented on skid row, the Irish, is perhaps the least likely to experience culture conflict in New York City.

Failure to realize ambitions also seems to be a fairly unimportant factor. It is discussed in detail in the chapter on aspirations and anomie. Here we merely note that the proportion of skid row men failing to achieve their aspirations is no higher than the proportion of Park Slope men. Finally, borderline intelligence, school problems, and truancy show little relationship with homelessness.

The factors that do seem to play a part in the life histories of homeless men in our sample include an unstable work history, heavy drinking, marital discord, low standard of living, public assistance, wanderlust and restlessness, reckless youth, poor health, physical disability, and repeated arrests for drinking offenses and other causes.

Separate chapters will be devoted to work history and drinking; we note here in passing that backgrounds of irregular employment and heavy drinking are recorded about twice as often for skid row men as in the settled sample.

On the face of it, skid row men show only slightly more marital discord than the Park Slope men (17 percent versus 11 percent); but only about half of the skid row men have ever been married. Hence the fact that the skid row sample shows a higher proportion of marital discord is striking. Marital discord seems to be about three times as frequent in the marriages of skid row men as in other marriages.

Almost all of the skid row men have had a low standard of living throughout their life histories. Public assistance has played a much more prominent part in their lives than in the lives of Park Slope respondents. More than 80 percent of the skid row men have received welfare, mission, or shelter assistance at some time, compared to one-fourth of the Park Slope men.

Wandering and restlessness, as indicated both by the number of different places a man has lived and the number of moves he has made, are reported to a much greater extent by skid row men than by Park Slope men. Poor health and disabilities are about twice as frequent on skid row as on Park Slope.

To be considered a reckless youth a respondent had to have been arrested before age 20, kicked out of school, or had to have started drinking heavily before age 20. Skid row men far outnumber Park Slope respondents in this category.

The greatest proportionate differences between the skid row and the Park Slope men involved drinking offenses. Almost half of the skid row men reported such arrests, as opposed to only 3 percent of the Park Slope men. Part of the differential is due to arrests occurring after arrival on skid row (that is, one has many arrests because he lives on skid row, rather than living on skid row because he has many arrests). But apart from drinking arrests, skid row men are also more likely to have, or to admit to having, criminal records.

Thus, only about half of the factors identified by previous investigators as associated with the development of homelessness distinguish the skid row men from the settled men in our sample. Furthermore, some of those items—such as public assistance support and arrests for drunkenness—reflect differences associated with the skid row phase of a man's life rather than antedating it.

Let us comment briefly on the findings reported in this chapter. There is some evidence that skid row men are more prone to the institutional life than other low-income men, although the differences are small. Institutional living was as common among Park Avenue men as skid row men, but the institutions involved were different. There is evidence that patterns of affiliation in formal organizations may be passed from parent to child, but the parents of skid row men were not less affiliated than the parents of other low-income respondents. Immigrant status does not account for skid row residence or disaffiliation, nor had the fathers of skid row men been poorer than the fathers of Park Slope men.

We did discover that the occupational-status histories of the skid row men were different from those of Park Slope and Park Avenue men, and that within each sample men with higher-status occupational histories tended to be more affiliated than men with lower status. Thus, insofar as the marginality hypothesis concerns economic marginality of the respondent himself, it is supported. There is evidence that the homeless man is distinctive in his occupational status, his mobility history, and in the apparent absence on skid row of the general relationship between occupational status and affiliation that prevails in other sectors of the community.

Finally, we have noted that when skid row men are compared to a low-income control sample, about half of the factors previously identified as antecedents of sociopathy or of skid row residence prove to be merely characteristics of growing up in poverty. Factors that did not distinguish Bowery men from Park Slope men included poverty in childhood, social maladjustment (as indicated by attitudes expressed at the time of the interview), lack of friends, a broken home, cultural conflict, failure to realize ambitions, borderline intelligence, and school problems. Factors that did seem to make a difference were an unstable work history, heavy drinking, marital discord, low standard of living, a history of public assistance, wanderlust, a reckless youth, poor health, and repeated arrests for drinking and other offenses.

NOTES

1. David J. Pittman and C. Wayne Gordon, *Revolving Door* (New York: The Free Press, 1958), pp. 11, 64-66.
2. *Ibid.*, p. 10.
3. *Ibid.*, pp. 65-67.
4. *Ibid.*, p. 67.
5. Donald J. Bogue, *Skid Row in American Cities* (Chicago: Community and Family Study Center, Univ. of Chicago, 1963), p. 180.
6. Robert Straus, "The Homeless Alcoholic, Who He Is, His Locale, His Personality, The Approach to His Rehabilitation," in *The Homeless Alcoholic: Report of the First International Institute on the Homeless Alcoholic* (Lansing: Michigan State Board of Alcoholism, 1955), p. 13.
7. C. Wayne Gordon, "Social Characteristics and Life Career Patterns of the Skid Row Alcoholic," in *Institute on the Skid Row Alcoholic, Annual Conference* (New York: National Committee on Alcoholism, 1956), pp. 6-9.
8. Margaret Mary Wood, *Paths of Loneliness* (New York: Columbia Univ., 1953), p. 27.
9. To distinguish skid row life from the occupational patterns of community living defined as institutional, periods of residence in skid row lodging houses and at Camp LaGuardia were coded as living alone.
10. We have said before that as a rule the findings for Camp LaGuardia men parallel those for Bowery men. In the following discussion

and throughout the book, we will usually refer in the text only to Bowery men. When it is not appropriate to include Camp LaGuardia men in this category, they will be considered separately.

11. Samuel E. Wallace, *Skid Row as a Way of Life* (Totowa, N.J.: The Bedminister Press, 1965), p. 165.

12. Pittman and Gordon, *op. cit.*, p. 65; Straus, *op. cit.*, p. 13.

13. George C. Homans, *The Human Group* (New York: Harcourt Brace Jovanovich, 1950), p. 457.

14. U.S. Bureau of the Census, *U.S. Censuses of Population and Housing: 1960 Census Tracts,* Final Report PHC (1)-104 (Washington, D.C.: U.S. Government Printing Office, 1962), Part 1, Table P-1.

15. Lee N. Robins, *Deviant Children Grown Up* (Baltimore: Williams and Williams, 1966), pp. 292-296, 301-303.

16. *Ibid.*, pp. 74-76, 79-81, 342-343. The criteria are listed in Table 4-7.

17. Bogue, *op. cit.*, pp. 402-404.

Homeless men in overnight lodgings at the Oak Street police station, New York City, late 1880s. (Jacob A. Riis)

The Bowery, 1886. (Jacob A. Riis)

The Bowery, 1973. (Robert F. Crawford)

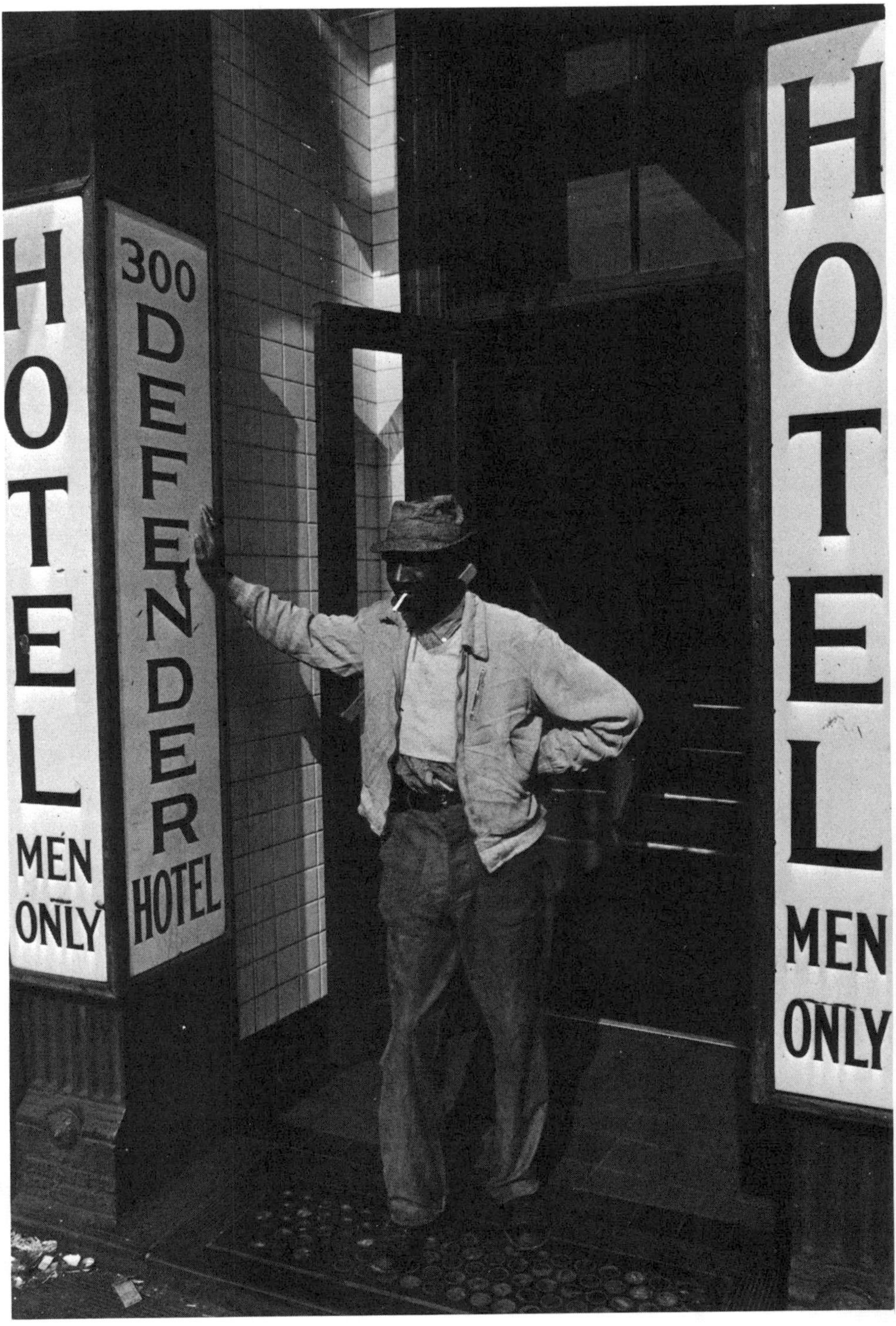

Near Houston Street, 1966. Bowery lodging houses such as the one shown charged about $1.50 per room in 1966. (Robert F. Crawford)

The Bowery, 1966. This homeless man worked at odd jobs at the Men's Shelter of the New York City Department of Welfare; the light bulb he wears is for circuit testing. (Robert F. Crawford)

On the Bowery, near Bleeker Street, 1965. This man pushes his baby carriage around all day, collecting rags, boxes, and scrap metal. (Robert F. Crawford)

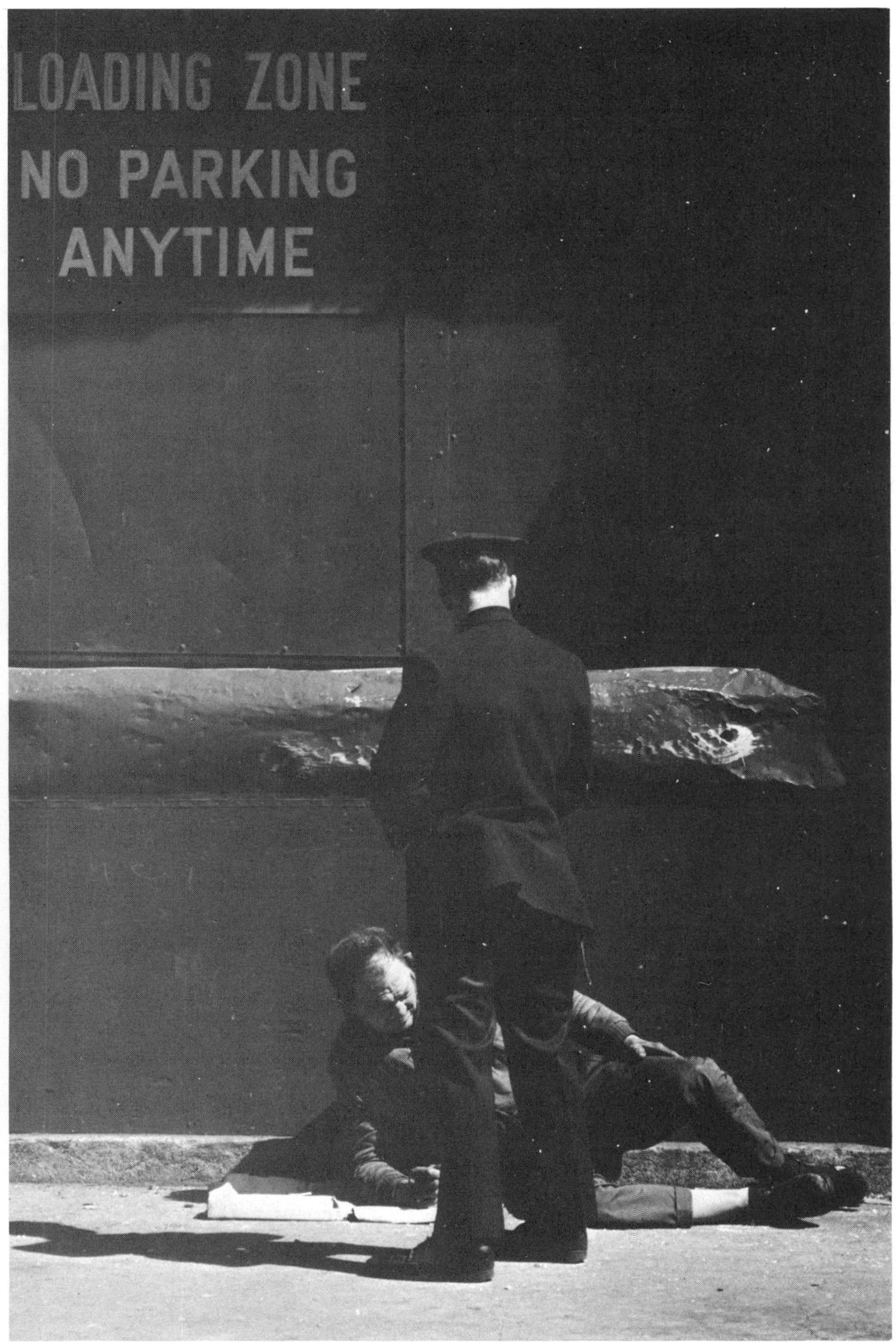

At the Bowery and East Third Street, near Men's Shelter, 1965. (Robert F. Crawford)

Near the Bowery and First Street, 1965. (Robert F. Crawford)

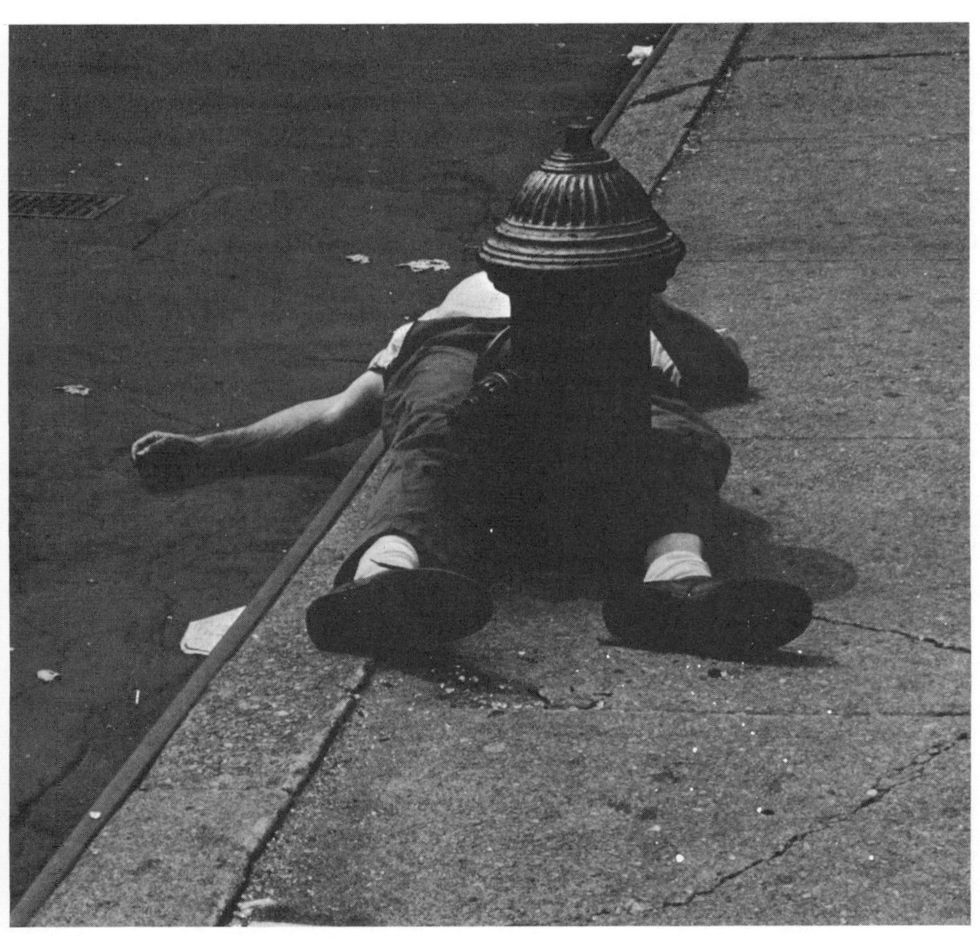

The Bowery, near Rivington Street, 1966. (Robert F. Crawford)

The Bowery and Elizabeth Street, 1960. (Robert F. Crawford)

PART II

THE LIFETIME EXPERIENCE OF HOMELESS AND SETTLED MEN

CHAPTER 5

FAMILIES OF ORIENTATION *

This chapter is concerned with three attributes of the respondent's family of orientation, namely, family stability, family size, and his ordinal birth position. These attributes have been linked to alcoholism and other antisocial behavior, including the social withdrawal typified by skid row men. The present analysis is a reevaluation of that linkage.

FAMILY STABILITY

The broken home is a traditional explanation for social pathology. Delinquency, crime, drug addiction, and alcoholism have all been viewed as consequences of broken homes.[1] With reference to homeless men, this point of view is elaborated in the undersocialization hypothesis used by Pittman and Gordon to explain the etiology of chronic alcoholism.[2] According to this hypothesis, inadequate socialization in early life leads to alcoholism, social withdrawal, and other types of unsavory behavior. One source of undersocialization is instability in the family of orientation—a broken home. Pittman and Gordon observe that while a stable home does not guarantee adequate socialization, its absence creates serious, sometimes lifelong, liabilities, especially among lower-class persons whose environment does not include other resources which reduce the impact of family disorganization. They summarize:

> The absence of one or both parents creates a condition in which the problems of socialization are multiplied, especially in the economic sphere and the realm of identification models, ego ideals and role conceptions.[3]

* Portions of this chapter are adapted from Howard M. Bahr's "Birth Order and Failure: The Evidence from Skid Row," *Quarterly Journal of Studies on Alcohol,* 32 (September 1971) pp. 669-686 and "Family Size and Stability as Antecedents of Homelessness and Excessive Drinking," *Journal of Marriage and the Family,* 31 (August 1969), pp. 477-483, with the permission of the publishers.

Pittman and Gordon indicate that deficiencies in family setting contribute to undersocialization among chronic police case inebriates and cite as evidence the finding that among their sample of 187 incarcerated inebriates, "the structural continuity of the family units was broken by death, divorce, or separation before the inebriates' fifteenth birthday in 39 percent of the cases." [4]

Other researchers have noted a relation between the broken home and alcoholism. Wahl studied family histories of 109 alcoholics and discovered that 37 percent of them had lost at least one parent before age 15; he concluded that parental loss was a significant factor in the etiology of alcoholism.[5] In numerous studies of alcoholics a median proportion of over 40 percent of the subjects have been found to come from broken homes,[6] and researchers have assessed such rates as high, indicating a connection between family instability and excessive drinking.

The determination of what constitutes a high rate of family instability should rest on comparisons with nonalcoholic populations of similar class background. A finding that about 40 percent of the alcoholics come from broken homes is insufficient by itself to demonstrate a causal linkage between broken homes and alcoholism since lower-class populations often show family instability rates of 40 percent or higher. Thus, Spergel found that approximately half of the delinquent and nondelinquent subjects he studied came from broken homes.[7] In the Cambridge-Somerville youth study, 28 percent of the lower-class subjects in the experimental group and the same proportion of the entire control group were from broken homes; [8] among the lower-class subjects in the control group, the proportion from broken homes was undoubtedly higher. Hollingshead and Redlich reported that among Class V persons in New Haven, 41 percent of the children under 17 years of age come from broken homes.[9] Thus, studies of alcoholics showing that 40 percent of them come from broken homes cannot be accepted as evidence that instability of the parental home leads to alcoholism.

One of the more compelling pieces of evidence in support of this position is a study in which the rates of parental deprivation among alcoholic patients were compared with those for a control group of hospital employees. The rates were similar (33 percent for alcoholics, 32 percent for employees), and the authors concluded that "stress of parental deprivation and the broken home does not loom with undue frequency in the life histories of alcohol addicts."[10]

Straus observed a positive relationship between instability of the parental home and subsequent homelessness,[11] and Dunham asserted that the usual background of the homeless man included a broken home.[12] However, Bogue found that only 24 percent of his respondents came from broken homes.[13] Since skid row men have predominantly lower-class backgrounds, we would expect a sizable proportion of them to be from broken homes. The finding that one-fourth of the men on Chicago's skid row are from broken homes does not establish a firm connection between broken homes and skid row residence

The conventional viewpoint about the effect of broken homes on skid row resistance, disaffiliation, and alcoholism may be restated formally as three hypotheses: men from broken homes are overrepresented (1) on skid row, (2) among disaffiliates, and (3) among heavy drinkers.

Our indicator of family stability is the question, Did your parents always live together until you were 16 years old? Men who answered negatively were asked about the nature of the parental separation and how old they were when it occurred. Our indices of affiliation are the current and past memberships mentioned in the preceding chapters. The measure of drinking status is the drinking count described in detail in Chapter 13. This index is based on a man's estimate of the frequency and extent of his drinking. Initially there were five categories: spree drinkers, three types of steady drinkers (heavy, moderate, and light), and abstainers. For the present analysis these were combined into three classes: spree and heavy drinkers, moderate drinkers, light drinkers and abstainers.

Thirty-five percent of the skid row men and 31 percent of the Park Slope men come from broken homes. However, both groups report higher rates of family instability than the Park Avenue men, of whom only 18 percent came from broken homes. Thus, when socioeconomic level is controlled, skid row men are not much more likely to come from a broken home than other low-income men.

The expected association between family stability and affiliation did not materialize either. In all of our samples men from broken homes reported about the same level of affiliation as men from stable homes. Only two statistically significant differences appeared. First, in the Bowery and Park Slope samples (but not in the Camp LaGuardia sample) men from broken homes were less educated than men from stable homes. Second, Park Slope men from stable homes reported much more church attendance than those from broken homes. But the preponderance of evidence does not support the hypothesized linkage between a respondent's adult affiliations and the stability of his family of orientation.

Nor do the results support the view that broken homes produce heavy drinkers. In the Bowery and Park Slope samples the proportion of heavy drinkers was slightly higher among men who came from broken homes, but the difference was not statistically significant. In the Camp LaGuardia sample the distributions were almost identical, and in the Park Avenue sample there were only two heavy drinkers, both of whom were from stable families.

Much of the apparent evidence for an association between broken parental homes and alcoholism or homelessness is probably based on a misperception of what constitutes a high rate of family instability, a misperception mainly due to the lack of comparative data from control samples. Witness Pittman and Gordon's interpretation of the finding that 39 percent of their sample come from broken homes:

> This seems to be an extremely high percentage of families whose structure collapsed. . . . Unfortunately, we do not possess exact comparable information concerning the general population, although data on other problem groups are available.[14]

They then cite a finding that 43 percent of a sample of juvenile delinquents came from broken homes. Having stated that the 39 percent *seemed* high, having admitted that they lacked the information necessary to determine just how high it was, and having cited one study showing a *higher* rate among delinquents (a lower rate would have been much more convincing evidence), in the following paragraph they then leap from a finding that *may* be a high rate to the assumption that they in fact *have* found a high rate: "What significance can be attached to the high rate of broken family structures among the incarcerated inebriates?" [15] Thus, the focus has subtly moved from the question of whether or not a rate is high (a question of descriptive fact) to the problem of the significance of the (undemonstrated) high rate of broken homes.

FAMILY SIZE

Assuming an inverse relationship between the number of children and the economic power available to launch each child in the world, one may infer that children from large families begin life at a disadvantage, and hence that a higher proportion of them can be expected to fail economically. It has also been suggested that children of small families are most likely to be oriented toward status-striving,[16] and that "the smaller the family, the more likely the [upward] mobility of the children." [17]

Skid row represents the failure end of the failure-success continuum. By the above argument men from large families ought to be overrepresented. Bogue reports that this is the case among skid row men in Chicago.[18] However, he notes that while men from large families are overrepresented on skid row, they are not overrepresented among heavy drinkers there. This last finding is at odds with some earlier research on family size and drinking. For example, Peterson found that "winos came from large families," [19] and Wahl reported that among alcoholic hospital patients "more than three times as many members of this alcoholic group originated from large families than do persons in the general population." [20]

These observations suggest that men from large families are overrepresented on skid row and among heavy drinkers.

Family-size and skid row residence. Table 5-1 shows the distribution of respondents by size of family of orientation for three skid row samples—statistics on Chicago's skid row are included—and for our control samples. The most obvious feature of the table is that in contrast to the four other samples, Park Avenue respondents tend to come from small families. But in comparison with the Park Slope sample, men from large families do not appear to be overrepresented in the three skid row samples. This finding prompts us to reexamine Bogue's finding of a positive relationship between family size and residence on skid row.

In evaluating figures on family size from different populations, one must maintain a constant reference point. Data on the size of families of procreation from the reference point of the mother must be clearly

Table 5-1

NUMBER OF CHILDREN IN FAMILY OF ORIENTATION (IN PERCENTAGES)

Number of Children	Chicago[a]	Bowery	Camp LaGuardia	Park Slope	Park Avenue
1	8	12	10	5	17
2	8	10	10	13	23
3	9	11	13	11	20
4	15	17	15	14	16
5-6	20	24	21	21	16
7-9	27	15	23	18	10
10 or more	13	10	9	19	0
N	613	192	197	123	102

a. This column based on Donald J. Bogue, *Skid Row in American Cities* (Chicago: Community and Family Study Center, Univ. of Chicago, 1963), p. 345.

distinguished from those on size of families of orientation from the reference point of the offspring. By way of illustration suppose seven women are distributed evenly among the categories listing number of children in Table 5-2. These seven mothers have a total of 33 offspring (see column 3). Although each woman represents one-seventh of the total population of mothers, the proportion of children coming from families of a given size varies from 3 percent to 30 percent; in the population of the children of these seven mothers, 3 percent are only children, 6 percent are offspring of two-child families, and so forth (column 4 in Table 5-2). Determination of whether families of orientation of a given sample differ in size from this hypothetical distribution requires a comparison of the distribution of respondents by family size with the distribution in column 5.

The reported positive association between family size and skid row residence is based on a comparison of the family sizes of skid row men with those of native White women 45 to 49 years of age in 1940. The data used in this comparison are reproduced in the first two columns of Table 5-3.

Table 5-2

HYPOTHETICAL DISTRIBUTION OF MOTHERS AND OFFSPRING, BY NUMBER OF CHILDREN

Number of Children	(1) Number of Mothers	(2) Percentage of All Mothers	(3) Number of Children	(4) Percentage of All Children
1	1	14	1	3
2	1	14	2	6
3	1	14	3	10
4	1	14	4	12
5-6	1	14	5	15
7-9	1	14	8	24
10 or more	1	14	10	30
Total	7	98	33	100

At first glance these figures support the conclusion that "a disproportionately large share of the Skid Row men come from families with seven or more children, and a disproportionately small share come from families with one to four children." [21] But note that the first column refers to the number of children in the family of orientation of *each individual respondent,* while the second is a distribution of *mothers* according to the size of their families of procreation. Thus, 12.7 percent of the native White women had only one child, 17.5 percent had two children, and 15.3 percent had three children. However, in a population composed of the children of these women, for every 13 only children there are 35 children from two-child families and 46 children from three-child families.

What Bogue has done is to compare the percentage of women with families of varying size with the proportion of the skid row population derived from families of varying size. Naturally, there are more men who come *from* large families than there are women who *have* large families, and hence he reaches the erroneous conclusion that men from large families are overrepresented on skid row. The distribution by family size of offspring from the families of procreation

Table 5-3

NUMBER OF CHILDREN IN THE FAMILIES OF CHICAGO SKID ROW MEN, AND IN THE FAMILIES OF LOWER-CLASS MOTHERS IN THE NATIONAL POPULATION (IN PERCENTAGES)

Number of Children	(1) Families of Orientation, Skid Row Men[a]	(2) Families of Procreation, Native White Mothers 45-49 Years of Age in 1940, with 5-6 Years of School[a]	(3) Families of Orientation, Children of Native White Mothers 45-49 Years of Age in 1940, with 5-6 Years of School[b]
1	8.3	12.7	2.9
2	7.7	17.5	7.9
3	9.0	15.3	10.4
4	15.2	13.8	12.5
5-6	20.0	18.9	23.6
7-9	27.3	14.8	26.8
10 or more	12.6	7.0	15.9
Totals	100.1	100.0	100.0

a. Figures are from Donald J. Bogue, *Skid Row in American Cities* (Chicago: Community and Family Study Center, Univ. of Chicago, 1963), p. 345.

b. Computed from the figures in column 2.

represented in column 2 of Table 5-3 appears in column 3 of the same table. These are the data Bogue should have used. Comparison of this distribution with the skid row distribution (column 1) does not reveal a positive association between family size and residence on skid row.

Incidentally, Wahl's conclusion that alcoholics tend to come from large families is based on the same faulty reasoning. Forty-nine percent of his sample of alcoholics were from families having four or more children. He cites a statistic that only 13.7 percent of the nation's families with children have that many offspring and divides that percentage into the 49 percent to obtain the finding that alcoholics are three times as likely as members of the general population to derive from large families.[22] Observe, however, that in the first instance (49 percent) he is speaking of the proportion of a sample of alcoholics who are *children* from large families, while the national statistic (13.7 percent) refers to the proportion of *families* (or mothers) having four or more children.

Refer back to the hypothetical distribution in Table 5-2, and assume that half of all children become alcoholics, regardless of family size. There are thus 16 alcoholics in the population. Note that while just over half (four-sevenths or 57 percent) of the families have four or more children, almost all of the alcoholics (thirteen-sixteenths or 81 percent) are from these large families. According to Wahl's procedure, the 81 percent would be divided by 57 percent to yield the finding that alcoholics are 1.4 times as apt to derive from large families as from the general population. Of course this is not so, since the distribution of alcoholics is based on the initial condition that regardless of family size every other child becomes an alcoholic.

Using the national figures on family size cited by Wahl, it can be demonstrated that in any randomly selected population more than one-third of the children would come from large families, despite the fact that such families make up only about one-seventh of all families with children. Contrasting the finding that 49 percent of the patients Wahl studied were from large families with the fact that at least one-third of the general population come from large families, it is apparent that the evidence for the conclusion that children from large families are overrepresented among alcoholics needs to be reexamined.

The national figures we have used in the evaluation of the family-size distributions of our four samples refer to an older cohort of mothers than the figures Bogue used. The reasons for selecting the older cohort—women aged 55 to 64 in 1940—are as follows.

The median age of the Bowery men was 52 years. Assuming that the births of Bowery men were distributed normally throughout their mothers' reproductive years, from age 15 to age 45, the average mother of a respondent would have been 30 years old in 1914 (1966 minus 52 = 1914). She would have completed her childbearing by 1929 and would have been 56 in 1940. Accordingly, the number of children ever born to women in the category including age 56 in the 1940 census was used to compute the expected size of family for the general population.

National figures for size of family in this cohort of mothers are presented in Table 5-4. Column 1 pertains to the general population, and column 2 to urban native Whites in the lowest socioeconomic stratum (using rental value of home as the index). The national figures are congruent with those for Park Slope (column 6), indicating that the Park Slope sample is an adequate control group. Whether the skid row men are compared to the national population or to the Park Slope respondents, the conclusion is the same: men from large families are *not* overrepresented in the skid row population. If anything, the reverse is the case. The three skid row samples show *smaller* proportions of respondents from families of seven or more children

Table 5-4

NUMBER OF CHILDREN IN FAMILY OF ORIENTATION, FOR SELECTED NATIONAL SKID ROW AND CONTROL POPULATIONS (IN PERCENTAGES)

	Children of Mothers Aged 55-64 in 1940, National Population[a]		Skid Row Samples			Our Control Samples	
Number of Children	(1) Total	(2) Urban Lower Class[b]	(3) Chicago[c]	(4) Bowery	(5) Camp LaGuardia	(6) Park Slope	(7) Park Avenue
1	4	3	8	12	10	5	17
2-3	23	15	17	21	23	24	42
4-6	36	33	35	41	36	35	31
7 and over	37	49	40	25	32	37	10
Total	100	100	100	99	101	101	100

a. Computed from U.S. Bureau of the Census, *Sixteenth Census of the United States: 1940, Population; Differential Fertility, 1940 and 1910, Women by Number of Children Ever Born* (Washington, D.C.: U.S. Government Printing Office, 1945), Tables 1-3 and 57-59. Non-Whites other than Blacks are not included in these figures.

b. Native Whites only. Monthly rental value of home was $5.00 or less.

c. Computed from figures in Table 5-3.

than would be expected among offspring of a lower-class urban sample, and there is a substantial overrepresentation of men who were only children in the skid row samples.

Family size and drinking. The hypothesized relation between drinking and family size did not appear in any of the samples. In fact, in two of the four samples there was a slight (and nonsignificant) negative relationship between family size and extent of drinking. Thus, the findings support Bogue's conclusion that coming from a large family does not necessarily predispose one to heavy drinking.

In sum, not only are offspring from large families not overrepresented among skid row men or heavy drinkers in our samples, but even in some of the earlier studies purporting to show a direct relation between family size on the one hand and skid row residence or alcoholism on the other hand, the relation, upon closer analysis, seems an artifact of a faulty analytical procedure.

THE EFFECTS OF BIRTH ORDER

Investigations of the relationship between success and birth order have generally found that success, however measured, attends firstborn and only children more than persons in other birth ranks. A related question—less well covered in the research literature—is the possible association between birth order and failure.

It has been suggested that firstborn children are the carriers of traditional culture in that they are socialized to be the passers-on of the social heritage to a greater extent than later-born children.[23] Firstborns are said to be more highly socialized than later-borns, and to be more responsible.[24] In contrast, skid row men withdraw from the traditional culture, if they do not actively reject it, and are the ultimate noncarriers of the cultural heritage. Moreover, they have been identified as undersocialized.[25]

Rosen summarized several studies showing that firstborn or only children are likely to have socialization experiences that are conducive to the transmission of values, and in his own research found that firstborn or only children were more likely than intermediate or youngest children to have values like those of their mothers. Other researchers have observed that ordinal position and sibling sex status involve distinctive social learnings, and that the social learning among firstborns in the two-child family includes strong identification with the parents and leads to academic success and a readiness to take parent-surrogate roles.[26]

One review of the literature on birth order and eminence concluded that eminence, however defined, was related to birth order: firstborns tend to achieve greater eminence than the later-born.[27] It has been argued also that the eldest child is particularly vulnerable to introversion, aloofness, and introspection because of his progressive displacement from primary parental attention by subsequent siblings.[28] A contrary argument is that the status and authority of the eldest sibling with respect to later-born children give him a sense of security and adequacy.

Schachter postulated a stronger affiliative tendency among the early-born subjects which results in their joining more voluntary associations than later-born subjects. Early-born children, he argued, are more likely to seek social means for solving problems, while the later-born choose nonsocial means. Thus, disturbed firstborn individuals are more likely to seek out psychotherapists to help them with their problems, while later-born individuals are more susceptible to alcoholism.[29]

As evidence for the presumed linkage between birth order and alcoholism, Schachter cites data on alcoholism and birth rank published by Bakan, which purport to show that youngest and later-born children are overrepresented among men convicted for crimes involving alcohol abuse.[30] Bakan did not attempt to account for his findings, but it has been suggested that a special factor in the etiology of alcoholism may be "a family constellation in which the patient tends to be the youngest, or the most protected, in the sense of prolonging his dependency and denying his gradual and smooth individualization." [31] The alleged association between alcoholism and birth order was challenged by Smart, who said that the results were not based on a sample of alcoholics but rather of persons convicted for public intoxication. Further, he questioned Schachter's assumption that regardless of size of family, children in birth order 1, 2, and 3 are earlyborn and other birth orders are laterborn.[32] Smart's position is consistent with some earlier research showing no relation between sibling position and the genesis of alcoholism.[33]

Although Schachter's work stimulated many studies of birth order and affiliative behavior, most of these studies were of small samples. Warren reviewed the literature and concluded that only one study gives clear-cut evidence that firstborns have a stronger affiliative tendency than later-borns, and the evidence from that study holds only for women.[34] Schooler used hospital records in a study of birth order and schizophrenia and concluded that compared to their own firstborn siblings, lastborns are less likely to be married, have lower occupational and educational levels, and have more personality disorders.[35] Recent studies have shown that later-borns are more likely to affiliate with a fraternity, that firstborn males anticipate higher occupational status than later-borns, and that firstborns are more conforming only under certain conditions.[36]

Among the hypotheses emerging from the foregoing discussion are these: (1) firstborn and only children tend to be more successful than other birth ranks (for example, they should be less likely to end up on skid row); (2) early-born siblings are more affiliated than later-born siblings; and (3) later-born siblings are heavier drinkers than early-born siblings.

Birth order and skid row residence. According to the first hypothesis, firstborn and only children should be underrepresented on skid row. The birth order distribution of our skid row and Park Slope samples are summarized in Table 5-5, and the proportions there do not support the hypothesis. In fact, the most striking thing about the table is the apparent overrepresentation of only children in the skid row sample.

It is possible, however, that it is the Park Slope population that is deviant rather than the skid row population. That is, for some reason there may be an underrepresentation of only children in Park Slope. This possibility was checked by computing the expected proportion of only children among various segments of the United States population, using census data from a cohort of mothers about the same age as the mothers of the skid row respondents.

As we noted in our discussion of family size, the proportion of only-born males in a population may vary with the age and socioeconomic characteristics of their mothers, and hence statements about the expected proportions of only-borns, or about any birth order distribution, for that matter, should specify the cohort of mothers used as the standard. The recently reported value of 10 percent as a

Table 5-5

BIRTH-ORDER DISTRIBUTIONS

	Bowery		Camp LaGuardia		Park Slope		Park Avenue	
	N	%	N	%	N	%	N	%
Only child	23	12	19	10	6	5	17	17
First-born	42	22	36	18	26	21	27	26
Last-born	37	19	55	28	27	22	27	26
Middle-born	90	47	87	44	63	52	31	30
Total[a]	192	100	197	100	122	100	102	99

a. Total Ns are slightly smaller than total sample size because of incomplete information.

standard total frequency of only children was determined by combining subjects from seven previous studies of alcoholics, and it represents the offspring of several different cohorts of mothers.[37] Judging from statistics about the national population, 10 percent is too high. We estimated expected proportions of only-borns on the basis of census reports of fertility by age.[38] For example, the proportions of only children from the combined offspring of all White women ever married (as reported in 1960) by five-year age intervals beginning with mothers aged 35-39 years were 6, 7, 8, 9, 8, 7, and 5 percent, respectively, the last percentage representing children of mothers aged 65 and over in 1960.

None of the cohorts of mothers considered thus far is as old as the mothers of the average respondents in the skid row samples. We demonstrated earlier in this chapter that the appropriate cohort for the present samples is mothers aged 55 to 64 in 1940, and computations based on the data in the 1940 census reports revealed that of the offspring of native White mothers aged 55 to 64 in 1940 only 5 percent were only children. For the offspring of foreign-born White or Black mothers in the general population the percentage of only children was even lower (3 percent), and among the lower classes, more comparable to the families of skid row men than other segments of the population, only about 2 percent.

If the national proportion (5 percent) of only children among offspring of native White mothers in the appropriate cohort is used to estimate expected frequencies of only-born and other children, and the observed frequencies of only and other children in the combined Bowery and Camp LaGuardia samples are compared with these theoretical frequencies in a chi-square test of goodness-of-fit, the observed frequencies in skid row samples differ from the expected frequencies at the .01 level.

Thus, youngest children do not appear to be substantially overrepresented on skid row, but only children are. Between 8 percent[39] and 12 percent of the men on skid row are only children, while the proportion of only children in the Park Slope sample is half that, and in comparable categories of the national population the proportion is even less. There seem to be about three times as many only children on skid row as in the general population of offspring from the same cohort of mothers, and if controls for economic status of mothers are added, skid row appears even more atypical.

Before moving to the other two hypotheses, a variation of the first deserves attention. Rather than focusing on firstborn and last-born siblings, the hypothesis may be restated in terms of birth order as an interval measurement. In other words the question is, given the family sizes claimed by the skid row men, are certain birth orders found on skid row more frequently than others?

The importance of correcting for family size in analyses of effects of birth has been stressed by several writers.[40] The argument is as follows. If a characteristic is unrelated to birth order, it should be distributed evenly among the birth ranks of families of the same size. But because of variations in family size there may be variation in the expected number of children of any particular birth rank, and an apparently skewed distribution of birth ranks with reference to some characteristic may be typical and in no way extraordinary. Without knowing the family size of respondents making up a population, no inference can be made about the expected distribution of a given characteristic.

There are several methods of correcting for family size. Smart describes the Greenwood-Yule reconstruction of sibships, used with the chi-square test to determine whether observed sibship frequencies deviate from expectations.[41] An alternative method is described by Keeping, who maintains that the chi-square test may underestimate the significance of the effects of birth order on a given population. In Keeping's test the sum of the birth ranks on N individuals affected by some characteristic is defined as the total birth rank and is used in conjunction with information on family size to determine whether the sample departs from randomness.[42]

An application of the Keeping test revealed that among the Bowery respondents birth rank is not related to residence on skid row ($Z = 0.45$; $.30 < p < .40$). However, a similar test for Camp LaGuardia residence and birth rank yielded a Z-score of 3.22, significant at the .01 level. A test of the hypothesis using the Greenwood-Yule correction and chi-square test yielded similar results: for the Bowery, chi-square = 5.90, 7 df, $.50 < p < .70$; for Camp LaGuardia, chi-square = 14.08, 8 df, $.05 < p < .10$. Thus, the hypothesis that failure, as indicated by presence on skid row, is more likely to attend later-born than firstborn sibs is supported for the respondents at Camp LaGuardia but not for Bowery men. It might be argued that life at Camp LaGuardia represents a purer form of withdrawal with fewer responsibilities than life on the Bowery and that whatever relation exists between birth order and retreatism is obscured on the Bowery by the diversity there.

In his study of birth order, eminence, and higher education, Schachter suggested that to prove that firstborns were more likely than their siblings to become scholars, it would be necessary to show either that they were underrepresented among nonscholars or that in the general population there was no birth-order effect.[43] In the present discussion the continuum has been success-failure rather than scholarship-nonscholarship, and Schachter's first suggestion has been followed, that is, it was hypothesized that firstborns were underrepresented among skid row men. However, this proved not to be the case. Instead, no consistent pattern was evident, except for a striking overrepresentation of only-born respondents. The explanation for this finding seems to lie in the relation between family structure and the development of dependency. It is true that an only child may have a marked advantage over children from multichild families of the same social class, but because he is a solitary child there may be other family structural factors which predispose him to weak affiliation outside the family or to overdependency. Furthermore, in some cases unreasonably high parental expectations might foster the type of retreat that would eventually produce a disaffiliate. These are speculations, but they serve as a reminder that the same family structure which produces an extremely high proportion of eminent men also produces relatively high proportions of failures. Apparently the success distribution of only children is skewed at both extremes.

Birth order and affiliation. Part of the confusion in the literature on birth order and social behavior is due to inconsistencies in classifying only children. Sometimes they have been classed with eldest children, and sometimes they have been studied separately. Warren has criticized the former practice, noting that there is as much justification for considering only children last-born as firstborn.[44] The best strategy seems to be to distinguish only children from children with siblings and to treat them as a separate category. The present analysis lends support to Warren's argument, and the following brief digression presents evidence for that position.

The relation between birth order and affiliation was assessed by computing for four positions—only child, firstborn with siblings, middle-born, last-born with siblings—the percentage of affiliated respondents for each of the 14 measures of affiliation. These percentages are given in Table 5-6. Values for only children and middle-born children in the control samples do not appear in the table because there were too few only children to permit meaningful comparisons of affiliation rates. However, the values for first- and last-born Park Slope Avenue respondents are included because they are referred to later.

The data in Table 5-6 were used to compute the extent of difference between all possible pairs of birth positions. For each measure of affiliation the absolute differences among the four birth positions were calculated. Consequently there were six values for each measure of affiliation, that is, absolute values for the percentage differences between only and firstborn children, only and middle-born, only and last-born, firstborn and middle-born, firstborn and last-born, and middle-born and last-born. These six values were then ranked by extent of difference. Thus, the largest of the six, or that pair of birth positions that were most different, received rank one; the next most different received rank two, and so on through rank six. Gross measures of the extent of difference between any two positions were obtained by summing the rank scores for each pair of birth positions; the lower the total, the greater the difference between the positions. Among Bowery men, the two positions most different on these fourteen measures of affiliation were only child and firstborn child, and

Table 5-6

PERCENTAGE OF RESPONDENTS AFFILIATED, BY BIRTH ORDER

Measures of Affiliation	Bowery				Camp LaGuardia				Park Slope		Park Avenue	
	Only child	First-born	Middle-born	Last-born	Only child	First-born	Middle-born	Last-born	First-born	Last-born	First-born	Last-born
Lifetime measures												
Ever married	36	52	49	32	53	53	44	49	77	56	77	74
Ever voted	70	67	60	73	74	78	62	80	73	52	96	96
Over 8 years education	52	57	44	64	58	43	37	48	56	46	96	100
Organizational affiliations in youth[a]	52	60	51	54	53	50	48	62	42	37	74	89
Current measures												
Currently employed	39	52	32	38	—	—	—	—	77	82	89	89
Saw family member within past year	9	56	33	24	21	26	17	20	73	48	89	96
Attends church at least twicc a month	17	31	26	25	22	28	37	30	36	30	7	29
Belongs to informal group[b]	39	24	33	30	58	22	38	31	40	52	63	81
Has organizational affiliation(s)[c]	4	24	32	16	21	17	18	14	65	44	56	63

Table 5-6 (Continued)

Measures of Affiliation	Bowery				Camp LaGuardia				Park Slope		Park Avenue	
	Only child	First-born	Middle-born	Last-born	Only child	First-born	Middle-born	Last-born	First-born	Last-born	First-born	Last-born
Has close friend(s) in New York City	22	31	39	32	26	19	16	24	58	56	74	70
Knows names of more than 5 neighbors	44	60	48	46	68	63	52	58	31	63	78	52
Would like to know more neighbors	22	12	29	21	17	20	29	21	31	38	20	28
Would join a neighborhood organization	65	64	73	57	44	34	55	52	65	73	61	45
Conversed with more than 6 people yesterday	52	52	43	35	42	47	46	46	54	50	86	67
Lowest N[d]	22	39	85	33	16	34	83	50	25	24	21	22

a. Refers primarily to membership in voluntary organizations; jobs, church membership, family affiliation, and school excluded. Youth is defined as before age 20.

b. Men responding affirmatively to the question, Are there certain men you often hang around with? were considered as belonging to an informal group.

c. Refers primarily to voluntary organizations.

d. Number of cases varies slightly due to incomplete information.

the next most different were only child and middle-born child. Among Camp LaGuardia respondents, the positions of only child and middle-born child were most different, and only children resembled youngest children as much as eldest children. In neither sample were the only children most similar to the firstborn children. Hence, the assumption that only children and firstborn children are so alike that they may be combined in a single category for comparison with other birth positions is untenable. Using different data, the rankings undoubtedly would be different, but for present purposes and these variables, it clearly would be a mistake to lump only children and firstborn children into a single type.

In light of the above, tests of the relationship between birth order and affiliation were limited to comparisons between firstborn and last-born respondents with siblings. Since the probability of being firstborn is the same as being last-born, limiting the tests to comparisons of these two positions makes it possible to test the hypothesis without adding controls for family size.

According to the second hypothesis, firstborn children should be more affiliated than last-born children. Table 5-6 includes affiliation rates of respondents in these two birth ranks.[45]

If the hypothesis were supported, the percentages in the second, sixth, ninth, and eleventh columns should be higher than their respective counterparts in the fourth, eighth, tenth, and twelfth columns. The hypothesis receives the most support in the Park Slope sample, where on nine of the twelve types of affiliation the firstborns are more affiliated than the last-borns. Among Bowery men many of the differences between first- and last-borns are extremely small. In the Camp LaGuardia sample the anticipated greater affiliation of the firstborns is not at all in evidence. Nevertheless, for some types of affiliation the four samples showed consistent results. In all, firstborns were more likely to have married, to have seen a family member within the past year, to maintain current membership in a voluntary association, and to have conversed with many people on the day preceding the interview. On the other hand, in all four samples the last-borns were more likely to affirm that they belonged to an informal group of men who often got together. It may be that firstborns are more likely to attempt the affiliation linked to the greatest social responsibility, namely, establishment of a family of procreation, while the more dependent last-borns tend to avoid such heavy commitment but do participate more in certain less demanding types of affiliation, such as membership in an informal group. In any case, considering the four samples and all the measures of affiliation, the hypothesized relationship between birth order and affiliation is not apparent. Most of the observed differences simply are not large enough to warrant acceptance of the hypothesis.

Birth order and drinking. Comparisons of the distribution for firstborn and last-born children among the three drinking categories (spree and heavy drinkers, moderate drinkers, and light drinkers and abstainers) reveals that in two of the three lower-income samples last-borns appeared to be overrepresented among spree and heavy drinkers. Thus, 22 percent of last-borns in the Park Slope sample were spree and heavy drinkers compared to only 12 percent of the firstborns in that sample. Among Camp LaGuardia men, 56 percent of the last-borns were spree and heavy drinkers compared to 34 percent of the firstborns. The Bowery sample was the negative case: there the proportion of spree and heavy drinkers was about one-third among both first- and last-born respondents. Although two of the three lower-income samples show percentage differences in the expected directions, those differences were based on subsamples consisting only of firstborn and last-born sons and were not large enough to reach statistical significance even if significance tests were appropriate. Heavy and spree drinkers in the Park Slope and Park Avenue sample were so few as to preclude more detailed analysis. But in the skid row samples there were enough respondents who drank heavily to permit a test of whether later birth orders were overrepresented among heavy drinkers. Matrices were prepared showing the distribution of heavy and spree drinkers among Bowery and Camp LaGuardia respondents by birth order and family size, and the Keeping test was applied to determine whether the observed distribution of ordinal birth positions deviated from randomness after controls for family size were taken into account.[46] Among the Bowery men no birth-order effects were apparent, but among Camp LaGuardia respondents there was a significant relationship between birth order and heavy drinking: the later-borns were substantially overrepresented among the heavy and spree drinkers ($Z = 3.62$; $p < .001$). Thus we are left with equivocal findings: the evidence from Camp LaGuardia supports the hypothesis, that from the Bowery does not.

NOTES

1. For evidence that broken homes, per se, do not necessarily lead to maladjustment, see F. Ivan Nye, "Child Adjustment in Broken and in Unhappy Homes," *Marriage and Family Living,* 19 (November 1957), pp. 356-361; Lee Burchinal, "Characteristics of Adolescents from Unbroken, Broken, and Reconstituted Families," *Journal of Marriage and the Family,* 26 (February 1964), pp. 44-51.

2. David J. Pittman and C. Wayne Gordon, *Revolving Door: A Study of the Chronic Police Case Inebriate* (New York: The Free Press, 1958).

3. *Ibid.,* p. 81.

4. *Ibid.,* pp. 79-80, 93.

5. C. W. Wahl, "Some Antecedent Factors in the Family Histories of 109 Alcoholics," *Quarterly Journal of Studies on Alcohol,* 17 (December 1956), pp. 645-646, 649-650.

6. For example, see Robert A. Moore and Frieda Ramseur, "A Study of the Background of 100 Hospitalized Veterans with Alcoholism," *Quarterly Journal of Studies on Alcohol,* 21 (March 1960), pp. 51-67; Edith S. Lisansky, "Alcoholism in Women: Social and Psychological Concomitants," *Quarterly Journal of Studies on Alcohol,* 18 (December 1957), pp. 588-623; and William Jack Peterson, "The Culture of the Skid Road Wino," master's thesis, State College of Washington 1955, p. 26.

7. Irving Spergel, *Racketville, Slumtown, Haulburg: An Exploratory Study of Delinquent Subcultures* (Chicago: Univ. of Chicago Press, 1964), p. 7.

8. William McCord and Joan McCord, *Origins of Crime: A New Evaluation of the Cambridge-Somerville Youth Study* (New York: Columbia Univ. Press, 1959), p. 85.

9. August B. Hollingshead and Frederick C. Redlich, *Social Class and Mental Illness: A Community Study* (New York: John Wiley & Sons, 1958), p. 124.

10. Jane E. Oltman and Samuel Friedman, "A Consideration of Parental Deprivation and Other Factors in Alcohol Addicts," *Quarterly Journal of Studies on Alcohol,* 14 (March 1953), p. 56.

11. Robert Straus ,"Alcohol and the Homeless Man," *Quarterly Journal of Studies on Alcohol,* 7 (December 1946), p. 383.

12. H. Warren Dunham, *Homeless Men and Their Habitats* (Detroit: Wayne Univ., 1953).

13. Donald J. Bogue, *Skid Row in American Cities* (Chicago: Community and Family Study Center, Univ. of Chicago, 1963), p. 351.

14. Pittman and Gordon, *op. cit.,* p. 79.

15. *Ibid.,* p. 80.

16. Bernard C. Rosen, "Family Structure and Value Transmission," *Merrill-Palmer Quarterly,* 10 (January 1964), p. 68.

17. Bernard Berelson and Gary A. Steiner, *Human Behavior* (New York: Harcourt Brace Jovanovich, 1964), p. 469.

18. Bogue, *op. cit.,* p. 345.

19. Peterson, *op. cit.,* p. 26.

20. Wahl, *op. cit.,* p. 646.

21. Bogue, *op. cit.,* p. 345.

22. Wahl, *op. cit.,* pp. 645-646.

23. Kenneth Kammeyer, "Birth Order and the Feminine Sex Role Among College Women," *American Sociological Review,* 31 (August 1966), pp. 508-515.

24. A. P. MacDonald, Jr., "Manifestations of Differential Levels of Socialization by Birth Order," *Developmental Psychology,* 1 (September 1969), pp. 485-492; A. P. MacDonald, Jr., "Birth Order and Religious Affiliation," *Developmental Psychology,* 1 (September 1969), p. 628.

25. Pittman and Gordon, *op. cit.*

26. Rosen, *op. cit.,* pp. 59-76; B. Sutton-Smith, J. M. Roberts, and B. G. Rosenberg, "Sibling Associations and Role Involvement," *Merrill-Palmer Quarterly,* 10 (January 1964), p. 36.

27. William D. Altus, "Birth Order and Its Sequelae," *Science,* 151 (January 1966), pp. 44-49.

28. Wahl, *op. cit.,* pp. 643-654.

29. Stanley Schachter, *The Psychology of Affiliation* (Stanford, Calif.: Stanford Univ. Press, 1959), p. 78.

30. David Bakan, "The Relationship Between Alcoholism and Birth Rank," *Quarterly Journal of Studies on Alcohol,* 10 (December 1949), pp. 434-440.

31. Alan D. Button, "The Genesis and Development of Alcoholism: An Empirically Based Scheme," *Quarterly Journal of Studies on Alcohol,* 17 (December 1956), pp. 671-675.

32. Reginald G. Smart, "Alcoholism, Birth Order, and Family Size," *Journal of Abnormal and Social Psychology,* 66 (January 1963), p. 17.

33. Wahl, *op. cit.,* p. 645.

34. Jonathan R. Warren, "Birth Order and Social Behavior," *Psycho-*

logical Bulletin, 65 (January 1966), pp. 40-43; H. B. Gerard and J. M. Rabbie, "Fear and Social Comparison," *Journal of Abnormal and Social Psychology,* 62 (May 1961), pp. 586-592.

35. C. Schooler, "Birth Order and Hospitalization for Schizophrenia," *Journal of Abnormal and Social Psychology,* 69 (November 1964), pp. 574-579.

36. F. Baker and G. M. O'Brien, "Birth Order and Fraternity Affiliation," *Journal of Social Psychology,* 78 (June 1969), pp. 41-43; J. J. Platt, D. D. Moskalski, and R. Eisenmen, "Sex and Birth Order, and Future Expectations of Occupational Status and Salary," *Journal of Individual Psychology,* 24 (November 1968), pp. 170-173; W. R. Rhine, "Birth Order Differences in Conformity and Level of Achievement Arousal," *Child Development,* 39 (September 1968), pp. 987-996.

37. H. Barry, Jr., H. Barry, III, and H. T. Blane, "Birth Order of Delinquent Boys with Alcohol Involvement," *Quarterly Journal of Studies on Alcohol,* 30 (June 1969), p. 410.

38. U.S. Department of Commerce, Bureau of the Census, *1960 Census of Population, Subject Reports, Women by Number of Children Ever Born* (Washington, D.C.: U.S. Government Printing Office, 1964), p. 6.

39. Bogue, *op. cit.,* p. 345.

40. Smart, *op. cit.,* pp. 17 and 23; and U.S. Department of Census, *op. cit.*

41. Smart, *op. cit.*

42. E. S. Keeping, "The Problem of Birth Ranks," *Biometrics,* 8 (March 1952), pp. 112-119. The total birth rank (x) is the sum of each individual's birth order. Thus, the total birth rank of a population consisting of two only children, two second-born children, and a third-born child would be nine. For sibships of a given size (s), keeping present formulas for expected total birth rank and its variance: $E(X_s) = N_s(s + 1)/2$ and $V(X_s) = N(s^2 - 1)/12$. A Z-score is obtained by dividing the difference between the summation of the observed total birth ranks and the summation of the expected total birth rank by the square root of the summation of the variance:

$$Z = [\Sigma(X_s) - \Sigma E(X_s)]/([\Sigma V(X_s)]^{1/2})$$

To determine the significance of the deviation of an observed distribution of birth ranks from the expected, the Z-score is evaluated in a table of areas under the normal curve.

43. Stanley Schachter, "Birth Order, Eminence and Higher Education," *American Sociological Review,* 28 (October 1963), pp. 757-768.

44. Warren, *op. cit.*, pp. 38, 48.

45. In tests of Hypothesis 2 we are comparing extreme categories (first- and last-born siblings) after deleting the intermediate categories. There is serious question about the applicability of tests of significance under these conditions. Moreover, in the process the number of respondents included in any comparison is reduced considerably so that sizable percentage differences do not achieve statistical significance. However, note that if the appropriateness of significance tests be granted, the differences between first- and last-born siblings in Table 5-6 are significant only for two variables: Saw family member within past year (.01 level for Bowery men, .05 level for Park Slope men); and Knows names of more than five neighbors (.05 level for Park Slope men).

46. For details see Howard M. Bahr, "Birth Order and Failure: The Evidence from Skid Row," *Quarterly Journal of Studies on Alcohol,* 32 (September 1971), pp. 682-683.

CHAPTER 6

FAMILIES OF PROCREATION

We noted in Chapter 2 that recent studies of skid row men showed that approximately half of them had never married, and of those who had married, all but a small fraction were widowed, divorced, or separated from their spouses. There is no doubt that these rates are among the most distinctive characteristics of a skid row neighborhood.

Bogue characterized skid row as containing a large group of undersexed or sexually shy men, a small but significant group of homosexuals, and a group of never-married alcoholics who are active sexually but believe they would fail in marriage because of alcoholism. Among the formerly married, the path to skid row is described as a flight in confusion and disorganization as a result of the failure of their marriages.[1]

A few decades ago the predominance of single men on the Bowery was even more striking than at present. Early in the depression Anderson reported that between 12 and 20 percent of the homeless men were, or had been, married and added that "the proportion on good terms with their wives is negligible." Of the more than 14,000 men enumerated in the Bowery area in the 1930 decennial census, 83 percent were single. Anderson compared marital-status rates for several New York City homeless populations, including men enumerated in speakeasies, lodgers at missions, commercial lodging house residents, applicants at the Bowery YMCA, and residents at Salvation Army industrial plants, and concluded that almost three-fourths of the homeless men had not been married.[2] Records of the Greater New York Gospel Mission and the Salvation Army reveal a comparable percentage—fewer than 20 percent of the clients reported having been married.[3]

The importance of marital instability as an indicator of the distinctive deviant status of homeless men was remarked by Pittman and Gordon, who wrote that "marriage instability is most marked among the homeless and the chronic police case inebriates, who have generally reached the bottom of the social escalator and are no longer completely functioning members of the society or the community." The complexity of the relationship between homelessness, chronic inebriety, and marriage was also noted by them:

> Marital status, of course, is only one indication, but still an extremely important index, of social integration. . . . Many individuals do not possess the competences in interpersonal relations or in personality traits that are associated with entrance into marriage; or, once involved in marriage, these individuals do not possess the requisite skills for continuing the marriage. Excessive drinking, which eventually causes disruptions in all areas of the social life space of the individual, is destructive of the marriage relationship itself.[4]

In the present chapter we shall compare the characteristics of the marriages of skid row men to those of respondents in the two control samples. Special attention will be paid to the marital problems of skid row men. Finally, we shall compare lifetime patterns of affiliation in families, contrasting experience in family of orientation with that in family of procreation, and noting how involvement with family members changes with age.

MARRIAGE RATES AND PATTERNS

Forty-nine percent of our Bowery respondents had been married, and 8 percent had been married more than once. The corresponding proportions in Park Slope were 71 percent and 8 percent, and on Park Avenue, 77 percent and 24 percent. Thus, compared to Park Slope men, the skid row respondents were less likely to have married, and those who had married were more likely to have had a second or a third marriage. Compared to all three low-income samples, the Park Avenue respondents were more apt to have married, to have married more than once, and to be married at the time of the interview. When we used the proportion *ever married* as the percentage base, the rates of second or subsequent marriages were as follows: Park Slope, 11 percent; Bowery sample, 18 percent; and Park Avenue, 31 percent. What these figures do not reveal is that among Bowery men the second or third marriage had been dissolved, and the respondent was living alone; among Park Avenue men, the men whose marriages had terminated had made new marriages. In a way, the frequency of second or third marriages is an index of marital instability; if this is so, the Park Avenue men may be said to have manifested higher rates of marital instability than the other samples. But that the single state is a temporary one among these upper-income men was apparent in the contrast between the combined proportions of currently divorced, separated, or widowed among them (11 percent) and among the low-income samples (Park Slope, 17 percent; Bowery, 44 percent; Camp LaGuardia, 47 percent).

Men in the control samples married later than the skid row men. In both Park Slope and Park Avenue the median age at first marriage was 26, compared to 23 for the Bowery and 24 for Camp LaGuardia residents. Late marriages were most common among Park Slope men, 37 percent of whom postponed marriage until age 30 or later. The corresponding proportions for Park Avenue, Camp LaGuardia, and the Bowery were, respectively, 25 percent, 23 percent and 22 percent.

Following marriage, a majority of the wives worked outside the home. The low-income samples were consistent in this; the proportion of those men who said their wives worked outside the home while they lived together ranged from 59 to 62 percent. Among wives of the Park Avenue men the proportion was somewhat lower (52 percent). Of those who worked, two-thirds of the control respondents' wives and almost three-fourths of the skid row men's wives had held full-time jobs at some time during their marriages.

Another similarity between the skid row and control samples is in the proportion of childless couples. About one-third of the reported (first) marriages had no offspring; the range was from 28 percent (Park Avenue) to 34 percent (Camp LaGuardia). However, the Park Slope men with children had more children than either the skid row men or the Park Avenue men. One-sixth of the fathers in Park Slope had five or more children in the course of their first marriage, but only one in ten skid row fathers had so large a family. The large family was even rarer among the Park Avenue men. Of the 58 fathers in that sample, only one had as many as five children.

Over 60 percent of the Park Slope and Park Avenue men were still living with their first wives, whereas less than 1 percent of the Bowery and Camp LaGuardia men reported that they still lived with their first wives. Among Bowery men the median length of marriage was seven years; among Camp LaGuardia men it was ten years. The average length of marriage was considerably greater for Park Slope men (median was 15 years). However, it is interesting that the Park Slope men who stopped living with their wives did so at about the same age as the Bowery men; the median age when respondents stopped living with their wives was 34 for the Bowery and Park Slope, 35 for camp men, and 39 for Park Avenue men.

None of the low-income samples was characterized by much joint participation in voluntary associations by husbands and wives. This kind of activity was about as frequent among skid row men as among Park Slope men. The proportion of formerly (or presently) married respondents reporting joint organizational activity with their wives was 8 percent among Bowery men and 11 percent among Park Slope men. But among the Park Avenue men, 40 percent said they had participated in one or more voluntary associations as a couple.

MARITAL PROBLEMS

An attempt was made to determine the types of problems the respondents had encountered in marriage by presenting them with a list of problems and asking which of these had rarely or often been problems in their marriages. The items included respondents' absence from home, nagging wife, drinking wife, respondent's drinking, in-law problems, and disagreements over friends.

Several findings stand out in the distribution of marital problems reported in Table 6-1. First, with one minor exception, the proportion of skid row men reporting a given problem is higher, usually much higher, than the proportion of men in the control samples who reported that problem in their marriages. Second, there is a ranking of importance of problem in the skid row distributions, with respondent's drinking, his absence from home, and his wife's nagging being identifiied, in that order, as the dominant problems. In the control samples, the clear distinctions among the major problems are not as sharp; in the upper-income sample, the range between the problem mentioned most frequently and the next four problems is only 6 percent; in Park Slope a range of 9 percent includes the four problems mentioned most frequently.

Table 6-1

TYPES OF ISSUES REPORTED AS OFTEN A PROBLEM IN RESPONDENTS' FIRST MARRIAGES (IN PERCENTAGES)

Type of Problem	Bowery	Camp LaGuardia	Park Slope	Park Avenue
Respondent's absence from home	37	30	20	12
Wife's nagging	26	19	17	14
Wife's drinking	8	14	2	3
Respondent's drinking	45	52	14	8
In-Laws	24	16	11	12
Friends	26	6	8	9
Lowest N[a]	89	93	87	76

a. Number of cases varies slightly due to incomplete information.

As the stereotype of the skid row man suggests, the item most frequently mentioned as often a problem in the marriages of Bowery and Camp LaGuardia men is the respondent's drinking. Half of the skid row men who had been married mentioned this as a marital problem. Drinking is mentioned more than three times as often by skid row men as by Park Slope men. Among the latter it is the third most frequent marital problem, the first being respondent's absence from home, the second being nagging wife. Among the Park Avenue men it ranked number five in frequency of mention.

Most of the respondents in the three low-income samples have always been poor. Thus we may expect that financial difficulties were almost universal in their marriages. Unfortunately this item was not included in the checklist of problems read to respondents, but it was a frequent response to the probe that followed the checklist: Were there other important problems in your marriage?

Another common problem was marital infidelity. Among the skid row respondents it was mentioned almost as frequently as financial difficulties. Because these items were not included in the list, there is no way of knowing their importance relative to the other types of problems. It is felt, however, that only respondent's drinking, itself usually associated with financial and emotional crises, was a more frequent problem than family finances and marital infidelity.

Financial problems and marital infidelity appear together in several of the histories. For example, there is the Bowery man, a former lathe operator, who began to lose his eyesight. "My eyes were going bad," he states, "I couldn't work and bring money home." His first wife divorced him after seven years of marriage. He was twenty-four years old at the time. The next year he remarried, and this time the marriage lasted only a year. Again there were financial problems, and when he returned from a six-month job as a lathe operator in a California aircraft plant, his wife asked for a divorce. She wanted to marry a neighbor.

Another Bowery man described his wife's expensive tastes as an important problem in their marriage: "My wife liked expensive clothes. If she couldn't afford expensive things she would wear rags; and I liked to see her look nice, but could not afford it." Finances were not the only problems in the marriage; his wife thought he was away from home too much, and they disagreed about in-laws, his drinking, and whose friends they should see. Despite these problems, the marriage lasted for sixteen years. He described the end of the marriage: "Jealousy; something was going on. She had other men. When we separated I went to New York. When I came back a few years later, she had two more kids. So we got a divorce." That was in 1942. The following year, he began living on the Bowery, and he has lived there ever since.

Often the infidelity was imputed to the respondent. Note the following comments about additional problems in the marriage:

> "My wife thought I ran around too much with other women."
>
> "She thought I gave other women too much attention."
>
> "She thought I was stepping out, jumping the fence."

Most often, the respondents were much more explicit about their wives' sexual infidelities than their own, although there were exceptions, such as the man who stated that his sister-in-law "had designs" on him. He said he kept his wife drunk while carrying on an affair with her sister.

A variety of other marital problems were reported by the skid row men. For example:

> "She stabbed me. We had a general argument about drinking and a lot of little things."

> "She was much too young for me. She was sixteen [he was twenty-five] and over at her folks' too much."

> "My drinking caused my wife to use barbiturates. She started using barbiturates because of ulcers."

> "My mother and sister died. I was sick. My wife wanted to go to her own people, and that ended it."

> "She was a cold woman emotionally."

> "I never had problems with my first wife. I never bothered with her. The second wife was a schizophrenic. She tried to commit suicide."

> "I wanted to leave the South, and my wife wanted to stay."

> "We never had any problems. I hardly knew her. I went with a band to New York. We were never legally separated. I just lost interest in her."

Before moving to a discussion of lifetime patterns of family affiliation, a brief summing up is in order. How different are the marital histories of skid row men? First and foremost, the majority of skid row men have *no* marital history. Second, there has been an extraordinary rate of marital dissolution among those skid row men who have been married, three or four times higher than in the control samples. The skid row men tend to have married earlier than the others, and if they had children, they had fewer than their low-income counterparts off skid row (but more than the upper-income men). When compared to men in the other samples whose marriages had terminated, it was plain that the skid row men's unions did not last as long. Finally, the proportion who reported problems in their marriages were much higher in the skid row samples than in the control samples, and there were important differences in the nature of the problems they remembered. Skid row men cited their own drinking as the most important problem, and absence from home as second in importance. In the control samples, drinking was much less of a marital problem, and absence from home less important.

In some ways, the skid row men who had been married were not very different from married men in the control samples. First, their wives worked outside the home to about the same extent as the wives of the Park Slope men. Second, they were no more likely to be childless than were control sample respondents, although they differed in the number of children fathered. Third, they were as likely to have participated with their wives in activities outside the home as the Park Slope respondents.

THE FAMILY AFFILIATION PROFILE

One method of life-history analysis we used consisted of constructing a series of profiles for each respondent. The profiles represented the degree of affiliation in a given sector at specified intervals throughout the life history. Individual profiles may be summarized in a single measure, or combined into a profile of a person's total affiliation at successive ages. An alternative strategy, the one we will use here, is to summarize across the sample for a given age or age interval. The result is an index of the composition of the sample. A series of these indices may form a profile of compositional changes in the sample as a whole or in subsamples. Thus, one may note the proportion of respondents affiliated at a given age and trace changes in that proportion over the entire life span.

The respondents were asked whom they had lived with during each year of their lives. In addition, another portion of the interview covered marital histories and still another dealt with visits or other contacts with family members. These data were used to draw a profile of family affiiliation for the respondent's entire life. For each year it could be determined whether he was living with members of his family of orientation or his family of procreation, and if with neither, what contacts he had with them. These profiles were then summarized to provide information on the sample as a whole at a given age.

In constructing the profiles reproduced in Figure 6-1, family affiliation was treated as a dichotomous variable. Men living with their families of orientation or procreation were considered affiliated. Men not living in their own family unit, no matter how frequent their contacts with relatives, were classified as disaffiliated in this sector. When we have compared the four samples on this general measure of family affiliation, we shall turn to profiles showing lifetime affiliation with parents' family (family of orientation) and with respondent's own family (family of procreation). In each case, we shall treat the control samples as standards against which the degree of deviance of skid row affiliation patterns may be judged.

To highlight the differences among the three types of samples—skid row, low-income settled, and high-income settled—and to keep the figures as simple as possible, we have omitted the profiles of Camp LaGuardia men. They parallel those of Bowery men in almost every particular, and in cases where a profile for Camp LaGuardia men does differ, we will point out the difference.

LIFETIME PATTERNS OF AFFILIATION

With respect to the percentage of respondents living with family members at various ages, the high-income respondents are unlike either of the low-income samples. Until age 20, Park Avenue men were not more affiiliated with their families than Bowery or Park Slope men, but from that time on, throughout life, they became increasingly affiliated. Their period of least affiliation was at age 20, when most of them were away from home at college. Beyond that age the families of orientation they left were promptly replaced by families of procreation. Of particular interest is the fact that even late in life the proportion of high-income men living with family members increases with age. Peak family affiliation is at age 65—the last age that appears on the figure—when more than 85 percent of the Park Avenue men were living with family members. In contrast, age 65 is the time of lowest affiliation for the low-income samples. Thus, at the stage of life when the low-income samples are

Figure 6-1.

PERCENTAGE OF RESPONDENTS LIVING WITH FAMILY, BY RETROSPECTIVE AGE, FOR PARK AVENUE, PARK SLOPE, AND BOWERY

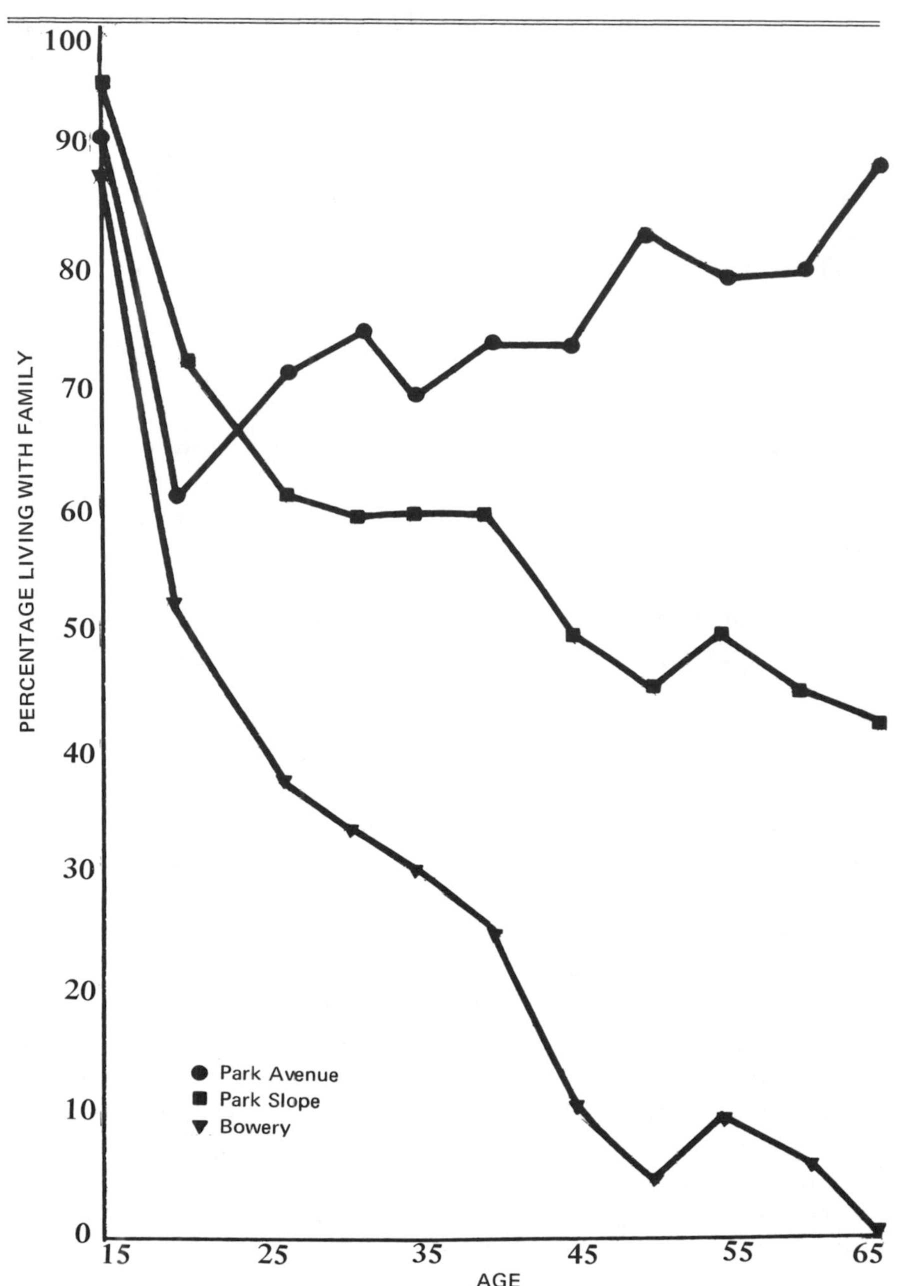

gradually losing family affiliations, the high-income men are still gaining them.

At age 15, 95 percent of the Park Slope sample lived in families, as did 87 percent of the Bowery men. Five years later only about half of the Bowery men were living in families, compared to almost three-fourths of the Park Slope men. From age 25 until middle age, the Park Slope sample was stable, with about 60 percent of the sample living in families at any given time. The proportion living in families drops to 45 percent by age 50 and from age 50 to 65 it fluctuates between 45 and 50 percent.

The Bowery sample shows a continuing decline in family affiliation through life. The decline is rapid, and there are no reversals in the trend. By age 40 only about one-fourth of the men were living in families; by age 60 the proportion was one in twenty.

The intersample differences in family affiliation at the later ages do not seem attributable to the slight differences in family affiliation during youth. Control-sample respondents and Bowery men leave their families of orientation. But the latter are less likely to establish new family bonds, and when they do, their ties to wives and children are tenuous. The Bowery men who do not marry still lose contact with their families of orientation. Separating the combined measure of family affiliation into its components will make this point more obvious.

Profiles similar to Figure 6-1 were prepared for family of orientation and family of procreation. With respect to the former, the general pattern of disaffiliation was the same for all four samples. That pattern was a sharp decline—from about 90 percent to between 10 and 20 percent—in the proportion of men living with parents or siblings between ages 15 and 30, a continuing decline at a slower rate until ages 35 to 40, and after that general stability (between 0 and 10 percent) until age 65. At every age between 15 and 65 the proportion of Bowery men living with their parents or siblings was smaller than in any other sample.[5] At almost every age the Park Slope men were the most likely to be living with parents or siblings.

Even greater differences pertained to the family of procreation. From age 25 on, the Park Avenue men were much more likely than men in other samples to be living with wives or children. At age 25 the figure was 36 percent, compared to 18 percent for Bowery men; and the discrepancy between the Bowery and Park Avenue samples increased with age, until at age 65 *none* of the Bowery men were living with family members, but 84 percent of the Park Avenue men were doing so. The Park Slope men occupied a middle position between the profiles for Bowery men and for Park Avenue men. The peak proportion of Park Slope men living with wives or children occurred at age 40. Beyond that there was a gentle decline until age 50, followed by relative stability. At age 40, 47 percent of the Park Slope men were living with their wives or children; at age 65 the figure had dropped only to 35 percent.

In marked contrast, the profile for Bowery men was an almost symmetrical curve, with the proportion of men living with wives or children rising from 1 percent at age 15 to a high of 22 percent at ages 30 to 35,[6] then dwindling to practically nothing through the next 15 years. By age 50 only 3 percent of the Bowery men were living with members of their family of procreation. From early adulthood on, the skid row men were very different from the control samples with respect to involvement in a procreative family. Also significant, although unrelated to the major theme of this investigation, were the substantial and increasing differences between the Park Slope and Park Avenue samples in family affiliation; throughout most of the life history the differences between Park Avenue and Park Slope were nearly as great as Park Slope and the Bowery.

Contact with kin. Let us illustrate the striking differences among the samples with respect to family affiliation by using another indicator of the strength of family ties—frequency of contact with relatives. The men were asked, Do you frequently see any of your relatives or family, other than those you are living with? Then, regardless of what they had answered, they were asked, When was the last time you saw any relatives or family? On the first question slightly more than one-fourth of the Bowery men answered positively, compared to half of the Park Slope men and 87 percent of the Park Avenue men. Responses to the following question revealed that the Camp LaGuardia men were most detached from their kin; only one-fifth of them claimed a visit or telephone call to relatives during the past year, compared to 35 percent for Bowery men. Sixty-eight percent of the Park Slope men had seen or spoken to their relatives within the past year, and almost all of the Park Avenue men (90 percent) claimed such contact. The striking thing about these findings is the strong positive relationship between interaction with kin (and hence the possibility of both psychic and economic support from them) and the economic status of the sample. Almost all of the upper-income respondents saw their relatives frequently; few of the impoverished skid row men did. The contrast is even more striking if we remember that most of the control sample respondents were living with someone—usually a spouse—and so had daily contact with a family member, a fact which the above percentages do not reflect.

The intersample differences in kin contact may be highlighted by looking at the other end of the continuum. Only 2 percent of the Park Avenue men had not seen their relatives for at least ten years, but one-fifth of the Park Avenue men had experienced at least a ten-year hiatus in kin relationships, as had 32 percent of the Bowery men and 43 percent of the Camp LaGuardia men. One of every eight skid row residents had not seen a relative for 30 years or more.

NOTES

1. Donald J. Bogue, *Skid Row in American Cities* (Chicago: Community and Family Study Center, Univ. of Chicago, 1963), p. 371.

2. Nels Anderson, *Homeless in New York City* (New York: Board of Charity, 1934), pp. 172-173, 400.

3. Thomas L. Logan, "Report on the Greater New York Gospel Mission" (New York: Welfare Council of New York City Research Bureau, September 1931), p. 26.

4. David J. Pittman and T. Wayne Gordon, *Revolving Door: A Study of the Chronic Police Case Inebriate* (New York: The Free Press, 1958), p. 32.

5. Thus, the extended case history of "Thomas Finn" in Elmer Bendiner's *The Bowery Man* (New York: Thomas Nelson and Sons, 1961) represents an atypical pattern of disaffiliation.

6. The highest level of affiliation with wives and/or children occurred a decade earlier for skid row men than for the Park Slope men (ages 30 and 40, respectively).

CHAPTER 7

EDUCATIONAL EXPERIENCE

It is a truism that formal education is linked to occupational mobility and success. Thus, when confronting skid row—an assemblage of spectacularly unsuccessful men—one is immediately curious about educational achievement.

Among the questions bearing on the relationship of educational achievement to disaffiliation are these:

1. How well educated are skid row men?

2. Are relatively affiliated skid row men better educated than the more disaffiliated?

3. How important is school performance in the explanation of disaffiliated careers?

4. How was the formal education of skid row men terminated?

5. Did they want more education than they received?

6. Did they take advantage of adult education programs following the termination of their formal schooling?

The answers to these questions are summarized below.

EXTENT OF FORMAL EDUCATION

Bogue concluded from a comparison of the educational attainment of skid row men with that of a national sample of low-income workmen that the educational composition of skid row was about average for the occupational position of its residents.[1] In Chapter 2 we contrasted the educational attainment of skid row and control samples and reached the same conclusion: there were no substantial differences between the Bowery and Park Slope samples, and Camp LaGuardia men were only slightly lower in educational attainment. The educational attainment of Camp LaGuardia men is about the same as Bogue reported for men on Chicago's skid row in 1958.[2] One-fifth of the Camp LaGuardia men graduated from high school, compared with about one-fourth of the Bowery and Park Slope men.

The atypicality of the Park Avenue sample with respect to educational attainment was mentioned in Chapter 2. For emphasis, we note again that 50 percent of all Bowery men and 53 percent of the Park Slope men had from zero to eight years of school, while only 5 percent of the Park Avenue men were limited to this educational level. At the other end of the continuum, only 8 percent of the Bowery men and the same percentage of the Park Slope men have had some college education, whereas the figure for the Park Avenue men is 71 percent. This great disparity in educational attainment meant that analytical categories which fit the low-income samples may be inappropriate for the Park Avenue sample. Some of the major topics in the following pages, such as the reasons for termination of formal education, are simply not relevant for the Park Avenue men. Consequently, in the remainder of this chapter the discussion focuses on the low-income samples.

The similarity of the Bowery and Park Slope samples in educational attainment suggests that inferior formal education is *not* a dominant factor bringing men into skid row. However, the question of the influence of education on affiliation remains to be answered.

EDUCATION AND AFFILIATION

It was expected that educational achievement would vary directly with affiliation, and the data support this expectation (See Table 7-1). In all three low-income samples the more educated respondents were more likely to have been married, to have voted, and to have maintained organizational memberships earlier in life. These correlations carry into the present. The better-educated Bowery respondent is more apt to belong to an informal group of friends, to maintain organizational affiliations, to have close friends in the city, to know his neighbors by name, and to talk with many men in the course of a day. One of the few areas in which the influence of education was

Table 7-1

PERCENTAGE OF RESPONDENTS AFFILIATED, BY EXTENT OF EDUCATION, FOR VARIOUS MEASURES OF LIFETIME AND CURRENT AFFILIATION*

Measures of Affiliation — Years Education:	Bowery 0-8	Bowery 9+	Camp LaGuardia 0-8	Camp LaGuardia 9+	Park Slope 0-8	Park Slope 9+
Lifetime measures						
Ever married	44	48	38	61	68	74
Ever voted	57	73	66	80	60	84
Organization affiliation(s) in youth[a]	33	73	37	74	40	47
Current measures						
Currently employed	34	46	—	—	70	84
Saw family member within past year	32	36	20	18	65	74
Attends church at least twice a month	21	29	36	26	37	43
Belongs to informal group[b]	27	36	32	40	27	47
Has organizational affiliation(s)[c]	14	32	13	24	45	62
Has close friend(s) in New York City	30	37	17	24	52	53
Knows names of more than 5 neighbors	43	54	46	74	44	47
Would like to know more neighbors	27	19	29	16	37	24
Would join a neighborhood organization	68	66	52	46	73	63
Conversed with 7+ people yesterday	40	50	39	58	47	51
Lowest N[d]	92	96	105	77	59	51

*Underscoring denotes differences significant at the .05 level.

a. Refers primarily to membership in voluntary organizations; jobs, church membership, family affiliation, and school attendance are excluded. Youth is defined as before age 20.

b. Men responding affirmatively to the question, Are there certain men you often hang around with? were considered as belonging to an informal group.

c. Refers primarily to voluntary organizations.

d. Number of cases varies slightly due to incomplete information.

not apparent was organizational valence: better-educated men are no more likely than other Bowery men to say that they would join an organization for neighborhood improvement if one were formed in their area. But otherwise, there is a definite association between education and all types of affiliation.

There is some evidence that the less-educated men feel relatively isolated. In all three low-income samples they were more likely to respond that they would like to know more of their neighbors, and in the Camp LaGuardia and Park Slope samples they expressed greater willingness to join neighborhood organizations.

The effects of education were not as obvious in the Park Slope sample as in the skid row samples. The better-educated Park Slope men were more likely to get together with an informal group of friends and to have organizational affiliations, but they were not more likely to have friends in the city, to know neighbors' names, or to have conversed with many people on the day preceding the interview. However, as in the skid row samples, men with little education seemed lonelier than other men; they were more likely to wish to know their neighbors.

IMPORTANCE OF SCHOOL PERFORMANCE

The low-income samples do not differ in reported school performance. Between 7 and 10 percent of respondents in all three samples reported that they ranked in the lower third of their classes, about a third indicated they were in the upper third, and between 50 and 60 percent reported themselves in the middle third. The contrast between the low-income and Park Avenue men is striking: 65 percent of the latter said they were in the upper third of their classes, and *none* of them placed themselves in the lower third.

School performance is attached to educational achievement, however, and cannot be considered separately. That a person was at the top of his class takes on greater significance if he graduated from high school than if he only finished the third grade. Combining their educational achievement and school performance, the respondents were grouped into four categories: (1) men with fewer than eight years of schooling and low class rank, (2) men with fewer than eight years of schooling and high (upper third) class rank, (3) men with more than eight years of schooling and low class rank, and (4) men with more than eight years of schooling and high class rank.

The distribution of men among these categories is shown in Table 7-2. There were few intersample differences in this distribution. One of every four Bowery men had more than eight years of education and claimed to have been in the upper third of his class, compared to one of every six Camp LaGuardia and Park Slope men. There was a corresponding underrepresentation of Bowery men in the low education, high class-rank category. But the important finding in Table 7-2 is that in terms of the combination of years of school completed and perceived academic performance, there is no evidence that skid row men are more disadvantaged than the lower-income control sample. If anything, Bowery men had better educational preparation than Park Slope men.

REASONS FOR TERMINATING FORMAL EDUCATION

The low-income samples differed very little in the distribution of responses to the question, Why did you leave school when you did? Most frequently, economic factors of some kind had drawn the respondent away from school: he wanted to go to work, or he had to support himself or help support his family. About two-thirds of the

Table 7-2

EDUCATIONAL PERFORMANCE AND ATTAINMENT (IN PERCENTAGES)

Educational Attainment	Perceived Rank	Bowery	Camp LaGuardia	Park Slope
0-8 years	Lower 2/3	36	39	32
0-8 years	Upper 1/3	11	16	21
9+ years	Lower 2/3	30	29	30
9+ years	Upper 1/3	24	15	16
Total		101	99	99
N		186	188	118

Table 7-3

REASONS FOR LEAVING SCHOOL (IN PERCENTAGES)

Reasons for Leaving School	Bowery	Camp LaGuardia	Park Slope	Park Avenue
Graduated or finished all available schooling	14	13	16	53
Didn't like school, doing badly, or expelled	17	13	14	6
Left home	5	3	2	1
Wanted to work	18	10	4	9
Went to work, had to help support family, other financial reasons	43	52	59	18
Other	12	13	13	16
Total[a]	109	104	108	103
N	193	194	119	103

a. Total of the percentages exceeds 100 because some respondents gave more than one answer.

low-income men gave reasons of this kind. Bowery men were more likely to stress that they *wanted* to go to work.

Involuntary deprivation was not very evident; only one-third of the low-income respondents (in Park Slope, 40 percent) indicated that at the time they left school they wanted more education.

Between 13 and 16 percent of the low-income men terminated their schooling after graduating or after completing all the schooling available to them. A similar proportion left school because they did not like it, were doing badly, or were expelled, and a like number gave other explanations for dropping out. Negative experiences with school were not uncommon even among the high-income men. Six percent of them said their schooling ended because of expulsion, poor performance, or simple dislike for school.

Among the other reasons for terminating education were military service, personal health, family problems, and social upheavals. The nature and variety of these responses are illustrated below.

Bowery sample—wanted more schooling:

> "Cause the girl got pregnant. She quit so I quit too."

> "I started messing around playing baseball."

> "My brother died. I took his job over."

Bowery sample—did not want more schooling:

> "I was young and impetuous and academically lazy. I became a patriot and fought for my country."

> "Teacher hit me with a ruler and hurt me."

> "I was scared of examinations, everybody said I had to get high marks. I went to the waterfront and shipped out."

Camp LaGuardia sample—wanted more schooling:

> "Shortage of books, wouldn't let me sit with other students, so I played hooky."

> "I couldn't go anymore because of the revolution. The whole country was paralyzed."

> "I went to the Marines. My father couldn't support all of us. We needed money and had to work or join the army."

> "I didn't leave. They told me to leave. I don't know why."

> "Father wanted me to learn bricklaying."

Camp LaGuardia sample—did not want more schooling:

> "Got girls in my head, and put away the books."

> "I ran away. I wanted to see the world. I did, too."

"When war started, everyone went wild. Broke my hip during school, and drifted from school after that."

"Because it got to be a bore."

Park Slope sample—wanted more schooling:

"I disliked the principal."

"I don't know, health never good, I was always sick. I wanted to stay in school. I wanted to go to college. Stomach trouble, indigestion, diarrhea. It was too hard for me to go to school."

"My father forced me out."

Park Slope sample—did not want more schooling:

"They wanted me to be a priest, I didn't want it."

"I wanted to concentrate on music—the harp."

"My eyes were bad."

Park Avenue sample—wanted more schooling:

"I ran away from home. My father argued a lot. He told me, 'you're getting too big for your pants.' "

"Money was needed at home."

Park Avenue sample—did not want more schooling:

"I was drafted. I hated school. Still do, as a matter of fact."

"I wanted to get into active life. . . . I got most of my education outside school."

"I got enough degrees in school, sufficient education."

"Who wants more after that [Ph.D.]?"

"I was making too much money. My time was too valuable to go to school."

ADULT EDUCATION

The Bowery and Park Slope samples did not differ in the proportion of men who had attended adult-education courses. But while there were no differences among the low-income samples in the incidence of adult education, there were differences in its duration. In Park Slope, 56 percent of the men with adult-education experience had attended classes for two years or more; the comparable proportions in the Bowery and Camp LaGuardia samples were 42 and 31 percent respectively. Again, the Park Avenue sample differed sharply; 83 percent of the men reporting some adult education said they had attended classes for two years or more.

In comparison with the other low-income respondents skid row men are not particularly unschooled. Not only are there no differ-

Table 7-4

DURATION OF ADULT EDUCATION (IN PERCENTAGES)

Period Attended Classes	Bowery	Camp LaGuardia	Park Slope	Park Avenue
Less than 6 months	15	20	11	6
1 year	43	49	33	11
2 years	18	20	28	26
3 years	7	9	8	17
4 years	7	—	8	17
5 or more years	10	2	11	23
Total	100	100	99	100
N	60	45	36	53

ences in educational achievement, but the samples are not significantly differentiated in quality of school performance, in reasons for leaving school, or in proportions of men attending adult-education courses. It appears that education is linked to other kinds of affiliation; the better-educated respondents report more affiliations.

Most skid row men have lower-class backgrounds, and their educational histories seem quite normal for their early circumstances. Although the adult-educational experience of skid row men seems to indicate less persistence in remedying educational deficiencies than appears in the control samples, the educational experience of skid row men is not sufficiently different from that of the low-income control sample for educational deficiency to be conceived as a major causal factor pushing men to skid row.

The similarity in educational attainment between Bowery men and Park Slope men must be emphasized. One of the most influential books about skid row men, Pittman and Gordon's *Revolving Door,* stated that "on the whole, the incarcerated inebriates are an educationally disadvantaged group." [3] Later, a report on Philadelphia's skid row men stated that "comparison with the over-all United States male population indicates that skid row men have had less education," and went on to suggest the need for comparisons of the educational attainment of skid row men and working-class populations.[4]

Bogue's *Skid Row in American Cities* provided the suggested comparison with working-class populations, using national statistics on educational attainment for male operatives, service workers, and nonfarm laborers to create a composite national figure for low-income occupations. He concluded that the educational attainment of residents of Chicago's skid row was about average for low-income workingmen.[5] The same finding had been reported for skid row men in Minneapolis five years earlier:

> . . . while skid row residents tend to be underprivileged with respect to education . . . if we take account of the unusual age distribution and the tendency for older men to show lower levels of achievement, the difference in educational level between the skid row population and the U.S. average virtually disappears.[6]

We compared the Bowery men's educational distribution with that of all male Manhattan residents and reached essentially the same conclusion: when they are compared with the population in general, they appear to be slightly disadvantaged; but when age and social-class controls are added, the educational differences disappear. The burden of this chapter is that residents of skid row do not end up there because of their low educational attainment. Skid row men may need adult-education programs to upgrade their occupational skills, but so does a sizeable proportion of the nation's unskilled and semi-skilled workers.

NOTES

1. Donald J. Bogue, *Skid Row in American Cities* (Chicago: Community and Family Study Center, Univ. of Chicago, 1963), pp. 109-110.
2. *Ibid.*
3. David J. Pittman and C. Wayne Gordon, *Revolving Door: A Study of the Chronic Police Case Inebriate* (New York: The Free Press, 1958), pp. 33, 57.
4. Leonard Blumberg *et al., The Men on Skid Row* (Philadelphia: Department of Psychiatry, Temple Univ. School of Medicine, 1960), p. 5.
5. Bogue, *op. cit.,* pp. 109-110.
6. Theodore Caplow, Keith A. Lovald, and Samuel E. Wallace, *A General Report on the Problem of Relocating the Population of the Lower Loop Redevelopment Area* (Minneapolis: Minneapolis Housing and Redevelopment Authority, 1958), pp. 75, 77.

CHAPTER 8

OCCUPATIONAL EXPERIENCE *

The current employment status of Bowery men was discussed in Chapter 2. In the present chapter we shall contrast the lifetime employment and occupational mobility profiles of Bowery men with those of our other respondents. We shall also review the explanations they themselves give for their downward occupational mobility. Finally, there are several case histories which illustrate the interplay of various elements in producing a given mobility trend.

EMPLOYMENT PROFILES

An extensive employment history was obtained from each man interviewed, including for each job the nature of work, when employment began and ended, the type of business or industry, the location of the job, the hours worked, and the pay. For present purposes, a man was considered employed during a given year if he worked most of that year, even if only at spot jobs. However, men who specified that they worked only part of the year were not coded as employed unless they held relatively long-term jobs (six months or more). The emphasis is on a definite commitment to a job or series of jobs. Note that in this chapter *unemployment* refers not only to total (every day, all year) unemployment, but also to temporary, sporadic work alternating with periods of unemployment.

Analytical procedures were similar to those outlined in the discussion of family affiliation. A profile was prepared for each respondent, showing whether he was employed or unemployed in each year of his life. Summarizing these by single years, profiles showing trends in employment by age were obtained for each sample.

The rank order of the samples in employment corresponds to their

* Portions of this chapter are adapted from Howard M. Bahr, "Worklife Mobility Among Bowery Men," *Social Science Quarterly,* 49 (June 1968), pp. 128-141 and from Howard M. Bahr and Theodore Caplow, "Homelessness, Affiliation, and Occupational Mobility," *Social Forces,* 47 (September 1968), pp. 28-33, with the permission of the publishers.

rank order in family affiliation, with Park Avenue men reporting almost 100 percent employment throughout their adult lives (see Figure 8-1). They entered the labor force later than the low-income men—at age 15 only one in ten of them was employed, compared to a third or more of the low-income men—but by age 25 the Park Avenue men had finished their schooling and joined the labor force, and throughout the rest of their adult lives they have remained employed. Betwen ages 30 and 65 there are never less than 95 percent of them employed, and there is no sign of declining employment with age. In contrast, the low-income samples show a peak employment rate fairly early in life, followed by a steady decline.

Despite the gentle decline after age 30, most of the Park Slope respondents were employed throughout adult life. At age 30, over 90 percent of them were employed; even at age 65 well over half of them were. In contrast, a substantial proportion of the skid row men were unemployed at every age, and from age 45 on, more than half of them were unemployed.

In the skid row samples the age of peak employment occurred even earlier than in the Park Slope sample. Thereafter, there was a steady decline in the proportion of respondents employed. By age 45 only about half of the skid row men were employed.

PREVIOUS STUDIES OF LIFETIME MOBILITY

There have been frequent studies of occupational mobility among manual workers,[1] but few of these have been concerned with mobility among the lowest classes of unskilled workers. There are worklife histories of business executives, scientists, tool and die makers, electronics technicians, molders and core makers, radio workers, weavers and loom fixers, machinists, hosiery workers, and government clerical employees, but not of unskilled workers.[2] Even studies which attempt to describe the mobility experiences of cross sections of the population often neglect the lowest socioeconomic groups, or else their statements about lower-class mobility patterns are limited because of few respondents in the lower occupational categories. Thus, Davidson and Anderson present some case histories but report that their data are too limited for a detailed study of unskilled workers' career patterns; also it seems likely that their sample, drawn from the

Figure 8-1.
PERCENTAGE OF RESPONDENTS EMPLOYED
BY RETROSPECTIVE AGE
FOR PARK AVENUE, PARK SLOPE, AND BOWERY

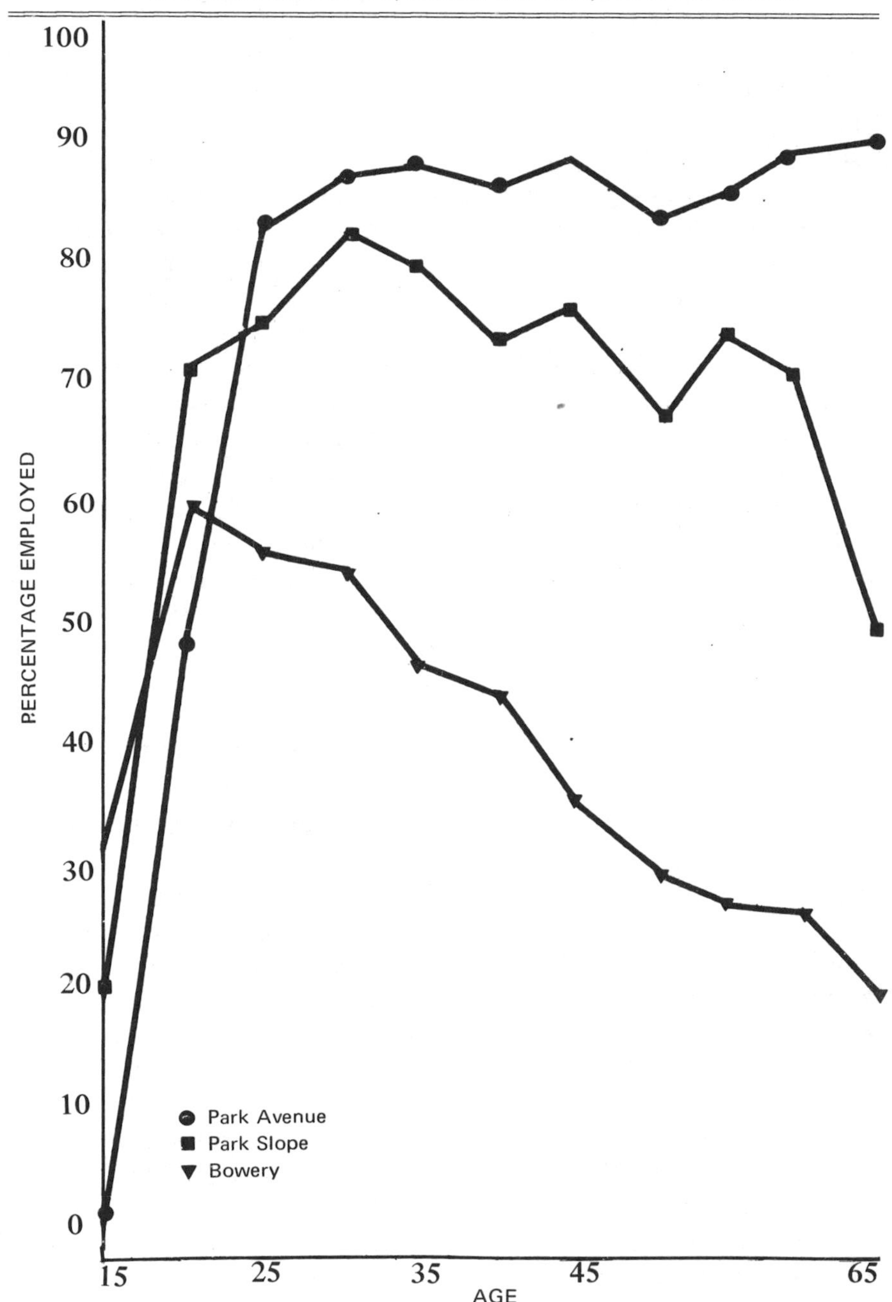

membership of various formal organizations (although some jail and poor-farm inmates were included), underrepresents the unskilled.[3] Miller and Form's detailed analysis of the career patterns of a cross section of the Ohio population was based on interviews with 276 respondents, only 19 percent of whom were unskilled workers.[4] Lipset and Bendix purposely omitted census tracts of highest and lowest socioeconomic levels from their sample, and thus can say little about mobility of unskilled persons; only 44 (out of 639) of their respondents held jobs which could be considered "unskilled." [5]

Some information about the lifetime mobility patterns of unskilled workers is available in three other works. When Reynolds studied the life histories of 450 manual workers in New Haven, 21 percent (95) of his respondents were unskilled workers. Consequently he was able to make some generalizations about worklife mobility among the unskilled: "downward movement seems . . . to result from a combination of personal shortcomings and economic mischance." [6] Also, there are several reports describing the findings of a six-city survey of occupational mobility in which 13,000 work histories for the decade 1940 to 1950 were collected.[7] Finally, there is an early work consisting of 100 detailed histories of persons given unemployment assistance in Bloomington, Indiana, in 1930 to 1931.[8] Unfortunately, little text or analysis is included; the author merely presents raw data and some summary tables.

In the past decade or so there have been important studies of occupational mobility by Wilensky, Gusfield, Breed, Bogue, and many others.[9] But the focus of mobility research continues to be on intergenerational mobility; [10] when worklife mobility is studied, it is usually in terms of a few selected points in an individual's work history. For instance, the first Census Bureau report of lifetime occupational mobility (1964) has only three points of reference: respondent's first job, his current job, and his father's job.[11] Consequently the analysis of lifetime mobility is limited to comparisons between first job and current job. The same data (respondent's major occupation in 1962 compared to major occupational group of his father, and respondent's occupation in 1962 compared to occupational group of his own first job) form the basis for two recent papers which focus on relations among occupational groups rather than on career experience of individuals and for the assessment of occuptional mobility in Blau and Duncan's *The American Occupational Structure*.[12]

Of the four recent studies of worklife mobility in individual life histories cited above, only one (Bogue) dealt explicitly with individuals of low socioeconomic status. Wilensky was concerned with the "middle mass"; Gusfield studied professionals, managers, sales workers, and trained (skilled) laborers; and Breed interviewed relatives and associates of male suicides.[13]

Measuring mobility. There appears to be moderate consensus about relative prestige or status-ranking of occupations, and to a certain degree this consensus extends over both time and space—that is, in the same country it extends over considerable time periods, and even countries at different stages of industrialization have similar occupational status hierarchies.[14]

A number of methods of stratifying occupations appear in the literature. Among the most detailed systems of ranking are the Duncan Socioeconomic Index (SEI) and the Bogue Index of Socioeconomic Status (SES). Bogue cross-classified occupations by educational and individual income; his SES is a weighted average of these measures.[15] The Duncan scores combine the purely socioeconomic approach of Bogue and the prestige rankings of the North-Hatt scale, using the North-Hatt rankings as criteria in deriving weights for the education and income components of the scale. The income and education indicators are adjusted for differences in age distribution among the various occupations.[16] There are SEI scores, ranging from 0 to 96, for each of the detailed occupational categories listed by the United States Census; the SES scale scores for each detailed occupation range from 44 to 184. In the present analysis occupational status is measured in terms of the Duncan SEI.

Duncan stresses that the SEI should not be considered accurate to the second digit; there are errors in the original census data from which it was computed, and slight changes in the computational routine would alter the score by plus or minus one. Further, the index may be seriously biased for certain occupations. Census figures on income, for example, do not include nonmonetary perquisites or make allowances for cost-of-living differentials.[17] In sum, the SEI is only an approximation based on national data, and differences of one or two points are for practical purposes meaningless.

PATTERNS OF OCCUPATIONAL MOBILITY AMONG SKID ROW MEN

One of the stereotypes associated with skid row men is that they have skidded, or have been downwardly mobile in occupation. On skid row, allegedly, may be found men who once held normal jobs but who now eke out subsistence by panhandling, dishwashing, and occasional labor, or are supported by charity.

Bogue's *Skid Row in American Cities* seems to include the only study of occupational mobility among skid row men published prior to our New York studies. The findings he reports are based on more than 600 "complete occupational histories" of men interviewed on Chicago's skid row. A mobility profile was prepared for each respondent, based on five points in his occupational history (first regular full-time job, current or last job, and three other points defined as "principal jobs between the first and last that portrayed the mobility pattern of achievement"). The profile included the SES score of each job, its duration, and the age when the respondent entered it.[18] Analysis of these mobility profiles led to the following generalizations about worklife occupational mobility among homeless men.

1. In comparison with the SES distribution of the male labor force of the United States, the status of the current or last job of homeless men is very low.

2. "The average lifetime mobility pattern of homeless men is one of a small rise in status from an initial low-status point, and then a steady decline to a point even lower than the first job."

3. Homeless men achieve their peak SES fairly early, usually at their second job, and the status of their subsequent jobs is successively lower.

4. In terms of lifetime net mobility (difference in occupational status between first and last or current job) almost half (45 percent) of the homeless men experience a decline, while 22 percent remain stable and 33 percent rise in status.

5. Almost all homeless men arrive on skid row by loss of some higher status.

6. Of the five over-all patterns which a man's mobility could take (considering his career in terms of four principal jobs), there are two patterns typical of skid row: upward mobility followed by downward mobility, and continuous downward mobility.

7. In general, skid row men have lower status than their fathers.[19]

We shall use these seven statements to organize our own findings on patterns of occupational mobility in our four New York samples. Hopefully, an analysis of lifetime patterns of occupational mobility based on complete occupational histories rather than on a few selected points in a career should give us more precise results than the findings cited above.

Only those occupations lasting a year or more are included in the mobility profiles. To minimize the unreliability involved in assigning status scores to specific occupations, the Census Bureau's *Alphabetical Index of Occupations and Industries* was consulted as an intermediate step in coding the SEI score of each occupation.[20] As a further precaution, two sets of profiles were prepared by coders who worked separately, then compared their work and resolved the differences.

Comparative status. In Table 8-1 the occupational-status scores (abbreviated SEI) of first, highest, average, and current or last jobs of the men in each sample are compared to the occupational-status distribution of the male labor force of the United States (1950). These data corroborate Bogue's finding that compared with the nation's labor force, the occupational status of homeless men is very low. However, the present low status of skid row men does not necessarily imply skidding in their work histories. The occupational status of the first job held by these respondents was almost as low as that of their most recent job, and so is the mean occupational status that summarizes all the jobs they have ever held.

With respect to mean lifetime occupational status and status of their first and last jobs, Park Slope men are fairly similar to the national labor force in 1950. Indeed, the jobs of highest status ever

Table 8-1

OCCUPATIONAL STATUS OF RESPONDENTS AT SELECTED POINTS IN THEIR WORK HISTORIES, COMPARED TO THE UNITED STATES MALE LABOR FORCE (1950) (IN PERCENTAGES)

	Selected Points in Work History												Mean Occupational Status				
	First Job				Highest Status Job				Current or Last Job								
Socio Economic Index	Bowery	Camp La Guardia	Park Slope	Park Avenue	Bowery	Camp La Guardia	Park Slope	Park Avenue	Bowery	Camp La Guardia	Park Slope	Park Avenue	Bowery	Camp La Guardia	Park Slope	Park Avenue	U. S. Labor Force 1950[a]
0-9	26	22	15	3	6	1	—	—	33	22	11	2	18	10	5	—	15
10-19	51	44	52	10	33	34	23	1	51	63	45	—	55	61	45	2	34
20-29	9	12	10	10	17	15	11	1	5	8	13	—	19	18	23	—	11
30-39	8	11	5	5	23	22	22	—	10	3	11	1	6	5	11	1	11
40-49	4	5	10	11	11	12	21	1	1	3	10	2	2	2	10	3	9
50-99	3	5	8	62	11	17	23	97	1	2	10	95	1	3	6	94	20
Totals	101	99	100	101	101	101	100	100	101	101	100	100	101	99	100	100	100
N	180	185	125	104	180	185	125	104	180	185	125	104	180	185	125	104	—
Mean	18	20	23	54	29	33	38	78	14	14	25	75	16	18	25	69	30

a. Albert J. Reiss, Jr., *et al., Occupations and Social Status* (New York: The Free Press, 1961), p. 147.

held by Park Slope men show a more favorable distribution than the national labor force.

The Park Avenue men occupy a distinctive position on all four variables in Table 8-1; almost all of them began their occupational careers in high-status occupations, and their mean occupational status is more than twice as high as the Park Slope sample or the national labor force.

Average mobility patterns. The average lifetime mobility pattern for respondents in the three samples is graphed in Figure 8-2. The yearly figures represent the mean occupational status of all respondents who worked during that year of their lives.

Between ages 20 and 25 the mean occupational status of Bowery men fluctuates between 17 and 18. From this point on, the general trend is downward. By age 60 the mean occupational status of Bowery men is 14, and by age 65 it is 12. The Camp LaGuardia men (not included in Figure 8-2) show a similar pattern. However, throughout the pattern their scores are somewhat higher. From age 20 to 30 the mean occupational status of Camp LaGuardia men is over 20 and at age 65 their mean occupational status is 15.

Comparing the skid row samples with the control samples, the increasing divergence of their statuses in early adulthood is apparent, as is the lateness of the peak status among control sample respondents. By age 65 the difference in mean occupational status between the Park Slope and skid row samples is as much as 20 points.

The Park Avenue men begin working at higher-status jobs, and their mean occupational status continues to increase throughout life, while that of Park Slope men rises, declines, and then rises again, and that of skid row men steadily declines. For the Park Avenue men the rate of status gain slackens after age 40; by then, many of them are settled in a high-status occupation, and their increased income and responsibility beyond that point are not reflected in their occupational-status scores (for example, the SEI has one score for lawyer; whether he is just beginning a practice or has a wide reputation, any lawyer's score is the same). Thus, at the later ages, the real differences in status—measured by income, prestige, or power—are greater than the profiles indicate.

Peak status. In Bogue's Chicago study, the coding of occupational

Figure 8-2.

MEAN SOCIOECONOMIC STATUS, BY RETROSPECTIVE AGE, PARK AVENUE, PARK SLOPE, AND BOWERY MEN

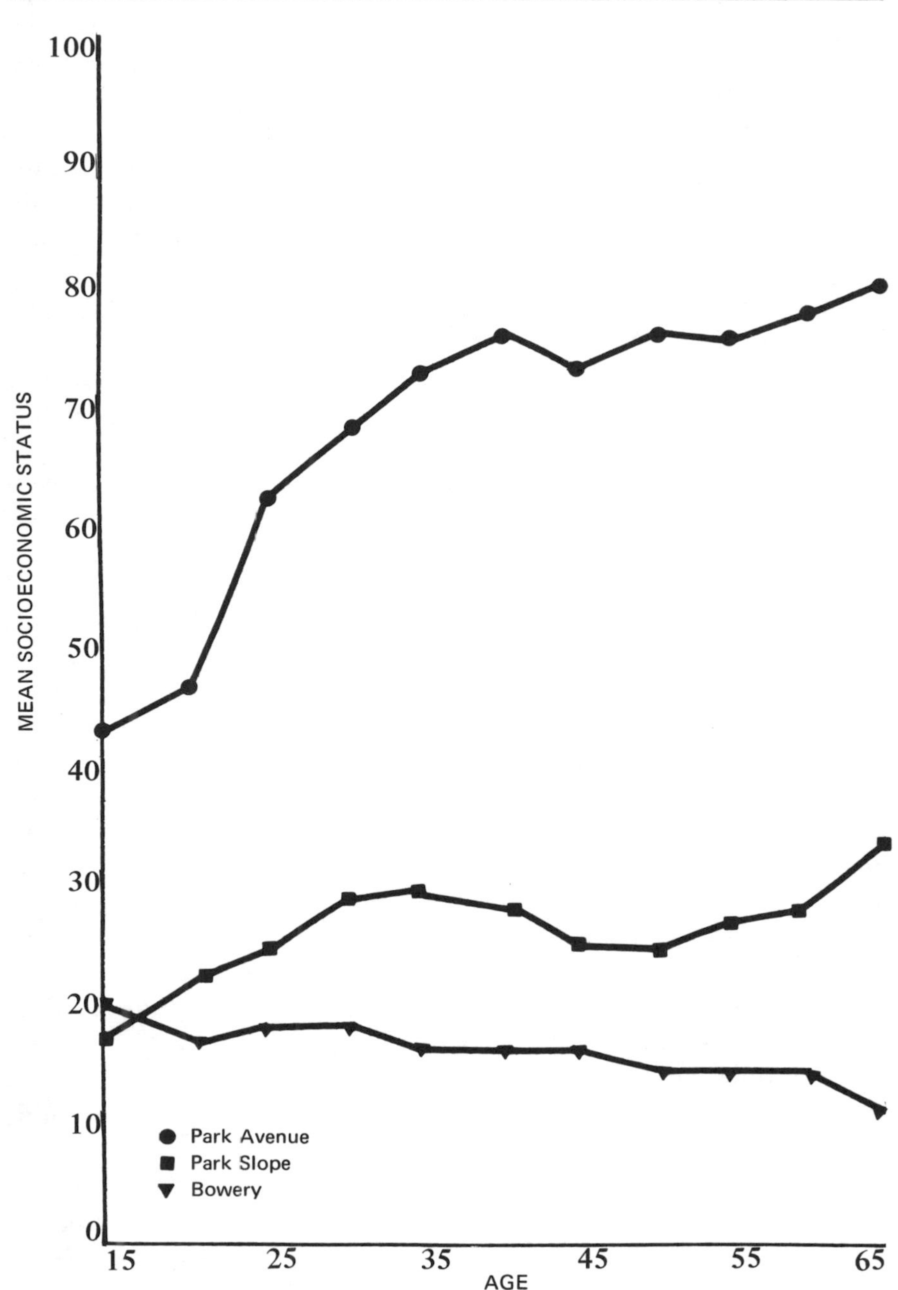

histories was based on "five points that best represented each man's work career." These points included first full-time job, current or last job, and three jobs between the first and last that coders felt best portrayed the mobility pattern. Thus, when Bogue reports that the men achieved their highest status on the second job, it is understood that he is talking about the second point in the five-point job history, rather than the second job ever held by the respondent.[21] In other words, when the occupational histories of the Chicago respondents were coded in terms of the five most representative occupations in each man's history, the peak status tended to appear at the second point coded.

In our New York study we attempted to gather complete occupational histories and to code them in their entirety. Nevertheless, it was not always possible to separate jobs within an occupation; for example, a man might say that he worked as a railroad laborer for three years, and then became a grocery clerk. During his period as a railroad laborer he might have worked for several different railroad companies; therefore grocery clerk would be his second occupation but not his second job. In attempting to compare the samples in terms of peak status, we decided to avoid the issue of whether a man's highest status was in his second, third, or *n*th occupation or job, and to focus instead on his age at first attainment of peak status.

On the basis of Bogue's work, it was expected that skid row men would reach peak status sooner than men in the control samples, and this proved to be the case. Like the Chicago skid row men, Bowery and Camp LaGuardia men achieved peak status fairly early in life, most of them by their early twenties (at a median age of 22); men in the control samples were older at their first attainment of peak status (median age of 24 for Park Slope men and 26 for Park Avenue men).

Not only does the skid row man achieve his peak status earlier, but he holds it for a shorter time. For Bowery men, who attained peak status at a median age of 22, the median age for losing it was 31. The Camp LaGuardia men are similar in this respect (age 22 for attainment and age 32 for loss of highest status). However, among Park Slope respondents the median age for losing peak status was 37, and among Park Avenue men it was 49.

Lifetime mobility. The Bowery and Camp LaGuardia men differ from the Chicago men studied by Bogue in that more of the New

York men show no net lifetime mobility. This means that the status of their most recent jobs is approximately the same (not more than four points higher or lower on the Duncan SEI scale) as that of the jobs they held at age 20. About a fifth of Bogue's respondents were at approximately the same status when interviewed as when they entered the labor force, compared to more than a third of the Bowery, Camp LaGuardia, and Park Slope men (see Table 8-2).

With respect to the proportion of men with downward net mobility, the findings are remarkably similar to Bogue's: about 46 percent of the Camp LaGuardia and Bowery men were downwardly mobile; the figure for the Chicago sample was 45 percent. The proportion of downwardly mobile men in the control samples was much lower; in Park Slope only 27 percent of the respondents were working at jobs five or more points lower in status than their jobs at age 20, and among the Park Avenue men the proportion in this condition was only 7 percent.

Status loss. Bogue's finding that almost all homeless men had held higher occupational status earlier in their lives was supported in the present study. He reported that 83 percent of the Chicago skid row men had fallen one or more points from their peak lifetime status. Corresponding figures for the Bowery and Camp LaGuardia samples are 82 percent and 85 percent (see Table 8-2). When only those men who had lost five or more status points were considered as downwardly mobile, about three-fourths of the skid row men fell into that category. In contrast, about half of the Park Slope men and only one-fifth of the Park Avenue men had lost this much ground occupationally.

On the face of it, extensive downward mobility appears slightly more often among the Chicago skid row men than in the New York samples. Almost one-third of Bogue's respondents had skidded 30 or more points, compared to between one-fifth and one-fourth of the New York respondents. Note, however, that Bogue used a different index of occupational status, one that has a range of 140 points rather than the 96-point range of the Duncan Index used in this study. Thus the apparent difference in the proportions of the samples having extensive downward mobility is of no consequence.

Mobility patterns. A statistical summary of the lifetime mobility

Table 8-2

TWO MEASURES OF LIFETIME MOBILITY, FOR NEW YORK AND CHICAGO SKID ROW SAMPLES (IN PERCENTAGES)

Mobility	Chicago[a]	Bowery	Camp LaGuardia	Park Slope	Park Avenue
Lifetime Net Mobility					
Rise	33	18	18	38	68
No change	22	37	35	35	25
Fall	45	46	47	27	7
Total	100	101	100	100	100
N		180	185	124	104
Points Fall from Lifetime Peak (Net Status Loss)					
None	17	18	15	40	75
1-4	9	8	12	9	4
5-9	6	18	15	5	8
10-14	10	13	8	10	4
15-19	12	12	10	10	6
20-24	7	9	10	7	2
25-29	10	5	7	6	1
30 or more	29	18	23	15	1
Total	100	101	100	102	101
N		180	185	124	104

a. Bogue, *Skid Row in American Cities* (Chicago: Community and Family Study Center, Univ. of Chicago, 1963), p. 325.

Table 8-3

STATISTICAL SUMMARY OF LIFETIME OCCUPATIONAL MOBILITY PROFILES

Number of Significant[a] Changes of Direction in the Mobility Profile	Direction of Change[b]	Idealized Pictorial Representation	Bowery	Camp LaGuardia	Park Slope	Park Avenue
0	None	—	13%	9%	10%	8%
0	R	/	7	6	17	36
0	F	\	19	16	7	4
1	RF	/\	16	15	18	4
1	FR	\/	5	11	15	14
2	RFR	/\/	8	11	9	16
2	FRF	\/\	12	10	8	4
3	RFRF	/\/\	6	7	6	3
3	FRFR	\/\/	4	6	5	5
4	RFRFR	/\/\/	2	1	2	6
4	FRFRF	\/\/\	3	4	1	0
5+	RFRFRF . . .	/\/\/\	4	3	0	1
5+	FRFRFR . . .	\/\/\/	1	2	2	0
Total			100	101	100	101
N			180	185	124	104

a. A significant change is five or more points on the Duncan Socioeconomic Index.

b. R = rise, F = fall.

patterns of the New York respondents appears in Table 8-3. Before commenting on these findings, some comments on method are in order.

It was assumed there were typical mobility patterns in the histories of skid row men, and an attempt was made to distinguish them by counting the number of changes of direction in the profiles. The number of significant changes (five or more points on the SEI) in a man's status history may be viewed as a measure of the "disorderliness" of his career. A profile congruent with the universal ideal of occupational success would be an orderly progression of jobs of increasingly higher status. Orderly movement in a downward direction is also possible, as when each job has a lower status than the one that preceded it. A somewhat less orderly profile would show one or two ups and downs, and a disorderly profile would manifest a succession of increases and decreases.

For the moment, the focus will be on significant changes of direction. Thus, if a man held a series of jobs, each lower in status than the preceding one, his profile would reflect a constant fall in status, and might be pictorially represented like this: ╲.

This method differs slightly from Bogue's, and therefore these results are not entirely comparable to those he reports for Chicago skid row men. Since the career mobility patterns outlined by Bogue are based on only four points in the respondent's career—first job, last job, and two intermediate jobs [22]—there are only five possible mobility patterns (stability, up only, down only, up-then-down, and down-then-up). In the present analysis every variation of five or more points in status was noted separately, and the number of possible patterns is much greater.

The patterns typical of skid row men, according to Bogue, are down only and up-then-down. In the Chicago study these two patterns accounted for two-thirds of the sample.[23] However, the heavy representation of Bogue's respondents in these two categories is partly a function of the method, with its restriction to only four points. In the data from our New York samples (summarized in Table 8-3) there is no typical pattern that fits a large proportion of the men in any of the samples.

Among skid row men the most frequent mobility pattern is down only. Almost one-fifth of the skid row men have had this type of mobility experience. The next most common pattern, characteristic of another sixth of the population, is up-then-down. These two patterns are the ones Bogue reported to be typical of skid row men in Chicago; they are frequent if not typical in the Bowery and Camp LaGuardia samples. Two other patterns often reported among Bowery men are stability and down-then-up-then-down. Between 30 and 45 percent of the respondents have more complicated mobility patterns, ranging from two to eight significant changes in direction of occupational mobility in the course of a worklife history.

Inspection of Table 8-3 reveals several important differences between control sample respondents and skid row men. The more complex mobility patterns occur somewhat more frequently in skid row than in the control samples, and the latter have fewer downwardly mobile and more upwardly mobile respondents. In fact, there are twice as many men with up only patterns in Park Avenue as in Park Slope, and Park Slope has more than twice as many up onlys as the skid row samples. The probabilities that the last significant change in direction of occupational mobility was positive is 77 percent in Park Avenue, 50 percent in Park Slope, 37 percent at Camp LaGuardia and 27 percent on the Bowery.

Intergenerational mobility. Neither the skid row nor the Park Slope samples showed much intergenerational upward mobility. The mean lifetime occupational status of the Bowery men was approximately ten points lower than that of their fathers, and the mean lifetime status of the Park Slope men was about three points lower. About half of the Bowery men had clearly lower status than their fathers, and about one-fifth of them had higher status. Thus, Bogue's finding that the occupational status of most skid row men is lower than that of their fathers is supported. By contrast, the mean lifetime status of the Park Avenue men was 11 points higher than that of their fathers, and 55 percent of them had occupations at least five points higher than their fathers' occupations.

After summarizing these occupational mobility patterns, let us return to the question, How different is the skid row man? In the light of the intersample contrasts discussed above, the answer is, Very different indeed. At any point in the skid row man's employment history his occupational status is lower than that of the Park Avenue or Park Slope man; his mean occupational status declines through adult life, while that of the more settled men increases during at least part of the life span; his peak status is lower, he attains it sooner, and holds it more briefly. His lifetime net mobility is likely to be downward, whereas Park Avenue and Park Slope men experience more upward than downward mobility; his career patterns are more disorderly than those of other men, and he is significantly worse off than was his father, whereas the Park Slope man has at least maintained his father's status, and the Park Avenue man is distinctly better off than his father. In sum, with respect to his occupational life history the skid row man is dramatically disadvantaged.

OCCUPATIONAL MOBILITY AND DISAFFILIATION

Vertical mobility is a potentially disruptive process. Blau has observed that the conditions accompanying occupational mobility are not conducive to the development of integrative social bonds.[24] Wilensky and Edwards take a similar position, asserting that the mobile person "tends to lack firm ties to either the groups he has left behind or those into which he is moving." [25]

If downward mobility weakens or destroys the affiliative bonds that link persons to organizations in their social environment, the homelessness of skid row men is not surprising; it is the natural consequence of their downward mobility. We can test the hypothesis that downward occupational mobility is directly associated with loss of affiliation, drawing the data from the Bowery and Park Slope samples.

Earlier in this chapter we introduced two measures of worklife mobility: status loss and lifetime mobiilty. Status loss is the difference between the status of a man's most recent job and the job of highest status in his history. Lifetime mobility is the difference between the status of a man's first job and his most recent job. Among Bowery men lifetime mobility ranges from —71 to +30, with a mean of —4.6; among Park Slope men the range is from —68 to +68, with a mean of 2.5. Approximately the same proportion of both samples had stable worklives (see Table 8-2), but more than one-third of the Park Slope men had been upwardly mobile, compared to about a sixth of the Bowery men. Almost half (46 percent) of the Bowery men but only 27 percent of the Park Slope men experienced net downward mobility.

With respect to status loss, the range of values for the two samples were comparable: 0 to 73 for Bowery men, and 0 to 77 for Park Slope men. The mean status loss of Bowery men was slightly greater than that of Park Slope men (15.6 and 12.6, respectively). However, Table 8-2 reveals that the differences between the samples are at the upper levels, that is, more Park Slope men are upwardly mobile or stable, and more Bowery men have histories of *slight* downward mobility. There is little difference between the samples in the proportion of respondents whose histories show substantial or extreme status loss. Inspection of the distribution of lifetime mobility reveals the same thing: there were as many substantial and extreme skidders in Park Slope as on the Bowery—15 percent of both samples had lifetime mobility scores of −15 or lower. In other words, there are more skidders on the Bowery than in Park Slope, but most of the Bowery skidders have not skidded very far. Men who have experienced substantial downward mobility are as common in the settled lower-class neighborhood as in skid row.

In testing the relation between affiliation and mobility, churches,[26] labor unions, and other voluntary associations were combined into a single category—other affiliations. Consequently we had three types of affiliation: family, occupation, and other. Each of these types was subdivided into categories of high, moderate, and low affiliation. With regard to family, high affiliation denotes that in a given year the respondent was living with at least one member of his family of orientation or family of procreation; moderate affiliation means that he saw at least one close relative at least once a month; and low affiliation includes all less frequent contact. Occupationally, high affiliation means the respondent worked the entire year at short-term or long-term jobs; moderate affiliation means that he worked part of the year at short-term or long-term jobs or the full year at day-to-day jobs; and low affiliation means he worked part of the year at day-to-day jobs or was unemployed.[27] High affiliation in the category of other affiliations denotes membership in at least two of the three types of organizations included in the category, for example, in a church and a labor union, a church and a voluntary association, or a labor union and a voluntary association. Moderate affiliation refers to membership in a single type of organization and low affiliation denotes no organizational memberships.

We attempted to control for the influence of aging on affiliation by comparing respondents' affiliations and occupational status at two specific points, ages 30 and 50. In Table 8-4 we present information on changes in affiliation in the three organizational types between these two points. A change was defined as movement from one category to another, for example, from high to moderate or low, or from moderate to low or high. Observe that in their other affiliations the samples are alike but that changes in the family and occupational affiliation in the Park Slope sample differ significantly from those in the Bowery sample. Loss of family affiliations between age 30 and age 50 is almost twice as common among Bowery men as Park Slope men. Only a few of the Park Slope men but more than a third of the Bowery men showed a decrease in occupational affiliation for the same period.

The samples manifest different histories of affiliation change but

Table 8-4

CHANGES IN AFFILIATION AND OCCUPATIONAL STATUS, AGES 30 AND 50 (IN PERCENTAGES)

Type of Affiliation	Change	Bowery	Park Slope
Family	Increase	7	26
	No Change	59	54
	Decrease	34	19
$x^2 = 12.51$, df=2, $p < .01$			
Job	Increase	7	4
	No Change	57	88
	Decrease	37	9
$x^2 = 14.25$, df=2, $p < .001$			
Other Affiliations	Increase	19	28
	No Change	67	63
	Decrease	14	9
$x^2 = 2.29$, df=2, $p < .50$			
Direction of Occupational Mobility	Upward	16	21
	No Change	52	53
	Downward	32	26
$x^2 = 1.01$, df=2, $p < .70$			
N		90	57

similar mobility patterns. Comparison of occupational status at ages 30 and 50 reveals no change for the majority of respondents, and shows downward mobility to have occurred for about the same proportion of respondents in each sample. But comparison of affiliation changes for the same period shows greater losses in family and occupational affiliation for Bowery men than for Park Slope men. Therefore, we conclude that the disaffiliation of the Bowery respondents was not attributable to their downward mobility.

Despite this finding, it is possible that occupational skidding may accompany loss of affiliation within a given sample. If downward mobility combines with another factor to produce disaffiliation, and that factor does not appear in the life histories of Park Slope men, downward mobility would not then be associated with disaffiliation, even though it were an important element in the combination of factors producing disaffiliation on skid row. In other words, if an unknown factor combines with downward mobility to produce disaffiliation, we would expect the association between downward mobility and disaffiliation to be stronger for the Bowery sample than for the Park Slope sample.

Among the 29 Bowery respondents who skidded, 13 lost family affiliation, 20 lost job affiliation, and 8 lost other affiliations (45 percent, 69 percent, and 28 percent, respectively). Corresponding figures for the 15 Park Slope skidders are 6, 2, and 1 (40 percent, 13 percent, and 7 percent, respectively). Thus, the expectation that the association between downward mobility and disaffiliation would be stronger in the Bowery than in Park Slope is supported. But the association between downward mobility and affiliation loss is not very marked in either of the samples. Even in the Bowery sample downward mobility seems, at best, merely a factor contributing to disaffiliation.

Thus, the hypothesis that downward occupational mobility is associated with loss of affiliation was not supported. When the samples as a whole were considered, Bowery men were significantly different from Park Slope men both in patterns of affiliation and in mobility histories, but when controls for age were added, the differences in occupational mobility disappeared; the skid row men had not skidded much more than the Park Slope men. In the light of these findings it seems unlikely that the disaffiliation of Bowery men is a consequence of their downward mobility.

These findings have implications for the study of aging as well as for theories of homelessness. Whether downward mobility is accompanied by disaffiliation seems to depend on the social context in which the mobility occurs. Apparently the tendencies to disaffiliation that derive from downward mobility may be neutralized by other elements of the life history.

SOME OCCUPATIONAL CASE HISTORIES

Periodically, the stereotype of skid row as a habitat of former professional men who have "hit the skids" is reinforced by pieces in newspapers and magazines about former executives or professional men who have ended their careers on skid row. Accounts like these have wide appeal. There is drama in remarkable change of any kind, and the tale of a fall from high status is as interesting as the story of a meteoric rise. Usually the journalistic accounts of the skid to the bottom do not stress the atypicality of their subjects. The journalist may be excused for his selective perception; he needs interesting material, and the life history of the typical Bowery man is a dull account of poverty, drink, hard work, and hopelessness.

Few Bowery men have ever held positions of power or responsibility, so not many of them have skidded extensively. In the present analysis a loss of 50 or more points in occupational status was arbitrarily designated as an extreme status loss. It may be illustrated by the status difference between a social worker and a taxicab driver (54 points). Using the 50-point standard, only 4 percent of the Bowery men, 8 percent of the Camp LaGuardia men, 3 percent of the Park Slope men, and 1 percent of the Park Avenue men have suffered extreme status loss.

Several major patterns appear in the histories of the extreme skidders. First, several of their histories reveal a general deterioration of social relationships accompanied by excessive drinking, and culminating in loss of job and family, arrests for drunkenness, and dependence on skid row facilities. The histories of Robert Kelly and John Van Leer illustrate this pattern. (Names are fictitious in all case histories, both here and throughout this report.) Kelly and Van Leer are late skidders; in their early adult lives they were highly affiliated. Donald O'Laughlin and James Reardon illustrate another pattern; that of relatively low affiliation in adult life despite a fairly high-status occupation. Neither of these men has ever married. The former, a fairly young man, exemplifies the early skid career.

Robert Kelly, youngest son of an insurance and real estate agent, was born on Long Island in 1907. As a youth he was active in many organizations. In high school he belonged to the swimming and rifle teams and the Junior Naval Reserve, and for several years in high school and college he worked on weekends as a caddy. During his college years, Kelly pledged a fraternity and remained an active member until 1934. In 1929 he left college without receiving his degree because he had been offered a job as an electrical engineer in Manhattan. He held the job for twenty-two years, becoming chief engineer in a subsidiary company and vice-president in charge of engineering.

Six years after leaving school he married a college graduate. She worked full time for two years after their marriage. He considers this the happiest period of his life—"When I started work and my first marriage and everything was so new." Later they had three children.

By 1943 Kelly was drinking heavily. He reports that his normal day's consumption at that time was about sixteen shots of whiskey. Drinking became a major problem in his marriage; he and his wife were divorced in 1951. He joined Alcoholics Anonymous, but his drinking continued. Soon afterward, Kelly lost his job, stopped going to church regularly, and first spent a night on the Bowery.

In 1952 he married a second time, once again to a college graduate. He held another job as electrical engineer throughout most of this second marriage. Financial problems led to a separation in 1959. During his second marriage Kelly began to go on long drinking sprees, and he was arrested twice for being drunk and disorderly. Since the separation from his second wife his jobs have been irregular; he lives by dishwashing or loading trucks one or two days a week. In 1961 the Men's Shelter suggested that Kelly go to Camp LaGuardia. He went and has returned to the camp six times since then. He likes the camp because of the "security and no drinking and hope for the future," but finds it "too secluded, not enough room for a man to expand in his mental and spiritual directions."

Kelly considers the present the least happy period of his life. The interviewer commented: "Articulate and educated but extremely frightened . . . very sad, this one."

John Van Leer, the eldest son of a building contractor, was born in Westchester County, New York, in 1900. In school his marks were about average, and he participated in high school athletics (basketball and baseball teams). Van Leer wanted to be an engineer, and after graduating from high school in 1917, he attended college for four years, but did not graduate.

He married in 1922 and took a job with a Wall Street firm as a runner and assistant statistician. Then he was an autombile salesman in Connecticut for a year. In 1926 he was hired by the New York Telephone Company as an engineer. He says that while he was with the telephone company, he studied probability theory at MIT. In 1929 he returned to Wall Street as a statistician. He left again in 1932 to become a branch manager for an insurance concern. In 1934 and 1935 he had a relief job as a recreation commissioner in Westchester County. About this time he was divorced. Both he and his wife were drinking heavily, and the family was having financial difficulties. After the divorce he did not contribute to the support of his children.

Van Leer resumed working for the telephone company in 1935, this time selling directory advertising. He left in 1940 to join the British army and was stationed in Calcutta for three years. He says that the happiest time in his life was on the ship coming home from Calcutta in 1943. In that year he took a job as a civil engineer in Florida and remarried. Two years later he separated from his second wife. He says that his drinking had been a problem, but he also blames her: "The whole thing was no good. I left. She was a tramp all her life."

After the termination of his second marriage, Van Leer moved to New York. He spent his first night on the Bowery about then. However, his professional career lasted three more years; he held a job as a senior staff engineer for a firm of engineering consultants until 1948. By that time he had been drinking heavily for more than fifteen years. He joined Alcoholics Anonymous in 1945 and was a member "off and on" until 1952. In 1950 he was arrested for being drunk and disorderly, and since then he has been arrested nine more times. By 1955 he was going on sprees that lasted three days or more. He was sent to Camp LaGuardia in 1957 and has gone there voluntarily several times since. In 1961-62 he stayed at the camp almost a year. Since 1961 he has been drinking two pints of wine every day. He considers himself a light drinker: "If I have money, I'll drink heavy; I'm a light drinker by Bowery standards." From 1948 to 1963 he worked sporadically at odd jobs: kitchen helper, porter, or maintenance man. He has been unemployed since 1963.

Van Leer has lived on the Bowery or at Camp LaGuardia for ten years now. He has no illusions about getting away. When asked where he thought he would be a year from now, his first reply was "dead." He says "survival is the only thing that's important. I'm on the Bowery, not in a penthouse." He lives on Social Security. At the conclusion of the interview he stated his guiding principles. Among them was "Take what comes—never cry."

Donald O'Laughlin, born in 1930 in a small North Carolina town, was the eldest of three children. His father was a petty officer in the navy when Donald was growing up, and was away from home for long periods. The O'Laughlins moved every two or three years, living in Florida, California, and Virginia, but returned several times to Donald's birthplace. As a boy he was active in the YMCA and belonged to the Boy Scouts. At the age of 15 he went to work part-time in a supermarket. He was hoping to become a writer.

After graduating from high school, O'Laughlin entered the University of North Carolina at Chapel Hill and majored in psychology. He says he did his best in college and received fairly high grades. By this time his father had left the navy and ran an oil business.

Following graduation from college, O'Laughlin served in the navy for three years. He began drinking heavily after his discharge from the navy, and since that time has gone on a five-day spree about once a month. When not on a spree, he drinks two glasses of wine a day.

In 1957 O'Laughlin took courses at an electronics school in Danville, Virginia, and the following year he went to work as a technician in North Carolina. After nine months at that job he signed a contract to teach high school mathematics and taught mathematics in North Carolina and Virginia for two years. He says that these were his happiest years: "I was working at a trade I was best at."

He apparently lost his teaching job in 1962 and then worked short-term as a grill cook and as a handyman. In 1964 he left North Carolina and moved to Manhattan, where he obtained a series of unskilled temporary jobs through an employment agency. Less than a year later he spent his first night on the Bowery and was given meals and lodging by the Men's Shelter. O'Laughlin still lives on the Bowery, but appears to have achieved a measure of occupational stability. He works in a Bowery employment agency processing papers. He has worked there for about a year and makes $200 a month.

O'Laughlin says he has never been married and has never lived with a woman. He commented: "Many people bug me; I don't like close attachments." He has been a loner most of his life although he does claim to have a close friend whom he sees every night and a group of friends who meet to drink and talk several times a month.

He considers "peace of mind, adequate income, self-respect, and love" the most important things in life, and offers the statement "do justly, love mercy, and walk humbly with our God" as his guiding principle.

O'Laughlin is only 35 years old, and he still hopes to escape the Bowery. He told the interviewer that in a few months he planned to return to North Carolina and become a high school teacher again. The interviewer described him as a "quiet, well-mannered man," who offered to buy him a soda.

James Reardon, the youngest of five children, was born in Argentina in 1905. When he was five years old, his family moved to a farm in Ireland. He views his school days in Ireland as the happiest part of his life. He left school at age 18 and went to work as an assistant bookkeeper in a hardware store. A year later, in 1924, he immigrated to the United States. Living in Philadelphia with a cousin, he took a job as a clerk in a chain grocery store. Later he became manager of the store. After seven years in Philadelphia he moved to New York and managed a chain grocery store.

Reardon was in the army from 1941 to 1945, serving in Africa and Europe. After his discharge he was unemployed for six months and lived with his father in Philadelphia. Then he was employed as a machine operator in a carpet factory, a job he held until 1948. About that time his father died, and Reardon went to live with his brother. For a year he was unemployed; then he went to work as a kitchen helper. In 1952 he again moved to New York and again found the same kind of work he had had in Philadelphia. After about two years in the city he began receiving assistance from the Men's Shelter on the Bowery.

He maintained membership in the Veterans of Foreign Wars and a Democratic Club until 1955. He marks that year as the beginning of his heaviest drinking, and claims to have drunk three quarts of whiskey a day for a considerable period of time. Simultaneously, he began attending Alcoholics Anonymous meetings, and he continued to attend them for three or four years. He first stayed at Camp La-Guardia in 1955 and since then has returned 13 times. His current stay at the camp is his longest; he has been there for a year, although he does not like it: "Things get too boring here, and a change does you good. I want to get away from here, to get out and see the public." Reardon has lived in rooming houses most of his life, has never married, and has no close friends at the camp.

There are not many extreme skidders on skid row. The mobility profiles of most Bowery men show low-level stability or minor fluctuations. Three of these stable career patterns are illustrated in the case histories below. Kurt Holtz, the subject of the first history, is one of the light-drinking, lifetime isolates who arrive on skid row after retirement. The other men were more affiliated than Holtz, and heavy drinking appears as an important factor in their disaffiliation.

Kurt Holtz was born in Bavaria in 1881. His father was a railroad man and his mother was a cleaning woman. He completed six grades and then left school because "in Germany, when you are 14, you have to leave school and learn a job." Kurt would have liked to stay in school but "you had to be rich to go to college."

In 1901, when he was 20 years old, he entered the German army and was stationed in Nuremburg until 1904. After his discharge he traveled around Europe for two years and then emigrated to the United States. He moved to Long Island and found work as a farm laborer. Except for a short period in 1908 when he shoveled snow in New York City, he spent his entire worklife as a farm laborer in New York and New Jersey. He quit working in 1946, when he was sixty-five years old, and moved into Manhattan, living in nursing homes and hospitals. In 1951 he had a bladder operation which completely disabled him.

Holtz spent his first night on the Bowery in 1964 at the age of 83. He says he leaves the Bowery every day and does not know anyone in the neighborhood by name: "Why should I? I'm always alone. The less men you know, you always have a dollar in your pocket. I don't want to know them. I want to be left alone."

He has been on welfare since 1946. He receives no Social Security and has never been a client at the Men's Shelter. When he was asked if he would be willing to join an organization to improve the condition of Bowery men he answered: "But there are not many around here that you could call men. I drank too, but I always was on the job in the morning." He has been an abstainer since 1946, and before that drank only two glasses of beer a week.

Holtz has been a loner all his adult life. In his early teens he belonged to a wrestling and weight-lifting club and a dancing club, but as an adult he has never been affiliated with any organization. He has no family ties. He never married, has not seen any of his relatives since 1904, and has no close friends or regular associates.

Jussi Virtanen. Born in 1905 in Finland, his family migrated to the United States and settled in Pittsfield, Massachusetts when he was two years old. He completed the eighth grade and then left school permanently because "I just wanted to have money in my pocket." His first job was in a gun factory as a material handler. At age 15 he went into his father's occupation of boilermaker as a helper.

In 1923 he joined the merchant marine in coastal shipping. As a sailor, he traveled "all over the U.S.—West Coast, East Coast, Great Lakes." He remained in the merchant marine until 1937, living in Boston, New York, Savannah, Jacksonville, San Francisco, Portland, Seattle, and other cities. The interviewer notes: "His job history is sketchy because a good part of his life has been spent traveling on and off ships, in jobs of about one or two weeks." During this period he spent his first night on the Bowery in 1931.

He has never been married, although he lived with a woman for six months in 1931. He said, "She was paying our expenses and I was just drinking and so we fought a lot. . . . I just packed up and left Portland and shipped out of Seattle." Since 1933 he has worked sporadically as a trucker's helper and in warehouses and railroad camps, besides occasional sea voyages. He last saw his mother and father in 1934, and he has had no family contacts since.

Virtanen claims to have been a moderate drinker all of his adult life: "I'm not a heavy drinker. It doesn't pay to put yourself into the gutter." However, he was arrested in 1935 on charges of being drunk and disorderly, the first of six such arrests. In 1955 he joined Alcoholics Anonymous and remained with them for two years.

In 1941 he stayed at Camp LaGuardia for six weeks. The next year he first received assistance from the Men's Shelter. He has returned to the camp only once, for his present stay of nine months. He considers the most important thing in life to be "getting by from day to day without extending yourself too much."

Bill O'Malley. He was born in Connecticut in 1896, and when he was four years old, his father died. After completing ten grades of school, he terminated his formal education and became an apprentice machinist. He continued in this line of work for 43 years, coming to the Bowery in 1956.

He married in 1919 and remained married for 36 years. While married he belonged to an amateur orchestra and managed a baseball team. The couple had four children. They were divorced in 1935. He said he continued to support the children for five years after the divorce, until they were "pretty well grown."

O'Malley began to drink heavily about 1941. In 1946 he joined Alcoholics Anonymous for six months, but his drinking continued until 1958. Since that time he has been an abstainer.

In 1956 he spent his first night on the Bowery. Since 1959 he has worked as a clerk in a Bowery hotel.

Many skid row men have disorderly work histories, with numerous job changes and zigzag mobility profiles. This series of brief work histories concludes with an example of this pattern, the case of Harold Rice.

Harold Rice. One of eleven children of a construction worker, Rice was born in Boston in 1919. When he was ten years old, his family moved to Tennessee, where he quit school at age 14, after completing only three grades, because "I got tired." Then the family moved to Alabama, and Rice took his first job in a funeral parlor. His youthful ambition was to be a mortician. He worked at the funeral home for two years and then entered the army. He served for eight years and was discharged in 1946 at the age of 27. He married that year. His wife was a high school graduate, and she worked full-time during their entire marriage. Rice was unemployed for six months after his marriage; then he worked for about a year as a spike driver on a railroad crew.

During the rest of his married life he worked sporadically loading freight for a trucking company in Tennessee and New York. He also spent two years in Pittsburgh (1951-1952). No employment is listed for that period, but while there he lived with another woman. In 1952: "I just got tired and hit the road." He does not cite any serious problems in this consensual union, but says that drinking was a problem in his marriage. He was definitely separated from his wife in 1953. "My wife got sick. Her mother carried her to her home and that was it." He last saw his wife in 1956, but reports that he still contributes to the support of their two children.

Following his separation, he was a hobo, in upstate New York, Rochester, Florida, New York City, and Tennessee. In 1955 he went to work as a grinder for a sink company in Tennessee and joined a union.

He first spent a night on the Bowery in 1956 and was first arrested as drunk and disorderly that same year. He has since been arrested 20 times on similar charges. He is a spree drinker; his sprees last two or three weeks each. He claims to have gone on 20 sprees in a single year. When not on a spree, he says, he drinks four pints of wine a day.

Since first coming to the Bowery he has continued his traveling, taking to the road every summer and often making several trips a year. During the summers of 1958 to 1965 he worked on the road, taking casual jobs unloading trucks, packing rags, and helping in construction. He first visited Camp LaGuardia in 1964 and has returned several times, but never for longer than a month. His last job was in 1965 when he worked as a potwasher in Kiamesha, New York, for six months "during the season." That same year he attended meetings of Alcoholics Anonymous. He first received assistance from the Men's Shelter in 1966, and he now lives on public assistance.

He claims that a year from now he will be in Tennessee, "with my wife and children." He considers the years of his marriage the happiest in his life and the time he started drinking as the least happy. The interviewer commented: "Respondent never faced me. He always managed to wind up sideways or with his back toward me, speaking in a muffled voice."

NOTES

1. In 1954 Parnes observed that most empirical studies of labor mobility had focused on manual workers, and that the mobility patterns and labor market behavior of nonmanual workers were relatively unexplored; see Herbert S. Parnes, *Research on Labor Mobility* (New York: Social Science Research Council, 1954), p. 36.

2. Harold L. Wilensky, "Work, Careers, and Social Integration," *International Social Science Journal,* 12, No. 4 (1960), p. 553.

3. Percy E. Davidson and H. Dewey Anderson, *Occupational Mobility in an American Community* (Stanford, Calif.: Stanford Univ. Press, 1937), pp. 3-6, 84-86, and 103-104.

4. Delbert C. Miller and William H. Form, "Measuring Patterns of Occupational Security," *Sociometry,* 10 (November 1947), p. 366.

5. Seymour M. Lipset and Reinhard Bendix, "Social Mobility and Occupational Career Patterns," *American Journal of Sociology,* 57 (January-March 1952), pp. 369 and 503.

6. Lloyd G. Reynolds, *The Structure of Labor Markets* (New York: Harper & Row, 1951), pp. 139 and 296.

7. For lists of publications and reports stemming from the Six-City Survey, see Gladys L. Palmer, *Labor Mobility in Six Cities* (New York: Social Science Research Council, 1954), pp. 9, 139-141 and Wilensky, *op. cit.,* pp. 553-554.

8. Thomas Wesley Rogers, *The Occupational Experience of One Hundred Unemployed Persons in Bloomington, Indiana* (Bloomington: Indiana Univ., Bureau of Business Research, 1931).

9. Harold L. Wilensky, "Orderly Careers and Social Participation: The Impact of Work History on Social Integration in the Middle Mass, *American Sociological Review,* 26 (August 1961), pp. 521-539; Joseph R. Gusfield, "Occupational Roles and Forms of Enterprise," *American Journal of Sociology,* 66 (May 1961), pp. 571-580; Warren Breed, "Occupational Mobility and Suicide among White Males," *American Sociological Review,* 28 (April 1963), pp. 179-188; Donald J. Bogue, *Skid Row in American Cities* (Chicago: Community and Family Study Center, Univ. of Chicago, 1963), pp. 315-329.

10. During the period 1960 to 1965, the *American Sociological Review* and the *American Journal of Sociology* published 26 articles which, judging from their titles, dealt with occupational mobility. Of these,

19 discuss intergenerational mobility only, 4 consider both inter- and intragenerational mobility, and 3 are concerned with intragenerational mobility alone.

11. United States Bureau of the Census, "Lifetime Occupational Mobility of Adult Males, March 1962," *Current Population Reports,* Series P-23, No. 11, May 12, 1964 (Washington, D.C.: U.S. Government Printing Office, 1964).

12. Otis Dudley Duncan, "The Trend of Occupational Mobility in the United States," *American Sociological Review,* 30 (August 1965), pp. 491-498; Peter M. Blau, "The Flow of Occupational Supply and Recruitment," *American Sociological Review,* 30 (August 1965), pp. 475-490; Peter M. Blau and Otis Dudley Duncan, *The American Occupational Structure* (New York: John Wiley and Sons, 1967).

13. Wilensky defines "middle mass" as the lower middle class and the upper working class (Wilensky, "Orderly Careers," p. 524); 49 of Gusfield's sample of 195 were skilled laborers (Gusfield, *op. cit.,* 572); 32 of the 103 suicides studied by Breed were in service or labor occupations (Breed, *op. cit.,* p. 181).

14. See, for example, Robert W. Hodge, Paul M. Siegel, and Peter H. Rossi, "Occupational Prestige in the United States, 1925-63," *American Journal of Sociology,* 70 (November 1964), pp. 286-302; Alex Inkeles and Peter H. Rossi, "National Comparisons of Occupational Prestige," *American Journal of Sociology,* 61 (January 1956), pp. 329-339; Allan W. Eister, "Evaluations of Selected Jobs and Occupations by University Students in a Developing Country: Pakistan," *Social Forces,* 44 (September 1965), pp. 66-73.

15. Bogue, *op. cit.,* pp. 317-318.

16. Albert J. Reiss, Jr., Otis Dudley Duncan, Paul K. Hatt, and Cecil C. North, *Occupations and Social Status* (New York: The Free Press, 1961), pp. 109-138, especially pp. 114-115. For examples of the use of Duncan's index, see Bruce K. Eckland, "Academic Ability, Higher Education, and Occupational Mobility," *American Sociological Review,* 30 (October 1965), pp. 735-746; Louis Guttman and Edward O. Laumann, "The Relative Associational Contiguity of Occupations in an Urban Setting," *American Sociological Review,* 31 (April 1966), pp. 169-178; Donald G. McTavish, "A Method for More Reliably Coding Detailed Occupations into Duncan's Socio-Economic Categories," *American Sociological Review,* 29 (June 1964), pp. 402-406; Peter M. Blau and Otis Dudley Duncan, *op. cit.*

17. Reiss, *op. cit.,* pp. 130-131.

18. Bogue, *op. cit.,* pp. 320-322.

19. *Ibid.,* pp. 322, 324, 325-326, 327-328, and 324, respectively.

20. United States Bureau of the Census, *Alphabetical Index of Occupations and Industries* (Washington, D.C.: U.S. Government Printing Office, 1950); see also McTavish, *op. cit.*

21. Bogue, *op. cit.,* pp. 320, 325.

22. *Ibid.,* pp. 327-328.

23. *Ibid.*

24. Peter M. Blau, "Social Mobility and Interpersonal Relations," *American Sociological Review,* 21 (June 1956), p. 290.

25. Harold L. Wilensky and Hugh Edwards, "The Skidder: Ideological Adjustments of Downward Mobile Workers," *American Sociological Review,* 24 (April 1959), p. 216.

26. A respondent was classified as belonging to a church in a given year if (a) he attended regularly, whether or not he claimed to be a member, or (b) he attended sporadically (at least once a year) and claimed membership.

27. Long-term jobs lasted six months or more; short-term jobs lasted at least one week but less than six months; day-to-day jobs are those for which a man was hired to work less than a week and was paid every day. Generally, in day-to-day jobs, neither employee nor employer is committed to more than one day's employment.

CHAPTER 9

ASPIRATION, ACHIEVEMENT, AND ANOMIE

Anomie, in current usage, refers to "a breakdown in the cultural structure, occurring particularly when there is an acute disjunction between the cultural norms and goals and the socially structured capacities of members of the group to act in accord with them." [1] This disjunction is said to occur because persons at all socioeconomic levels internalize the dominant cultural goals, but social-class differences limit the accessibility of the goals.[2] One of the modes of adaptation to anomie is retreatism or rejection of both the cultural goals and the institutionalized means for attaining them. According to Merton,

> People who adapt (or maladapt) in this fashion are, strictly speaking, *in* the society but not of it. Sociologically, these constitute the true aliens. Not sharing the common frame of values, they can be included as members of the *society* (in distinction from the *population*) only in a fictional sense.[3]

Skid row, with its peculiar subculture, is obviously an environment conducive to retreatism. However, not all skid row men are retreatists, and it remains to be demonstrated that anomie is more prevalent among skid row men than in other low-income populations. The present chapter considers the relationships among anomie (defined as the disparity between aspiration and achievement), skid row residence, and disaffiliation.

YOUTHFUL ASPIRATIONS

Respondents in the four samples were asked, When you were a young man, did you have any ambitions about what you wanted to be in life? If a man answered affirmatively, he was asked a second question: What did you want to be? On the basis of their replies respondents were divided into five categories as follows: (1) men who aspired to a specific high-status occupation, (2) men who aspired to a specific low-status occupation, 3) men who aspired to general success—wealth, fame, or power, (4) men whose aspirations were not specifically occupational or oriented to success, and (5) men having no specific aims.

Table 9-1 summarizes the occupational aspirations of those respondents reporting specific occupational goals. Occupations that seemed to belong together have been combined. At least half of the men aspired to be professional men or artists and performers. The control sample respondents were most likely to aspire to these occupations; 60 percent of the Park Slope men and 82 percent of the Park Avenue men with specific aspirations wanted to be professionals or artists, compared with about half of the Bowery and Camp LaGuardia men.

Physician and engineer were the most frequently mentioned occupations. Bowery men wanted to be physicians, engineers, clergymen, and lawyers, in that order. Camp LaGuardia and Park Slope men more often aspired to be engineers than to be physicians. Between 15 and 25 percent of the men in all four samples had aspired to be artists, writers, performers, or professional athletes. The more fre-

Table 9-1

TYPE OF ASPIRATION, FOR RESPONDENTS REPORTING SPECIFIC OCCUPATIONAL ASPIRATIONS (IN PERCENTAGES)

Type of Aspiration	Bowery	Camp LaGuardia	Park Slope	Park Avenue
Professional workers	36	30	45	58
Performers or artists	18	19	15	24
Skilled workers	20	25	15	0
Semiskilled workers	12	10	7	0
Businessmen	8	15	5	20
Government employees	11	8	15	4
Totals[a]	105	107	102	106
N	121	110	74	71

a. Percentage totals are greater than 100 because some respondents reported more than one aspiration.

quent choices in all three low-income samples were skilled occupations in the construction trades (carpenters, electricians, plumbers, and bricklayers) and auto mechanics. Among the respondents who aspired to semiskilled occupations, the most frequent choices were seaman, farmer, and truck (or bus) driver. Owning or managing a business was a youthful aspiration reported by 20 percent of the Park Avenue men, 15 percent of the Camp LaGuardia men, 8 percent of the Bowery men, and 5 percent of the Park Slope men; among the specific positions mentioned were real estate owner, circus owner, banker, contractor, and hotel owner. Finally, sizeable proportions of the three lower-income samples aspired to public service as policemen, firemen, or soldiers.

No attempt was made to measure individual variations in opportunity structure, apart from the assumption that achievement is an ex post facto indicator of opportunities. The higher the achieved status, the greater the opportunity must have been. If this assumption is permissible, the probability of disaffiliation might be expected to vary directly with the disparity between aspiration and achievement.

First, the respondents' educational attainment and their levels of aspiration will be compared, and then the achievement of aspirations will be discussed. This will enable us to test the hypothesis that the greater the disparity between aspiration and attainment, the greater the disaffiliation.

EDUCATIONAL ASPIRATION AND ACHIEVEMENT

Skid row men did not aspire higher than men in the control samples. In fact, the distribution of responses by sample (Table 9-2) reveals that they were more often victims of low aspiration or lack of aspiration than of frustrated aspirations. Sixty-nine percent of the Park Avenue men aspired to high-status occupations,[4] compared with 41 percent of the Park Slope men, 35 percent of the Bowery men, and 29 percent of the Camp LaGuardia men.

We speculated that men with high aspirations in youth would be better educated than men with low aspirations. Ideally, the process of education exposes the student to an increasing number of occupational alternatives and also encourages him to strive for high-status positions. On the other hand, occupational aspirations may

Table 9-2

TYPE OF ASPIRATION IN YOUTH
(IN PERCENTAGES)

Type of Aspiration	Bowery	Camp LaGuardia	Park Slope	Park Avenue
High Aspirations[a]	35	29	41	69
Low Aspirations	28	28	25	7
Other Aspirations	3	2	2	0
None	34	42	32	24
Totals	100	101	100	100
N	197	195	121	99

a. Aspirations to general success or to specific occupations having status scores of 50 or above on the Duncan Socioeconomic Index are considered high.

explain continued attendance at school. Undoubtedly the process works both ways: education stimulates aspiration, and aspiration encourages scholastic effort.

In part, the data support these expectations. The high aspirers in the skid row samples were better educated than the low aspirers or the men reporting no aspirations (see Table 9-3). But in the control samples the educational attainment of high aspirers was no greater than that of low aspirers.

In the three low-income samples the high aspirers were most likely to report that they desired more education at the end of their schooling. Despite the positive correlation between desire for more education and level of aspiration, it should be noted that in neither the Bowery nor Camp LaGuardia sample did more than half of the high aspirers desire further education at the conclusion of their schooling. Among the Park Slope men 59 percent of the high aspirers wanted more education. They seem to be more aware than skid row men of the utility of education for occupational mobility.

In all four samples there was a positive relation between desire for additional education and actual participation in adult-education programs. Of those Park Avenue respondents who desired further

Table 9-3

LEVEL OF ASPIRATION BY EDUCATIONAL ACHIEVEMENT AND DESIRE FOR MORE EDUCATION AT END OF FORMAL SCHOOLING (IN PERCENTAGES)

	Bowery Aspiration			Camp LaGuardia Aspiration			Park Slope Aspiration			Park Avenue Aspiration		
Educational Achievement	High[a]	Low	None	High	Low	None	High	Low	None	High	Low	None
High (9+ years)	60	46	46	63	35	33	51	52	38	96	100	88
Low (0-8 years)	40	54	54	37	65	67	49	48	62	4	0	12
Totals	100	100	100	100	100	100	100	100	100	100	100	100
N	68	56	66	57	54	78	47	29	39	68	7	24
	gamma = .20			gamma = .38*			gamma = .17			gamma = .54		
Desired Further Education at End of Formal Schooling												
Yes	47	36	24	50	35	19	59	36	22	29	57	46
No	53	64	76	50	65	81	41	64	78	71	43	54
Totals	100	100	100	100	100	100	100	100	100	100	100	100
N	60	52	53	50	52	78	46	28	36	65	7	22
	gamma = .32			gamma = .45*			gamma = .52*			gamma = .09		

a. Aspirations to general success or to specific occupations having status scores of 50 or above on the Duncan Socioeconomic Index are considered high in all the samples.

* Significant at the .05 level.

education at the termination of their formal schooling, over 60 percent later participated in adult education programs, as did about 40 percent of the Bowery and Park Slope men who wanted more education when they first left school. About one-fourth of the Park Slope men who initially had not wanted further schooling later took some adult education, as did half of the Park Avenue men in that category. Rates for Camp LaGuardia men were somewhat lower than those of the other low-income samples.

AGE, RACE, AND ASPIRATION

In the skid row samples there was a strong relation between age and reported levels of youthful aspiration. Almost half of the younger Bowery men but only a fourth of the older men reported high youthful aspirations. The pattern was even stronger at Camp LaGuardia, where more than half of the younger men reported high youthful aspirations. However, in the control samples this relation between age and aspiration did not appear (see Table 9-4).

Adding controls for race had little effect on the relation between age and aspirations (see Table 9-5). Among both Whites and Blacks on skid row, about three-fourths of the old men had had low aspirations or none at all, and the modal response among young skid row men fell in the high-aspiration category. In Park Slope about half of the old men of both races and half of the young Blacks had had high aspirations, as did one-third of the young whites. In all three samples high-aspiration responses were more frequent among Blacks than among Whites. (There were no Blacks in the Park Avenue sample, so all assessment of racial effects apply only to the low-income samples.)

Having shown how level of aspiration varies by age and race, we may now describe how differences in age and race affect the achievement of aspirations. Given the American system of institutionalized racial inequality, Blacks were expected to be less successful than Whites in achieving their youthful ambitions. The fact that more Blacks than Whites had had high aspirations was expected to make the racial differences in achievement even more striking. In the discussion about age and aspiration it was noted that younger men on skid row tended to report higher youthful aspirations than the old men there. Presumably the goals of the old men, being lower, had

Table 9-4

LEVEL OF ASPIRATION BY AGE (IN PERCENTAGES)

	Bowery		Camp LaGuardia		Park Slope		Park Avenue	
	Age		Age		Age		Age	
Level of Aspiration	55+	0-54	55+	0-54	55+	0-54	55+	0-54
High[a]	25	45	21	52	47	39	74	62
Low	32	27	30	22	16	31	7	7
None	42	28	49	26	38	30	19	31
Totals	99	100	100	100	101	100	100	100
N	87	104	138	54	45	74	54	45
	gamma = .33*		gamma = .48*		gamma = .00		gamma = .26	

a. Aspirations to general success or to specific occupations having status scores of 50 or above on the Duncan Socioeconomic Index are considered high.

* Significant at the .05 level.

Table 9-5

LEVEL OF ASPIRATION BY AGE AND RACE (IN PERCENTAGES)

	Bowery							
	White				Black			
	55+		0-54		55+		0-54	
Level of Aspiration	%	N	%	N	%	N	%	N
High[a]	25	19	37	22	30	3	56	24
Low	30	23	30	18	40	4	23	10
None	45	34	33	20	30	3	21	9
Total	100	76	100	60	100	10	100	43
	gamma = –.22				gamma = –.36			

	Camp LaGuardia							
	White				Black			
	55+		0-54		55+		0-54	
Level of Aspiration	%	N	%	N	%	N	%	N
High	21	24	47	14	23	5	58	14
Low	29	33	17	5	36	8	29	7
None	50	58	37	11	41	9	12	3
Total	100	115	101	30	100	22	99	24
	gamma = –.35*				gamma = –.60*			

	Park Slope							
	White				Black			
	55+		0-54		55+		0-54	
Level of Aspiration	%	N	%	N	%	N	%	N
High	46	16	33	13	50	5	46	16
Low	14	5	33	13	20	2	29	10
None	40	14	33	13	30	3	26	9
Total	100	35	99	39	100	10	101	35
	gamma = .06				gamma = .01			

a. Aspirations to general success or to specific occupations having status scores of 50 or above on the Duncan Socioeconomic Index are considered high in all three samples.

* Significant at the .05 level.

been more easily reached. In Park Slope the younger men had not had higher youthful aspirations, so there was no basis for prediction. The expected ranking of the skid row subpopulations in terms of the proportion of men achieving their aspirations was older Whites, younger Whites, older Blacks, and younger Blacks.

Table 9-6

ACHIEVEMENT OF ASPIRATIONS BY AGE AND RACE (IN PERCENTAGES)

Whether Aspirations Achieved	Bowery							
	White				Black			
	55+		0-54		55+		0-54	
	%	N	%	N	%	N	%	N
Yes	30	13	22	9	14	1	12	4
No	70	31	78	31	86	6	88	30
Total	100	44	100	40	100	7	100	34
	gamma = .18				gamma = .11			

Whether Aspirations Achieved	Camp LaGuardia							
	White				Black			
	55+		0-54		55+		0-54	
	%	N	%	N	%	N	%	N
Yes	19	11	5	1	21	3	18	4
No	81	47	95	18	79	11	82	18
Total	100	58	100	19	100	14	100	22
	gamma = .62				gamma = .10			

Whether Aspirations Achieved	Park Slope							
	White				Black			
	55+		0-54		55+		0-54	
	%	N	%	N	%	N	%	N
Yes	24	5	12	3	—	—	26	7
No	76	16	88	23	100	7	74	20
Total	100	21	100	26	100	7	100	27
	gamma = .41				gamma = −1.00			

In fact, as may be seen from the percentages in Table 9-6, the ranking for the three samples by proportion of successful [5] men were as follows:

For the Bowery, older Whites, younger Whites, older Blacks, younger Blacks; for Camp LaGuardia, older Blacks, older Whites, younger Blacks, younger Whites; and for Park Slope, younger Blacks, older Whites, younger Whites, and older Blacks. Thus, in terms of reaching their goals, the older men had been somewhat more successful than the younger men; the only exception to this pattern was the Black population of Park Slope. Moreover, as expected, the Bowery Whites were more successful than the Bowery Blacks; twice as many of them had achieved their aspirations at some time in their lives. This pattern is not apparent in the other two samples.

In summation, in each sample more Blacks than Whites had aspirations to high status, and these interracial differences in aspiration for high status were greatest among Bowery men. Further, Bowery Blacks were less successful than Bowery Whites in achieving their aspirations, although Blacks in the other samples were not notably unsuccessful. The combination of higher aspirations and lower (or even equal) attainment among Blacks in all the samples suggests that the Blacks experienced more anomie than the Whites. Finally, because the interracial difference in the gap between aspirations and achievement appears greatest on the Bowery, one would expect the Black-White differentials in anomie to be greatest in the Bowery sample.

Using the Srole scale [6] as a measure of anomie, these hypotheses were tested. In all three samples Blacks were found to be more anomic than Whites. Using a three-level classification of anomie (low, medium, and high), the proportion of Blacks in the high-anomie category was 59 percent on the Bowery, 45 percent at Camp LaGuardia, and 42 percent in Park Slope. The corresponding figures for Whites were 36, 27, and 30 percent. In the skid row samples the relation between race and anomie was statistically significant (at the .01 level for Bowery men and at the .07 level for Camp LaGuardia men). Not only are Blacks more anomic than Whites, but, as expected, the Black-White discrepancy was greatest among Bowery men. Thus, interracial differentials in aspiration and achievement are associated with interracial differences in anomie as measured by an attitude scale.

DISAFFILIATION AND THE DISCREPANCY BETWEEN ASPIRATION AND ACHIEVEMENT

About half the respondents reported specific occupational aspirations that could be assigned status scores, and this section is based upon those cases only. This population was dichotomized with respect to the discrepancy between the status of each man's specific occupational aspiration and the highest occupational status he ever held. This measure, the aspiration-achievement discrepancy, is hereafter abbreviated AAD.

High discrepancy was defined as 20 or more points on the Duncan Socioeconomic Index. According to the theory of anomie, men with high AADs should be more retreatist, that is, less affiliated, than men with low AADs. The 20-point definition divided the three low-income samples into high AAD and low AAD segments of approximately equal size. However, among the Park Avenue respondents only 8 percent of the men had AADs of 20 or more, making intra-sample comparisons meaningless. Accordingly, the following discussion pertains only to the three low-income samples. Comparisons of their affiliative patterns does not support the hypothesis. Within each sample the differences in affiliation between the high and low AAD segments were small or inconsistent (see Table 9-7). For example, the AAD is not related to whether a respondent is currently employed, has seen family members (apart from those in his household) during the past year, attends church regularly, or belongs to an informal group. Low-AAD men are no more likely than high-AAD men to belong to voluntary organization, to have close friends in New York, or to know the names of their neighbors. In fact, in the Bowery sample it is the men with high AADs who are more likely to have close friends in the city; 51 percent of them claim one such friend, compared to only 37 percent of the low-AAD men. The skid row samples reveal no differences between men with high and low AADs in number of conversations on the day previous to the interview, although Park Slope men with low AADs seem to talk with more people than men with high AADs. If one assumes that the men with high AADs desire more social interaction than they maintain—that they have retreated but regret their loneliness—then the finding that twice as many of the high-AAD respondents expressed a desire to get

Table 9-7

VARIOUS MEASURES OF CURRENT AFFILIATION BY DISCREPANCY BETWEEN ASPIRATION AND ACHIEVEMENT (AAD) (IN PERCENTAGES)

	AAD					
	Bowery		Camp LaGuardia		Park Slope	
	High	Low	High	Low	High	Low
Measures of Affiliation	(20+)	(0-19)	(20+)	(0-19)	(20+)	(0-19)
Currently employed	40	39	—	—	76	77
Saw family member within past year	42	35	18	20	73	70
Attends church at least twice a month	22	29	27	32	37	42
Belongs to informal group[a]	33	33	41	44	27	43
Has organizational affiliation(s)[b]	29	21	23	19	59	69
Has close friend(s) in New York City	51	37	27	24	55	54
Knows names of more than 5 neighbors	56	44	61	59	50	51
Would like to know more neighbors	24	29	31	26	47	22
Would join a neighborhood organization	77	77	44	56	78	61
Conversed with 7+ people yesterday	50	42	48	48	<u>37</u>	<u>63</u>
Lowest N[c]	52	55	41	55	34	32

Underscoring denotes differences significant at the .05 level.

a. Men responding affirmatively to the question, Are there certain men you often hang around with? were considered as belonging to an informal group.

b. Refers primarily to voluntary organizations.

c. Number of cases varies slightly due to incomplete information.

to know more of their neighbors may be seen as providing support for the hypothesis. However, a more valid interpretation might be that a true retreatist does not want to know his neighbors, and hence the finding that high-AAD respondents would like to know more of their neighbors is a further refutation of the hypothesis.

A more general evaluation of the findings is in order. There are ten current-affiliation variables in Table 9-7. Considering all three samples, and excluding current employment for the Camp LaGuardia sample, there are 29 relationships. In only one of these is the intra-sample differences between the high and low AAD categories significant at the .05 level, and only 12 of the 29 relationships were even in the expected direction. These findings are evidence that to the extent that disaffiliation reflects retreatism, the discrepancy between occupational aspiration and achievement is not related to retreat.

EFFECTS OF STATUS LOSS

Although a discrepancy between aspirations and achievements (AAD) is not closely associated with retreatism in our samples, we should point out that we measured the discrepancy between aspiration and achievement in a manner that minimized it. The AAD was calculated by subtracting the highest occupational status *ever* achieved by the respondent from the status of the occupation to which he aspired. In most cases, the respondent's employment at the time of the interview did not represent the highest status of his career. The extent of this decline—status loss—was discussed in Chapter 8, on occupational mobility. Briefly, it refers to the number of points of decline between one's highest occupational status and his current or last status.

If discrepancy between aspiration and achievement is a factor leading to retreatism, downward mobility ought to have a similar effect. Consequently, it seemed essential to pay attention to the discrepancy between a man's highest occupational status and his current or last status, in addition to the discrepancy between aspiration and achievement.

A single measure of status deprivation was computed by adding together each respondent's scores for AAD and status loss. It was hypothesized that status deprivation would be greater among skid row men than among Park Slope respondents, but no significant differences were found among the samples. About one-half of the respondents in each sample had histories of high (40 points or more) status deprivation. To our surprise there were *no* important differences with respect to affiliation between men with high and low status deprivation, although there are sizable intersample differences in extent of current affiliation. To cite two examples. men with high status deprivation were no less likely than men with little status deprivation to have interacted with one of more members of their families in the past year; and in the Camp LaGuardia and Park Slope samples, men with high status discrepancy were more, not less likely, to attend church regularly.

Of course, most of these findings are based on old men's responses about their aspirations during youth. Retrospective data like these are always suspect. Even if the men had perfect memories, the question asked was intentionally phrased so that some might respond in terms of hopes and dreams, while others replied more literally.

We conclude that if anomie is conceptualized as the disparity between occupational achievements and aspirations, it is not related to disaffiliation; skid row men—who do not differ from other low-income men in the discrepancy between aspiration and achievement—do differ in the extent of their affiliations. Accordingly, the theory of anomie does not seem to explain the disaffiliation of skid row men.

NOTES

1. Robert K. Merton, *Social Theory and Social Structure* (New York: The Free Press, 1957), p. 162.
2. *Ibid.,* p. 146.
3. *Ibid.,* p. 153.
4. High occupational status was arbitrarily defined as an occupation with a score of 50 or more points on the Duncan Socioeconomic Index. See Albert J. Reiss, Jr., ed., *Occupations and Social Status* (New York: The Free Press, 1961), pp. 263-275.
5. Success was defined as the respondent's achieving, even for a brief time, that objective identified as what he wanted to be in life.
6. Leo Srole, "Social Integration and Certain Corollaries: An Exploratory Study," *American Sociological Review,* 21 (December 1956), pp. 709-716. Srole's items have been modified somewhat since their original publication. The present study used the version of the scale described in Ephraim Harold Mizruchi, *Success and Opportunity* (New York: The Free Press, 1964), p. 162.

CHAPTER 10

RELIGIOUS EXPERIENCE *

Our examination of the relation between aging, church attendance, and affiliation in voluntary associations is based on our respondent's retrospective account of church attendance throughout their lives. We are principally concerned with two questions: (1) How do the lifetime patterns of church attendance of skid row men differ from those of the men in the control samples, and (2) how does the relation between church attendance and other forms of affiliation vary with age?

We noted earlier that between 80 and 90 percent of skid row men list themselves as either Catholic or Protestant, with Catholics outnumbering Protestants. Of the Bowery men 53 percent were Catholics and 37 percent were Protestants. The proportions in Park Slope were almost the same (55 percent and 32 percent respectively). However, in the Park Avenue sample the order of religious preference was Jewish, Protestant, and Catholic (48 percent, 36 percent, and 10 percent, respectively).

The Park Avenue sample had the lowest level of church (including synagogue) attendance at the time of the interview. Only 22 percent claimed to attend religious services regularly or often, compared to almost twice that proportion in Park Slope (39 percent). The skid row samples fall in between, with one-fourth of the Bowery men and 31 percent of the Camp LaGuardia men reporting regular attendance.

The discussion of religious affiliation which follows is concerned only with the extent of church attendance and religious participation and does not take into account qualitative denominational differences. However, most of the time we shall be concerned with intersample differences in lifetime profiles of religious participation—with trends rather than absolute differences—and so the disparity in denominational composition between the upper-income sample and the other samples should not matter too much.

* Part of this chapter is adapted from Howard M. Bahr, "Aging and Religious Disaffiliation," *Social Forces,* 49 (September 1970), pp. 59-71, with the permission of the University of North Carolina Press.

AGE AND CHURCH ATTENDANCE

Most studies of age and religious attendance have been cross-sectional.[1] A few researchers have used retrospective data from questions comparing present attendance with a reference point in the past, either a specified number of years earlier or a specified younger age.[2]

Research on the relation between age and church attendance may be interpreted with reference to four distinct models, which we designate at the traditional model, the stability model, the family-cycle model, and the disengagement model (see Table 10-1). Each of them is described below.

According to the traditional model there is a sharp decline in religious activity between the ages of 18 and 30, and the lowest level in the life cycle is reached between 30 and 35. Beyond age 35 there is a steady increase in religious activity until old age. This model is supported by the research of Fichter, Cauter and Downham, Mauss, Glock, and others.[3]

The lifetime stability model of church attendance assumes that aging and church attendance are not related. Some evidence for this is found in cross-sectional data from several national surveys and in a survey of Detroit.[4] In attempting to interpret the findings of lifetime stability, Laserwitz suggested that "perhaps church attendance is based upon patterns established fairly early in life and subject to little (if any) change with aging." [5] The stability model receives further support from an examination of American studies of participation in formal associations by Wilensky. He reviewed the variations in religious participation by age as reported in thirteen studies and found that "church membership and attendance, while they may or may not increase slightly in the middle years, do not drop off until after 70 or 75." [6]

The family-cycle model assumes that stages of the family life cycle are related to religious activity. Albrecht's analysis of church attendance [7] among 404 families in the "Bible Belt" supports this model, and Lazerwitz reports that it fits the church attendance of Protestants elsewhere. He describes the pattern as follows:

Table 10-1

SUMMARY OF PATTERNS OF AGING AND CHURCH ATTENDANCE FROM SELECTED RESEARCH STUDIES

Source	Sample			Model Supported
	Type[a]	Size	Characteristics	
Cavan *et al.* (1949)	X	1258	Adults aged 60 and over	Stability[b]
Fichter (1952; 1954)	X	8363	White Catholics aged 10 and over in 3 urban parishes	Traditional[b]
Catholic Digest (1953)	X	–	Adults, national sample	Stability
Hunter and Maurice (1953)	R	151	Adults aged 65 and over, Grand Rapids, Michigan	Disengagement
Cauter and Downham (1954)	X	1200	Adult residents of Derby, England	Traditional
McCann (1955)	R	606	Adults aged 65 and over, Long Beach, California	Disengagement
Catholic Charities of St. Louis (1955)	R	437	Catholics aged 60 and over, largely women	Disengagement
Albrecht (1958)	X	404[c]	Parents in 7 Alabama counties	Family-cycle
collected 1967)	X	959	Adult Mormons in Salt Lake City	Traditional

Table 10-1 (Continued)

Barron (1958, 1961)	R	1206	Adults aged 60 and over, national sample, mostly men	Disengagement
Orbach (1961)	X	6911	Adults in Detroit	Stability[b]
Lazerwitz (1961)	X	7312	Adults in 3 national samples	Stability Family-cycle[d]
Catholic Digest (1966)	X	–	Adults, national sample	Stability
Glock, Ringer, and Babbie (1967)	X	765	Adults, national sample of Episcopalians	Traditional[b]
Mauss (unpublished, collected 1967)	X	959	Adult Mormons in Salt Lake City	Traditional

a. R = retrospective, X = cross-sectional; studies classified as retrospective used a question of the order, Do you attend services more or less often than when you were fifty?

b. The published findings include evidence that the pattern held for men and women considered separately.

c. The sample consisted of parents in 404 families.

d. Protestants only.

> After marriage, regularity of church attendance rises, and it peaks for Protestants having children five years old or over. Apparently, when children are old enough to be sent to Sunday School, their parents tend to stay for religious services. With children no longer in the home, regularity of attendance drops.[8]

The fourth model, progressive disengagement, is linked to the disengagement theory of aging; the basic idea is that normal aging involves a progressive reduction of social ties. This process is conceived as normal and healthy. Aging is described as "an inevitable mutual withdrawal or disengagement" resulting in decreased interaction between the aging person and other members of his social systems.[9] Applied to church attendance, the disengagement model leads us to expect decreasing attendance after middle age. Research findings which support this model have been summarized by Maves and, more recently, by Riley and Foner, who conclude that "the evidence, though slight, suggests that more individuals decrease than increase their attendance as they reach old age." [10]

The four models of the relationship between aging and church attendance are sketched in Figure 10-1. Observe that there is no incongruity between the family-cycle model and the disengagement model; the latter merely applies to the ages beyond 50, while the family-cycle model covers the entire span of adult life. However, note that while research supporting the family-cycle model also supports the disengagement model, research supporting the disengagement model does not necessarily support the family-cycle model.

Measurement of church affiliation. Our information on church attendance was based on a sequence of questions. The first was, Has there ever been a time, from your childhood until now, when you went to church regularly—say, almost every week? Persons responding negatively were asked, Could you give me a general idea about how much you have attended church throughout your life? Those who answered in the affirmative were asked, How old were you when you first began to go that often? How long did that last? Was there another time after that when you went almost every week? The questioning continued until the respondent had reported all episodes of regular attendance and specified their duration.

In the present analysis church attendance was treated as a dichoto-

Figure 10-1.

FOUR MODELS OF THE RELATIONSHIP BETWEEN AGING AND CHURCH ATTENDANCE

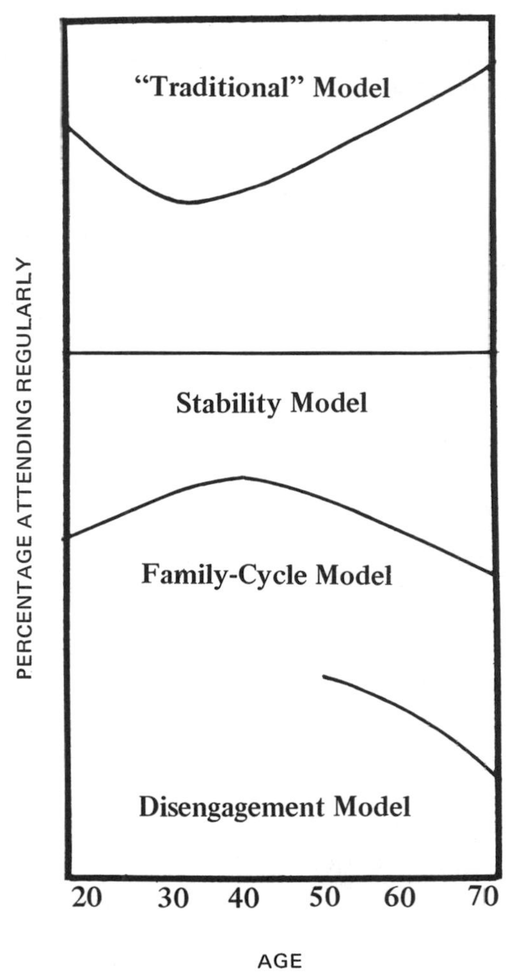

mous variable, with regular attenders (including those who attend often as well as regularly) distinguished from those who attended sporadically or not at all. Other profiles were prepared showing the extent of church membership and activity for each year of life.

Church attendance profiles for the four samples appear in Figure 10-2. The level of regular church attendance for the four samples varies from between 35 and 50 percent at age 20 to between 20 and 40 percent at age 65. In general, the highest rates of regular attendance are reported by the Park Slope sample, and the lowest by the Park Avenue sample. The Bowery and Camp LaGuardia samples are not persistently distinctive in their profiles. Throughout most of adult life, their attendance trends seem to parallel those of control samples.

The congruence of the lifetime profiles with each of the four models may be determined by comparing Figures 10-1 and 10-2. The traditional model is not supported by any of these profiles. There is no evidence in any of the noninstitutionalized samples, low-income or high-income, that church attendance increases with age. In the Camp LaGuardia sample there is a slight increase between ages 50 and 65, but this is probably explained by the convenience of chapel services at Camp LaGuardia.

The stability model receives some support from the two skid row samples. Between ages 25 and 65 the proportion of regular church attenders at Camp LaGuardia varies between 40 and 34 percent, and for Bowery men, between 40 and 30 percent. But even for these samples, the profile can be divided into two distinct phases, a steady decline (ages 20 to 35 for Camp LaGuardia men and 20 to 45 for Bowery men), followed by fluctuation in both directions. Church attendance patterns in the control samples definitely do not support the stability model. For the high-income men there is a decline until age 40, then an apparent increase until a peak at age 50, and beyond that a gradual decline. The Park Slope profile shows a continual decline throughout life.

The family-cycle model is not clearly supported by any of the profiles. The least congruent is the Park Slope profile in which there is no sign of the change in church attendance that might be expected to accompany socialization of children. The Bowery and Camp LaGuardia samples do not provide much evidence either way because

Figure 10-2.

PERCENTAGE OF RESPONDENTS REPORTING REGULAR* CHURCH ATTENDANCE, BY RETROSPECTIVE AGE

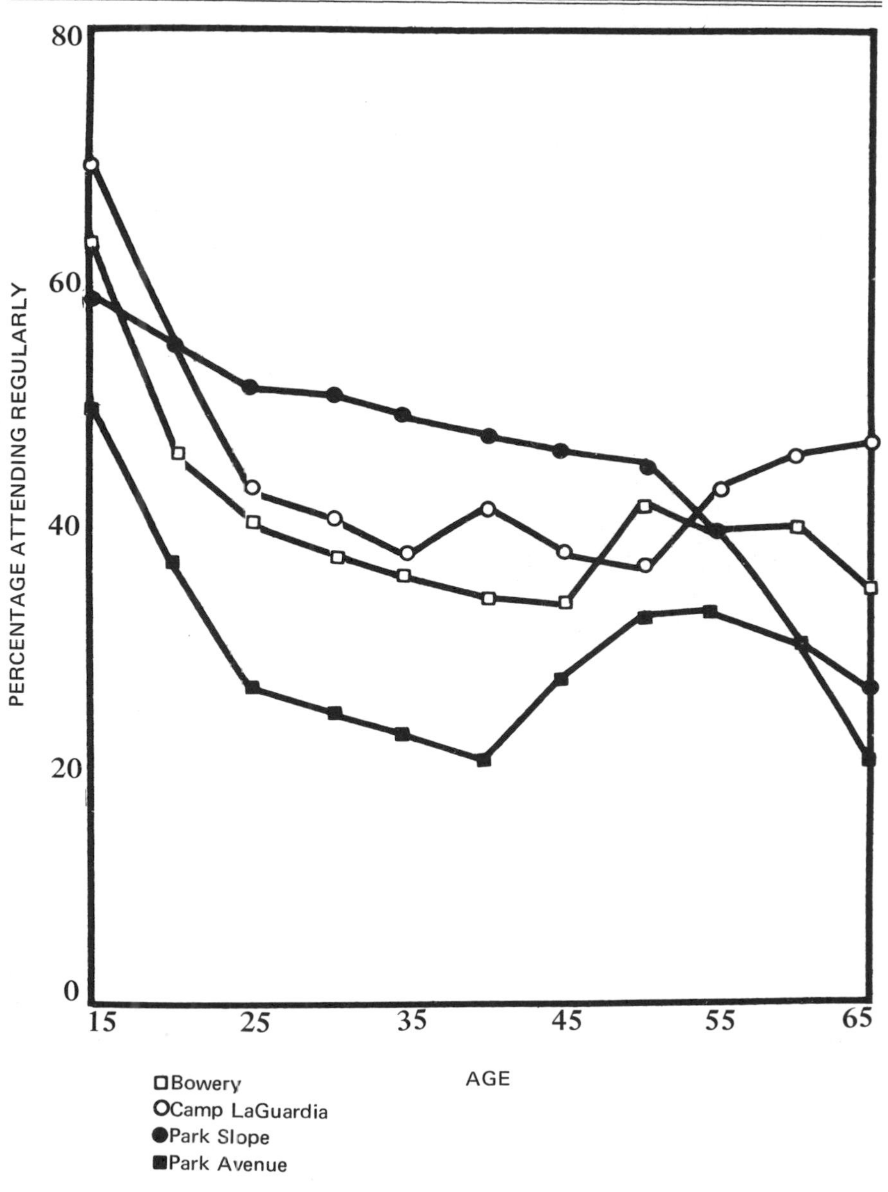

*Men who reported that they often attended are included.

of the high proportion of men with atypical marital histories or no marital histories.

The disengagement model receives the greatest support. Profiles for all except the Camp LaGuardia sample manifest decreasing attendance between ages 50 and 65. A possible reason for the unexpected slight increase in church attendance among aged men at Camp LaGuardia was noted in the discussion of the traditional model.

The early years of the profiles in Figure 10-2 may be biased by the presence of the younger respondents who are not represented in the later years of the profiles. This possibility was examined by dividing the samples into a younger category of respondents (under 50) and an older category (50 and over). For each category the proportion of respondents attending church regularly was computed for five-year intervals between ages 20 and 45 (see Table 10-2).

With one exception (in Park Slope) there were substantial differences

Table 10-2

PERCENTAGE REPORTING REGULAR CHURCH ATTENDANCE FOR YOUNGER (UNDER 50) AND OLDER (50 AND OVER) RESPONDENTS[a]

Sample	Respondent's Age at Interview	Age 20	25	30	35	40	45
Bowery	Under 50	35	32	31	30	24	8
	50 and over	51	44	39	38	36	36
Camp La Guardia	Under 50	47	23	20	14	17	12
	50 and over	52	44	42	39	42	37
Park Slope	Under 50	45	45	48	44	46	47
	50 and over	59	53	47	47	44	42
Park Avenue	Under 50	32	16	16	11	5	8
	50 and over	36	35	33	32	27	32

a. Men who reported that they often attended are included.

between the younger and older men in extent of church attendance during the twenty-five year period: the younger men were much less likely to attend regularly. However, the developmental pattern was similar for both age groups; only the level of attendance differed. The usual patterns are a continued decline, or a decline combined with stability during early middle age. There is no evidence of an upswing in attendance late in life. In fact, comparison of attendance rates in Table 10-2 with the profiles in Figure 10-2 reveals that the apparent increase in church attendance between ages 40 and 50 for the Bowery and Park Avenue samples can be explained by the progressive loss of the younger respondents with their lower levels of attendance. For the older skid row respondents the bulk of the decline in regular attendance occurs before age 30, followed by a period of relative stability or slow decline that continues throughout life. The older men in the Park Slope and Park Avenue samples show a marked decline in attendance after the age of 50.

Thus application of a gross, dichotomous age control reveals that the age of the respondent at the time of the interview has a biasing effect on the profiles and that the direction of that bias is to increase artificially the rates of attendance for the later years. Stated differently, the profiles in Figure 10-2 tend to understate the degree of disaffiliation; the extent of decline in church attendance with age is somewhat greater than it appears.

The differences in church attendance between younger and older respondents may reflect a historical decline of religious activity in America, or it may indicate that the older men in the samples had different cultural origins than the younger men. The latter hypothesis has already received some support with respect to skid row men, and it seems probable that the same kind of differential recruitment may explain the age-linked differences in religious activity on Park Avenue. The supposition that American society has experienced a long-term decline in church attendance which is reflected in current disparities between age groups in extent of regular attendance is supported by some studies of attitudes toward organized religion, but is called into question by at least one national survey showing that patterns of church attendance by age did not change much between 1952 and 1966.[11]

CHURCH ATTENDANCE, VOLUNTARY AFFILIATION, AND AGING

Analysis of the relation between religious affiliation and other types of voluntary affiliation leads us to the unexpected finding that for "normal" (Park Slope and Park Avenue) respondents the salience of religion seems to decline with age. The decline occurs not only in the high-income sample with its continuing increase in proportion of respondents having voluntary affiliations, but also in the low-income sample. The decline in the salience of religious affiliation may be illustrated by computing for each age interval the proportion of respondents with at least one voluntary affiliation who maintain an active religious affiliation (see Table 10-3). At age 20 over 90 percent of the respondents in the Park Slope sample who have at least one voluntary affiliation of any kind maintain regular church attendance; at age 65, barely half of them do so. The corresponding figures for the Park Avenue sample are 54 percent at age 20, and 24 percent at age 65.

Table 10-3

PERCENTAGE OF RESPONDENTS WITH ONE OR MORE VOLUNTARY AFFILIATIONS (INCLUDING CHURCH) REPORTING REGULAR CHURCH ATTENDANCE AT VARIOUS RETROSPECTIVE AGES[a]

	Age										
Sample	15	20	25	30	35	40	45	50	55	60	65
Bowery	84	80	75	69	69	63	61	69	66	74	75
Camp La Guardia	91	89	75	76	77	75	74	77	86	91	95
Park Slope	89	91	84	76	73	68	69	68	59	47	53
Park Avenue	71	54	52	42	39	34	37	38	37	32	24

a. Men who reported that they often attended are included.

It is clear that in both the low- and high-income samples participation in organized religion becomes less salient with age. For the skid row men the pattern is somewhat different. The salience of church attendance decreases or remains stable until age 45, after which it increases. In other words, among skid row men a church tie is frequently the only voluntary affiliation that is maintained into later life. At age 65 over 70 percent of the Bowery men who maintain any voluntary affiliations at all are regular church attenders. For Camp LaGuardia men the corresponding figure is over 90 percent.

Skid row men belong to few organizations, but when they do maintain a voluntary affiliation, there is a high probability that it will be a church affiliation. Apparently ties to a church are easier to maintain than ties with most other kinds of organizations, given the multiproblem condition of most skid row men. Or skid row men may find the church ties the most difficult to let go. In any case, it seems clear that for many skid row men the church is their last formal link with the wider society.

CROSS-SECTIONAL VERSUS RETROSPECTIVE DATA

Researchers who use cross-sectional data to make generalizations about the relationship between aging and church attendance sometimes assume that the age-linked variations in current church attendance are congruent with the patterns of church attendance and aging that would appear in longitudinal or life-history data. As a test of the validity of this assumption, figures on current church attendance and age were prepared by dividing the samples into age categories and computing the proportion of men in each category who reported regular church attendance (cross-sectional data). These proportions appear in Table 10-4. In the same table, for comparison, are figures representing the proportion of regular attenders at each age, based on a summary across the individual life-history profiles (retrospective data).

The discrepancies are sizeable; in three of the four samples, use of cross-sectional data rather than retrospective data leads to the selection of a different model as the best fit. Thus, among Bowery respondents the retrospective data seem to suggest the stability pattern, while the cross-sectional data seem to support a somewhat tardy ver-

Table 10-4

RETROSPECTIVE VERSUS CROSS-SECTIONAL DATA: PERCENTAGE OF RESPONDENTS REPORTING REGULAR CHURCH ATTENDANCE, BY AGE[a]

Sample	Type of Data	Age[b]			
		Under 40	40-49	50-59	60-69
Bowery	Retrospective	35	31	33	30
	Cross-sectional	12	15	38	30
Camp LaGuardia	Retrospective	36	35	38	39
	Cross-sectional	14	9	28	41
Park Slope	Retrospective	46	44	33	23
	Cross-sectional	43	41	50	32
Park Avenue	Retrospective	24	28	30	20
	Cross-sectional	19	5	38	21

a. Men who reported that they often attended are included.

b. Retrospective data are based on reported attendance at age 35, 45, 55, and 65.

sion of the family-cycle pattern, with a sharp increase in attendance between the ages of 35 and 55, followed by a slight decline thereafter. For the Camp LaGuardia respondents the pattern obtained from the cross-sectional data supports the traditional model. There is a sharp increase in attendance after a low point at age 45. In contrast, the retrospective data suggest stability; there is a slight increase in attendance, but not enough to justify accepting the traditional model.

On the basis of the retrospective data, the experience of the Park Slope sample strongly supports the disengagement model. But the cross-sectional data manifest a substantial increase in attendance after age 45 and a peak at age 55, followed by a decline. For the Park Avenue sample, the retrospective data show a slight increase in regular attendance between ages 35 and 55. followed by a decline; the cross-sectional data, on the other hand, show a decline in attendance between ages 35 and 45, followed by a sizeable increase to a high point at age 55, then a decline. Observe that except in the Camp LaGuardia sample, the cross-sectional data support the notion of a late-adulthood cycle in church attendance, with sizeable increases between ages 45 and 55 and declining attendance thereafter. Clearly, the relationship between aging and church attendance apparent in cross-sectional data is not necessarily congruent with the patterns that appear in retrospective data obtained from the same respondents.

These observed incongruities between profiles based on cross-sectional data and those based on retrospective data have two important implications for research. First, increased research attention should be devoted to longitudinal and retrospective studies of membership and participation in various types of voluntary association. Second, there is a need for regional or national studies of the relationship between current and previous patterns of participation in church and other associations. The present study is limited to small samples of males in one metropolitan area; the need for wider studies is obvious.

The burden of the present analysis is that little confidence can be placed in the extant generalizations about aging and church attendance until extensive retrospective or longitudinal research reveals the degree to which variations now attributed to aging are merely reflections of age-specific patterns of current attendance without direct counterpart in the personal histories of older respondents. Developmental patterns must be distinguished from variations due to societal change, and the different effects of change upon specific subcultures need to be identified.

"GUIDING PRINCIPLES" AND "MOST IMPORTANT THINGS"

In a paper on "Preferences for Moral Norms in Three Problem Areas" Robert C. Angell introduced two measures of religiosity in addition to church attendance, based on these questions: "What do you feel are the most important things in life?" and "Do you have any guiding principle in life? What is it?" [12] We incorporated these questions in our interview. The responses permit us to tap dimensions of religiosity besides church attendance.

The responses to the question about guiding principles were

Table 10-5

PERCENTAGE OF RESPONDENTS MENTIONING SELECTED GUIDING PRINCIPLES AND MOST IMPORTANT THINGS IN LIFE[a]

	Bowery	Camp LaGuardia	Park Slope	Park Avenue
Guiding Principles				
None	36	51	31	11
Formal religious statements	16	10	12	3
Humanistic concerns, general good will	23	25	28	45
Other	26	15	31	42
N	192	194	116	100
Most Important Things				
Basic necessities, survival	26	17	9	6
Health	25	34	33	30
Job, occupational success	18	21	16	14
Happiness, peace of mind, self respect	17	24	27	38
Money	17	14	22	10
Family	13	12	20	26
Religious prescriptions, God's will	4	6	5	3
Drink	4	1	—	—
N	191	189	118	100

a. Columns total more than 100 percent because multiple responses were allowed.

grouped into four categories: (1) men who reported *no* guiding principles, (2) those who identified some aspect of formal worship or organized religion, (3) those who did not make direct reference to symbols of formal religion but exhibited a positive concern for others, and (4) a residual category consisting of men who mentioned a guiding principle not directly tied to religious symbols or concern for others. The distribution of respondents among these four categories, given in Table 10-5, reveals that poor men are less likely to claim a guiding principle than rich men. There were more than three times as many men with no guiding principles in the low-income samples as on Park Avenue. Note that in this case the skid row men are like the Park Slope respondents, but different from the Park Avenue sample.

The Park Avenue respondents were the least likely to respond in statements denoting direct religious symbolism or ritual, but they were more "religious" than men in the other samples in the frequency of responses suggesting concern for others. Almost half (45 percent) of the Park Avenue sample might be said to have a religious-humanistic outlook, compared to about one-fourth of the low-income samples. Again, the important point is that the skid row men do not differ from the Park Slope respondents in these matters, but all three low-income samples differ from the Park Avenue men. Needless to say, these differences are as likely to be explained by differences of ethnic and religious composition between the Park Avenue sample and the three other samples as by the income factor alone.

Table 10-5 also contains the distribution of responses to the question on the most important things in life. Responses definitely containing symbols of religion were infrequent in all samples; the incidence of such statements ranged from 3 percent in the Park Avenue sample to 6 percent in the Camp LaGuardia sample. Responses with definite religious content are illustrated by the following:

"Take Christ as your personal savior [Bowery]."

"Life of Christ, clean living, helping others [Bowery]."

"Will power, strength to overcome weakness, and my belief in God [Camp LaGuardia]."

"Honesty and faith in good qualities of character [Camp LaGuardia]."

> "Health, serving God, faith in God [Park Slope]."

> "The belief in the Bible [Park Slope]."

> "Religion and honesty; a godly and honest life [Park Avenue]."

> "You've got to have religion or the belief in God even if you don't go to church [Park Avenue]."

Let us digress briefly to comment about some of the other findings on most important things. First, statements about health as one of the most important things in life were as common among Park Avenue men as among skid row men. In fact, the range among all four samples in proportion of men mentioning health was very narrow, from 25 percent on the Bowery to 34 percent at Camp LaGuardia. Another topic on which the four samples agreed was the importance of employment (the frequency of mention ranged from 14 percent among Park Avenue men to 21 percent among Camp LaGuardia men).

Interesting differences in statements about most important things are also apparent in Table 10-5. For example, concern about basic necessities, or survival seems to vary inversely with the economic status and settled conditions of the sample. Thus, over one-fourth of the Bowery men gave a response that included some reference to getting by, for example:

> "A place to sleep, something to eat, happiness, health."

> "A place to sleep, to eat, clothes, money. If you have money, you can get everything."

> "Waking up in the morning, knowing you're alive. Put in a day's work so you can eat and sleep."

But at Camp LaGuardia, where food, clothing, and a place to sleep are taken for granted, only one-sixth of the men mentioned them among the most important things in life. In the Park Slope sample 9 percent mentioned the basic necessities, and on Park Avenue, only 6 percent.

Family was mentioned as one of the most important things in life about twice as often in the Park Slope and Park Avenue samples as among skid row men. Similarly, self-respect and peace of mind were more frequently mentioned by the control sample respondents, although the differences between the Camp LaGuardia men and the Park Slope men were not significant. There were two types of responses which were not given by the control samples at all; none of them included alcohol among the most important things in life, but 4 percent of the Bowery men did so. The other type of response heard only from skid row men—and that only rarely—was a denial that anything is important, for example: "I'm ready to die any week; there's nothing to live for."

NOTES

1. An innovative attempt to supplement the static views drawn from cross-sectional studies of voluntary associations is the recent work of Babchuk and Booth, who consider membership in church-related organizations but not church attendance per se; Nicholas Babchuk and A. Booth, "Voluntary Association Membership: A Longitudinal Analysis," *American Sociological Review,* 34 (February 1969), pp. 31-45.

2. Milton L. Barron, *The Aging American: An Introduction to Social Gerontology and Geriatrics* (New York: Thomas Y. Crowell, 1961); C. W. McCann, *Long Beach Senior Citizens' Survey* (Long Beach, Calif.: Community Welfare Council, 1955); W. W. Hunter and H. Maurice, *Older People Tell Their Story* (Ann Arbor: Institute for Human Adjustment, Division of Gerontology, Univ. of Michigan, 1953).

3. Joseph H. Fichter, "The Profile of Catholic Religious Life," American Journal of Sociology, 58 (September 1953), pp. 145-150; *Social Relations in the Urban Parish* (Chicago: Univ. of Chicago Press, 1954), p. 91; T. Cauter and J. S. Downham, *The Communication of Ideas* (London: Chatto & Windus, 1954); Charles Y. Glock, B. B. Ringer, and E. R. Babbie, *To Comfort and Challenge* (Berkeley: Univ. of California Press, 1967), pp. 38-59; Armand Mauss, unpublished table from the project "Mormonism and Urbanism," a project of the Research Program in Religion and Society, directed by Charles Y. Glock, Survey Research Center, University of California, Berkeley.

4. "How Important Religion is to Americans," *Catholic Digest,* 17 (February 1953), pp. 7-12; "Do Americans Go to Church?," *Catholic*

Digest, 33 (July 1966), pp. 24-32; Ruth S. Cavan, Ernest W. Burgess, R. J. Havighurst, and H. Goldhamer, *Personal Adjustment in Old Age* (Chicago: Science Research Associates, 1949); H. Orbach, "Aging and Religion: Church Attendance in the Detroit Metropolitan Area," *Geriatrics,* 16 (October 1961), pp. 530-540; Bernard Lazerwitz, "Some Factors Associated with Variations in Church Attendance," *Social Forces* 39 (May 1961), pp. 301-309.

5. Bernard Lazerwitz, "Religion and Social Structure in the United States," *Religion, Culture, and Society,* ed. Louis Schneider (New York: John Wiley & Sons, 1964), pp. 426-439.

6. Harold L. Wilensky, "Life Cycle, Work Situation, and Participation in Formal Associations," in *Aging and Leisure,* ed. Robert W. Kleemeier (New York: Oxford Univ. Press, 1961), pp. 213-242.

7. R. E. Albrecht, "The Meaning of Religion to Older People—The Social Aspect," in *Organized Religion and the Older Person,* ed. Delton L. Scudder (Gainesville: Univ. of Florida Press, 1958), pp. 53-70.

8. Lazerwitz, "Religion and Social Structure in the United States," p. 432.

9. Elaine Cumming and W. E. Henry, *Growing Old* (New York: Basic Books, 1961), p. 14.

10. P. B. Maves, "Aging, Religion, and the Church," in *Handbook of Social Gerontology,* ed. Clark Tibbetts (Chicago: Univ. of Chicago Press, 1960), pp. 698-749; Matilda White Riley and A. Foner, *Aging and Society, Volume 1: An Inventory of Research Findings* (New York: Russell Sage Foundation, 1968), pp. 489-490.

11. R. K. Young, D. S. Dustin, and W. H. Holtzman, "Change in Attitude Toward Religion in a Southern University," *Psychological Reports,* 18 (February 1966), pp. 39-46; "How Important Religion is to Americans," *Catholic Digest,* 17 (February 1953), pp. 7-12; "Do Americans Go to Church?" *Catholic Digest,* (July 1966), pp. 24-32.

12. Robert C. Angell, "Preferences for Moral Norms in Three Problem Areas," *American Journal of Sociology,* 67 (May 1962) pp. 650-660.

CHAPTER 11

PARTICIPATION IN VOLUNTARY ASSOCIATIONS *

Sociologists often assume that participation in organizations other than economic and family institutions is good for the individual and for society. Nisbet refers to "organizations of the middle range" which provide protection against political enslavement by the state, and Rose maintained that voluntary associations support democracy by distributing power widely and providing mechanisms for change.[1] There is evidence that persons with voluntary affiliations are more involved in political activity, have more positive attitudes toward their life situations, and are less likely to show anomie than the unaffiliated.[2]

In earlier chapters we discussed the attenuation of the family ties of skid row men and their disadvantaged position with respect to employment. In the light of the relative weakness of their family and occupational ties, the voluntary affiliations of skid row men take on added significance. Conceivably, their involvement in voluntary associations could substitute for the family and employment ties they lack.

This chapter will include (1) a comparison of the four samples regarding current and past involvement in voluntary associations, including youth organizations, (2) intersample comparisons of patterns of lifetime affiliation in voluntary associations, and (3) discussion of age-linked affiliation trends in specific types of voluntary associations.

Most of the data on voluntary affiliations come from two sections of the questionnaire. First, there was a question about voluntary participation in adult life: Let me list a few kinds of organizations. Thinking of the time since you left school, I want to know if you have ever been a member or if you've ever had anything to do with them, even if you weren't a member. There followed a list of types of associations, including church groups, clubs, lodges, veterans'

* Part of this chapter is adapted from Howard M. Bahr, "Aging and Religious Disaffiliation," *Social Forces,* 49 (September 1970), pp. 59-71, with the permission of the University of North Carolina Press.

groups, unions, ball teams, bowling leagues, political organizations or action groups, music or other hobby groups, and community and neighborhood organizations. For each organization identified as relevant to a man's life history, there was an adult-organization chart containing questions about the name of the organization, whether the respondent's name was on the membership roster, when he joined or began taking part, how long and how often he participated, and whether he had any special positions or duties.

Then there was a question about youth organizations, followed by specific probes: As a boy or a teenager, were you ever a member, or did you ever take part in: clubs or extracurricular activities in school, organized athletic teams, Boy Scouts, YMCA, a gang, political clubs or action groups, 4-H clubs or other outdoor or handicraft groups, Boy's Club, or church groups or clubs? As with adult affiliations, for each type of organization receiving a positive response, there was a youth-organization chart containing questions about nature and duration of participation. Late in the interview schedule, there was the specific question, Have you ever gone to meetings of Alcoholics Anonymous? When a respondent said yes, the interviewers were instructed to fill out an adult-organization chart.

The term *voluntary affiliation* thus refers to a residual category containing all types of affiliation except work and family ties. A respondent's total affiliative network was conceived as the sum of his familial, occupational, and voluntary memberships.

CURRENT AND PAST VOLUNTARY AFFILIATIONS

Voluntary affiliations are important in the lives of Bowery men. Nearly one-fourth of them reported at least one such affiliation at the time of the interview, and almost four-fifths had belonged to at least one voluntary association as an adult (see Table 11-1). However, the Bowery men had far fewer voluntary affiliations than men in the control samples. Twenty-three percent of the Bowery men had at least one affiliation, compared to 52 percent of the Park Slope men and 63 percent of the Park Avenue men. The mean number of current affiliations was 0.3 for Bowery men, 0.2 for Camp LaGuardia men, 0.6 for Park Slope men, and 2.1 for Park Avenue men. Twenty-two percent of the Park Avenue men had four or more current

Table 11-1

NUMBER OF CURRENT AND PAST VOLUNTARY AFFILIATIONS (IN PERCENTAGES)

	Bowery	Camp LaGuardia	Park Slope	Park Avenue
Number of current affiliations				
0	77	83	48	37
1	16	16	43	18
2	4	2	7	16
3	2	—	2	8
4	—	—	—	7
5+	—	—	—	15
Totals	99	101	100	101
N	202	199	122	103
Mean	0.3	0.2	0.6	2.1
Number of adult affiliations				
0	21	24	25	11
1	29	29	35	11
2	22	22	19	16
3	11	14	10	11
4	9	7	5	14
5+	6	4	6	39
Totals	98	100	100	102
N	202	198	124	103
Mean	1.8	1.7	1.6	5.2
Number of voluntary affiliations during youth				
0	46	47	58	26
1	18	23	19	17
2	17	14	8	17
3	8	7	7	8
4	3	7	4	10
5+	7	3	4	22
Totals	99	101	100	100
N	200	198	122	103
Mean	1.3	1.1	.9	2.6

affiliations; none of the Camp LaGuardia or Park Slope men, and only one of the Bowery men, had that many.

Although the Bowery men are currently less affiliated than the Park Slope men, they have not always been so. When we added up the number of associations to which each man had belonged as an adult, the Bowery sample had a larger total than the Park Slope sample. The mean number of adult affiliations was 1.8 for Bowery men, 1.6 for Park Slope men, and 5.2 for Park Avenue men.

Of course this simple count of voluntary affiliations does not reflect the duration or intensity of participation. A Bowery man might have belonged to several associations at various times and yet have very few affiliation man-years. The duration of affiliation is, however, reflected in the lifetime affiliation profiles discussed below.

Inspection of voluntary affiliations during youth revealed that the Bowery men had been somewhat more affiliated than the Park Slope men, while the Park Avenue men had been much more affiliated than either. Thus, at the time of the interview the Bowery and Camp LaGuardia men were less affiliated than either the Park Slope or Park Avenue samples, but in the affiliative histories they were comparable to the Park Slope men. The sharp difference in affiliation is not between homeless and settled men, but between low-income and high-income men.

LIFETIME AFFILIATION PROFILES

Previous studies of the relationship between aging and voluntary participation have revealed a distinct pattern: low affiliation in the early adult years, increasing affiliation during the middle years, and declining affiliation in the fifties and sixties. Wilensky describes the pattern as follows:

> Where studies lump *all* formal organizations together—church, church-related, and labor unions as well as other more voluntary associations—the proportions reporting two or more memberships appear to be lowest among young people under 30. The membership peak is among those 30 to 44. There is a slight decline in subsequent years which becomes definite after 60 or so. Meeting attendance shows a similar curve.[3]

Bell and Force found that part of their sample showed a different pattern: among high-status respondents the number of memberships did not decrease with age, even in the sixties and seventies. For persons of lower status, however, their findings are consistent with the description above.[4]

Summary profiles showing by age the proportion of respondents maintaining one or more voluntary affiliations were prepared and are presented in Figure 11-1. Similar profiles showing the mean number of voluntary affiliations maintained at various ages were prepared and are discussed below.

The Park Slope profile in Figure 11-1 shows a lifetime pattern of affiliation that approximates the rise-then-fall life cycle previously mentioned. In contrast, the Bowery and Camp LaGuardia men had not experienced any increase in voluntary affiliations during their middle years, but following middle age they show a clear decline of affiliation that parallels the Park Slope profile.

The Park Avenue profile shows the expected low affiliation in the early adult years, but thereafter, a trend toward increasing affiliation, which accelerates after age 40. These respondents reported their highest level of voluntary affiliations at age 65, the most advanced age for which information was charted. Thus, the present findings support the work of previous investigators who reported that among persons of high economic status voluntary affiliations may increase throughout life.

When we measured the mean number of voluntary affiliations, rather than the proportion of respondents having at least one affiliation, the pattern was much the same. All the low-income samples showed declines in the mean number of association membership after age 45, but Park Slope men at age 65 maintained approximately the same number of voluntary affiliations as Bowery men in the prime of life. The peak for Park Avenue men occurs at age 65, when they average 2.7 affiliations. At that age the mean number of affiliations for Park Slope men is 0.7, and for the Bowery men it is 0.5.

AFFILIATION BY TYPE OF ASSOCIATION

We may now ask which kinds of voluntary association contributed most to the differences in total affiliation. The various types of youth

Figure 11-1.

PERCENTAGE OF RESPONDENTS AFFILIATED WITH VOLUNTARY ASSOCIATIONS, BY RETROSPECTIVE AGE

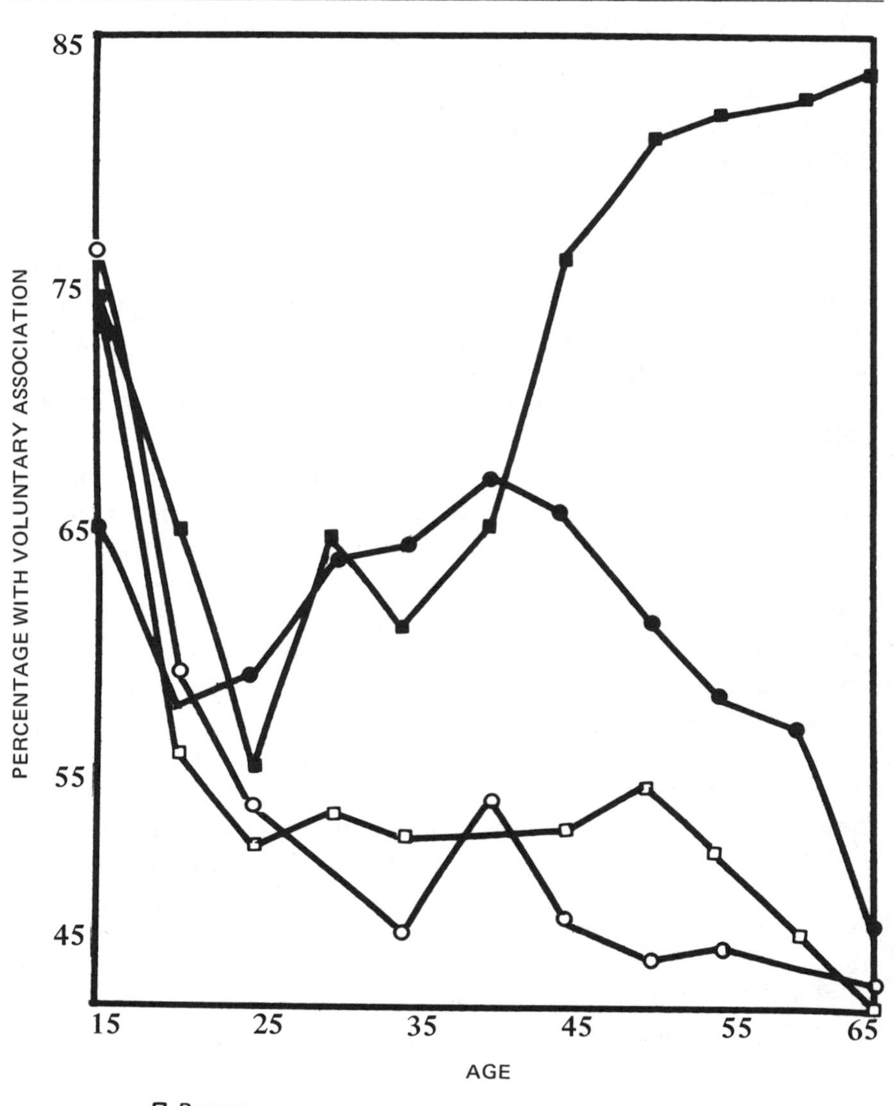

organizations identified by the respondents were divided into six categories: (1) school teams, clubs, and extracurricular groups; (2) Boy Scouts, 4-H, and YMCA; (3) neighborhood gangs: (4) political clubs or action groups; (5) church groups; and (6) other youth organizations. For each sample we computed the mean number of affiliations in each of these six categories. Only one significant intersample difference appeared: the Park Avenue men had belonged to from three to six times as many school teams and extracurricular groups as had men in the lower-income samples. Their mean number of such affiliations was 1.8, compared to 0.3 for Park Slope men, 0.4 for Camp LaGuardia men, and 0.6 for Bowery men. For the other five types of youth organization, the number of affiliations reported by Park Avenue men was comparable to that reported by other respondents.

For adult affiliations the contrasts in mean number of memberships by type of organization were sharper. But, as in the youth organizations, the main differences were between the low-income and high-income samples. The range among the three low-income samples in mean number of adult affiliations by type of organization varied from between 0.0 and 0.1 for hobby groups to between 0.5 (Camp LaGuardia) and 0.7 (Park Slope) for labor unions and professional organizations. The mean number of union or professional association memberships held by the Park Avenue men in adult life was 0.9, compared to 0.7 for Park Slope and 0.6 for Bowery men. For every other type of voluntary affiliation in adult life, the mean number of memberships reported by the Park Avenue men was from two to ten times higher than the number reported by the low-income respondents.

Numerically, the most important type of voluntary association for the low-income respondents was the labor union, followed by lodges and recreational associations. For the Park Avenue sample the same three types of association ranked highest, but more memberships were reported in recreational associations (a mean of 1.3) than in labor unions (0.9) or lodges (0.9).

The same general results were obtained when we controlled for age by preparing lifetime profiles for specific type of affiliation. For unions and professional associations the differences were small but consistent: beyond age 35 the Park Avenue men maintained a mean of between 0.4 and 0.5, the rate for the Park Slope men varied between 0.3 and 0.4, and that for Bowery men ranged between 0.1 and 0.2. Very little political affiliation was reported, but the Park Avenue men were higher than the other samples in this respect, with an annual mean of about 0.1. The most striking differences—and these were very large—were in the profiles showing lifetime membership rates in recreational associations, including fellowship, music, hobby, and other recreational groups. The Bowery and Park Slope samples demonstrated relative stability throughout adult life, although a slight downward trend was evident in the later years; the mean number of recreational organizational memberships ranged between 0.2 and 0.3 during the age 30 to age 40 decade, and thereafter fluctuated between 0.1 and 0.2. In contrast, the mean number of such affiliations for Park Avenue men increased from 0.6 at age 25 to 1.5 at age 50, then dropped off slightly for a decade before reaching a peak of 1.6 at age 65. From age 45 on, the mean number of recreational affiliations reported by the Park Avenue men is between 9 and 12 times higher than those reported by the Park Slope or the Bowery men. It is plain that with respect to lifetime patterns of voluntary affiliation, the striking differences are between poor and rich men rather than between homeless and settled men.

REFLECTIONS ON CONTRASTS IN PARTICIPATION PROFILES

Intersample variations in lifetime patterns of family, job, and voluntary affiliation have now been described. Let us pause briefly and review some the implications of these findings for understanding the disaffiliation of skid row men.

At the end of adolescence all the samples showed sharp declines in family affiliation, lesser declines in affiliation with voluntary associations, and increasing employment. These are signs of the attenuation of ties to families of orientation and the concomitant assumption of adult occupational roles.

In the control samples, the losses of affiliation associated with the transition from youth to adulthood had run their course by age 25. By that age many of the respondents had formed new family ties so that the percentage of respondents living in families stabilized and showed little change until middle age. By age 25 almost all of the men in the control samples were employed, and even Park Slope men maintained a high level of employment throughout the middle years. Clearly the attenuation of ties to parents and siblings was balanced by new ties to wives and children, and the loss of youthful affiliations was followed by the acquisition of adult affiliations. In the Park Avenue sample these affiliations continue to increase until after age 65; among Park Slope men family, employment, and associational ties begin to erode at age 40 or 45. Thus, their profiles show three major phases corresponding to youth, adulthood, and old age.

However, when the affiliation profiles of skid row men are examined, the adult phase is missing or vestigial. For example, with respect to family affiliation the decline begun at the end of adolescence continues through life, and the attenuation of ties to parents and siblings is not compensated by the formation of ties to wives and children. With respect to employment the skid row profiles show the beginning of the adult phase, but only for a short time. As a group, skid row men never achieve the stability of employment that characterizes the control samples. Shortly after they have assumed their first occupational ties, they begin losing them, and the attenuation continues throughout life. Similarly the skid row pattern reveals the shucking off of voluntary affiliations related to home and school without the acquisition of enough new affiliations to reverse the downward trend.

It is as if the skid row men had gotten trapped in the "attrition of affiliation" phase that marks the end of adolescence. They lose family ties but do not establish new ones; they begin occupational careers but abandon them; they leave voluntary associations and do not join others. Their affiliation profiles are like those of settled adolescents and old men, without the intervening adult phase.

Skid row men have high morbidity and mortality rates; they are old before their time. Our review of their participation in voluntary associations suggests that in affiliation patterns, as in physical health, they are prematurely aged.

In all of the affiliation profiles, whether referring to family affiliation, employment, membership in voluntary association, or occupational status, the relative positions of the samples are the same, with skid row men at the bottom and Park Avenue men at the top. Furthermore, the general trends during adult life are the same regardless of the subject of the profile. High-income men gain affiliations throughout life; skid row men lose them; and poor men in settled neighborhoods gain affiliations and then lose them again.

The operation of what Robert Merton has called the Matthew Effect[5]—"to them that have shall be given"—is apparent in the affiliation profiles. The Park Avenue men start with an advantage and increase it; the older they get, the more affiliations they have. The Bowery men begin adult life with relatively few affiliations and lose them as they go along. The Park Slope men acquire affiliations as adults, but begin to lose them as they approach old age.

NOTES

1. Robert A. Nisbet, *The Quest for Community* (New York: Oxford Univ. Press, 1963); Arnold M. Rose, *Theory and Method in the Social Sciences* (Minneapolis: Univ. of Minnesota Press, 1954).

2. See, for example, William Erbe, "Social Involvement and Political Activity: A Replication and Elaboration," *American Sociological Review,* 29 (April 1964), pp. 198-215; Scott Greer and Peter Orleans, "The Mass Society and the Parapolitical Structure," *American Sociological Review,* 27 (August 1962), pp. 634-646; Herbert Maccoby, "The Differential Political Activity of Participants in a Voluntary Association," *American Sociological Review,* 23 (October 1958), pp. 524-532; and Arnold M. Rose, "Attitudinal Correlates of Social Participation," *Social Forces,* 37 (March 1959), pp. 202-206.

3. Harold L. Wilensky, "Life Cycle, Work Situation, and Participation in Formal Associations," in *Aging and Leisure,* ed. Robert W. Kleemeier (New York: Oxford Univ. Press, 1961), p. 218.

4. Wendell Bell and Maryanne Force, "Urban Neighborhood Types and Participation in Formal Associations," *American Sociological Review,* 21 (February 1956), p. 32; Nicholas Babchuk and A. Booth, "Voluntary Association Membership: A Longitudinal Analysis," *American Sociological Review,* 34 (February 1969), p. 35.

5. Robert K. Merton, "The Matthew Effect in Science," *Science,* 159 (January 5, 1968), pp. 56-63.

CHAPTER 12

SOCIALIZATION INTO SKID ROW *

How does one become part of the deviant world of skid row? Let us begin with the assumption that the fundamental process of socialization into a stable, deviant community is not very different from the process of socialization into a normal community. There is, in both cases, a sequence of "progressively increasing commitments to conventional norms and institutions." [1]

THE SOCIALIZATION PROCESS

Skid row may be described as a community of stigmatized persons. Stigmas are discrediting visible attributes on the basis of which a wide range of other imperfections are imputed to an individual. Often blemishes of individual character, such as weak will and dishonesty, are associated with the word stigma. Some stigmatized persons sustain a community life, or at least a distinctive subculture. Goffman describes urban milieus having a nucleus of service institutions which provide a territorial base for "shamed groups," such as homosexuals and alcoholics. A skid row is such a milieu. Persons having particular stigmas form recruitment bases for these ecologically consolidated communities; [2] on skid row, alcoholics or heavy drinkers form one such base.

Residence on skid row is a stigma. The skid row man lives among others who share his predicament, and may use his disadvantage as a basis for his life organization, but "he must resign himself to a half-world to do so." In this half-world he may develop a myth of how he came to be stigmatized, explaining that although he is here, he does not belong here.[3]

There is a tendency for a stigma to spread from the stigmatized individual to his close connections. As a result, "such relations tend

* Portions of this chapter are adapted from Howard M. Bahr, "Drinking, Interaction, and Identification: Notes on Socialization into Skid Row," *Journal of Health and Social Behavior,* 8 (December 1967), pp. 272-285, and used by permission of the American Sociological Association.

either to be avoided or to be terminated, where existing." [4] Thus the skid row man, whose only deviance may be his address, is likely to have character defects ascribed by outsiders. Consequently his social world outside of skid row shrinks, and his skid row identity comes to dominate his life.

It should be emphasized that many skid row men are isolates long before they arrive on skid row; their social relations may have attenuated to nothing in other settings. Presumably such men do not experience a sense of social withdrawal when they move to skid row. But the newcomer to skid row who still has social ties with the outside is likely to find these ties strained by the stigma of a skid row identity.

As the skid row man's normal social relations contract, he has the choice of becoming an isolate or associating with his own. Skid row men usually acquire their stigmatized selves late in life, and the uneasiness they feel about their new associates is often paralleled by an uneasiness about their old, more conventional associates. His ambivalence about attachment to a stigmatized category may lead the skid row man to oscillate toward and away from identification with skid row. Goffman states that the relation between the stigmatized individual and his peers depends, in part, on the extent to which he can find a new "we" among others like himself, that is, whether he finds himself part of a well-organized community with long-standing traditions.[5] Those who live on skid row but don't conform to its stereotypical drinking patterns are in a way "double deviants," estranged from the skid row culture with its emphasis on primary drinking groups, as well as from the normal community.

Socialization always requires the abandonment of old relationships as well as the development of new ones. Accompanying changes in the type of one's involvements are changes in self-image as recognition of oneself as a member of the new subculture gradually develops.[6] In the following pages we shall label the gradually developing awareness that one belongs to a given subculture as *identification;* active involvement in a subculture we shall call *interaction.*

Those who conform to expected modes of behavior may find support and satisfaction in a subculture, and those who do not conform are likely to feel isolated. One of the dominant patterns of the skid row subculture is heavy drinking. In fact, Wallace goes so far as to identify the drunk as the only fully acculturated member of the skid row subculture and the status of drunk as the essential core of the subculture.[7] This being so, we would expect that the heavy drinker on skid row derives more support and satisfaction from the subculture than the man who does not drink heavily—that the heavy drinker is more likely to feel that skid row is home and that nice people live there. This expectation seems to be borne out. Abstainers, light drinkers, and moderate drinkers on skid row often express negative attitudes toward heavy drinkers. Bogue reported that more than one-third of the men he interviewed said they disliked living on skid row because of the drunkenness and heavy drinking:

> This dislike by persons who are not chronic alcoholics for those who are probably is as intense as any racial or ethnic prejudice in the city . . . roughly one-half of Skid Row's residents are forced by simple poverty . . . to live among a group of people it dislikes, fears and avoids. . . . They resent the low social status that their Skid Row address gives them because of its connotations of alcoholism.[8]

One of the best-established principles of social interaction is that an increase of interaction between peers increases their liking for one another.[9] If interaction and positive sentiments vary together, then identification with a deviant subculture should be related positively to the amount of interaction an individual sustains with members of that subculture. Group solidarity is the product of sentiments generated by interaction.

Interaction also seems to be associated with conformity. Hopkins cites several studies of small groups which lend support to the notion that interaction has "more or less subtle" socializing effects so that the more one interacts with others in his group, the more he conforms to the group.[10]

Other things being equal, an individual's identification with a subculture should vary with the length of time he has been exposed to it. If nothing else, as the amount of time he has invested increases, his commitment increases. But exposure is only one factor affecting commitment; the nature of the participation is more important.

When a man arrives on skid row, he may already have values and attitudes which adapt him for skid row life. Participation in drinking groups is one of the major forms of sociable activity on skid row.[11] Abstainers and light drinkers are less likely to participate in these groups and hence may be socialized less readily than the heavy drinkers. Stated differently, newcomers to skid row whose drinking does not conform to the skid row pattern should be less likely to accept a skid row identity than men already accustomed to skid row drinking patterns.

To the extent that the skid row man retains the standards of normal society, he will reject his skid row peers or regard them ambivalently. It has been suggested that social distance between an individual and one or more strangers varies inversely with the relative prestige of the stranger's group.[12] The nonconformist (light-drinking or abstaining) newcomer to skid row is likely to put considerable social distance between himself and the strangers he encounters there because he perceives them as members of a low-status group. The nonconformist newcomer is likely to spend much of his time away from skid row and to avoid interaction with skid row men beyond a superficial level.

However, continued exposure to the skid row way of life may result in gradual socialization; even if he maintains his nonconformity with respect to drinking, long residence on skid row may bring about a gradual change in his self-image until he identifies with the area and accepts his neighbors. As the stigma of skid row residence spreads to the man's other social relations, skid row life may come to seem more attractive.

On the basis of the foregoing reflections, we formulated seven hypotheses. We expected that a skid row man's identification with skid row should (1) vary inversely with the extent of his interaction with people off skid row, that it would vary directly with (2) his conformity to skid row drinking patterns, (3) his interaction with other skid row men, and (4) the length of time he has spent on skid row. Also we expected that a skid row man's interaction with other skid row men would (5) vary directly with his conformity to skid row drinking patterns, and (6) vary inversely with the extent of his interaction with people off skid row. Finally, we expected that his conformity to skid row drinking patterns would (7) vary inversely with the degree of his isolation.

EVIDENCE FROM AN EXPLORATORY STUDY

The test of these seven hypotheses drew upon data collected in one of the exploratory studies prior to the major survey of the Bowery and Camp LaGuardia in 1966. In fact, the instrument used in the major survey did not include the direct measures of identification with the Bowery used in the exploratory study. Consequently our discussion of socialization and identification with skid row is based upon the earlier study; the sample consisted of 92 men selected randomly from the guest registers of four Bowery lodging houses.[13] Interviews were conducted by Patricia Nash in the fall of 1964.

Variables. The hypotheses of the exploratory study were based on six variables: identification with skid row, conformity to skid row drinking patterns, interaction with other skid row men, length of time on skid row, interaction with "normals," and alienation.

Identification with the Bowery area was measured by responses to four questions: (1) Is this your home? (2) What kinds of people live here (friendly, grouchy)? (3) Are the other fellows here about the same kind of fellow as you are? and (4) How many people in this house would you call good friends? The sample was almost evenly divided on the first question, with 53 percent of the men answering affirmatively. A majority (59 percent) reported that their neighbors were friendly. A majority (60 percent)said that they felt other Bowery dwellers were like themselves, and about the same proportion (64 percent) said they had at least one good friend in the lodging house where they were staying. On all these questions, positive responses (people here are friendly, this is home, I am like others here, I have good friends here) are assumed to denote greater identification with skid row than noncommittal or negative responses.

As an indication of conformity to skid row drinking patterns we used only one item, the respondent's perception of the extent of his drinking. Each man was asked whether he was a teetotaler, a light drinker, went on drinking sprees, drank daily, or got drunk daily. The first two categories are considered as not conforming to the stereotyped Bowery drinking pattern, while the last three are viewed as conforming. By these standards, 48 men (15 spree drinkers, 17 who were drunk daily, and 16 who drank daily) were classed as conformists and 38 (12 teetotalers and 26 light drinkers) as nonconformists.

Four questions were asked concerning aspects of a respondent's interaction with his Bowery peers: (1) About how many fellows who live in this area (the Bowery) but who are not now staying at this lodging house did you have a conversation with yesterday? (2) Do friends who don't live in this lodging come and spend time here with you? (3) Do you visit friends in other lodging houses? (4) Do you ever do anything outside of the Bowery with people from the Bowery? Seventy-one percent reported participating in at least one conversation with a fellow lodger during the previous day, and a similar proportion, 68 percent, said they had conversed with someone living in the Bowery but not in their lodging house. Only 24 percent reported that friends visited them in their lodging houses, and an even smaller number stated that they visited friends in other lodging houses. Most Bowery men (75 percent) do not participate in off-Bowery activities with people from the Bowery.

The duration of Bowery experience—hereafter labeled "exposure"—was obtained by the question, How much time have you spent on the Bowery? Forty-nine percent of the sample had been on the Bowery nine years or less. For convenience we shall refer to these men as newcomers, and to men who had been on the Bowery ten years or more as oldtimers.

To indicate interaction with people off the Bowery, we used responses to the question, How often do you leave the Bowery to work, visit friends or relatives? We reasoned that men who leave to work or visit are maintaining some ties with the outside, and that the strength of these ties is likely to vary with the frequency of interaction with the persons involved. Forty-four percent of the sample reported that they leave the Bowery daily to work or visit friends or relatives. These men are considered more closely identified with normal society than men who leave the Bowery less often.

To indicate perceived alienation from other people, we used the question, Who, would you say, takes a personal interest in you? Responses were dichotomized. If the respondent said that one or more persons took an interest in him (a relative, friend, fellow lodger, lodging house clerk or owner, bartender, boss), he was given a low-alienation classification. Only those respondents who answered "no one" or whose answers indicated themselves or nonhuman subjects (my money, God) were considered alienated. By these standards, 45 percent of the sample were alienated.

On the basis of their responses to four of the interaction questions, we divided the sample into three types of men: isolates, interactors, and intermediates. *Isolates* are men who reported that they talked to no one in the Bowery (outside their lodging house) on the previous day, said that they neither visit friends at their lodging houses nor receive friends, and do not leave the Bowery in the company of other Bowery men. *Interactors,* on the other hand, not only *did* talk with other Bowery men on the previous day, but also reported that they engage in active socializing with skid row men, either visiting men in other lodging houses, being visited, or going off the Bowery with companions from the Bowery. Of the 92 respondents, 28 were classified as interactors and 21 as isolates.

Each of the four indicators of identification with Bowery subculture was divided into categories of high identification and low identification, and the same procedure was followed with the variables extent of drinking, interaction, interaction with normals, alienation, and exposure. The several indicators of interaction and identification were treated as separate variables. The degree of association among the variables was measured by Goodman and Kruskal's *gamma* computed without controls (Table 12-1) and controlling for exposure and extent of drinking.[14]

For two of the variables, interaction and identification, there were multiple indicators, that is, four questions were assumed to measure aspects of identification with the Bowery, and five referred to dimensions of interaction with other skid row men. Before proceeding to a discussion of the tests of the hypotheses, we examine the interrelations among the indicators of each of these variables.

Interrelations among the indicators. Measures of association (gamma) among the several indicators of identification and interaction are presented in Table 12-1. For the identification variables the gammas range from .25 to .72. Gammas among the interaction variables are likewise positive, ranging from .06 to .88.

Two contrasting assumptions can be made about the interrelations among the several indicators of each of these variables. First, the relatively low correlations among the indicators of identification (or interaction) may reflect variations in validity, that is, some of them

Table 12-1

MEASURES OF ASSOCIATION (GAMMA) AMONG VARIABLES RELATED TO SOCIALIZATION INTO SKID ROW SUBCULTURE, FOR 92 BOWERY MEN

	Identification					Interaction							
	1	2	3	4	5	6	7	8	9	10	11	12	13
1 Drinking	..	—.28	.68**	.57**	.01	.29	.41	.32	.19	.48*	.51**	—.30	.20
Identification													
2 Is Bowery home?	..	...	.28	.50**	.28	.17	.08	.06	—.13	—.03	—.42*	—.31	.60**
3 Favorable evaluation of neighbors	..	...	...	.72**	.25	.19	—.02	.27	—.01	.48	—.58**	—.64**	.00
4 Similarity to neighbors	..	...	...	...	.34	.20	.38	.41	—.40	.67**	—.63**	.06	.40
5 Presence of friends	..	...	...	...	...	.75**	.30	.36	.35	.54*	—.07	—.53**	—.19
Interaction													
6 Lodging house conversations	..	...	...	...	...	...	.56**	.29	.06	.46	—.31	—.62**	—.26
7 Bowery conversations	..	...	...	...	...	...	...	.45	.44	.32	—.66**	—.49**	—.02
8 Visited by Bowery friends	..	...	...	...	...	...	...	...	.88**	.80**	—.20	—.24	.00
9 Visits Bowery friends	..	...	...	...	...	...	...	...	...	.67**	—.36	—.25	.22
10 Goes off Bowery with Bowery men	..	...	...	...	...	...	...	...	...	...	—.32	—.32	.00

Table 12-1 (Continued)

	Identification					Interaction							
	1	2	3	4	5	6	7	8	9	10	11	12	13
11 Interaction with normals	.	...	...	...	...	...	...	...	...	...	...	.27	−.43*
12 Alienation	..	...	...	...	...	...	...	...	...	...	...	...	.23
13 Exposure	..	...	...	...	...	...	...	...	...	...	...	...	...

* Denotes significance at the .10 level.

** Denotes significance at the .05 level.

are better measures of the underlying variable of identification with the Bowery than others. Under this assumption it can be argued that the indicator that correlates most highly with all the other measures of identification is in fact the best indicator. The same argument can be applied to the interaction variables: they are more or less valid in reflecting interaction in general, and the one most highly associated with all the others is the most accurate indicator of interaction. If we accept this assumption, we need only test the propositions and corollaries using the best measures of identification and interaction.

There is an alternative position, however: interaction and identification are complex, many-faceted variables, and differences among the indicators not only reflect inadequacies in the indicators but also suggest that interaction and identification are not all of a piece. With this assumption we are led to test the hypotheses separately for each indicator.

For the reader wishing to evaluate the hypotheses on the basis of a best indicator, we note that the best indicator of identification is similarity to neighbors, and the best indicator of interaction is whether friends visit the respondent at his lodging house. The ranking of indicators of identification (that is, the extent to which they are associated with the other identification indicators) in terms of mean gamma among the possible interrelations, computed from the measures of association in Table 12-1, is as follows:

Similarity to neighbors	.52
Evaluation of neighbors	.42
Is Bowery home?	.35
Presence of friends	.29

The corresponding ranking of mean gammas among possible interrelations of interaction indicators is:

Visited by Bowery friends	.60
Goes off Bowery with Bowery men	.56
Visits Bowery friends	.51
Bowery conversation	.44
Lodging house conversations	.34

The correlates of identification with skid row. The findings are presented in the following order. For each hypothesis we first consider Table 12-1, which pertains to the entire sample, without controls. Next, where applicable, we discuss the evidence for the hypothesis after the imposition of controls.[14]

With respect to the predicted inverse relation between identification with the Bowery and interaction with normals (Hypothesis 1), all of the relevant measures of association were in the expected direction. The more frequently one leaves the Bowery to work or visit friends or relatives, the less likely he is to consider the Bowery home, to evaluate other Bowery men favorably, to consider himself similar to them, or to feel that he has good friends in his lodging house. Thus the data support Hypothesis 1.

Adding controls for exposure did not change this result. When we controlled for drinking, however, for heavy drinkers we find an unexpected positive association between interaction with normals and one identification indicator: heavy drinkers who frequently leave the Bowery to work or visit friends were more apt to have good friends in their lodging houses than were the heavy drinkers who seldom leave the area. Also, the predicted inverse relationship between the two variables—feelings of similarity to neighbors, and interaction with normals—was much stronger for indifferent drinkers than for heavy drinkers.

The expected relation between conformity to Bowery drinking patterns and identification with the Bowery (Hypothesis 2) appeared for two of the four indicators of identification—evaluation of neighbors and perceived similarity to other Bowery men. For the other measures of identification the data did not support the hypothesis. Adding controls for exposure made no drastic changes in the negative relation between drinking and identification of the Bowery as home, but there was a difference between newcomers and oldtimers in the relationship between drinking and presence of friends. Without controls gamma was .01, but when we controlled for exposure it became negative (—.27) for oldtimers and positive (.38) for newcomers.

Hypothesis 3 (identification with Bowery life is directly associated with interaction with skid row men) received partial support from our analysis. We will consider each of the four identification variables separately.

Interaction with other Bowery men seemed to have little effect on whether a man considered the Bowery home. When controls for exposure were added, the most striking difference that appeared was that among oldtimers the relation between considering the Bowery home and Bowery conversations was negative, while for newcomers it was positive. Controlling for drinking, we found that among indifferent drinkers interaction and identification of the Bowery as home varied as predicted, but among heavy drinkers all but one of the interaction variables were inversely related to identification of the Bowery as home.

Returning to Table 12-1 and considering the next indicator of identification—evaluation of neighbors—we find that three of the five interaction variables are positively related to the favorableness of one's evaluation of his neighbors. A man's conversing with his fellow lodgers apparently had a positive effect on his evaluation of them, but whether or not he talked to men elsewhere on the Bowery had little effect on his evaluation of his fellow lodgers. It is also of interest that the Bowery man who went to see other Bowery residents at their lodging houses was less likely to evaluate his neighbors favorably than was the man who received visitors. Controlling for exposure revealed that the relation between evaluation of neighbors and interaction was stronger for the oldtimers than for newcomers.

Several changes in the relation between interaction variables and evaluation of neighbors appeared when controls for extent of drinking were added. Among indifferent drinkers only two measures of interaction—lodging house conversations, and leaving the Bowery in the company of other Bowery men—were positively related to favorable evaluations of neighbors; for the other interaction variables—conversations on the Bowery, and being visited by or visiting other Bowery men—the relation was inverse. Among heavy drinkers, on the other hand, both lodging house and Bowery conversations were unrelated to evaluation of neighbors, but being visited and leaving the Bowery in company with other Bowery men were directly related to favorable evaluations of Bowery neighbors.

Except for the variable on visiting Bowery friends, the relationship between interaction indicators and feelings of similarity to Bowery neighbors was as predicted. The interaction variable most highly associated both with evaluation of Bowery neighbors and with feelings of similarity to Bowery men was whether a man was accompanied by Bowery men in off-Bowery activities. The relation between interaction and feelings of similarity to other Bowery men was stronger among newcomers than among oldtimers. Among the latter only two variables—going off the Bowery with Bowery men, and Bowery conversations—were positively related to feelings of similarity, while among newcomers all five interaction variables were positively related to feelings of similarity to Bowery neighbors. Adding controls for drinking revealed sizable differences between heavy drinkers and indifferent drinkers in the relationship of feelings of similarity to neighbors and conversations either in lodging houses or elsewhere in the Bowery (for heavy drinkers, gammas were —.53 and —.14 respectively; for indifferent drinkers, .38 and .74). Thus, heavy drinkers may converse with Bowery men and still not consider themselves to be like other Bowery men; but indifferent drinkers who converse with other Bowery men do view themselves as similar to their neighbors.

All of the interaction variables were associated positively with the final identification variable, presence of good friends in one's lodging house. The relation was found to be stronger among the newcomers than the oldtimers. Among indifferent drinkers the feeling that one has friends in his lodging house was directly related to all five forms of interaction, but for heavy drinkers feeling that one has friends correlated highly with only two interaction variables—lodging house conversations, and leaving the Bowery area with other Bowery men. In other words, among heavy drinkers there may be interaction without friendship or friendship without interaction, but among the indifferent drinkers, those who do not report having friends in the area seem to get by with a minimum of interaction. Also, it may be that the lodging house is less important in the social life of heavy drinkers. Their friends are in the bars, and thus the association between interaction and presence of friends in lodging houses is lower among them than among indifferent drinkers.

With respect to the polar types, interactors consistently identified with the Bowery more than isolates did (see Table 12-2). As compared with the isolates, they were more likely to consider the Bowery home, to evaluate their neighbors favorably, to perceive themselves as similar to their neighbors, and to feel that they had good friends in their lodging house.

Hypothesis 4 predicted that identification with the Bowery was directly related to the length of time one had lived there. Two measures of identification with skid row—whether one considered it

Table 12-2

IDENTIFICATION WITH THE BOWERY, DRINKING, AND INTERACTION WITH NORMALS AMONG 49 RESPONDENTS CLASSIFIED AS INTERACTORS AND ISOLATES

Indicators of Identification, Drinking, and Interaction with Normals	Positive Responses				
	Interactors		Isolates		
	Percentage	N	Percentage	N	Gamma
Indicators of Identification					
Is Bowery home?	57	16	48	10	.19
Favorable evaluation of neighbors	68	17	62	10	.12
Similarity to neighbors	69	18	41	7	.52
Presence of friends	78	21	45	9	.62*
Conformity to skid row drinking patterns	74	20	37	7	.66*
Interaction with normals	21	6	70	14	.79*

* Denotes significance at the .05 level.

home, and whether one thought himself similar to his neighbors—varied directly with length of time on the Bowery; but the other measures of identification were not related to duration of exposure to Bowery subculture. Controlling for drinking status produced the following results: for indifferent drinkers all of the relevant gammas were positive and the hypothesis was supported; for heavy drinkers two variables—evaluation of neighbors, and presence of friends—were inversely related to exposure. In other words, the longer indifferent drinkers remain on the Bowery, the more likely they are to identify with the area. The longer a heavy drinker remains on the Bowery, the more likely he is to consider it home and to perceive himself as similar to other Bowery men, but the less likely he is to evaluate his neighbors favorably or to feel that he has good friends among them.

Conformity and interaction patterns. The predicted direct relationship between interaction and drinking (Hypothesis 5) was supported. In all cases the relevant gammas were positive, ranging from .19 to .48. Adding controls for exposure revealed that the relation was stronger among newcomers than for oldtimers.

According to Hypothesis 6, interaction with skid row men varies inversely with the extent of interaction with people off skid row. The data supported this hypothesis: relevant gammas in Table 12-1 range from —.20 to —.66. When controls are added for exposure, we found that the relation did not appear for two of the interaction variables. The hypothesis also was supported after extent of drinking was taken into account: for indifferent drinkers all of the gammas were in the expected direction, and so were all but one of the gammas for heavy drinkers.

A comparison of Bowery isolates and interactors also supports hypotheses 5 and 6 (see Table 12-2). Interactors were twice as likely as isolates to be heavy drinkers and were much less likely to leave the Bowery daily (21 percent of the interactors leave the Bowery daily but 70 percent of the isolates do so).

The final hypothesis, that conformity to skid row drinking patterns varies inversely with feelings of alienation from other people, was supported (gamma is —.30). Controlling for exposure enhanced the relationship among newcomers and reversed it for the oldtimers: among newcomers indifferent drinkers are much more likely than heavy drinkers to be alienated, but among oldtimers the heavy drinkers are more likely to be alienated.

Summary. Before summarizing the findings, some limitations of the exploratory study should be emphasized. First, we were limited to data from the original interviews which happened to be relevant to the variables we wished to study. The sample was small and was drawn from a universe of approximately 400 men, less than one-tenth of the total population of the Bowery. In addition, the method of analysis was relatively gross: we used dichotomized variables throughout. Therefore, the findings must be considered tentative, and further tests of the hypotheses are in order.

Tests of the hypotheses may be summarized as follows. For the uncontrolled sample, out of a total of 43 predictions, 35 (81 percent) were in the direction predicted. For two of the subsamples, indifferent drinkers and newcomers, higher proportions of correct predictions were obtained: of the 33 predictions which applied to indifferent drinkers, 29 of the observed relationships were in the expected direction; for newcomers, 34 of 39 were as predicted.

Two hypotheses were clearly supported: identification with skid row varies inversely with interaction with normals (Hypothesis 1), and interaction with other skid row men varies directly with the extent of a subject's drinking (Hypothesis 5).

The expected inverse relation between interaction with normals and interaction with Bowery men (Hypothesis 6) held for the sample as a whole and for the subpopulations of oldtimers and indifferent drinkers. For newcomers and heavy drinkers it held for most but not all of the measures of interaction with Bowery men.

The remaining four hypotheses received partial support. The expectation that identification with skid row would vary directly with drinking (Hypothesis 2) held for some indicators of identification but not others. Similarly, the associations between identification with skid row and interaction with skid row men (Hypothesis 3) and between identification with skid row and duration of skid row residence (Hypothesis 4) were supported for some but not all the identification indicators. Finally, the predicted inverse relation between extent of drinking and alienation (Hypothesis 7) was supported for the entire sample and for men who had lived on the Bowery less than ten years, but not for Bowery oldtimers.

Support for the hypotheses was greater among indifferent drinkers and, with the exception of Hypothesis 6, among newcomers. In other words, the hypotheses about socialization into skid row draw their greatest support from reports of behavior of men who are currently in the process of socialization.

The fact that the least support for the hypotheses was obtained for heavy drinkers and oldtimers suggests that the relation between identification and interaction need not be current. It appears that after the socialization process has run its course, continued interaction may not be necessary for identification to persist. For example, the heavy drinker who has lived on skid row for many years may have formerly interacted with other skid row men more than he does now, and his current identification with skid row is partly a result of that interaction. Once socialized, a decline in the extent of his interaction need not be accompanied by a corresponding decline in his identification with skid row.

NOTES

1. Howard S. Becker, *Outsiders: Studies in the Sociology of Deviance* (New York: The Free Press, 1963), pp. 27 and 31.

2. Erving Goffman, *Stigma: Notes on the Management of Spoiled Identity* (Englewood Cliffs: Prentice-Hall, 1963), pp. 3-4, 22-24.

3. *Ibid.*, p. 21.

4. *Ibid.*, p. 30.

5. *Ibid.*, pp. 34-35, 38-39.

6. Theodore Caplow, *Principles of Organization* (New York: Harcourt Brace Jovanovich, 1964), pp. 170-171.

7. Samuel E. Wallace, *Skid Row as a Way of Life* (Totowa, N. J.: The Bedminster Press, 1965), pp. 187-188.

8. Donald J. Bogue, *Skid Row in American Cities* (Chicago: Community and Family Study Center, Univ. of Chicago, 1963), p. 170.

9. See, for example, George C. Homans, *The Human Group* (New York: Harcourt Brace Jovanovich, pp. 111-113; and Caplow, *op. cit.*, pp. 91-97, 105.

10. Terence K. Hopkins, *The Exercise of Influence in Small Groups* (Totowa, N. J.: The Bedminster Press, 1964), pp. 62-65.

11. See, for example, Elmer Bendiner, *The Bowery Man* (New York: Thomas Nelson and Sons, 1961), pp. 91-92; Joan K. Jackson and Ralph G. Connor, "The Skid Road Alcoholic," *Quarterly Journal of Studies on Alcohol,* 14 (September 1953), pp. 468-486; James F. Rooney, "Group Processes Among Skid Row Winos," *Quarterly Journal of Studies on Alcohol,* 22 (September 1961), pp. 444-460.

12. Michael Banton, "Sociology and Race Relations," *Race,* 1 (November 1959), p. 10.

13. The 92 men were a 25 percent sample of residents in four diverse types of lodging house. The houses were selected systematically to maximize variation in certain characteristics (e.g., size, racial composition, and turnover) and to represent the entire range of Bowery lodging houses.

14. Readers wishing to examine the tables showing the effects of controls for exposure and extent of drinking on the relationships given in Table 12-1 are referred to Howard M. Bahr, "Drinking, Interaction, and Identification: Notes on Socialization into Skid Row," *Journal of Health and Social Behavior,* 8 (December 1967), pp. 279-280.

CHAPTER 13

DRINKING PATTERNS *

In the popular imagination, skid row is a center of excessive drinking, and all of its residents are drunks or alcoholics. Like many other stereotypes this one is partly true. Numerous studies have shown that high proportions of skid row men are heavy drinkers, although many skid row men drink moderately or not at all.

In this chapter the drinking habits of Bowery men are described and compared with the drinking habits of men in the control samples. The relationship between drinking and social affiliation is considered at some length, and age at the onset of excessive drinking is identified as an important variable affecting skid row career patterns. Lastly we will discuss the question of who drinks with whom.

CURRENT DRINKING HABITS

Two measures of current drinking habits were obtained. Both derived from respondents' reports about their drinking, but one—the drinking count—was a classification by researchers on the basis of reported frequencies and amounts of alcohol consumption, while the other—the drinking self-rating—was the respondents' current classification of themselves as drinkers. (For Camp LaGuardia men "current" drinking referred to the period immediately preceding their most recent arrival at the camp.)

At the beginning of a series of questions about drinking, respondents were asked, Do you drink the same way all the time, or do you ever go on benders or sprees lasting several days or longer? Men who said they went on sprees were asked about the frequency and duration

* Portions of this chapter are adapted from two previously published papers: Howard M. Bahr, "Lifetime Affiliation Patterns of Early- and Late-Onset Heavy Drinkers on Skid Row," *Quarterly Journal of Studies on Alcohol,* 30 (September 1969), pp. 645-656; and Howard M. Bahr and Stephen J. Langfur, "Social Attachment and Drinking in Skid-Row Life Histories," *Social Problems,* 14 (Spring 1967), pp. 464-472, by permission of the Journal of Studies on Alcohol, Inc., and the Society for the Study of Social Problems.

of their sprees and about the extent of their drinking at other times. Subjects reporting that they were not spree drinkers were questioned about the frequency and extent of their drinking. This information was used in determining the drinking count. After a respondent had described the types of alcoholic beverage he drank and how much and how often he drank them, he provided the drinking rating by tagging himself as a heavy drinker, a moderate drinker, or a light drinker.

No attempt was made to determine how much spree drinkers drank. Because of the uncontrolled nature of spree drinking and the foggy memory associated with long drinking bouts, spree drinkers were automatically classified as heavy drinkers. Men who reported they did not go on sprees were classified as heavy, moderate, or light drinkers according to the following procedures.

Beverages were translated into ounce equivalents of alcohol according to this standard: 1 oz. of beer = 1 oz. equivalent; 1 oz. of wine = 4 oz. equivalents; and 1 oz. of distilled spirits = 10 oz. equivalents. The men reported the extent of their drinking in terms of popular measures of various beverages. The following standards were used in converting these measures to ounces of beverage for subsequent conversion into ounce equivalents of alcohol: 1 cocktail or shot of whiskey = 1.5 oz. of whiskey; 1 glass of whiskey = 2 oz. of whiskey; I glass of wine = 4 oz. of wine; 1 glass of beer = 7 oz. of beer; 1 can or bottle of beer = 12 oz. of beer; 1 fifth (1/5 of a U.S. gallon) of whiskey = 26 oz. of whiskey; and 1 bottle of wine = 16 oz. of wine.

The questions on extent of drinking applied to drinking days only. When respondents reported varying drinking days and beverages, coders averaged quantities. Thus, if a respondent said he drank beer every day, wine several times a week, and whiskey on weekends, he was coded as a daily drinker, and the beverages consumed less frequently were prorated on a daily basis.

Taking both amounts (ounce equivalents of alcohol) and frequencies (daily, several times a week, or less often) of drinking into account, the following criteria were set up. In order to be counted as a heavy drinker, a respondent had to (1) drink 160 ounce equivalents of alcohol or more daily, or (2) drink 240 ounce equivalents several times a week, or (3) drink 320 ounce equivalents on drinking days if he drank less often than several times a week. A respondent was classified as a light drinker if he (1) drank 20 ounce equivalents or less daily, or (2) drank 30 ounce equivalents or less on drinking days several times a week, or (3) drank 60 ounce equivalents or less on drinking days that occurred less frequently than several times a week. The category of moderate drinkers was a residual one including all respondents classified as steady drinkers who did not meet the criteria for inclusion in the heavy or light categories.

More than a third of the Bowery men and almost half of the Camp LaGuardia men were counted as heavy drinkers, compared to only one out of eight Park Slope men and one out of fifty Park Avenue men. Approximately two-thirds of all the heavy drinkers were spree drinkers. It should be remembered that the drinking categories were developed for describing skid row men, and that the moderate-drinking category allows considerable intake of alcohol.

The finding that about one-third of the Bowery men are heavy drinkers is congruent with the results of other skid row surveys (Table 13-1.) One-third of the respondents in the Chicago study and 38 percent of the residents of the Minneapolis skid row were classified as heavy drinkers. The Philadelphia survey did not distinguish between heavy and moderate drinkers; however, 29 percent of the Philadelphia respondents were spree drinkers (compared to 26 percent on the Bowery), and the proportion of nonspree drinkers was precisely the same as among Bowery men (54 percent). Thus, the results of four major skid row surveys agree that something over a third of skid row men are heavy drinkers.

In addition to questions on current drinking, the interview inquired about the nature and extent of previous drinking. Of the Bowery men, 14 percent were not heavy drinkers at the time of the interview, but reported heavy drinking earlier in life. Combining these with current heavy drinkers, precisely half of the Bowery men were or had been heavy drinkers. The proportion in Camp LaGuardia was similar (54 percent). Data from the Chicago study are not exactly comparable, but it is possible to arrive at an approximation. Bogue states that 29 percent of the men classified as teetotalers had formerly been heavy drinkers.[1] If the same proportion applies to the moderate and light drinkers, the total of men who at the time of the Chicago survey were not heavy drinkers but who had drunk heavily in the past would have been 19 percent. Adding this to the 33 percent who were current heavy or spree drinkers at the time of his study yields a total of 52 percent. Thus the Chicago and New York studies support

Table 13-1

EXTENT OF DRINKING IN VARIOUS SKID ROW POPULATIONS[a] (IN PERCENTAGES)

Drinking	Bowery	Camp La Guardia	Phila-delphia	Chicago	Minne-apolis
Heavy	26	32	29		
Heavy nonspree	10	15			
All heavy	36	47		33	38
Moderate	30	26		24	
Light	14	10		28	
Moderate or light	44	36	54[b]	52	34
Abstainers	20	17	17	15	28
Totals	100	100	100	100	100
N	194	196	2213	613	280

a. Sources: for Bowery and Camp LaGuardia, present study; for Philadelphia, Temple Univ. School of Medicine, Department of Psychiatry, *The Men on Skid Row* (Philadelphia: Greater Philadelphia Movement, 1960), percentages and total N adjusted for nonresponses; for Chicago, Donald J. Bogue, *Skid Row in American Cities* (Chicago: Univ. of Chicago, Community and Family Study Center, 1963); For Minneapolis, Theodore Caplow, Keith A. Lovald, and Samuel E. Wallace, *A General Report on the Problem of Relocating the Population of the Lower Loop Redevelopment Area* (Minneapolis: Minneapolis Housing and Redevelopment Authority, 1958).

b. Includes nonspree heavy drinkers.

the generalization that about half of the residents of skid row are or have been heavy drinkers. The Minneapolis and Philadelphia reports do not include information on previous drinking patterns.

More than a fourth of the Bowery and Camp LaGuardia men said they went on sprees or benders, compared to fewer than a tenth of the Park Slope men and none of the Park Avenue men. Of the 111 Bowery and Camp LaGuardia men who were spree drinkers, half said their sprees lasted two weeks or more, and half of these claimed sprees of a month or longer (for spree drinkers at Camp LaGuardia, the question referred to the year before they last came to the camp). By contrast, almost all of the spree drinkers in Park Slope limited their sprees to a week or less.

Thus, many more skid row than Park Slope men go on sprees, and their sprees last much longer. However, in the average number of sprees reported in the past year by spree drinkers, the low-income samples did not differ. Most of the spree drinkers are relatively heavy drinkers even when not on a spree. This was particularly true of Park Slope drinkers, 70 percent of whom drink daily when not on a spree, compared to a sixth of the Bowery spree drinkers.

Congruence of the self-rating and the count. The relation between the two drinking classifications may be seen in Table 13-2. The two classifications are most closely related in the Park Slope and Park Avenue samples (*gammas* are .80 and .78), but the skid row samples also show a fair correspondence between the counts and the self-rating (*gammas* are .64 and .58).

It was expected that the discrepancy between the count and the self-rating would vary directly with the degree to which the behavior was negatively sanctioned. For instance, heavy drinking is more strongly disapproved than moderate drinking, and moderate drinking probably evokes more disapproval than light drinking. Accordingly, light drinkers should be more apt to define their drinking status realistically than moderate drinkers, and moderate drinkers should be more willing to admit they are moderate drinkers than heavy drinkers are willing to admit to their excessive drinking.

The data support this expectation. Table 13-3 shows the proportion of respondents in each of the quantitative drinking categories who rated themselves in the corresponding qualitative self-category. Slightly less than half of the heavy drinkers (by count) on skid row rate themselves as heavy drinkers, and in Park Slope the proportion drops to less than a third. At the other end of the drinking scale, perceptions are more realistic. Almost all of the light drinkers rate themselves as light drinkers.

The apparent influence of the social context on self-perception may also be noted. In a milieu where heavy drinking is common, heavy drinkers are more apt to perceive themselves as heavy drinkers than in an environment where heavy drinking is not the rule. In fact,

Table 13-2

DRINKING COUNTS COMPARED TO SELF-RATINGS, FOR DRINKERS

Drinking Status (Self-Ratings)	Drinking Status (Counts)							
	Bowery				Camp LaGuardia			
	Spree	Heavy	Moderate	Light	Spree	Heavy	Moderate	Light
Heavy Drinkers	23	9	10	—	32	9	5	2
Moderate Drinkers	20	8	27	5	21	14	29	3
Light Drinkers	6	2	20	20	8	5	16	13
Total	49	19	57	25	61	28	50	18
	gamma = .64				gamma = .58			

Drinking Status (Self-Ratings)	Drinking Status (Counts)							
	Park Slope				Park Avenue			
	Spree	Heavy	Moderate	Light	Spree	Heavy	Moderate	Light
Heavy Drinkers	3	2	—	1	—	2	3	—
Moderate Drinkers	6	2	20	1	—	—	35	5
Light Drinkers	1	2	16	28	—	—	26	23
Total	10	6	36	30	—	2	64	28
	gamma = .80				gamma = .78			

Table 13-3

PERCENTAGES OF RESPONDENTS WHOSE DRINKING SELF-RATINGS CORRESPOND TO THEIR DRINKING COUNTS[a]

Drinking Status (Counts)	Percentage of Drinkers Self-Rated Correctly			
	Bowery	Camp LaGuardia	Park Slope	Park Avenue
Heavy or Spree Drinkers	47	46	31	—[b]
Moderate Drinkers	47	58	56	55
Light Drinkers	80	72	93	82

a. Source: Computed from figures in Table 13-2.

b. Two cases only.

the influence of the social context is such that a sizable proportion of skid row men perceive themselves to be heavier drinkers than their reported consumption warrants. By way of contrast, Park Slope men almost never perceive their drinking to be heavier than it is, and the majority of the Park Avenue men who perceived themselves as light drinkers were moderate drinkers by count.

In all the samples, men who said they are heavy drinkers probably speak truly and men whose drinking is actually light generally rate themselves as light drinkers. On the other hand, in the skid row samples about two-thirds of the men who say they are light drinkers probably are not, and even in Park Slope only 60 percent of the men who claim to be light drinkers would be so classified by our drinking count. Finally, in all the samples, a majority of the men whom we would count as heavy drinkers do not so rate themselves.

DRINKING AND AFFILIATION

Until about twenty years ago sociological research on alcoholism was based, for the most part, on interviews with homeless men, jail inmates, and other drinkers of low socioeconomic status. This research resulted in a stereotype of the alcoholic as a person whose experience in school, job, family, and recreation have left him with few stable ties to other persons.[2] According to this view, the heavy drinker was apt to be "undersocialized," with a life history "characterized by limited participation in the primary groups which are necessary for personality formation, by minimum participation in social activities, and by inadequate opportunities for sharing experiences with others." [3]

More recent studies have shown that heavy drinkers of higher status do not differ appreciably from their social-class peers in affiliative behavior. Bailey has asserted that "the more recent quantitative studies have effectively destroyed the oversimple characterization of alcoholics as a marginal, undersocialized and relatively homogeneous group of derelicts and chronic offenders." [4]

At present the two contradictory images of the heavy drinker continue to appear in the research literature; he is either undersocialized, and his drinking is presumed to be largely a result of this condition; or he is, or has been, normally affiliated, and the causes of his drinking are sought elsewhere than in his affiliative history.

In a pilot study conducted prior to the main wave of interviewing on the Bowery, we attempted a preliminary comparison of the life histories of heavy drinkers with those of moderate drinkers and abstainers in a sample drawn from Bowery lodging houses. We were thus reexamining the same type of population on which the original association between undersocialization and alcoholism had been based; more specifically, we wanted to test the hypothesis that heavy drinkers had experienced more affiliative deprivation than their less intemperate peers.

Pittman and Gordon have characterized the undersocialized life history as one "that has been deficient and continues to be deficient in membership in those associations of sharing that are found in the family of orientation and procreation, in the peer groups that stretch from pre-adolescence to old age, and in community activities." [5]

Much of the previous research on skid row alcoholism has focused on arrested inebriates or applicants for aid at mission or shelter facilities,[6] thus including especially high proportions of heavy drinkers.[7] In an attempt to secure a more representative sample than one composed of arrested inebriates or welfare applicants alone, we selected names randomly from the registers of six hotels and lodging houses on the Bowery.[8] Both paying lodgers and persons whose beds were provided by city welfare were included in the sample.

The questionnaire we used called for life histories [9] specifying the number and duration of each man's affiliations within seven "sectors of social attachment": family, school, job, union, church, recreation, and politics. Detailed information on the drinking history of each respondent was also obtained. For 63 respondents the data were complete enough to permit a drinking-count drinking status and measures of lifetime affiliation.[10]

A comparison of affiliation indices revealed that throughout their lives the heavy drinkers in the sample maintained greater attachment to the social environment than did moderate drinkers or abstainers (see Table 13-4). Thus, the relation between undersocialization and the development of drinking turned out to be the reverse of what the original hypothesis had led us to expect: as a group, heavy drinkers on the Bowery appeared to have histories of greater affiliation than did the moderate drinkers or abstainers. Conceivably, variations in age among the three categories of drinkers might account

Table 13-4

LIFETIME SOCIAL ATTACHMENT BY EXTENT OF CURRENT DRINKING, FOR 63 MEN LIVING ON THE BOWERY

Lifetime Social Attachment	Extent of Current Drinking			
	Heavy	Moderate Light	Abstainers	Total
High	9	8	1	18
Medium	7	10	1	18
Low	7	11	9	27
Total	23	29	11	63

gamma = .43.

tau = .28.

level of significance $P < .05$.

for differences in lifetime affiliation. The low indices of affiliation among abstainers, for example, might be explained by their having spent a greater proportion of their lives in old age, a period generally characterized by low levels of affiliation. To check this possibility, indices of affiliation were computed for the first twenty years of life separately. These (Table 13-5) indicated that even in youth the heavy drinkers of the sample had had higher levels of affiliation than the moderate drinkers and abstainers.

The association between drinking and affiliation also held when only current affiliations were taken into account: the heavy drinkers in the sample maintained a mean of 1.3 current affiliations, compared with 0.8 for moderate drinkers and 0.6 for abstainers.

A closer examination of the association between drinking and affiliation in each of the seven sectors of attachment indicated that heavy drinkers maintained their widest margin over moderate drinkers and abstainers in three sectors: recreation, church, and family. These three sectors correspond to those areas in which the undersocialized man's life history, according to Pittman and Gordon, is

Table 13-5

SOCIAL ATTACHMENT IN YOUTH, BY EXTENT OF CURRENT DRINKING, FOR 63 MEN LIVING ON THE BOWERY

Social Attachment in Youth	Extent of Current Drinking			
	Heavy	Moderate-Light	Abstainers	Total
High	9	11	1	21
Medium	8	8	4	20
Low	6	10	6	22
Total	23	29	11	63

gamma = .29.

tau = .19.

level of significance P < .10.

likely to be most deficient.[11] Only in the job sector were the abstainers the most highly affiliated of the three groups, followed by the moderate drinkers and then by the heavy drinkers. For the remaining sectors the data did not indicate any clear relation.

We concluded that the homeless man on skid row could not be unequivocally identified with the stereotype of the heavy drinker. There were Bowery men who had been undersocialized all their lives but who had never drunk to excess, even after long exposure to the Bowery. A condition, such as "undersocialization," cannot be the major factor in the development of a certain kind of behavior if it appears most consistently in the lives of those who do not exhibit the behavior. The heavy drinkers in our sample may indeed be undersocialized in comparison with the general population, but this deficiency cannot be the explanation for their excessive drinking if it is even more characteristic of abstainers and moderate drinkers on the Bowery.

The three sectors in which the heavy drinkers appeared to have been more affiliated than moderate drinkers and abstainers—family, church, and recreation—have to do with the development of primary relations.[12] On the other hand, heavy drinkers were less affiliated than moderate drinkers and abstainers in the job sector, where secondary relations might be more prominent. In comparison with the general population, of course, the heavy drinkers of the sample were relatively unaffiliated in all seven sectors; but this did not preclude the possibility that the affiliations they did maintain involved primary relations to a greater extent than did those of moderate drinkers and abstainers. This possibility would accord with Connor's observation that alcoholics are far more likely than nonalcoholics to describe themselves mainly in primary-relationship terms.[13]

Another of our pilot studies suggests that even after they arrived on the Bowery heavy drinkers engaged in primary relations to a greater extent than other residents. For example, Patricia Nash interviewed 92 men, selected at random from four Bowery lodging houses.[14] She divided her sample into light and heavy drinkers. Of the two groups, the heavy drinkers were more likely to talk with others during the course of the day, to have a best friend on the Bowery, and to feel that someone took an interest in them. In general, the heavy drinkers in this sample appeared more sociable, friendly, and outgoing than the light drinkers. Not only were they more likely to have friends on the Bowery, but they also tended to identify more closely with other Bowery men. In addition, the heavy drinkers were much more likely than light drinkers to perceive the basic attitude of their fellow lodgers as friendly, and to favor a particular lodging house because they liked the other lodgers.[15]

Roughly two-thirds of the heavy drinkers in the pilot study reported that they drink with others some or all of the time (several stated that they can't or hate to drink alone, that they must have others with them). By way of contrast, about two-thirds of the moderate drinkers reported that they never drink with others. It may be, therefore, that the heavy drinkers arrived on the Bowery relatively soon after the dissolution of social attachments because of the availability of both alcohol and drinking companions; the skid row setting allows them to maintain both their drinking patterns and some sociable relationships.

In contrast, most of the abstainers in the sample appeared to have experienced extremely low levels of affiliation throughout their lives, both in youth and adulthood. This was reflected in every sector of attachment, except the job sector, where they showed surprisingly steady employment histories. By the age of 25, most of these respondents had selected New York City as their home base, and most of them had continued to live in rooming houses until they arrived on the Bowery years later. Typically, they followed the same kind of job throughout their working lives—dishwasher, porter, handyman, or general laborer—but changed employers frequently. These abstainers apparently selected a limited living space and a limited kind of economic activity in early adulthood, and made few changes subsequently. Their arrival on the Bowery did not result from any particular crisis, but came about as the last of a number of moves from one rooming house to another within the city.

Thus, two distinct paths to skid row were distinguishable in the life histories of the heavy drinkers and of the abstainers. The heavy dranker maintained some close social relations throughout his life, but was liable to severe losses of affiliation during adulthood. In contrast, the skid row abstainer was often a man who never had been attached to any part of the social order; his arrival on skid row was a noneventful step in a career of nonattachment.

These findings from the pilot study were based on a small sample, but other findings from the major Bowery survey provided further evidence for the same pattern.

The five quantitative categories of the drinking count were condensed into two broader categories of heavy and light drinkers (the latter category including abstainers). When heavy and light drinkers were contrasted on fourteen measures of affiliation, it was found, as expected, that on skid row heavy drinkers were more affiliated than light drinkers.

The differences were not as large as anticipated, but both on the Bowery and at Camp LaGuardia the expected pattern appeared. The differences are most striking with respect to organizational affiliations in youth, acquaintance with neighbors, and (for the Bowery sample only) willingness to join a neighborhood organization, but heavy drinkers were also more likely than light drinkers to have married, to be currently employed, to have more than eight years of education, to maintain current organizational affiliations, to have close friends in New York City, and to have conversed with many people on the day preceding the interview. In fact, of the 14 measures of affiliation listed in Table 13-6, the Bowery light drinkers were more affiliated than the heavy drinkers on only one measure, current church attendance. The relationship between drinking and affiliation was stronger on the Bowery than at Camp LaGuardia, where light drinkers not only attended church more often than heavy drinkers, but were as likely to have seen members of their families within the year preceding the interview, to indicate a willingness to know more of their neighbors, or to join a neighborhood organization.

Since the greater affiliativeness of heavy drinkers is explained by the influx of two different types of men to the Bowery, there was no reason to expect that it would appear in Park Slope, and indeed it did not. There was no consistent pattern in Park Slope; on half of the indicators heavy drinkers were *less* affiliated than light drinkers. Heavy drinkers were more likely to have voted but less likely to have attended church regularly; they were more likely to have attended high school but less likely to be employed; more likely to know the names of their neighbors but less likely to have ever married. Thus it appears that the pattern of relatively strong affiliation among heavy drinkers may be peculiar to skid row, as it provides (1) a supportive environment for heavy drinking, (2) a place where one can live

Table 13-6

PERCENTAGE OF RESPONDENTS AFFILIATED, BY EXTENT OF CURRENT DRINKING (BY COUNT), FOR VARIOUS MEASURES OF LIFETIME AND CURRENT AFFILIATION*

Measures of Affiliation	Extent of Current Drinking					
	Bowery		Camp LaGuardia		Park Slope	
	High	Low	High	Low	High	Low
Lifetime measures						
Ever married	51	38	49	42	67	76
Ever voted	66	64	72	70	75	68
Over 8 years education	56	42	46	35	51	42
Organizational affiliation(s) in youth[a]	63	38	59	36	44	40
Current measures						
Currently employed	42	33	—	—	67	79
Saw family member within past year	35	31	19	21	69	66
Attends church at least twice a month	22	32	29	37	31	45
Belongs to informal group[b]	33	26	38	28	36	34
Has organizational affiliation(s)[c]	27	15	20	9	46	53
Has close friend(s) in New York City	37	26	20	17	46	55
Knows names of more than five neighbors	52	44	65	40	50	41
Would like to know more neighbors	25	17	23	26	26	36
Would join a neighborhood organization	72	53	50	51	69	69
Conversed with 6+ people yesterday	58	46	60	46	49	60
Lowest N[d]	123	58	137	49	48	62

*Underscoring denotes differences significant at the .05 level.

a. Refers primarily to membership in voluntary organizations; jobs, church membership, family affiliation, and school attendance are excluded. Youth is defined as before age 20.

b. Men responding affirmatively to the question, Are there certain men you often hang around with? were considered as belonging to an informal group.

c. Refers primarily to voluntary organizations.

d. Number of cases varies slightly due to incomplete information.

cheaply, and (3) a nondemanding environment [16] where one can withdraw socially, keep to himself, and avoid long-term commitments. People drawn by the last two reasons tend to be more disaffiliated than those drawn by the first two, and thus affiliated excessive drinkers and isolated light drinkers and abstainers live side by side on skid row.

THE ONSET OF EXCESSIVE DRINKING AND AFFILIATION

Life-history data may be used to assess the effects of age at the onset of heavy drinking on affiliative histories of skid row men. That heavy drinking attenuates social affiliations is not at issue; the role of excessive alcohol use in the disruption of affiliations has frequently been confirmed.[17] However, it has been suggested that the age of onset of excessive drinking is an important variable for distinguishing between career patterns in which drinking functions as a "primary causal influence" and those in which it is a "secondary cause," or a "consequence of earlier maladjustments." [18]

In the former pattern, the onset of excessive drinking is said to occur early (between ages 20 and 30), to be accompanied by arrests for public intoxication or other offenses involving drinking, and to be a primary cause of failure or to represent adaptation to early failures resulting from other handicaps. In the latter pattern, alcoholics have had relatively stable occupational and marital experiences, and the onset of inebriety follows some personal crisis or physical decline. These men have arrest records which begin later in life. For them, "alcohol functions to adapt the individual to the crisis and modes of marginal existence which become more acute with age." [19] In this career pattern excessive drinking usually begins somewhat later than age 30.

These observations are derived from interviews with incarcerated inebriates. If they apply to free men, the affiliative histories of primary excessive drinkers should be quite different from those of secondary excessive drinkers. Our hypothesis was that early-onset heavy drinkers would be less affiliated in families, jobs, and voluntary associations and have lower occupational status than late-onset heavy drinkers.

Table 13-7 presents the distribution of the heavy drinkers in our

Table 13-7

AGE AT ONSET OF EXCESSIVE DRINKING AMONG BOWERY AND CAMP LAGUARDIA RESPONDENTS WHO HAVE BEEN HEAVY DRINKERS, AND AMONG MODERATE, HEAVY, AND ALCOHOLIC-DERELICT DRINKERS IN THE CHICAGO SKID ROW SAMPLE (IN PERCENTAGES)

	Bowery	Camp LaGuardia	Chicago[a]
Under 20	32	16	28
20-24	18	25	
25-29	15	11	
30-34	9	13	
20-34	42	49	53
35-44	20	16	15
45 and over	7	20	4
Total	101	101	100
N	94	104	349

a. From Donald J. Bogue, *Skid Row in American Cities* (Chicago: Community and Family Study Center, Univ. of Chicago, 1963); the N was computed by multiplying the total sample size (613) by the proportion of moderate, heavy, and alcoholic-derelict drinkers.

skid row samples by age at onset of excessive drinking. Similar data from Bogue's study of a skid row population in Chicago are given for comparison. The Bowery and Chicago distributions are quite similar. Of the Bowery heavy drinkers, 32 percent began drinking heavily before age 20, compared to 28 percent of the Chicago heavy and moderate drinkers. At the other end of the scale, 7 percent of the Bowery and 4 percent of the Chicago men did not begin drinking heavily until age 45 or later. The distribution at Camp LaGuardia reflects its selective intake procedures. Camp LaGuardia men began drinking somewhat later in life than Bowery men.

If age at onset of excessive drinking distinguishes between two or more distinct career patterns, early-onset and late-onset heavy drinkers should manifest distinctive affiliation profiles. The heavy drinkers were therefore divided into two categories: men who began to drink excessively before age 30 (early-onset) and those who began later (late-onset). For these two classes of heavy drinkers, lifetime profiles were prepared showing changes in the proportion of men living with their families, employed all year (or part of the year at long-term jobs), or affiliated with one or more voluntary associations. Lifetime occupational mobility profiles were also constructed.[20]

A comparison of the family-affiliation profiles revealed the expected pattern. At all ages the late-onset heavy drinkers on the Bowery were more likely to live with their families. The disparity between the two groups was at a maximum around age 30, when twice as many late-onset as early-onset drinkers were living with their families. Thereafter the gap between the two groups narrowed until by age 50 there was essentially no difference between them. The pattern in the Camp LaGuardia sample was similar but the differences between early- and late-onset profiles did not become apparent until age 30, and by age 50 there was little difference between the two types of heavy drinkers.

That early-onset heavy drinkers are substantially less affiliated than late-onset heavy drinkers was equally evident in their employment histories. Beginning about age 20, early-onset heavy drinkers were less often steadily employed. Among Bowery men the differences were greatest during the 20 to 35 age span and practically disappeared by age 45. In fact, by age 55 the early-onset heavy drinkers were somewhat more likely to be employed than the late-onset drinkers. Among the Camp LaGuardia men the differences between early- and late-onset heavy drinkers extended throughout life.

Early- and late-onset heavy drinkers differ strikingly with regard to membership in voluntary associations, especially in the Camp LaGuardia sample. Among Bowery men the late-onset heavy drinkers also had had substantially higher levels of affiliation: about two-thirds of them had belonged to voluntary associations compared to about half of the early-onset heavy drinkers, and these differences persisted until after age 40.

Finally, the expected differences were observed between early- and late-onset heavy drinkers with respect to occupational mobility. Late-onset drinkers had enjoyed substantially higher status in early adulthood. Not until age 45 were the mean occupational statuses of the two groups comparable.

A brief summary is in order here. As the critical variable distinguishing the early-skid from the late-skid career, Pittman and Gordon used the age at which a man was committed the second time for public intoxication or an offense involving drinking.[21] The present analysis used age at onset of heavy drinking as the critical variable and focused on the process of disaffiliation from families, jobs, and voluntary associations. In both the Bowery and Camp LaGuardia samples the affiliation profiles of early-onset heavy drinkers (before age 30) manifested greater disaffiliation and lower occupational status than the profiles for late-onset heavy drinkers. In most cases the differences were large enough to support the late-skid and early-skid distinction quite independently of data on arrests. Thus, the distinctive career patterns noted by Pittman and Gordon among incarcerated inebriates are shown to apply to noninstitutionalized heavy drinkers on skid row and to inmates of a voluntary institution.

SOCIABLE AND SOLITARY DRINKING

Wallace's report of the extent of group drinking on skid row seems somewhat exaggerated. "Practically all drinking on skid row takes place in groups," he asserts, and "few men drink alone." [22] While some published descriptions of skid row bottle gangs would seem to support this view, the statistical evidence indicates that the importance of the bottle gang in skid row drinking has been overrated. Both the Chicago study and the present research found much solitary drinking on skid row. Only about one-sixth of the Chicago skid row drinkers studied by Bogue habitually bought bottles and drank their contents in company with others; [23] beer drinking was the predominant habit. Although drinking in a bar often takes place among strangers, the norms of bar sociability apply. This means that the persons present, regardless of their backgrounds or former acquaintance, are open to conversational interaction.[24]

Encounters in bars are tacitly understood to be short-lived. Conversation tends to be tentative and superficial, and the right of any party to terminate interaction at any time is understood.[25] Bar-drinking may be perceived by the drinker as either solitary or companionate. In one exploratory survey the respondents were questioned about where and with whom they drank. Half of the men who said that they usually drank in bars asserted that they usually drank alone; about a third of them said that they usually drank with friends.

In the main survey, the respondents were asked, Do you usually drink alone or with others? The majority of respondents in all three samples reported that they usually drank with others. One-third of the Bowery drinkers drink alone, about half of them drink with others, and one-fifth reported both patterns. The distributions of Camp LaGuardia and Park Slope respondents were about the same; Park Slope respondents showed a slightly higher proportion (60 percent) of men who usually drink with others. We conclude from these figures that skid row men are not much more likely to drink alone than are men in the control group, but neither are they more likely to drink with others. If anything, there is less drinking with others on skid row than in other lower-class urban contexts.

Nor did our participant observers' descriptions of activities in Bowery bars suggest much group behavior:

> I observed where the men sat in order to see if friendship patterns could be determined on this basis. The regulars ordered their drinks at the bar but drank them at their tables. However, there was no pattern as to where the men would sit. The men would sit at one table in a group; one by one they would get up and go to other tables and regroup. There never seemed to be any pattern at all during the entire day. All of the regulars behaved in an individualistic fashion. Despite the fact that some seemed to have best friends, they did not sit with them exclusively. The groupings occurred more or less by chance and shifted constantly. No one person always sat at the same table with any other. All or most of the men were friendly to one another. There were no signs of any small groups. During the course of the day I spoke to at least 25 different men. Many of the other men spoke to as many as 15 or 25 other men. The men came and went on an individual basis.
>
> Many of the men would go outside and sit on the sidewalk beside the building. Some of them lay down and slept beside the building. Again, there was no patterned grouping.[26]

It should be understood, then, that most skid row men drink in bars, that the context of their drinking is the skid row type of bar sociability, and that while the drinking occurs in the presence of others, it cannot be realistically viewed as group behavior.

NOTES

1. Donald J. Bogue, *Skid Row in American Cities* (Chicago: Community and Family Study Center, Univ. of Chicago, 1963).

2. This position grew out of the early work of Bacon, Straus, and Malzberg, and has been further elaborated by Pittman and Gordon. See Selden D. Bacon, "Inebriety, Social Integration and Marriage," *Quarterly Journal of Studies on Alcohol,* 5 (June and September 1944), pp. 86-125 and 303-339; Robert Straus, "Alcohol and the Homeless Man," *Quarterly Journal of Studies on Alcohol,* 7 (December 1946), pp. 360-404; Benjamin Malzberg, "A Study of First Admissions with Alcoholic Psychoses in New York State, 1943-1944," *Quarterly Journal of Studies on Alcohol,* 8 (September 1947), pp. 274-295; David J. Pittman and C. Wayne Gordon, *Revolving Door* (New York: The Free Press, 1958). The origins of the alcoholic-as-isolate stereotype are outlined in Margaret B. Bailey, "Alcoholism and Marriage," *Quarterly Journal of Studies on Alcohol,* 22 (March 1961), pp. 81-97.

3. Pittman and Gordon, *op. cit.,* p. 10.

4. Bailey, *op. cit.,* p. 83.

5. Pittman and Gordon, *op. cit.,* p. 10.

6. For example, Bacon studied inebriety among men arrested for drunkenness; Straus interviewed men admitted to the Salvation Army Men's Social Service Center in New Haven; Pittman and Gordon studied chronic inebriates in a county jail in New York State: Bacon, *op. cit.,* p. 303; Straus, *op. cit.,* p. 360; Pittman and Gordon, *op. cit.,* p. 1.

7. Straus reports that 57.7 percent of the men he interviewed were "steady excessive" drinkers and that another 20.9 percent were "regular excessive" drinkers; he generalizes that between 80 and 85 percent of the homeless men studied by earlier researchers (e.g., Solenberger, Laubach, and Anderson) were either alcoholics or excessive drinkers. Elsewhere, Straus and McCarthy state that out of 444 men using the facilities of a municipal men's shelter on the Bowery, 316 were "pathological" or heavy drinkers. By way of contrast, in a sample drawn primarily from lodging houses and hotels on Chicago's skid row, Bogue found that only

30 to 35 percent of the men could be called heavy or problem drinkers; Straus, *op. cit.,* p. 367; Robert Straus and Raymond G. McCarthy, "Nonaddictive Pathological Drinking Patterns of Homeless Men," *Quarterly Journal of Studies on Alcohol,* 12 (December 1951), p. 606; Bogue, *op cit.,* pp. 92-93.

8. Sampling procedures were similar to those described by Bogue, *op. cit.,* pp. 511-514.

9. It is generally assumed that men on skid row are extremely reticent about their personal histories; therefore, previous investigators interested in such information have almost always worked in the context of a special relationship; either they have devoted much time to the establishment of rapport with respondents, or they have interviewed persons who could be sanctioned for uncooperativeness (e.g., welfare clients and prisoners). For examples of both methods see Nels Anderson, *The Hobo: The Sociology on the Homeless Man* (Chicago: Univ. of Chicago Press, 1923); Bacon, *op. cit.;* Straus, "Alcohol and the Homeless Man," *op. cit.;* Pittman and Gordon, *op. cit.* Working without such a special relationship, our pilot study interviewers contacted each man in the sample, explained the purpose of the interview, and requested the man's cooperation. Out of the sample of 79, ten men refused to be interviewed. Although this refusal rate is fairly high (13 percent), it is comparable to those in some studies carried out in the special contexts described above. For example, Levinson had to schedule interviews with 57 men on the active case load of the New York City Men's Shelter in order to get 50 completed interviews. See Boris M. Levinson, "The Socio-economic Status, Intelligence, and Psychometric Patterns of Native-Born White Homeless Men," *Journal of Genetic Psychology,* 91 (December 1957), pp. 205-206.

10. For computational details see Howard M. Bahr and Stephen J. Langfur, "Social Attachment and Drinking in Skid-Row Life Histories," *Social Problems,* 14 (Spring 1967), pp. 464-472.

11. Pittman and Gordon, *op. cit.,* p. 10.

12. Primary relations may be distinguished from secondary relations as having *inter alia* less specificity of role and more immediacy of emotional gratification and frustration.

13. A major theme which Connor finds in the self-descriptions of alcoholics is "the pronounced emphasis the alcoholic places on primary-relationship terms when he undertakes to describe himself. This theme is important not only because it is the most emphatic and consistent among the several alcoholic subpopulations, but because it is the only aspect which remains stable through numerous analyses, and particu-

larly for the influence of sobriety on the self-concept." See Ralph G. Connor, "The Self-Concepts of Alcoholics," in *Society, Culture, and Drinking Patterns,* eds. Donald J. Pittman and C. R. Snyder (New York: John Wiley & Sons, 1962), p. 466.

14. Patricia Nash, "Homeless Men at Home," an unpublished project memorandum, Homelessness Project, Bureau of Applied Social Research, Columbia University, 1965. See also J. F. Rooney, "Group Processes Among Skid-Row Winos. A Re-evaluation of the Undersocialization Hypothesis," *Quarterly Journal of Studies on Alcohol,* 22 (September 1961), pp. 444-460; W. J. Peterson and M. A. Maxwell, "The Skid-Row 'Wino,'" *Social Problems,* 5 (Spring 1958), pp. 308-316.

15. Nash, *op. cit.*

16. See George Nash and Patricia Nash, "The Non-Demanding Society; An Analysis of the Social Structure of a Skid Row," paper read at the annual meeting of the Eastern Psychological Association in New York City, April 14, 1966.

17. Selden D. Bacon, "Alcohol and Complex Society," in *Society, Culture and Drinking Patterns,* eds. Donald J. Pittman and C. R. Snyder (New York: John Wiley & Sons, 1962), pp. 78-93; Joan K. Jackson, "Social Adjustment Preceding, During and Following the Onset of Alcoholism," Diss. Univ. of Washington 1955; Edwin M. Lemert, "The Occurrence and Sequence of Events in the Adjustment of Families to Alcoholism," *Quarterly Journal of Studeis on Alcohol,* 21 (December 1960), pp. 679-697; A. W. Stearns and Albert D. Ullman, "One Thousand Unsuccessful Careers," *The Amercan Journal of Psychiatry,* 105 (May 1949), pp. 801-810.

18. Pittman and Gordon, *op. cit.,* p. 127.

19. *Ibid.*

20. For details about construction of the profiles and reproductions of the profiles themselves, see Howard M. Bahr, "Lifetime Affiliation Patterns of Early- and Late-Onset Heavy Drinkers on Skid Row," *Quarterly Journal of Studies on Alcohol,* 30 (September 1969), pp. 645-656; and *Homelessness and Disaffiliation* (New York: Bureau of Applied Social Research, Columbia Univ. 1968).

21. Pittman and Gordon, *op. cit.,* p. 130.

22. Wallace, *op. cit.,* p. 184.

23. Bogue, *op. cit.,* p. 273.

24. See Sherri Cavan's discussion of bar sociability in *Liquor License* (Chicago: Aldine Publishing Co., 1966), pp. 49-66. Also see Erving Goffman, *Behavior in Public Places* (New York: The Free Press, 1963), pp. 131-132; and Matthew P. Dumont, "Tavern Culture: the Sustenance

of Homeless Men," *American Journal of Orthopsychiatry,* 37 (October 1967), pp. 938-945.

25. Cavan, *op. cit.,* pp. 49-66.

26. George Nash, "Bowery Bars," an unpublished project memorandum, Bowery Project, Bureau of Applied Social Research, Columbia Univ., 1964, pp. 20-21.

CHAPTER 14

ACTIVITIES AND ATTITUDES

We shall now examine what skid row men say they do, and contrast these activities with those reported by Park Slope and Park Avenue men. We shall also have something to say about our respondents' attitudes toward themselves and toward the world around them.

The treatment of the men's activities and attitudes will be selective. More thorough discussions of the activities and perspectives of homeless men are available elsewhere, for example, in Bogue's chapters "What Homeless Men Think of Living on Skid Row," "Recreation of Skid Row," and "The Skid Row Man's Image of Himself and His Aspirations." [1] The first of these contains special sections on "general attitudes toward Skid Row living," "attitudes toward the hotels in which they live," and "what homeless men think of each other." We have no reason to suppose that the attitudes of skid row men in New York differ drastically from those of skid row men in Chicago, and we shall not attempt to duplicate Bogue's analysis. Instead, using a few selected indicators of activity, interaction, and attitude, we shall continue the theme of this work: does the skid row man differ from the low-income settled man or the high-income man with respect to—in this case—his activities and attitudes?

ACTIVITIES

The skid row men were not uninformed about current events. Two-thirds of them said they read a newspaper daily, and the proportion of daily readers among Park Slope men was only slightly higher than that. However, all but 3 percent of the Park Avenue men claimed to read a newspaper daily.

The intersample differences in time spent watching television revealed a similar contrast between Park Avenue and the low-income samples, except that in this case the higher participation was on the low-income side. In response to a question about how many hours a day were spent in watching television, none of the Park Avenue men reported more than four hours of viewing, and one-fourth of them said they did not watch television at all; the mean number of viewing hours they reported was 1.2. Watching television was a more salient activity in the three low-income samples, but the differences among them were small: mean viewing hours per day for the Bowery, Camp LaGuardia, and Park Slope samples were, respectively, 1.9, 1.8, and 2.0.

The men were questioned about a third form of mass media exposure, attendance at motion pictures. The Bowery and Park Slope samples were similar in overall rates of film attendance during the month preceding the interview. Approximately two-thirds of both samples had not seen any movies, and at the other end of the scale, 8 percent of the Bowery men and 5 percent of the Park Slope men had seen nine or more movies during the past month. The Park Avenue men were most likely (51 percent) to have seen at least one film during the month preceding the interview, but they were less likely than the skid row men to have seen many films. The mean number of films seen by the Park Avenue men was 1.1, compared to 1.2 seen by the Camp LaGuardia and Park Slope men and 1.6 seen by Bowery men. Among those who saw some films, the Bowery men were by far the most avid show-goers. Sixteen of them saw nine or more films in the month preceding the interview; the highest number reported by anyone in the Park Avenue sample was six. When the mean number of films seen by those who went to films was computed separately, the intersample differences were more striking: the mean number for Park Avenue men was 2.1, compared to 3.6 for Park Slope and 4.4 for Bowery men.

The man who reads newspapers all day or watches television all day may be manifesting retreatist behavior rather than using the media as extensions of his nervous system in the McLuhan sense, but a case can be made for treating exposure to the mass media as an extension of the personal space of a respondent. And since that extension involves receiving the same communications as many others in the society, it can be interpreted as a form of social participation.

If a man can extend his personal space via participation in the mass media, he can also extend it by direct participation in, or observation of, neighborhoods or subcultures beyond his own. Whenever he leaves his own neighborhood, either vicariously via the mass media or in person, he tends to increase his involvement in the wider society. Half of the Bowery and Park Slope men reported that they left their neighborhood every day; two-thirds of the Park Avenue men did so. The insularity of Bowery and Park Slope men was more apparent at the other end of the scale. Twenty-two percent of the Bowery men and 24 percent of the Park Slope men said they went out of their neighborhoods once a month or less often. Only 2 percent of the Park Avenue men were so immobile.

We have touched upon two ways a man may extend himself and thereby achieve identification and integration with the wider society; by participation in the mass media, and by personal mobility into other social worlds. Talking with other men and learning about their experiences in the wider society may be a third type of extension. One of our interview questions asked: About how many people would you say you had conversations with yesterday? Eight percent of the Bowery and Camp LaGuardia men and 9 percent of the Park Slope men reported no conversations at all. But all of the Park Avenue men claimed a conversation with at least one person on the preceding day. The mean numbers of conversations reported by Bowery, Camp LaGuardia, Park Slope, and Park Avenue men were, respectively, 12, 12, 14, and 19; the median numbers were 6, 6, 6, and 14. Thus, the three low-income samples were very much alike in the extent of their conversational interaction with others, and the average number of other persons engaged in conversation was substantially less in these samples than among the Park Avenue men.

In addition to the questions about leaving the area, participating in the mass media, and talking with others, there were two direct questions about the way a man structured his time. One concerned activities with his closest friend, and the other referred to what the respondent and certain men he often hung around with did together. The wording of both questions—What sorts of things do you usually do together?—did not elicit responses from men who had no close friends or steady associates. Multiple responses were permitted; a man could list as many activities as were appropriate in describing his relationship with his friends. Thus the sheer number of different activities mentioned is one index of activity level, the mean number of activities per man is another, and the type of activities mentioned provides a third index of involvement in the wider society.

The most frequently mentioned activities with friends and ac-

Table 14-1

MOST FREQUENTLY MENTIONED TYPES OF ACTIVITIES WITH CLOSE FRIENDS AND IN INFORMAL GROUPS

	Percentage of Total Activities Mentioned							
	Bowery		Camp LaGuardia		Park Slope		Park Avenue	
Type of Activity	With Close Friends	With Informal Group	With Close Friends	With Informal Group	With Close Friends	With Informal Group	With Close Friends	With Informal Group
Formal entertainment (movies, concerts, art, etc.)	12	0	3	0	5	7	13	9
Eating (lunch, dinner, going out to restaurant)	4	4	—	2	4	7	24	22
Talking (joking, kidding around, criticizing the government)	30	38	37	46	28	25	19	32
Drinking (drinking, going out to bars)	21	24	8	7	12	16	6	7
Going around together (walks, go slumming, go to the park, ride around)	6	2	12	2	7	5	8	3
Sedentary activities (watching television, smoking, sitting, reading, listening to music)	6	9	15	13	2	5	—	—

Table 14-1 (Continued)

	Percentage of Total Activities Mentioned							
	Bowery		Camp LaGuardia		Park Slope		Park Avenue	
Type of Activity	With Close Friends	With Informal Group	With Close Friends	With Informal Group	With Close Friends	With Informal Group	With Close Friends	With Informal Group
Table games, indoor sports (cards, pool)	6	10	12	20	15	13	3	11
Outdoor sports (golf, swimming, softball, etc.)	3	4	1	4	7	7	8	11
Work	6	2	5	2	7	3	2	—
Sport events (prize fights, ball games, racetrack)	2	5	4	1	2	5	4	4
Parties and clubs (organized groups, entertaining, social clubs)	2	—	—	—	2	5	7	3
Other	3	2	3	2	9	3	7	1
Total	101	100	100	99	100	101	101	103
N (total activities)	138	82	75	85	136	61	193	114
N (respondents)	66	40	39	48	62	28	82	49
Mean (activities/respondent)	2.1	2.0	1.9	1.8	2.2	2.2	2.4	2.3

quaintances are shown in Table 14-1. For each sample there are two columns, each representing a selected activity's proportion of the total number of activities mentioned. The first column describes activities with close friends, and the second describes activities with the informal group.

One talks with a friend, and, if one can afford it, one goes to lunch or supper with him. The most frequently mentioned activity with close friends was talking, except in the Park Avenue sample; among the Park Avenue men it was mentioned almost as often as eating together.

The other frequently mentioned activities varied from sample to sample. Talking and drinking constituted over half of the activities with friends recorded by Bowery men. In Camp LaGuardia the types of activity mentioned most frequently were all sedentary; watching television together, smoking, sitting, or reading. In Park Slope, respondents often mentioned table games, like cards or pool.

Reports of activities with a group of acquaintances (columns 2, 4, 6, and 8 in Table 14-1) were fairly congruent with reports of activities with closest friends. In all the samples, talking was the most frequently mentioned activity. On the Bowery, informal groups engage in talking, drinking, and, to some extent, table games. At Camp LaGuardia, drinking drops out—because of institutional constraints—and is replaced by table games and sedentary activities. The activities of informal groups in Park Slope include talking, drinking together, and table games, in that order. The Park Avenue men are distinctive in their frequent dining out and their participation in more strenuous sports like golf, swimming, and tennis.

A comparison of the number of activities mentioned gives some sense of the scope of the respondents' worlds. It should be remembered that the Park Slope men are more likely than the Bowery men to have close friends in the city, and that the Park Avenue men are still more apt to claim close friends. Eighty percent of the latter said they had close friends, compared to 50 percent of the Park Slope men and 33 percent of the Bowery men. The non-skid row men participate in slightly more activities with their friends than do the skid row men. The mean number of activities with close friends reported by Bowery men was 2.1, by Park Slope men 2.2, and by Park Avenue men 2.4. For activities with one's informal group the mean numbers of activities were approximately the same: 2.0, 2.2, and 2.3, respectively.

A few other generalizations deriving from Table 14-1: sedentary activities were more frequently mentioned by the Bowery and Camp LaGuardia men than by the Park Slope and Park Avenue men; parties and clubs were mentioned by Park Slope and Park Avenue men, but not by any Bowery or Camp LaGuardia men; formal entertainment was not mentioned as a group activity by Bowery and Camp LaGuardia men, although some claimed to attend such spectacles in the company of their closest friends. The Bowery and Camp LaGuardia men participate in sports events as spectators as often as the Park Slope and Park Avenue men.

Conversation topics. Given the importance of talking as an activity, some description of the things talked about is in order. Interviewers inquired about eleven topics of conversation in the following manner: "Here are some things that men often talk about. I'm interested in what you usually talk about when you and your acquaintances get into conversations. As I mention each item, try to tell me if it is something you talk about very often, sometimes, or almost never. The eleven topics mentioned appear in Table 14-2.

It is apparent from the figures in Table 14-2 that men in the Park Slope, Bowery, and Camp LaGuardia samples were very similar in frequency of reported conversation topics. The most frequent topics, discussed very often by between 42 and 49 percent of the men in these three samples, were sports and jobs. In striking contrast was the Park Avenue sample, where the most frequent topic was politics—the least frequent topic among respondents in the other three samples—followed by money and financial problems.

To obtain a ranking which reflected the proportion of each of the three possible responses, index numbers were assigned to each response. Thus, if a man said that he very often talked about a topic, he was given a score of two for that item. A "sometimes" response was scored one, and "never" was scored zero.

Sample means were computed, creating a single index score which reflected the number of "never," "sometimes," and "very often" responses. Thus, a mean score of 2.0 would denote that all respondents in a given sample had said they talked about that topic very often;

Table 14-2

MEAN SCORES[a] FOR FREQUENCY OF CONVERSATION TOPICS, AND PERCENTAGE REPORTING THEY DISCUSSED A TOPIC VERY OFTEN

Topic	Bowery		Camp LaGuardia		Park Slope		Park Avenue	
Money and financial problems	1.02	40%	0.87	29%	1.03	38%	1.39	56%
Drinking	0.92	35	0.90	31	0.61	18	0.48	7
Sports	1.12	43	1.30	49	1.22	45	1.17	38
Politics	0.51	8	0.42	8	0.70	17	1.47	54
Sex	0.62	18	0.52	12	0.89	27	0.93	26
Jobs	1.18	43	1.22	43	1.15	42	0.89	30
Religion	0.51	11	0.39	8	0.74	20	0.49	8
Plans for the future	0.67	19	0.84	28	0.89	26	1.12	29
People you know in common	0.67	17	0.65	14	0.91	25	1.16	33
Your families	0.56	18	0.39	8	0.94	31	1.04	30
Improvements needed in this area	0.78	26	0.43	12	0.85	29	0.43	13
Mean for above 11 topics	0.78		0.72		0.90		0.96	

a. Computed from individual scores, where very often = 2; sometimes = 1; and almost never = 0.

if all respondents in a sample had said that they never discussed a topic, the sample mean for that topic would be zero. The closer the score to zero, the less frequently a given topic had been discussed. The index scores for the 11 topics are given in Table 14-2.

In all four samples money or financial problems and sports are among the most popular conversation topics. In the three low-income samples talk about jobs or occupation is also at or near the top of the ranking, but for the Park Avenue men talk about the job ranked eighth in the field of eleven topics. Drinking is near the top in the Bowery and Camp LaGuardia samples, but ranked low in the Park Slope and Park Avenue samples. Talk about plans for the future is ranked about the same in all four samples (between fifth and seventh) as is sex (between sixth and eighth). Religion is discussed infrequently, ranking between ninth and eleventh in all the samples. As anticipated, talk about one's family is much more common on Park Avenue and in Park Slope than on Skid Row.

We tried to find out whether there were identifiable clusters in conversational topics, that is, whether men who liked to talk about their families also liked to talk about plans for the future, or whether men who often talked about sex would also be likely to talk about money. To answer these questions, the conversation topics were assigned index numbers and a factor analysis was done for each sample separately. The factor loadings discussed below are derived from a varimax rotation.

Among the Bowery men, three dominant factors accounted for a total of 56 percent of the variance. Items loading on the first factor were religion, family, and plans for the future; on the second, money and drinking; and on the third, sex and plans for the future. For Camp LaGuardia respondents there were also three factors which accounted for 56 percent of the variance. The items loading on Factor I were plans for the future and family; on Factor II, money, drinking and sports; and on Factor III, politics.

Among Park Slope and Park Avenue men there were four identifiable factors having eigenvalues greater than 1.00. In the Park Slope data the four factors accounted for 63 percent of the variance in the correlation matrix for the 11 items. Items loading on the first were plans for the future and drinking (loading in opposite directions); on the second were jobs, religion, and plans for the future; and on the third, people known in common, families, and plans for the future. The fourth factor had only a single item loading on it, improvements needed in the area.

Among Park Avenue men, the four factors accounted for 56 percent of the variance. Items loading on the first factor were religion and improvements needed in the area; on the second, politics and jobs. The third and fourth were distinctive single items, drinking and politics, respectively.

In sum, among Bowery and Camp LaGuardia men there was some clustering of conversation topics; men who talked about their families also talked about their plans for the future or, on the Bowery, religion; men who talked about money and financial problems also tended to talk about drinking. But beyond those two factors no consistency was apparent. Furthermore, the clustering of topics that appears in the conversation of skid row men does not appear in the conversations of Park Slope and Park Avenue men.

ATTITUDES

The instrument contained four attitude scales developed by other researchers. These four scales, containing 27 items, were the Srole anomie scale (five items); two scales by Morris Rosenberg, misanthropy or faith in people (five items) and self-esteem (ten items); and a self-estrangement scale developed by Charles Bonjean (seven items).[2] Time pressures on the interview prevented the inclusion of other scales, but we did add three single items (making a total of 30 items in all), each reflecting some aspect of a man's perspective toward social problems: his fatalism, assessment of the honesty of skid row men, and estimation of the relative importance of poverty versus communism as a national problem. Respondents indicated whether they agreed, disagreed, or couldn't decide about each of the statements. For analysis the uncertain responses were assigned to either the agree or disagree category so as to minimize a respondent's apparent pathology. For example, a "cannot decide" response on a self-esteem question was coded as a high self-esteem response, and an uncertain response on a self-estrangement item was coded as a low self-estrangement answer.

All of the scales concern aspects of alienation. To determine if they do in fact represent distinct dimensions, a principal-axis factor analysis was performed on the matrix of intercorrelations among the 30 items, and seven factors with eigenvalues greater than 1.00 were identified. These seven factors accounted for 47 percent of the total variance.

The structure of the first unrotated factor is presented in Table 14-3. This unrotated factor accounted for 20 percent of the total variance and 42 percent of the variance explained by the first seven factors. The fact that only ten of the 30 items did not reach a loading of at least .35 on the first unrotated factor indicates that there is a great deal of common variance among the items. In short, while there appear to be several dimensions of alienation represented, each dimension seems to overlap considerably with the others.

To further delimit the various components of alienation, a varimax rotation was performed, and the results of that procedure will be discussed below. In other words, we shall show that some of the so-called anomie items are more closely related to certain misanthropy items than to the other anomie items with which they usually are grouped. But for the moment, let us proceed as if we had not done the factor analysis and found that some of the associations between items on different scales were stronger than those within scale separately, and note the variations in response patterns by sample.

Anomie. One of the dominant notions in that body of sociological theory deriving from Emile Durkheim and extended by Merton, Srole, and others is that a psychological state called *anomy, anomia,* or *anomie* is an intervening variable in the causal linkage between deviant behavior and social conditions. In fact, the description of anomic man bears remarkable resemblance to that of the skid row man. In MacIver's words, the anomic person is "spiritually sterile, responsive only to himself, responsible to no one." [3] Srole devised a five-item scale to measure anomie, and research has shown that anomie is related inversely to a variety of indicators of socioeconomic status.[4]

Some have suggested that anomie scores reflect deep-seated personality characteristics as well as social influences. Whether it is the sociocultural factors or the personality factors which are most important in producing the attitudes researchers identify as anomic,

Table 14-3

UNROTATED LOADINGS ON FACTOR I OF 30 ITEMS RELATED TO ALIENATION (COMBINED SAMPLES), AND PERCENTAGE OF RESPONDENTS AGREEING WITH ITEMS*

Scale Items	Loadings on Factor I	Percentage of Respondents Agreeing with Item			
		Bowery	Camp La Guardia	Park Slope	Park Avenue
Anomia					
1. Most public officials are not really interested in the problems of the average man.	.28	53	37	57	32
2. These days a person doesn't know whom he can count on.	.51	72	67	72	26
3. Nowadays a person has to live pretty much for today and let tomorrow take care of itself.	.53	62	59	41	16
4. In spite of what some people say, the lot of the average man is getting worse, not better.	.50	48	39	38	17
5. Most people don't really care what happens to the next fellow.	.60	67	60	62	34
Self-estrangement					
6. Sometimes I get restless because I can't express my real feelings when talking and doing things with others.	.53	54	46	40	16
7. I have found that just being your natural self won't get you very far in this world.	.51	46	41	46	16

Table 14-3 (Continued)

Scale Items	Loadings on Factor I	Percentage of Respondents Agreeing with Item: Bowery	Camp La Guardia	Park Slope	Park Avenue
8. I have found that more often than not the rules in our world go against human nature.	.45	42	34	45	23
9. When I am around other people, I try to keep in mind that saying what you really feel often gets you in trouble.	.58	72	78	59	31
10. I frequently have to do things to please others that I would rather not do.	.45	65	51	54	41
11. What others think I should do is usually not what I would really like to do.	.54	60	64	50	20
12. I have found that in order to get along in this world usually you have to put on an act instead of being able to be your real self.	.53	42	37	38	17
Misanthropy					
13. If you don't watch yourself, people will take advantage of you.	.59	89	86	83	50
14. No one is going to care much what happens to you, when you get right down to it.	.60	68	58	53	20
15. Some people say that most people can be trusted. Others say that you can't be too careful in your dealings with people. How do you feel about it? ("Most can be trusted" was the "agree" response).	−.48	22	33	30	64

Table 14-3 (Continued)

Scale Items	Loadings on Factor I	Percentage of Respondents Agreeing with Item: Bowery	Camp La Guardia	Park Slope	Park Avenue
16. Human nature is fundamentally cooperative.	–.01	69	73	62	69
17. Would you say that most people are more inclined to help others or more inclined to look out for themselves. ("Help others" was the "agree" response).	–.13	21	22	26	11
Self-esteem					
18. On the whole, I am satisfied with myself.	–.09	58	55	71	59
19. At times I think I am no good at all.	.53	44	40	26	17
20. I feel that I have a number of good qualities.	–.07	93	89	94	96
21. I am able to do things as well as most other people.	–.06	74	80	84	89
22. I feel I do not have much to be proud of.	.52	54	58	26	7
23. I certainly feel useless at times.	.59	63	63	36	18
24. I feel that I am a person of worth, at least on an equal plane with others.	–.11	85	84	88	97
25. I wish I could have more respect for myself.	.61	60	65	34	8
26. All in all, I am inclined to feel that I am a failure.	.52	42	49	12	3
27. I take a positive attitude toward myself.	–.09	69	74	73	95
Single-item indicators					
28. We will always have wars, depressions, corruption, and prejudice, and there is no					

Table 14-3 (Continued)

Scale Items	Loadings on Factor I	Percentage of Respondents Agreeing with Item: Bowery	Camp La Guardia	Park Slope	Park Avenue
point in trying to do anything about it.	.47	46	44	43	11
29. Men who live on the Bowery are basically honest.	−.26	38	29	33	20
30. Which is a greater problem facing the nation: fighting communism or fighting poverty? ("Fighting communism" was "agree" response).	.03	42	42	36	29
N	600	191[a]	195[a]	107[a]	100[a]

* Underscoring denotes Park Slope-Park Avenue differences significant at the .05 level; dotted line denotes Bowery-Park Slope and/or Camp LaGuardia-Park Slope differences significant at .05 level.

a. Lowest N; number of cases varies slightly due to incomplete information.

manifestations of these factors should be more prevalent on skid row than in more settled populations, and more prevalent among the poor than among the well-to-do.

The five items of Srole's anomie scale appear in the first five rows of Table 14-3, along with the proportion of respondents who agreed (gave the anomic response) with each item. Observe that the lowest rate of agreement for *any* item in the columns of the table representing the Bowery, Camp LaGuardia, and Park Slope samples is higher than the highest proportion of agreement among Park Avenue men. Moreover, the proportions of anomic responses for Bowery men are approximately the same as for Park Slope men; on only one item is there a significant difference between the Bowery and Park Slope samples. But on *every* item the Park Avenue men differ significantly from the Park Slope men. The conclusion is inescapable; the skid row men's responses to these items are no more anomic than those of the Park Slope men. In other words, in their responses to these five items the Park Slope men are much more like Bowery men than Park Avenue men. Apparently these items distinguish high-income from low-income men, but not skid row men from settled low-income men.

Self-estrangement. This variable refers to the situation that exists "when individuals feel that they must engage in behavior in which they are compelled by social situations to do violence to their own nature." [5] For our purposes, it is a particularly significant type of alienation because it represents a man's perceptions of the violations of his integrity of self. Part of the folklore about skid row is that a man may be free there, untrammeled by steady employment or family responsibility. Statements such as "nobody bothers me" or "I'm free to come and go" are fairly common responses to questions about why one lives in a skid row lodging house.[6] If, in fact, the skid row man experiences such freedom and integrity of self, his answers should reveal less self-estrangement than those of men burdened with the normal responsibilities of life in a mass society.

The self-estrangement scale we used was developed by Charles Bonjean and consists of the seven statements listed as items 6 through 12 in Table 14-3. As in the case of anomie, the major cleavage in the distribution of responses to the items is not found between skid row men and the Park Slope and Park Avenue men, but between the low-income samples (Bowery, Camp LaGuardia, and Park Slope) and the Park Avenue men. On six of the seven items the Park Avenue men manifested significantly less self-estrangement. On all but one of the items the highest proportion of self-estrangement responses ("agree" responses) appears in one of the skid row samples, but the differences between the skid row and the Park Slope respondents were very small. On only two of the seven items—"Sometimes I get restless because I can't express my real feelings. . . ." and ". . . saying what you really feel often gets you into trouble"—was the difference between the Bowery men and the Park Slope men statistically significant.

The absolute contrast between the proportion of estrangement responses in the three low-income samples and in the Park Avenue sample is revealing. For example, almost half of the Bowery and Park Slope men agreed that just being your natural self won't get you very far in this world, but only 16 percent of the Park Avenue men agreed with that statement. Three-fourths of the Bowery and Camp LaGuardia men, but less than a third of the Park Avenue men, agreed that saying what you really feel often gets you in trouble.

In sum, the responses to these seven items revealed substantial self-estrangement in the three low-income samples. There was no evidence that the skid row man, despite his relative freedom from responsibility for others, was less compelled by social situations to do violence to his own nature than the Park Slope man. The major finding seems to be that poor people, whether they live on skid row or in other neighborhoods, feel that they are compelled to do what they would rather not do and to be what they prefer not to be to a much greater degree than well-to-do people. The critical variable is not homelessness but affluence.

Misanthropy. In a 1956 article entitled "Misanthropy and Political Ideology" Morris Rosenberg described a five-item Guttman scale which reflected one's faith in people. His assessment of the association between misanthropy scores and attitudes toward political freedom led him to the conclusion that misanthropic attitudes had a significant effect upon political opinions. Rosenberg went on to suggest that the misanthropy variable was also relevant to nonpolitical attitudes and behavior. With respect to interpersonal relationships, he suggested that "the misanthrope may experience difficulty in establishing close, warm bonds of friendship because of his basic distrust of, and contempt for, other people." [7]

In the light of this hypothesis about a relationship between misanthropy and interpersonal relations, and considering the frequent observation by researchers and people who work among skid row men that many skid rowers have withdrawn from the human race or can't bear to have permanent ties to other people, the misanthropy scale was included in the interview schedule. Following Rosenberg, the working hypothesis was that skid row men would be more misanthropic than other men.

Responses to the five items on misanthropy are summarized in Table 14-3 (items 13 to 17). There is no evidence for the hypothesized greater misanthropy of skid row men. With one exception, the differences between the skid row men and Park Slope men are not significant. However, except for one item (human nature is fundamentally cooperative) which did not discriminate at all, the Park Avenue men *were* significantly different from men in the low-income samples. On three of the items they were significantly less misanthropic than the other respondents; at the same time, they were more apt to give the misanthropic response to the question, Would you say that most people are more inclined to help others or more inclined to look out for themselves? The important point is that with respect to the individual misanthropy items, the Bowery and Camp LaGuardia men are not different from the Park Slope men, but all of them are significantly different from the Park Avenue men. Again, socioeconomic status and not homelessness seems to be the important variable.

Self-esteem. Given the public image of skid row as the bottom and the stigma associated with living there, it was clear to us that some measure of self-esteem had to be included in the interview schedule. The scale we selected was developed by Morris Rosenberg, the same man who devised the misanthropy scale. It consisted of ten items, five denoting positive self-conceptions and five reflecting negative personal attributes.

Bowery men frequently refer to themselves, and even more frequently to their peers, as bums, failures, and forgotten men. It seemed reasonable to suppose that living in a stigmatized neighborhood would eventually have an effect on a man's self-concept. We anticipated that the skid row men would have lower self-esteem than men who lived in less demeaning settings.

The responses to the ten items on self-esteem (items 18 to 27 in Table 14-3) were in the expected direction. On seven of these ten items the Bowery men were significantly more apt to give the low self-esteem response than were Park Slope men. The self-esteem of Bowery and Camp LaGuardia men, as indicated by their responses to these questions, is significantly lower than that of Park Slope men, and the self-esteem of Park Slope men is significantly lower than that of Park Avenue men. In other words, socioeconomic status has a strong impact on self-esteem, but homelessness seems to have an independent influence of its own.

It is also interesting to note that the items on which the skid row men are not significantly different from men in the other samples are those which convey a positive image of self, such as the statement: "I feel that I have a number of good qualities." In contrast, the differences are greatest for items stated negatively, such as "I certainly feel useless at times." Apparently the skid row respondents endorse both positive and negative statements about themselves, while most men in the Park Slope and Park Avenue samples do not endorse negative statements. To be specific, five of the ten self-esteem items are stated negatively (items 19, 22, 23, 25, and 26 in Table 14-3). The proportion of Park Slope men agreeing with these negative self-conceptions ranged from 12 to 36 percent, and of Park Avenue men, 3 to 18 percent. In contrast, at least 40 percent of the Bowery and Camp LaGuardia men agreed with all of the negative statements, and on some of these items as many as two-thirds of the men agreed (for instance, 65 percent of the Camp LaGuardia men agreed with the statement "I wish I could have more respect for myself," and 63 percent of the Bowery men agreed with the statement: "I certainly feel useless at times").

Well over half of the men in all four samples agreed that "On the whole, I am satisfied with myself," yet 42 percent of the Bowery men and 49 percent of the Camp LaGuardia men also agreed that "All in all, I am inclined to feel that I am a failure." Thus, men in all the samples agreed that they had positive qualities, but the Bowery and Camp LaGuardia men were much more likely than the non-skid row respondents to admit negative self-conceptions. We concluded that skid row men are different from other men in self-esteem. To some degree they have accepted the attributes of failure and uselessness as part of their self-image. Even the poor men in Park Slope were unwilling to do that.

Fatalism, poverty, and the honesty of skid row men. The three single-item indicators of skid row men's attitudes were chosen with reference to some of our assumptions about homeless men. For example, several of the observers of homelessness have identified a basic inertness as one of the underlying characteristics of skid row men. A placid acceptance of things as they are and a spirit of spectatorship without participation was noted again and again by the field workers during the initial years of the research. Accordingly, we expected that skid row men would agree with statements expressing the futility of action. In terms of his own experience, the skid row man is living evidence that good intentions do not necessarily lead to success. Typically he has worked hard most of his life and has little to show for it. It might seem natural for him, in his powerless condition, to assert that there was no virtue in striving.

The statement we chose to elicit attitudes toward striving was verbally awkward because it expressed two thoughts, one having to do with the nature of the world and the other having to do with the probable efficacy of action. Despite the presence of these two separate ideas in the single item—we would split the question into two if we were to use it again—we felt that the combination of ideas would tap these attitudes. The item was worded, "We will always have wars, depressions, corruption and prejudice and there is no point in trying to do anything about it." Agreement with the statement was no more frequent among Bowery and Camp LaGuardia men than among Park Slope respondents. In all three of these samples, the proportion agreeing with the item was between 43 and 46 percent, but for Park Avenue men the rate of agreement was only 11 percent. Thus, the contrast is not between skid row and non-skid row men, but rather between the poor and the affluent. The poor, both skid row and non-skid row, are far more convinced of the inevitability of social problems than are the affluent.

A statement about the integrity of skid row men—"Men who live on the Bowery are basically honest"—also discriminated between the Park Avenue sample and the other three samples. Bowery men were somewhat more favorable toward their peers than were the other respondents. Only 20 percent of the Park Avenue men said that Bowery men were basically honest, compared to 38 percent, 29 percent, and 33 percent of the Bowery, Camp LaGuardia, and Park Slope samples, respectively.

Finally came the question, "Which is a greater problem facing the nation: fighting communism or fighting poverty?" Surprisingly, in the most impoverished of urban populations, poverty was singled out less often than in Park Slope or on Park Avenue. In fact, the Bowery men were evenly divided about the two problems, and the Camp LaGuardia men designated communism as the most critical problem by a five percent margin. In the two control samples, poverty was identified as the more important problem, and its most significant endorsement came not from the Park Slope men but from Park Avenue. Fifty-two percent of the Park Avenue men said fighting poverty was more critical than fighting communism. It is paradoxical that in this study, at least, the well-to-do were more likely to identify poverty as a critical problem than those who were living in poverty.

A reassessment of the attitudes represented. The results of the varimax rotation permit us to determine whether the item-clusters which "belonged" together—the anomie items, the self-estrangement items, etc.—actually were more closely associated with each other than with indicators of other attitudes.

Of the seven original factors, two (IV, VII) had only one item with a factor loading of .35 or greater, and one (III) had two items with significant factor loadings. These three single- or double-item factors will not be considered further. Items which loaded at the .35 level or higher on the remaining four factors are listed in Table 14-4.

Two items from the anomie scale, three from the misanthropy scale, and the single item about the honesty of Bowery men all had high loadings on Factor I. The common theme running through these items was a sense that most people did not care about other people, or, more specifically, that no one cared about the respondent. Items with positive loadings included statements that one did not know whom to count on, that most people do not care about other people, that one had to watch out or be taken advantage of, and that when you get right down to it, no one cares much about you. Items loading negatively (persons with high scores on Factor I were likely to disagree) included the statements that Bowery men were basically honest and that most people could be trusted. In view of the predominance of items from the misanthropy scale, and the lack of faith in people reflected in the anomie items loading on this factor, it seemed appropriate to designate Factor I as misanthropy.

Six of the eight items loading on Factor II were from the self-esteem scale, and so this factor was labeled as self esteem. All but one of the items loaded negatively, which means that men who disagreed with them had high scores on Factor II. The item from the self-estrangement scale was a statement about restlessness deriving from inability to express one's true feelings, and the item from the anomie scale asserted the futility of planning for tomorrow. The remainder of the items were negative self-evaluations: feeling useless, desiring more self-respect, and knowing that one was a failure or that one had little to be proud of.

The other two factors were components of self-estrangement. Four items had significant loadings on Factor V. One was the statement that things in the world are getting worse, and the others reflected

Table 14-4

ITEMS HAVING FACTOR WEIGHTS OF .35 AND OVER, VARIMAX SOLUTION, FACTORS I, II, V, AND VI, FOR 30 ITEMS RELATED TO ALIENATION (COMBINED SAMPLES, N=600)

Items	Loadings
Factor I	
2. These days a person doesn't know whom he can count on.	.61
15. Some people say that most people can be trusted. Others say that you can't be too careful in your dealings with people. How do you feel about it? ("Most can be trusted" was the "agree" response)	–.60
13. If you don't watch yourself, people will take advantage of you.	.58
29. Men who live on the Bowery are basically honest.	–.56
5. Most people don't really care what happens to the next fellow.	.50
14. No one is going to care much what happens to you, when you get right down to it.	.45
Factor II	
23. I certainly feel useless at times.	–.73
19. At times I think I am no good at all.	–.70
26. All in all, I am inclined to feel that I am a failure.	–.70
25. I wish I could have more respect for myself.	–.67
22. I feel I do not have much to be proud of.	–.61
6. Sometimes I get restless because I can't express my real feelings when talking and doing things with others.	–.42
3. Nowadays a person has to live pretty much for today and let tomorrow take care of itself.	–.36
18. On the whole, I am satisfied with myself.	.36
Factor V	
8. I have found that more often than not the rules in our would go against human nature.	.71

Table 14-4 (Continued)

Items	Loadings
7. I have found that just being your natural self won't get you very far in this world.	.61
4. In spite of what some people say, the lot of the average man is getting worse, not better.	.59
12. I have found that in order to get along in this world usually you have to put on an act instead of being able to be your real self.	.36
Factor VI	
10. I frequently have to do things to please others that I would rather not do.	.78
11. What others think I should do is usually not what I would really like to do.	.59
12. I have found that in order to get along in this world usually you have to put on an act instead of being able to be your real self.	.51

the alienation of the real self because the "rules in our world go against human nature," and because one has to put on an act to get along.

The difference between the items which loaded on Factor V and Factor VI (one item loaded on both factors) is that Factor VI seems related to making efforts on behalf of other people, while Factor V reflects the essential incompatibility between the natural self and human society. In other words, Factor VI is more specific to constraints which derive from one's desire to please others, while Factor V seems to apply to a more pervasive, general perception of the essential incompatibility between the self and the rules in our world.

Moreover, Factor VI has to do with personal behavior ("I frequently have to *do* things. . . ." or "What others think I should *do*. . . .") but Factor V summarizes a general orientation: it is not what the respondent does, but what he has learned that prevails in Factor V. Accordingly, for our purposes Factor V was designated as estrangement in orientation and Factor VI as estrangement in behavior.

Standardized factor indexes (scale scores) were computed on the basis of the factor weights; the frequency distributions and means by factor and sample appear in Table 14-5. Note that with respect to Factor I (misanthropy) the differences between the skid row samples

Table 14-5

DISTRIBUTION AND MEANS OF STANDARDIZED SCALE SCORES, BY SAMPLE, FOR FOUR TYPES OF ATTITUDE (FACTORS)

Factor I (Misanthrophy)

	Scale Scores	Bowery	Camp LaGuardia	Park Slope	Park Avenue
Low	4.0 to 4.9	3%	3%	5%	31%
	3.0 to 3.9	1	3	1	9
	2.0 to 2.9	5	5	13	15
	1.0 to 1.9	8	11	12	20
	−0.9 to 0.9	34	37	26	17
High	−1.0 to −1.9	29	26	39	7
	−2.0 to −2.9	20	16	5	2
Total		100	101	101	101
N		194	195	109	102
Mean score		−.38	−.17	.10	1.90

Factor II (Self-Esteem)

	Scale Scores	Bowery	Camp LaGuardia	Park Slope	Park Avenue
Low	5.0 to 5.9	6%	4%	—	1%
	4.0 to 4.9	11	12	5%	—
	3.0 to 3.0	14	14	6	1
	2.0 to 2.9	12	5	2	4
	1.0 to 1.9	12	11	7	—
	−0.9 to 0.9	16	24	17	8
	−1.0 to −1.9	9	7	14	10
High	−2.0 to −2.9	6	7	12	10
	−3.0 to −3.9	15	10	38	67
Total		101	99	101	101
N		194	195	109	102
Mean score		.86	.91	−1.05	−2.18

Table 14-5 (Continued)

Factor V (Estrangement in Orientation)

	Scale Scores	Bowery	Camp LaGuardia	Park Slope	Park Avenue
Low	1.0 to 1.9	28%	33%	30%	62%
	–0.9 to 0.9	41	43	39	31
	–1.0 to –1.9	10	10	14	4
High	–2.0 to –2.9	21	14	17	3
Total		100	100	100	100
N		194	195	109	102
Mean score		–.24	–.05	–.16	.52

Factor VI (Estrangement in Behavior)

	Scale Score	Bowery	Camp LaGuardia	Park Slope	Park Avenue
Low	1.0 to 1.9	14%	24%	25%	48%
	–0.9 to 0.9	59	54	52	48
	–1.0 to -1.9	27	22	23	4
Total		100	100	100	100
N		194	195	109	102
Mean score		–.13	.02	.02	.44

and Park Slope are small, but men in all three of these low-income samples show less faith in people than Park Avenue men. Thus the results of this more refined analysis, taking into account the differential weighting of the various misanthropy items, are in agreement with the impression obtained by simply comparing the items and weighting them equally: the low-income respondents (Bowery, Camp LaGuardia, and Park Slope samples) have less faith in people than do the Park Avenue men.

On Factor II (self-esteem) the standardized factor scores again produce results which paralleled those from the individual item analysis. Self-esteem scores for Park Slope men are much higher than for the skid row men, and they are higher still for the Park Avenue men.

For Factors V (estrangement in orientation) and VI (estrangement in behavior) the three lower-income samples had comparable means and distributions. In both cases, the significant differences appeared between the Park Avenue sample and the low-income samples, the poor men, skid row and non-skid row, showing comparable levels of estrangement.

Thus, whether based on the more conventional measures of anomie, self-estrangement, self-esteem, and misanthropy, or in terms of the modification of these measures accomplished by our own factor analyses and weighting scheme, the results of our assessment of the men's attitudes are the same: except for self-esteem, the responses of skid row men are not distinguishable from those of the Park Slope men. We would interpret the exception in light of the symbolic meaning of residence on skid row and interaction with its men. The stigma of skid row has its consequences for self-esteem, but not for self-estrangement, faith in people, or anomie.

The major attitudinal differences we have found are between the Park Avenue sample and the other three samples; most of the differences noted above are not attributable to homelessness but to degrees of affluence and poverty. In effect, we are talking about winners and losers in life, and the Park Slope man is a loser even though his self-concept does not include the stigma of residence in a community of failures. The lifetime of losing that produces an impoverished elderly resident of a low-income metropolitan neighborhood fosters attitudes not unlike those of a Bowery derelict.

ATTITUDES TOWARD THE FUTURE

Several skid row surveys have included questions about respondents' expectations for the future, with particular reference to relocation. Skid row men in Philadelphia were asked what their residential preferences would be if they had the means to move to a different neighborhood. About one-quarter said they would remain on skid row, more than half said they would move to another neighborhood in Philadelphia, and about one-sixth said they would move to a rural area or to another city.[8] These same respondents were asked where they would move if they were forcibly displaced by urban renewal. The answers were about the same as to the previous question; only 14 percent said they would move out of the city, and the authors concluded that at least 80 percent of the men would stay in Philadelphia.[9] The Minneapolis skid row survey showed similar results; about 80 percent of the men responding to a question about where they would move if skid row were razed expected to remain in Minneapolis.[10]

Bogue's discussion of the aspirations and intentions of Chicago skid row men was based on responses to a question about three wishes ("If you could make three wishes and they would all be granted, what would you wish for?") and a question about leaving skid row ("How long do you expect to stay here? Do you expect to move away from here? If so, when will it be?"). Three-fourths of the men wanted or expected to get away from skid row. Bogue estimated that about one-sixth of them had an intense desire to leave, and another 50 percent were serious about leaving.[11] Replies to the three wishes question indicated that the men were "overwhelmingly pro-rehabilitation." Their frequent wishes were for a job (or a better job), money or material wealth, better health, marriage and a happy home, a better place to live, and reunion with their families.[12]

Information relevant to these issues was obtained from Bowery men by a question that asked, Where do you think you will be a year from now? On its face, the question pertains to geographic location, and if a nongeographic answer was given, the interviewer probed: Do you think you'll be living here in the area, or somewhere else? Many respondents initially offered nongeographic answers which reflected their hopes or fears about the future. Some of these answers expressed the hope of reestablishing job and family ties, and others referred to the possibility of death within the coming year.

Some respondents had no idea about where they would be in a year, or refused to answer the question in locational terms. This proportion was higher at Camp LaGuardia (19 percent) than on the Bowery (9 percent). The largest proportion intended to remain where they were. Forty percent of the Bowery men expected to be on the Bowery the following year, and a third of the Camp LaGuardia men expected to remain at the camp. These findings are congruent with results from the Chicago survey. Between 30 and 40 percent of the men on the Chicago skid row intended to remain indefinitely. The remainder said that they expected to move within a year, but judging from the duration of their prior exposure to skid row, most of them would not succeed in doing so.

The transient character of skid row, at least in terms of wishful thinking, is evident when the proportion of Bowery respondents who expected to remain where they were is contrasted with the 70 percent of the Park Slope men and the 91 percent of the Park Avenue men who expected to remain where they were.

Men committed to skid row for at least a year expressed attitudes ranging from positive affirmation of the neighborhood's values to a sense of hopeless entrapment. More than one-fourth of the Bowery men and one-sixth of the Park Slope men said they planned to leave. Many of the Bowery men wanted to go to Florida, Arizona, or California or to return to places where they had relatives. A few hoped to be in Europe the following year, and some were seamen who planned to be back on ships. There were a few obvious fantasies, but most of the stated expectations for travel away from New York City appeared realistic.

In addition to the men who specifically planned to be living on the Bowery the following year, another third of the skid row men indicated that they would remain in New York City. Some specified particular neighborhoods, others just indicated they had no plans to leave.

Finally, there were men who indicated only where they intended *not* to be. These negative orientations to the neighborhood were much more common among skid row men than in Park Slope. Only 3 percent of the Park Slope men said that they were going to be somewhere else but did not specify where; in contrast, 14 percent of the Bowery men and 12 percent of the Camp LaGuardia men had such plans. One Bowery man wanted to be ". . . away from here—a good job and apartment. Please God—with a garden and a dog. Any job. I know I can make it, even if it's only a few dollars a week." Another said: "I hope I'll be out of here. I've just been here three days. I'd like to be any place but here."

INTEREST IN REAFFILIATION

One-fourth of the men in our skid row sample mentioned some aspect of reaffiliation when they were asked about where they would be next year. Most of them intended to find a job or to change jobs;

some planned to return to their families or wanted to establish a family. Respondents in the control samples did not mention reaffiliation nearly as often as skid row men; only eight Park Slope men and one of the Park Avenue men mentioned reaffiliation. Of course, most respondents in the control samples already had families, jobs, or both.

It should be emphasized that when our skid row respondents mentioned reaffiliation, they did so in reply to a question that plainly referred to geographic location. A higher proportion might have expressed proaffiliative attitudes had they been asked a more direct question, such as Do you plan to be working next year?

Table 14-6 shows how many respondents in various categories mentioned some type of reaffiliation in reply to the question about location. As one would expect, men who were fairly young, who were in good health, or who had been on skid row a relatively short time were most likely to have intentions for reaffiliation that were strong enough to be brought to the surface by this question. Heavy drinkers were somewhat more apt to mention reaffiliation than other men, perhaps because heavy drinkers had been more affiliated in the first place. Reading the statements that have to do with affiliation, it is clear that some of the men are engaging in fantasy when they speak of returning to their families or to their jobs. But in light of the respondents' histories, many of the intended reaffiliations do not seem too unrealistic.

Most of the men who talked about returning to their families had been on skid row a relatively short time. One man, 44 years old and a native of Manhattan, had never married but had maintained contact throughout his life with his brother and sister who lived in Queens. He had been on the Bowery for two years, but still saw his brother and sister every week. He did not know where he would be next year, but said he would remain near his family. A Black, 37, had lived on the Bowery only one year. In 1962 he returned from prison, found his wife pregnant by another man, and left her. Nevertheless, he answered the question about next year confidently: "I will have straightened myself out and be back with my wife and kid." Another Black, 41, said he slept in the lodging house so that he could get jobs on the Bowery early in the morning; his wife and six children lived in Brooklyn, and he saw them three or four times a week.

Table 14-6

PERCENTAGE OF RESPONDENTS WHO MENTIONED REAFFILIATION IN CONNECTION WITH EXPECTATIONS FOR THE COMING YEAR, BY CATEGORIES

	Bowery		Camp LaGuardia	
	Total Cases	Percentage Mentioning Reaffiliation	Total Cases	Percentage Mentioning Reaffiliation
Age				
0-49	78	30	29	17
50-59	47	21*	72	31*
60+	72	10	97	13
Race				
White	141	19	148	19
Black	55	22	49	22
Health				
Good	98	28	114	18
Poor	99	13*	84	24
Drinking rating				
Heavy	104	24	117	21
Other	86	14	75	16
Years on skid row[a]				
0-9	88	28	78	22
10+	104	14*	100	19

* The associations between reaffiliation and age (both samples), health, and years on skid row (Bowery sample) are significant at the .05 level.

a. Refers to the number of years elapsed since respondent first spent a night on skid row.

This man had been living on the Bowery on and off since 1964, but said that next year if his health were good he would be resettled with his family in Brooklyn.

Other men reported less plausible intentions to rejoin families with whom they had been out of touch for many years. One 47-year-old man had last lived with his family in 1953 when he "just got tired and hit the road." He had not seen any of them since 1955, the year before he started living on the Bowery. Nevertheless, he said that next year he would be in Tennessee with his wife and children. Another respondent had left his wife in 1952 and lived steadily on the Bowery and at Camp LaGuardia for at least twelve years. The last time he saw any of his relatives was ten years ago, but he said he intended to be back home in Florida next year.

For most of the men, the transition to more stable work would require less readaptation than a return to family life. Some men who were unemployed at the time of the interview planned to be working next year but intended to remain on skid row. Thus, an unemployed Puerto Rican, 61, who had spent most of his working life as a kitchen helper, salad man, and busboy said that if he were lucky, he would be working next year and that he would still be on the Bowery.

Several men had aspirations of getting away from the Bowery but continuing the same sort of work that maintained them on skid row. Others imagined a major change of life for themselves, including the start of a new career. A Latvian who had been a cook most of his adult life reported that his last job, three weeks before the interview, was with the South Shore Yacht Club. He spent his first night on the Bowery about 1952, and had lived on skid row or at the Seaman's Institute ever since. Nevertheless, he stated emphatically: "I'll be a cook in an upstate New York country club. I'm not sitting here for the rest of my life."

One man who arrived on the Bowery in 1961 after his wife died and who had lived in the New York metropolitan area all of his life, except for seven years in the Army, planned to go halfway around the world. At the time of the interview he was filling spot jobs as a general laborer, but he hoped to be working in Saudi Arabia the following year.

Among the more fantastic responses were those of a laborer, 50, who wanted, a year from now, to have a real estate business, a rooming house, and to give music lessons.

THE FEAR OF DEATH

According to the disengagement theory of aging, the perceived imminence of death is expected to increase with age. It was anticipated that skid row men, already disengaged to a large degree and living among sick and dying elderly men, would be more likely to mention death in connection with questions about the future than individuals living in more active and healthy neighborhoods. If we can assume that life on skid row is a form of social disengagement and heavy drinking a form of gradual suicide, there are further reasons to suppose that skid row men might react to a question about the future by expressing the anticipation of death.

As expected, Bowery men were more likely to respond to questions about the future in terms of the possibility of dying than were men in the control sample. Here are some typical responses:

> "A year from today, maybe alive, maybe dead. That belongs to God. Maybe in the grave."
>
> "Maybe dead. I've got no idea."
>
> "Hard to say . . . there's no guarantee on life."
>
> "I don't think I'll live that long."

Twenty-seven percent of the Bowery men mentioned the possibility of being dead next year. Among the Camp LaGuardia men, an older and supposedly a more derelict group, a slightly smaller proportion (19 percent) mentioned death. In response to the same question, 16 percent of the Park Slope men mentioned death, but only 6 percent of the Park Avenue men.

In all three low-income samples, old men were more likely than young men to mention death in connection with their expectations of the coming year. The intersample differences highlighted the inertness and resignation of Bowery residents (Table 14-7). One-fifth of the younger Bowery men (under age 50) mentioned death in connection with the coming year, compared to less than 4 percent of

Table 14-7

PERCENTAGE OF RESPONDENTS MENTIONING DEATH IN CONNECTION WITH EXPECTATIONS FOR THE COMING YEAR, BY CATEGORIES

	Bowery		Camp LaGuardia		Park Slope	
	Total Cases	Percentage Mentioning Death	Total Cases	Percentage Mentioning Death	Total Cases	Percentage Mentioning Death
Age						
0-49	75	20	27	4	59	3
50-59	44	30	63	16*	26	12*
60+	72	32	84	26	30	43
Race						
White	138	28	133	23	73	20
Negro	52	21	40	8	42	7
Health						
Good	94	23	97	14	80	10
Poor	97	30	77	25	35	29*
Drinking rating						
Heavy	102	26	105	17	34	12
Other	82	28	63	22	81	17
Years on skid row[a]						
0-9	86	26	65	15	—	—
10+	100	28	91	23	—	—

* For the Camp and Park Slope samples the association between mentioning death and age is significant at the .05 level, as is the association between health and mentioning death among Park Slope men.

a. Refers to years since respondent first spent a night on skid row.

the younger men at Camp LaGuardia and in Park Slope. In fact, the expectation of death among relatively young Bowery men was higher than among men aged 50 to 59 living at Camp LaGuardia or in Park Slope. The camp atmosphere seemed to have a salubrious effect on the outlook of the skid row men living there. For each category, the concern with death was less among Camp LaGuardia men than among Bowery men. In fact, concern with death among old men in Camp LaGuardia was less than that among middle-aged men on the Bowery. It may be that the official orientation of Camp LaGuardia—toward rehabilitation and rejoining the world—coupled with the better health care and nutrition available there and the affiliation, albeit minimal, that accompanies enrollment at the camp combine to create an environment where the expectation of death is somewhat reduced.

However, old men in Park Slope were more involved with thoughts of death than old men on skid row. Forty-three percent of the Park Slope respondents 60 and over mentioned death in connection with the coming year, compared to fewer than a third of the skid row respondents. In all the low-income samples, Whites were more likely than Blacks to mention impending death; the interracial disparity was greatest at Camp LaGuardia.

NOTES

1. Donald J. Bogue, *Skid Row in American Cities* (Chicago: Community and Family Study Center, Univ. of Chicago, 1963), pp. 134-171, 245-255, 392-401.

2. Leo Srole, "Social Integration and Certain Corollaries: An Exploratory Study," *American Sociological Review,* 21 (December 1956), pp. 709-716; see also Ephraim Harold Mizruchi, *Success and Opportunity* (New York: The Free Press, 1964), p. 162; Morris Rosenberg, "Misanthropy and Political Ideology," *American Sociological Review,* 21 (December 1956), p. 690; Morris Rosenberg, "Parental Interest and Children's Self-Conceptions," *Sociometry,* 26 (March 1963), pp. 35-36; and Charles M. Bonjean and Gary G. Vance, "Port Lavaca Community Survey: A Description and Comparison of Some Characteristics of Businessmen, Managers, and Workers," Department of Sociology and Hogg Foundation, Univ. of Texas, 1965, mimeographed, p. 29.

3. Robert M. MacIver, *The Ramparts We Guard* (New York: Crowell Collier and Macmillan, 1950), p. 84.

4. See, for example, Robert C. Angell, "Preferences for Moral Norms in Three Problem Areas," *American Journal of Sociology,* 67 (May 1962), pp. 650-660; Lewis M. Killian and Charles M. Grigg, "Urbanism, Race and Anomie," *American Journal of Sociology,* 7 (May 1962), pp. 661-665; Marshall B. Clinard, ed., *Anomie and Deviant Behavior* (New York: The Free Press, 1964); and Herbert McClosky and John H. Schaar, "Psychological Dimensions of Anomy," *American Sociological Review,* 30 (February 1965), pp. 14-40.

5. Bonjean and Vance, *op. cit.,* p. 29.

6. See, for example, Bogue, *op. cit.,* pp. 158-159; and Patricia Nash, 'The Methodology of the Study of Bowery Lodging Houses," Bureau of Applied Social Research, Columbia Univ., 1964, mimeographed, pp. 29-34.

7. Rosenberg, "Misanthropy and Political Ideology," p. 694.

8. Leonard Blumberg *et al., The Men on Skid Row* (Philadelphia: Temple Univ. School of Medicine, Department of Psychiatry, 1960), pp. 176 and 179.

9. *Ibid.,* pp. 182-183.

10. Theodore Caplow, Keith A. Lovald, and Samuel E. Wallace, *A General Report on the Problem of Relocating the Population of the Lower Loop Redevelopment Area* (Minneapolis: Minneapolis Housing and Redevelopment Authority, 1958), pp. 112-114.

11. Bogue, *op. cit.,* pp. 400-401.

12. *Ibid.,* pp. 394-395.

CHAPTER 15

HOW DISTINCTIVE ARE HOMELESS MEN?

We have tried to show how Bowery men differ from poor men in other neighborhoods. We have also tried to identify the characteristics which distinguish poor men, in skid row or out of it, from richer men, and have repeatedly found that the latter differences are greater than the former.

Let us first summarize some of the differences discussed in previous chapters, and then discuss the comparative happiness of the men.

A REVIEW OF DIFFERENCES FOUND

The Bowery has a higher proportion of White men than most low-income neighborhoods in New York City. Bowery men have atypical marital histories, with a high proportion never married and high incidences of separation, divorce, and widowhood. They are concentrated in low-status occupations: about two-thirds of them have been service workers and laborers.

Compared to Park Slope men, Bowery men are more likely to be unemployed; they are less likely to have visited relatives recently, to belong to formal organizations, to attend church, or to have close friends. In other words, the Bowery man is short on jobs, kin contacts, formal memberships, church attendance, and friendship. But in other ways, the Bowery man is not so different from his poor but settled counterpart. He is just as apt as the Park Slope man to be educated, to have participated in organizations or extracurricular activities in youth, to know the names of his neighbors and talk with them, to consider himself a part of an informal group of associates, and to vote. He has somewhat more institutional experience and is more likely to have experience in occupations like ranch hand, seaman, railroad worker, or lumberjack which now or formerly separated men from normal social activity and stable family life.

Despite our expectation that patterns of affiliation in formal organizations would have been passed from parent to child, the parents of the Bowery men were not less affiliated than the parents of Park Slope respondents. Immigrants are not overrepresented on the Bowery, and the fathers of Bowery men were not poorer than the fathers of Park Slope men.

In other populations there is a close relationship between occupational status and affiliation, but among skid row men occupational background is not a good predictor of affiliation.

Many of the factors conventionally identified as explaining the problems of skid row men prove on closer analysis to be generally characteristic of lives in poverty, although the skid row man *is* distinctive in his extraordinarily low occupational status and his extreme poverty. Other elements which distinguish the typical life history of the Bowery man from that of the Park Slope man were heavy drinking, marital instability, a history of public assistance, transiency in early life, poor health, and repeated arrests for drinking and other offenses. Some of these distinguishing factors, such as a history of public assistance and repeated arrests for drinking, stem from residence on skid row rather than from prior experience.

Our use of a low-income comparison sample enabled us to lay to rest some of the conventional explanations of homelessness in terms of deviant family structure. Men from broken homes are not overrepresented on skid row; nor are men from large families. The theory that later-born or youngest children are more apt to end up on skid row than those in other birth-order positions was not supported either. The only demonstrable birth-order effect we could find was an overrepresentation of only children among Bowery men.

The Bowery man's marital record is one of the few sectors of his life history that sets him off sharply from the Park Slope man. Most of the Bowery men have never married, and the marriages of the rest have been extraordinarily unstable. Given their high incidence of separation, divorce, and desertion, it is not surprising that Bowery men have many fewer children.

Their other family contacts are significantly sparse. About half of the Park Slope men see at least one relative frequently; less than a fourth of the Bowery men do so. About a third had not, at the time of the interview, seen any relative in the previous ten years.

Throughout life the Bowery man's occupational status is exceptionally low, and it declines over time, so that he becomes relatively worse off with increasing age. In comparison with his father, the typical Bowery man has lost status, while the Park Slope man has at least maintained the same level as his father.

In terms of current affiliation the Bowery men are clearly less affiliated than Park Slope men; more than three-fourths of them have no current voluntary affiliations at all. However, taking their entire adult lives, they have been as affiliated as the Park Slope men, and in early life more affiliated.

One obvious way that the skid row man differs from a man who is merely poor is that he lives in a stigmatized neighborhood and shares its subculture. According to one of our pilot studies, most respondents considered the Bowery to be home and other Bowery men to be like themselves. Much of the skid row subculture centers on excessive drinking, and Bowery men drink more, more often, and with less restraint than Park Slope men.

Although Bowery men identify with their neighborhood, they do not necessarily like it or approve of it. When asked where they intended to be a year later, only a minority said they would stay on the Bowery. They were eager to be somewhere else, but typically did not know where. When he tries to envisage the future, the Bowery man is more likely than the Park Slope man to think of death. The preoccupation with death among relatively young men on the Bowery was striking.

HAPPINESS ON THE BOWERY

How happy is the Bowery man? Is he significantly less happy than a poor man in a settled population? If so, then the arguments of those who plead that skid row men be left alone to enjoy their unique freedom from the shams and corruption of more conventional life-styles may rest on a misperception. Insofar as the responses to items in our interview schedule are relevant to the question, let us examine the comparative happiness of skid row men.

The best years of life. Toward the end of the interview schedule we asked, What was the happiest period in your life? and What was the least happy period in your life? Interviewers were instructed to probe so that the period could be identified by specific time references, and in doing so, they recorded data for most of the respondents on the nature of the periods of happiness and unhappiness.

More than a third of the 164 Bowery men who commented on the nature of their least happy period placed the present within that period. In Park Slope the proportion of men whose most unhappy time included the present was 13 percent; for Park Avenue men, this was true of only a single respondent. In other words, the present was perceived as the nadir, or part of the nadir, of life by many Bowery men, but by only a few men in the control samples. Even the Camp LaGuardia men were less unhappy; 22 percent of them put the present in their least happy period.

In all of the samples, youth or young manhood were the periods of life most frequently identified as the happiest time. The median ages of respondents at the end of their happiest periods were 25, 27.5, and 29.5 for Bowery, Park Slope, and Park Avenue men respectively. More relevant for our present purpose are the differences at the other end of the age continuum: *none* of the Bowery men put the end of their happiest period beyond age 50, but 5 percent of the Park Slope men and 11 percent of the Park Avenue men did so.

Knowing someone cares. One of the pilot studies contained the question, Who would you say takes a personal interest in you? The modal response (37 percent) was "no one"; one of every four men mentioned a relative.

In the same pilot study, one third of the men said that they did not have a best friend. We did not include the personal-interest question on the major survey, but the men's responses to questions about contact with relatives and having close friends suggests that the 37 percent figure for "no one" responses is not out of line. Two-thirds of the Bowery men did not have a close friend in New York City, compared to half of the Park Slope men and only one-fifth of the Park Avenue men; half of the Park Slope men said they frequently saw relatives and family other than those they were living with, compared to about one-fourth of the Bowery men. In addition, about 60 percent of the Park Slope men (but none of the Bowery men) were living with their wives. It is clear that the "no one" response is not atypical for skid row.

Although the Bowery man differs from most other men when he says that no one cares about him *personally*, his more general attitudes toward other people are not distinctive. Sixty-seven percent of the Bowery men agreed that most people don't really care what happens to the next fellow, but so did 62 percent of the Park Slope men, despite the fact that most of them had spouses, relatives, or close friends whom they thought really cared about them. The affection of friends or relatives does not make the Park Slope man more optimistic about mankind.

Feelings of self-worth. In Chapter 14 we described the self-concepts of Bowery men, and noted that the self-esteem scale was the only one of the four attitude scales in the study which significantly differentiated Bowery men from Park Slope men. Compared to Park Slope men, Bowery men are less satisfied with themselves and less likely to affirm that they can do things as well as other people. They sometimes have feelings of personal worthlessness; 44 percent said that at times they think they are no good at all, and almost two-thirds said that they certainly feel useless at times. These proportions are almost twice as high as the corresponding proportions among Park Slope men. The typical Bowery man agrees that he doesn't have much to be proud of. He would like to have more respect for himself, but finds it difficult: 42 percent of the Bowery men sum up their lives as failures, compared to 12 percent of the Park Slope men.

Freedom from pain. The first question in the interview concerned the respondent's health. On a four-point scale, with "excellent," "good," "fair," and "poor" as possible answers, the Bowery men reported themselves as less well than even the Camp LaGuardia men. This finding was unexpected since one of the qualifications for admission to Camp LaGuardia is ill health. Only 9 percent of the Bowery men claimed excellent health, compared to 14 percent of the Camp LaGuardia men, 33 percent of the Park Slope men, and 36 percent of the Park Avenue men. At the other end of the scale, 29 percent of the Bowery men, 11 percent of the Camp LaGuardia men, 12 percent of the Park Slope men, and only 3 percent of the Park Avenue men reported poor health. On a four-point scale ranging from 0 for poor health to 3 for excellent health, the respective means for the Bowery, Camp LaGuardia, Park Slope, and Park Avenue samples are 1.3, 1.6, 1.9, and 2.2. Thus the average state of health reported by the Bowery man is fair on a scale ranging from poor to excellent, and for Park Slope and Park Avenue men the average state is good.

Physical disabilities are related to the experience of illness or pain, and also to stigmatization. Respondents were asked if they had any physical disabilities, and if so, when they first became disabled. No one reported birth defects in answer to this question, but over half of the Bowery men reported at least one disability, as did 24 percent of the Park Slope men and 17 percent of the Park Avenue men.

When only significant disabilities were counted, the disadvantages of the Bowery men were even more apparent. After the respondent described the nature and duration of his disability, he was asked whether it had interfered with his working. Temporary disabilities were defined as those which interfered with work for less than two years. More lasting disabilities were placed in three categories: (1) unable to work since disability, (2) significantly handicapped since disability (deaf, for example, or missing an arm), (3) significantly disabled for two years or more but later able to work. Since our concern was with interference with work, men whose disabilities occurred after their retirement from the labor force were not included in this classification.

Thirty percent of the Bowery men had experienced significant disabilities, compared to 12 percent of the Park Slope men. The difference between the two samples was in the category of those significantly handicapped since disability, which included 18 percent of the Bowery men but only 3 percent of the Park Slope men. Also of interest was the relatively greater duration of disability among skid row men.

Freedom to act and not to be acted upon. The arm of the law leans more heavily on Bowery men than on other men. Their freedom is limited both with regard to legal assistance and to protection from personal indignities from policemen and others involved in the institutional pattern of the revolving door. Our survey did not focus on the relationship between skid row men and agents of the law, but several findings are relevant. First, with respect to frequency and reasons for arrests, the Bowery men are very different from the other samples.

Seven percent of the Park Slope men reported they had been arrested at least once for being drunk or disorderly or on a similar charge, but 50 percent of the Bowery men so reported, a proportion more than seven times higher. None of the Park Slope men had been arrested more than three times for such offenses, but 26 percent of the Bowery men had four or more such arrests, and 12 percent had ten or more arrests each!

A subsequent question about arrests for reasons unrelated to public drunkenness also revealed a disparity. Ten percent of the Park Slope men had been arrested on other charges, compared to 27 percent of the Bowery men. Six percent of the Bowery men had been arrested at least five times on other charges, but fewer than 2 percent of the Park Slope men had that many arrests.

Economic freedom. Happiness may also consist, in part, of being able to "do your own thing" and not having to conform to the wishes of others. The Bowery man's freedom from conventional expectations is not absolute, however. For one thing, he is frequently in the position of requesting food, clothing, and shelter from various social agencies, and when aid is granted, it is accompanied by communications which signal to him that the agents who serve him do not accept or approve of him. In Wiseman's words, the agents of the "helping" agencies for skid row men "view their clients with a combination of exasperation, anger and despair." [2] The costs of being served by these agents of social control is apparent in Bowery's men's comments about what they liked in a good lodging house clerk. The most important favorable comment was: "He treats me like a human being." [3]

The personal and psychological costs associated with dependence on the social agencies of skid row have been described by Wiseman:

> . . . any person who receives a gift is automatically at a status disadvantage. However, in the case of institutions that deal with deviants, another dimension must be added, that is, the lower status afforded automatically to deviants by reasons of their departure from normative behavior. . . . For those whose jobs require they help these deviant men, the assumption of superiority of the giver is much greater than might be expected in ordinary helping relationships. In these cases, there is the social class differential coupled with the impossibility of ever receiving adequate payment for such benevolence from such inadequate persons.[4]

One of the observers in our own project described the procedures of the Municipal Men's Shelter on the Bowery in graphic terms:

> The procedure for obtaining aid normally takes a client from one half to three hours. . . . The waiting clients usually do not talk to each other; when they do, they are sometimes told to be quiet.
>
> Eventually the client's turn comes, and he is interviewed at one of the windows like a bank customer standing at a teller's window. The clients' names are distributed randomly to the interviewers, so there is no continuity in the social worker-client relationship. The interviews average about three minutes, most of which time is spent by the interviewer in filling out forms. . . . Frequently the interview assumes the tone of a cross-examination in which the client tries to justify himself and the interviewer attempts to force some kind of admission or catch him in a contradiction.
>
> Relations between the social workers and clients are abrasive and sometimes hostile. Clients are expected to be respectful of officials, accurate in the information given, sober, and well-behaved. One client was told to say "sir" when addressing the interviewer. Another client who had last come to the Shelter in 1962 was severely reprimanded because he said he had never come before. One client, asked how to spell his name, said brashly, "That's what you're here for, isn't it?" The interviewer became furious, said something like "you've shot your wad, buster," and refused him service. On one client's record, it was noted that one evening he came to the Shelter intoxicated and attacked a particular policeman. When he returned to the Shelter a year later, he was not served until he apologized to the police officer.

The social workers do not appear to feel much pressure to shorten the time a client must wait to be interviewed. If the waiting room is full, the interviewers need not worry because any additional men will be kept out of sight on the first floor. A rule is in effect that not more than twenty clients per interviewer on duty will be allowed to wait on the third floor. The general attitude was illustrated by one social worker when a loud argument broke out next to him. He walked away from his client in the middle of the interview and said, "I can't work under these conditions." He lit a cigarette and chatted with a researcher for about half an hour without showing any concern for the client who was standing at his window.[5]

Despite the costs associated with receiving aid from social agencies, almost two-thirds of the Bowery men have received food or shelter from missions or public shelters, and one-third reported receiving assistance payments either in New York or elsewhere. Most of the reported episodes of assistance occurred within the twelve months prior to the interview.

Finally, there is the matter of income. The extremely low reported incomes of Bowery men suggest not happiness but insufficiency. The median monthly income of the Bowery men was $120; the Park Slope men, with $290, had more than twice as much, although the latter figure was still well below the poverty line for a metropolitan area like New York City.

The points just reviewed stand in sharp contrast to the rest of this book. We have found that in many ways the Park Slope man is like the Bowery man, and many of the supposed characteristics of skid row life are merely attributes of poverty and aging. The Bowery man's history is less distinctive than formerly supposed with respect, for example, to marginality, or undersocialization. But there is no doubt that, according to the indicators of well-being and happiness available to us, he is distinctly unhappy.

Compared to the Park Slope man, the Bowery man perceives the present as less happy; he is less likely to feel people care about him personally; he has lower self-esteem; he is more often ill and more likely to be disabled; he has been arrested much more often; he has fewer savings, a lower income, and is more often dependent on charity of a demeaning kind.

Most of these indicators are directly linked to the Bowery man's present location on skid row, his identity as a skid row man, and the stigmatization which accompanies that identity. Might the Bowery man be happier if he lived in a neighborhood equivalent to Park Slope? Certainly that move would decrease his vulnerability to arrest and to other treatment that reaffirms his image of inferiority, and would lessen the pain of his recognition that he lives on "the mile of forgotten men," with "bums and winos."

NOTES

1. For extensive documentation of this point, see James P. Spradley, *You Owe Yourself A Drunk* (Boston: Little, Brown, 1970) and Jacquelnie P. Wiseman, *Stations of the Lost* (Englewood Cliffs: Prentice-Hall, 1970).

2. Wiseman, *op. cit.*, p. 268; Wiseman's entire book is evidence for the costs involved in being "treated" by the "stations of the lost" which serve skid row men.

3. Patricia Nash, "Homeless Men at Home," an unpublished project memorandum, Homelessness Project, Bureau of Applied Social Research, Columbia Univ., December 1965, p. 37.

4. Wiseman, *op. cit.*, p. 251.

5. Stanley K. Henshaw, *Camp LaGuardia: A Voluntary Total Institution for Homeless Men* (New York: Bureau of Applied Social Research, Columbia Univ., 1968), pp. 154-156.

APPENDICES

APPENDIX I

RESEARCH PROCEDURES

The process of gathering life-history data via survey techniques can be divided into several distinct phases, including designing interview schedules, training interviewers, gaining access to the population, and, in the case of skid-row residents, maintaining satisfactory relations with the administrative staffs of the organizations which lodge the men, approaching and interviewing the men, and supervising interviewers. Each research setting—the Bowery, Camp LaGuardia, Park Slope, and Park Avenue—is considered separately in the following discussion of data-gathering procedure.

PREPARATION OF THE INTERVIEW SCHEDULE

During the first year of the Homelessness Project a pilot study was conducted in which life histories of 69 residents of skid row hotels were gathered. One of the products of this exploratory study was a life-history interview schedule which served as a basis for the more comprehensive instrument used in the major wave of interviewing. Before describing the survey methods, the development of that instrument will be briefly outlined.

We began with the interview schedule used in the pilot study, which focused on the history of a man's employment, migration, family experience, drinking, and participation in organizations. One staff member had the major responsibility for the first two drafts of the new interview schedule. Using the pilot-study instrument as a base, he added questions on topics neglected in the earlier version. In particular, items were added on the respondents' habits and attitudes, on the history of their participation in political and religious organizations, and on their income history.

The first two drafts included many questions that eventually were deleted. The procedure was to begin with an instrument that was too long and reduce it to the absolutely essential items, rather than to start with a shorter draft. After the second draft, the refinement of the interview schedule became the responsibility of the entire staff.

A group of four staff members worked full time in drafting and discussing the interview guide; several others participated occasionally. Although the four main participants were unequal in authority (one was project director, another director of a major portion of the project, the third was a full-time senior staff member, and the fourth a part-time research assistant) the fate of proposed items was usually decided by the one-man, one-vote principle.

The four main participants soon assumed distinct roles. The project director served as instrumental leader, paying more attention than the others to problems of finance and scheduling, and trying to limit the time and money spent in constructing the interview guide and to maximize the quality of the final product.

The second-ranking member of the group soon became an expressive leader; often he was a peacemaker, suggesting compromise or working in other ways to minimize friction aroused by the debate over various items. The third and fourth members of the group functioned as item appraisers, and concentrated on improving the interview schedule, regardless of the time or expense involved.

The group operated as a board of control, making decisions about items submitted to it by individual members. Sections of the interview schedule were assigned to individuals whose proposals were discussed among the group as a whole. Most final decisions were made in group session.

The third draft of the interview schedule was pretested on ten homeless men. Senior staff members did the interviewing. A fourth draft was given to thirty men. Some of the interviews were administered by interviewers-in-training and others by experienced staff members. A fifth draft was pretested on twenty men. Again, both experienced staff members and new interviewers did the interviewing. Following each pretest, the interview schedule was reappraised.

Fairly early in the process, the group split into two separate camps which maintained a tenuous identity throughout the construction of the interview schedule. Thus, coalitions tended to be predictable. The staff members had different theoretical interests, and often there was opposition to another person's favorite items. Considerable debate and argument usually preceded the tentative adoption or deletion of items. Sometimes there was tension as tempers wore thin after hours of discussion, but the debate was functional in that contested items were more carefully appraised and justified than they would otherwise have been.

Discussions were full of compromise, and various types of negotiation appeared. For example, one might agree to let an item he opposed remain in the schedule, providing its wording was changed. After making several concessions of this kind, one was in a favorable position to seek support for a favorite item of his own. Another device used to get specific items past the group was to feign intense interest in "decoy items" and then, after extended discussion, to allow those items to be eliminated on condition that other favorite items were allowed to remain. Still another gambit was the filibuster: sometimes when someone felt very strongly about an item he remained adamant until the others tired of talking about it and agreed to include the item simply so that the group could proceed to other business.

Hypothetical hysteria (a concept for which we are indebted to Michael Wild) played an important role in the decision making. The staff had interviewed homeless men before, and this experience made it easy to imagine diverse responses to a given question. Consequently proposed items were screened with reference to many outlandish possibilities. To a point, hypothetical hysteria is a valuable precursor to the actual pretest. However, if the discussion remains in the air too long, time is wasted preparing for imagined horrors that may never appear. It was the experience of the staff that an interplay between hypothetical hysteria and small-scale pretesting was most fruitful. A timely pretest of 20 interviews followed by a discussion of the findings, further revision of the interview schedule, and another pretest proved an excellent remedy for advanced cases of hypothetical hysteria. This procedure is recommended over that of massive pretest followed by revision without further pretest.

The staff was committed to administering the questionnaire to one or more control groups in addition to samples of the homeless population, and it recognized that unnecessary questions would increase the length of the interview and ultimately might necessitate decreasing the size of the sample. Therefore brevity was a guiding principle.

As discussions continued, it was found effective to delegate troublesome items to working groups of one or two persons. Only after definite proposals had been set down and agreed upon by the subgroup would the item be introduced again for general discussion.

When persons outside the regular members of the group were present during discussions, both beneficial and detrimental effects were observed. On the positive side, such observers or peripheral members sometimes added useful insights or made other valuable contributions. The fifth or sixth member sometimes sided with a particular subgroup and thus broke a deadlock. But the status of these relative outsiders was never clear, so the one-man-one-vote principle did not really apply to them, and no one defined what principle should. Confusion about their status as members of the group added somewhat to the tension when debates raged; having them as an audience often led to more stands for principle than occurred when the group met alone.

In general the one-man-one-vote principle was followed. Only a few sections of the interview schedule were not approved by at least three of the four main members, and usually final decisions were unanimous. When this was not the case, the issue was not the wording of items but rather their theoretical relevance; the disagreement was really about what was sociologically interesting.

The contributions of the principal investigator were mainly of two types. First, he criticized the early versions of the interview schedule, suggesting basic criteria for evaluation of items and noting the types of items that needed to be included or deleted. As preparation of the schedules progressed, he became a court of last resort. When the staff was divided about whether or not an item should be included, the critical question became, Is the issue important enough to take to the principal investigator? When the answer was no, further attempts at compromise were usually successful. In some cases the decision of the principal investigator resolved issues on which the rest of the staff had reached an impasse. It was found that involvement in the preparation of the interview schedule caused prejudice with regard to certain items. By having interviewers-in-training test the schedule, fresh observations and suggestions from "uncontaminated" investigators were gained without losing the insights of more experienced personnel, and at the end of the process the staff emerged with a core of experienced interviewers ready to begin the actual interviewing. Interviewers who participated in pretesting seemed to gain a sense of identification with the project and to believe that their opinions and experiences really mattered. The final version of the interview schedule contained a number of items that were changed or revised at the suggestion of these interviewers-in-training.

TRAINING INTERVIEWERS

There were several stages in the processing of training interviewers, including a general introduction to interviewing procedures, illustrative interviews by senior staff members, and practice interviewing among the interviewers until they were completely familiar with the interview schedule. This was followed by actual interviews with non-sample respondents. In preparation for interviewing the Bowery sample, for example, interviewers proceeded from interviewing their friends or co-workers to office interviews with actual Bowery men. Following that stage, they interviewed in practice lodging houses, that is, lodging houses not in the sample that were treated precisely as if they were. In these practice houses interviewers-in-training worked under conditions similar to those they would face later when interviewing the sample. They had to wait until a man on their list appeared, elicit a clerk's cooperation in identifying the man, approach him, explain the purpose of the interview, and attempt to gain his consent and maintain rapport throughout the interview.

During each of these stages, supervisors checked completed interviews for omissions and errors and instructed interviewers accordingly. Interviewers-in-training were not allowed to begin interviewing men in the sample until their practice interviews were on a par with those obtained by experienced interviewers in the field.

SURVEY METHODS ON THE BOWERY

Universe and sample. The Bowery provided a pool of homeless men from which the staff could draw a sample and test hypotheses about the antecedents and consequences of homelessness. The universe consisted of the residents in 41 housing facilities: 37 commercial lodging houses and hotels, the Bowery Mission, the Municipal Men's Shelter, and two Salvation Army facilities (a hotel and a rehabilitation center).

According to a February 1966 census of the area, there were about 5000 men living in the 41 housing facilities. By simple random sampling every *n*th lodger could have been selected from this population; but then it would have been necessary to interview in every lodging house or hotel on the Bowery. Simple cluster sampling, for example, taking every twenty-fourth, twenty-fifth, and twenty-sixth man, would not have improved the situation much; it still would have been necessary to interview in almost all of the lodging facilities. The problem was to draw a random sample from the entire Bowery population in such a way that every man on the Bowery had an equal chance of being included, and yet to limit the number of facilities in which the staff would be interviewing.

Between April 12 and April 14 the staff contacted each of these facilities and learned the number of men staying there on April 12. For each facility the population was rounded to the nearest ten. Total population of the area, in rounded figures, was 4820. This universe was divided into 482 units of ten men each. Each of these units was conceived as consisting of ten men drawn at random from the total population of the particular lodging house to which that unit belonged. The 482 units were then numbered consecutively, and a table of random numbers was used to select 24 of them. The 240 men represented by these units are the sample. Final statistics on the Bowery sample appear in Table I-1.

Approaching the houses. As a result of the pilot studies, friendly relations had been established with several of the owners and managers of the lodging houses. These owners were fairly familiar with the interviewing procedures, and in their houses few problems were encountered. It was in lodging houses where the staff had never worked before that there were more refusals and other problems.

When the interviewers were ready to begin in a particular lodging house, the project director met with the manager as well as the owner to explain the project and solicit their cooperation. All of the owners agreed to allow the field supervisors access to their guest registers and to set up interviewing stations in their lobbies.

Next, one of the field supervisors went to the hotel and drew a

Table I-1

DISPOSITION OF BOWERY SAMPLE

Sample drawn	240 men
Refusals	23
Not interviewed for other reasons[a]	14
Usable interviews	203

a. Other reasons include:

1. Interviewers could not contact the man, or were unable to contact him when interviewing was possible (8 men).

2. Men at houses that were closed to interviewers before contact could be made (4 men).

3. Deaf respondent (1 man).

4. Respondent who claimed to have been interviewed earlier (1 man).

random sample of the men who had spent the previous night there. This was done by giving all of them consecutive numbers according to the order in which they were listed in the guest register and then drawing random numbers until the desired number of respondents had been chosen. Copies of the list were given to the interviewers.

Two interviewers were continuously stationed at the house until it became difficult to locate enough respondents to keep both of them busy. Then one interviewer was assigned to the house at times when respondents might be available. In each house an attempt was made to complete the bulk of the interviewing in the first few days.

Approaching the men. After being admitted to a lodging house and given an interviewing station, the interviewer faced several problems. Having only the men's names and room numbers, he had to rely on the desk clerks or use some other strategy to identify the men on his list. Once a man was identified, the interviewer had to approach him and gain his cooperation. There was also the problem of maintaining sufficient rapport with the respondent to complete an interview sometimes lasting more than two hours.

The major obstacle confronting the interviewer on skid row is not persuading respondents to talk about themselves, but rather the difficulty of establishing initial contact and obtaining consent for an interview. Well-dressed strangers on skid row are often viewed with suspicion. The interviewer had to break through this suspicion and convince the respondent that he was sincere and that his inquiry was legitimate. Owners and clerks in the lodging houses, despite their own doubts, were very helpful in assuaging some of the men's suspicions.

The owners of the lodging houses agreed to provide a place where the interviews might be conducted in semiprivacy and to instruct their clerks to assist the interviewers by identifying the men in the sample when they appeared. In most cases owners and clerks were extremely helpful, going far beyond the limits of their initial agreement. Sometimes clerks and managers attempted to explain the purpose of the interviewing to a hesitant man or vouched for the legitimacy of the study.

It was not hard to identify men in houses where clerks were cooperative. When a man in the sample appeared, the clerk would point him out and the interviewer could make his approach. However, other strategies were needed because clerks might not pause from their work to tell an interviewer that a particular man had arrived, or might forget who was on the sample list, or overlook men for various reasons. Alternative methods of approach were particularly important in those lodging houses where the clerks were uncooperative. One method of approach was flagging room keys. When not interviewing, interviewers usually waited in or near the clerk's office at a place where they could see the rack of room keys. By placing a note on the keys of men in the sample it was possible to identify a man when he was handed a key with a note on it. Some notes were blank, others contained a brief message. When only a few men remained to be interviewed, it was possible to watch the critical keys without bothering to flag them.

Another strategy was to make periodic rounds of the cubicles. Where this was permitted by the management, the interviewer would go to the door of each respondent, watch for light under the door, and listen for sounds of activity within. Thus it was sometimes possible to find men who slipped in unnoticed during busy periods. These cubicle contacts were fruitful at times, but there was some danger that a man might refuse to open his door when the interviewer knocked, and without some face-to-face contact it was difficult to establish the rapport necessary for an interview. Moreover, men in nearby cubicles might hear the exchange and ridicule it or might decide to refuse an interview just as their neighbor was doing.

Although some interviews were obtained in the morning, the best time seemed to be in the evenings. During the first phase of interviewing, when the interviewer still had many men to contact, he could profitably spend all day at the lodging house. Later, when there were few men left, the usual procedure was to arrive at the lodging house late in the afternoon and spend the evening waiting and watching.

Sometimes men were contacted as they left the lodging houses in the morning; if it was impossible to arrange an immediate interview, appointments might be made for later in the day. Some men kept these appointments, but interviewers soon concluded that, if possible, it was best to interview a man on first contact. Otherwise the thought of a potentially unpleasant situation awaiting him at the lodging house might weigh on his mind all day and prompt him to avoid the interviewer.

Having identified his respondent, the interviewer had to be adept at getting an interview. Naturally, interviewers varied in their ability to do this. Usually a short approach was more effective than a long explanation. If men were interested, the reasons for the interview were explained, but usually simple statements like "we're interviewing men down here to find out what sort of jobs they've had and where they've been in their lives" were sufficient. Often an attempt was made to explain that the man's name had been chosen at random, and that interest was not in him personally but in one chosen by chance from a list representing all the residents of a particular lodging house. Some men were reassured when the interviewer explained that the information given would be completely confidential and that the respondent's name need not appear on the completed interview form. Bowery and Camp LaGuardia men are not unfamiliar with interviewing situations, and often they assented and were cooperative even though they had no interest in the purposes of the study.

Substitutions. Substitutions were made for men who moved out before an interviewer had a chance to contact them, and for men who moved out after being contacted but before being interviewed, provided that they had not refused to be interviewed. These were men who could not be interviewed when first approached, but who agreed that they were willing to be interviewed later. Substitutions were not made for men who were not interviewed for other reasons (men who were in the hospital, for instance, had died, refused, could not speak English, or ran away when approached). If a man moved out, the man who moved into his room was substituted. If no one was assigned to that room, the next man who had moved into the hotel was interviewed.

The interview. The impression that skid row men are unwilling to discuss their past lives, held by social workers, by skid row businessmen and employees, and by the men themselves, appears to be inaccurate. Once involved in an interview, the skid row man is not unwilling to discuss his past. No doubt, he conceals or distorts portions of it, but in this respect he does not differ from other men. Broad generalizations about the skid row population are usually ill-advised because many different types of men live there. But in its reaction to social research the population of skid row seems to vary little from other lower-class populations.

The interview was hard for many of the men. There were several tedious sections, including a detailed migration history and a section which called for the duration, location, and income of every job ever held. Some interviewers were more effective than others in justifying these sections, but most of them were able to complete an interview even if it meant returning for two or three sessions.

Initially, owners and clerks in the lodging houses almost unanimously agreed that the men would not consent. "He'll never talk to you," they would advise, or "no use wasting time trying to talk to him—he doesn't want to be bothered." One clerk averred that many men in the house would refuse to be interviewed because they were hiding from the police. Another clerk's certainty about this matter was based on his own experience: "Look, I've been here fifteen years and the men won't tell me nothing; so how do you expect them to talk to a stranger?"

Skid row men were of the same opinion. They believed most of the other men would probably refuse. Respondents were often surprised when they learned that almost all of the men in the sample had agreed to an interview.

Interviewers differed in their evaluation of interviews that took place in the men's cubicles. Some felt that this setting was ideal, provided entry could be gained. The respondent was likely to feel at ease since he could act as host in his own familiar setting, and the interview was more private than at interviewing stations. Others reported that a respondent was more likely to be domineering in his own cubicle than in neutral territory.

The length of the interview varied from 25 minutes to three and a half hours. The median was 90 minutes. Forty-two interviews were interrupted for various reasons; most of the interruptions were brief, for reasons like the following:

> Respondent was clerk in the hotel; he was constantly leaving for "five minutes."
>
> A drunken friend of the respondent interrupted for five minutes.
>
> Interviewer bought respondent two candy bars; man said he would not continue unless he was fed.
>
> Respondent started yelling. Would not answer questions, and was disturbing other lodgers; interviewer left. Later field supervisor apologized to the man and finished the interview.
>
> Respondent had to leave to get his meal. Interview resumed three weeks later.

In 75 interviews, someone besides the interviewer and respondent was present at least part of the time. Most of these bystanders were clerks or other lodgers. The interviewers generally considred the other persons present to have negligible effects on the interview situation.

The interviewers evaluated the attitudes of the Bowery respondents as follows: 51 percent very frank and cooperative, 22 percent average, 15 percent compliant but uncommunicative, and 12 percent resistant to the interview. Fourteen interviews were not evaluated.

The general impression of the staff is that most of the respondents found the interview more agreeable than they had anticipated, and a majority of them would willingly have granted a second session if the interviewer had requested it. Although "mind your own business" is generally the rule in skid row, the professional investigator is an outsider to whom the rule may not apply. The interviewing situation is not unfamiliar to skid row men, and if approached with respect and understanding they are at least as cooperative as most other low-status respondents.

Refusals. An initial refusal was never accepted as final. When a man appeared adamant, interviewers explained that they would be in the neighborhood again and might perhaps call on him when it was more convenient, or when he was feeling better, or had a chance to think about it, or had talked to other men who had been interviewed. Return calls were sometimes effective. Of the 29 men who initially refused to be interviewed, eight later agreed.

Relations with lodging house staff. The clerks in the lodging houses were not always cooperative. Although the approval of the management was obtained, some clerks took it upon themselves to protect men or to harass the interviewers. They could make it difficult for the interviewer to identify his men, to interview them in peace, or to endure the long waiting periods that were necessary. The problem of uncooperative clerks was dealt with by trying to avoid shifts when they were on duty, by requesting owners or managers to talk to them, and by noting which interviewers seemed to get along best with uncooperative clerks. One or more of these approaches worked in every case.

Other problems developed with owners and managers. For one thing, managers wanted the interviewing to be finished quickly. In three houses interviewers had to leave before completing all of the interviews because the owner began to feel that having interviewers continuously present was a nuisance. Some managers and owners were hypersensitive about continued attempts to contact refusals. Although managers were informed that interviewers would approach a man several times if he refused initially, some of them later objected to this procedure, stating that they had to guarantee their lodgers' privacy. Business is not good at the lodging houses. Most of them have many vacant rooms, and managers are concerned about losing steady tenants. Some managers feared that men might move out if they were approached repeatedly by interviewers. As a result, in some houses it was necessary to agree to approach refusals only one additional time.

It should be remembered that lodging house owners were under no obligation to allow interviews; they agreed to cooperate on a personal, voluntary basis. Their professional association had voted to cooperate with the Columbia University Homelessness Studies, but each owner or manager had a right to close his house to interviewers at any time. The staff remained on good terms with all managers and owners, and when the interviewing was completed, they departed with the understanding that there might be further interviewing in their lodging houses at some future time.

Interviewer supervision. Interviewers were supervised closely throughout the period of interviewing. Two full-time field supervisors trained and assigned interviewers, drew samples, received reports, and checked completed schedules. At night supervisors went from lodging house to lodging house ascertaining that all was well, seeing that interviewers were where they had been assigned, and assisting them where necessary. Interviewers checked out with the field supervisor before returning home after each night's work.

A pay scale based on a combination of piecework and an hourly minimum rate proved most effective in motivating interviewers and sustaining their morale. Interviewers could expect to make some money if they waited all evening in a lodging house and no respondent appeared, but the piecework rate focused their attention on completed interviews rather than on hours worked. An attempt was made to increase interviewer effectiveness by keeping a rough record of the number of hours worked for each completed interview and giving special attention to interviewers with a high ratio of hours per interview.

BOWERY LODGING HOUSES

Most of the interviewing took place in the lodging houses, a type of facility which may be unfamiliar to some readers. Therefore, the setting will be briefly described. Most Bowery lodging houses are in the upper stories of buildings that have bars, restaurants, or other business establishments on the ground floor. The entrance to a lodging house is usually a tiled stairway. Through the main door, one faces the clerk's cage; separated from this is the lobby, the center of lodging house social activity. There is great variety in cleanliness and general atmosphere among lodging houses, as well as in their clienteles. Some cater to older White men; in other houses Blacks predominate. Some admit men on tickets from the Municipal Men's Shelter, while others refuse to allow "ticket men." The houses vary in capacity from 79 to 566 beds. There is almost invariably a television set in the lobby. In some of the better houses there are soda, candy, and ice cream machines. During the day the lobbies are very quiet; they are noisier in the evening, especially on weekends.

Lodging houses provide many services for the men; the clerk or manager may help an inebriated lodger to his room, cash his checks, hold his mail and property for him, and lend him money. The clerks are themselves often Bowery men.

Interviewers were instructed to record their observations of the lodging houses, and the following excerpts from interviewer reports give some of the flavor of lodging house life.

> The setting is quite placid, approximately twenty men reading in the lobby, occasionally buying a Coke, smoking a cigarette. . . . Of the men who are lounging, several . . . are reading paperback novels. . . . Some are talking quietly while others are just sitting and staring.

> The lobby is entirely filled with an odor, the composition of which is approximately one part alcohol, two parts sweat, and one part urine.

> The lobby . . . is very large and dark. . . . It is fairly smoky but a few windows are open to dispel the smoke. The office is narrow but long and is well lighted. In the corner of the office are two [baseball] bats and some pieces of rope tied together. The whole place is fairly clean and there are no strong odors.

> They allow drinking on their main floor. . . . The lodgers frequently spit on the floor and there are broken bottles there. . . .

The lodgers were very friendly. A number of them offered themselves to be interviewed. They seemed to want someone to talk to.

Five men were eating cake and coffee in the lobby while talking and laughing. There is a "No Drinking" sign but one man was drinking in full view of the clerk.

The "No Drinking in the Lobby" sign seems to be strictly enforced and closely followed. However, on the beds and floors upstairs, there are empty and half-empty bottles of wine and liquor.

A few men were sitting in the lobby watching television. It is the only color television set up in any of the lodging houses. The men were watching a soap opera.

Men watching television. Not too crowded. One man sleeping in doorway. Bouncer got rid of him. Also got rid of a few other drunks that wandered up. Clerk not very cooperative. Worried about the men's privacy. Most men seem steady customers. Not much conversation.

The hotel seems to cater to a young, somewhat scruffy Black clientele. . . . Many of the men sit in the lobby playing cards and discussing world problems. A young Black clerk . . . attracts a group of men and lectures on "the art of being a bum."

Later in the evening the hot water went on in the showers causing an unbearable amount of humidity in the lobby and on the first floor. No one seemed to care and no one bothered to shut it off.

The lobby, while small, seems relatively clean and is not too much of a television hangout. . . . The rooms are microscopic but well-lighted and reasonably clean.

Large noisy place. Crowded. Clerks very cooperative. Took tour with clerk of dorm and rooms. There are two floors—Negroes are segregated. Clerk said this was voluntary.

Very quiet, About eight men here. . . . Music from the radio. Some men playing cards, reading papers; conversation was about a friend whose business failed. At six o'clock television went on for the news. Flies all over the place. They cannot get rid of them. Conversation about how important Negroes' vote will be in South.

The hotel has a number of kittens that roam the lobby. Men play with them. Clerk feeds them. They have their own corner and a bed is made for them.

The clerk is liked and respected by most of the men here. He is jovial and helpful to the men. He did evict one man who was very drunk and loud . . . by escorting him to the door. . . . When I came downstairs the clerk was throwing the same man out again. He gave him a choice of going out or going to his room but would not allow him to stay in the lobby because he had a bottle in his pocket and was drunk.

On the clerk's window are several magazine and newspaper clippings, mostly about Blacks. One of the articles featured a muscular female wrestler. Another article discussed alcoholic priests. There was also an advertisement cut out from last year's newspaper featuring "Susskind Interviews Six Bowery Bums."

. . . the clerk was selective about his clientele—he turned one man down and told him "no more rooms." But a few minutes later he sold another room to another man. The man he turned down was old, on crutches, and disheleveled:

> Lodger: What was the President's name in 1940?
> Clerk: FDR
> Lodger: You're wrong, you're so wrong.
> Clerk: Of course it was, you dope.
> Lodger: It was not! It was still LBJ.

Today several of the men sitting in the hotel lobbies were involved in more constructive activity than usual. One spent over an hour attempting to replace the hinge on the clerk's eyeglasses. Another, with a jeweler's magnifying glass set firmly in his eye, carefully studied a cigar-box full of watches. A third sat by a window . . . sewing his suit jacket.

Boys run in and out of the lobby. Most of them are Puerto Ricans. They come here to buy soda and ice cream in the machine.

Two young fellows came into the hotel to visit their invalid father. They took him for a walk.

. . . a tall, lean Black keeled over and at the same time vomited. . . . The clerk came out and took him up to his room. The other men in the lobby laughed.

A young man claiming to have a heart condition passed out on the floor in the lobby. Apparently a heart attack. He looked dead. Clerk called an ambulance. Man is not a guest at the hotel. The other men do not appear to be concerned at all. Everyone is still doing exactly what he was doing before the man collapsed. Two policemen come in and check his pulse. . . . Ambulance comes and all guests are very interested in what is happening. Policemen and ambulance attendant ask clerk for smelling salts and ammonia. No one has any. They put the man on a stretcher and take him to the ambulance.

One [drunk lodger] collapsed in the television room and was left alone. Another was so ill he was unable to walk and acted as a palsied victim. One man, while passing the candy machine, looked in the mirror and punched it as hard as he could but did not break it. . . . Twice the clerk . . . [went] downstairs to chase drunks away from the entrance of the house.

Room clerk says all men down here come because they hate women. No women can bother them down here.

SURVEY METHODS AT CAMP LaGUARDIA *

Approaching the camp. Camp LaGuardia was approached through Department of Welfare officials with whom staff members had worked during the Bowery Project. Permission was obtained from the commissioner of welfare to interview residents of the camp, and camp officials cooperated fully. Prior to the interviewing, the staff member who supervised the interviews spent several months in participant observation at the camp, and the rapport he developed with the staff, as well as his observations about the camp, was helpful in organizing the interviewing procedures.

Universe and sample. The sampling universe at Camp LaGuardia included the entire client population. The population fluctuates from day to day; once or twice a week a busload of men comes, and every day a few men leave. At the beginning of the interviewing there were more than 1020 men at the camp.

A simple random sample of the clients was drawn by sampling the beds. The camp has given an identification number to each bed in a dormitory. By listing the dormitories in sequence according to camp records, it was possible to assign the beds consecutive numbers from 1 to 1059. Three hundred random numbers between 0001 and 1059 were then drawn from a book of random numbers and these numbers were converted into camp bed numbers. The bed numbers were used in the order in which they were drawn from the random number table and were therefore in random order. Thus, at any cutoff point the numbers chosen constituted a random sample of the camp's beds. For example, if it had been necessary to stop interviewing when bed 150 on the list was reached, the project would still have had a random sample. As it happened, 295 bed numbers were used to obtain 199 interviews. The complete sample is not a cross section of the lodgers at any one point of time, but is the sum of many small daily samples, each of which is a random cross section of the camp as it was on the day the sample was drawn.

Each day approximately 20 bed numbers were checked against the

* Much of this section is adapted from a project memorandum by Stanley K. Henshaw.

Table I-2

DISPOSITION OF CAMP LAGUARDIA SAMPLE

Sample drawn	295 beds
Empty beds	61
Total effective sample	234 men
Refusals	22
Not interviewed for other reasons[a]	13
Usable interviews	199

a. Other reasons include:

1. Men who left the camp before they could be contacted (12 men).

2. Respondent had been interviewed on the Bowery (1 man).

camp bed list, and the occupants of these beds were requested to come the following day for an interview. This procedure minimized the problem of men leaving the camp after having been selected for the sample. Nevertheless, nine men left the camp on the day they were to be interviewed, and three others left after missing their appointments and before they could be contacted personally. The final disposition of the sample is summarized in Table I-2.

Approaching the men. An official communication channel was used to contact the men and request that they report to the interviewing site at a particular time. The camp has an official procedure for making appointments with the inmates. A slip of paper is placed on a man's bed, requesting him to please report to a particular place at a specified time on the following day. The form looks like this:

PLEASE REPORT
TO
NAME
BED NUMBER
TIME

The most common uses of this procedure are to ask men to do such things as pick up their mail, report for semiannual interviews with their social workers, or report for medical service.

The use of the official procedure had the obvious disadvantages of associating the interviewers with the camp administrators, thus putting respondents on guard not to say anything that might threaten their future career at the camp. To counter this, interviewers explained to each man before the interview that he had nothing to do with either the camp or the Department of Welfare, that the man's cooperation was voluntary, and that the interview was completely confidential. Most of the men accepted this explanation, and the word got around that the interview was voluntary, with the result that after the first few days men did not respond to the call slips as readily.

The advantage of using the camp call-slip system was its extreme simplicity and efficiency. One alternative would have been to send a special note to each respondent explaining the nature and purpose of the interview. However, there is reason to believe that this would have been less effective than the personal approach used on the Bowery. Another alternative would have been to have the interviewers locate each respondent and speak to him personally. This would have been extremely time-consuming, and many of the men would have been found in the company of other men, thus increasing the probability that they would not cooperate.

If a man did not appear on the day of his appointment, a second slip was sent to him requesting that he come to the Tap Room the next day or the day after. Most men responded to the second slip. If a man did not appear for his second appointment, his record was checked to ascertain his job at the camp, and he was approached by the interviewing supervisor.

The interview. Interviewing at Camp LaGuardia proceeded more smoothly than on the Bowery. For one thing, it followed the Bowery survey, and thus the interviewing staff was more experienced. For another, the interviewing station at the camp was more convenient than most of the Bowery stations.

The call slip asked the respondents to come to the Tap Room, where most of the interviewing took place. This was the only accommodation available, and it had the advantage of being separate from the camp's administrative offices. Undoubtedly, the Tap Room had more pleasant associations for the camp men than the rear of a clerk's office had for residents of a Bowery lodging house. Normally the

Tap Room is not open during the day; therefore, the interview gave the men a chance to enjoy the congenial surroundings of a favorite place.

Each interviewer occupied a separate corner of the Tap Room. Thus, there was a measure of social support for the men being interviewed. A respondent could observe other men being interviewed, but if he spoke softly he could not be overheard by the others. Some interviews were conducted outside on the grounds near the Tap Room, and a few took place in other locations.

The length of the interviews varied from 30 minutes to 3 hours and 45 minutes; the median was 70 minutes. Fifteen interviews were interrupted for one reason or another.

The men's reactions to the research project were mixed. Some of them received the interviewers cordially and encouraged their friends to cooperate; other reacted unfavorably. It was widely believed that the interviewers were conducting psychiatric research and that the interviewing supervisor was a psychiatrist. This belief seemed to increase the men's resistance. To counteract this, interviewers were instructed to explain to each respondent that we were sociologists, not psychiatrists or psychologists. However, this was not entirely effective in offsetting resistance because the men were more familiar with psychiatry and psychology than with sociology.

Reactions to the interview itself varied; some men enjoyed the experience while others were apprehensive throughout the interview. Most of them did not seem to mind revealing information about their lives or about their attitudes and self-perceptions. Probably the most unpleasant aspect of the interview for the respondents was being asked difficult questions: to remember exact dates and understand relatively abstract questions.

The interviewers' evaluation of the attitudes of camp men toward the interview situation revealed the following: 36 percent were classified as frank and cooperative, 45 percent as average, 13 percent compliant but uncommunicative, and 6 percent as resistant. Eight interviews were not evaluated.

During the course of the research it was noted that most people who deal with skid row men treat them as inferiors. One may often raise his voice at them, shout authoritative commands, and omit many of the courtesies accorded other people. This generalization applies to nurses, doctors, waitresses, bartenders, and the owners, managers, and clerks of lodging houses. At Camp LaGuardia the same habits began to appear among the interviewers. As they became more experienced, interviewers showed a tendency to become harsher with respondents. This was brought to staff attention when some respondents complained that the interviewers did not show proper respect for them.

Refusals. If a man refused to be interviewed, the field supervisor or a specially selected interviewer was sent to try to persuade him; but of the 18 men who initially refused, only two were subsequently persuaded to permit the interview. Those who refused usually failed to report for their appointments; only five men came to the Tap Room as scheduled and then said that they were unwilling to be interviewed.

Unfortunately, the refusals were not a cross section of the population; the client elite is overrepresented among the refusals and Blacks are underrepresented. Relatively submissive men agreed to be interviewed more readily than more aggressive men. This probably explains why the refusal rate was quite low at the camp and relatively low on the Bowery; acquiescent men are overrepresented on skid row. Responses to the attitude questions indicated that many of the men were cynical in their attitudes toward other people and toward society; their motivation for cooperating with the researchers was respect for authority rather than a desire to be helpful.

Relations with camp staff. The camp staff cooperated fully with the investigators, although they did not express much interest in the project and relations with them were not particularly close. Interviewers had little contact with staff members, except occasionally at lunch. The field supervisor attempted to keep the camp's executive director informed as to the project's progress and methods of operation.

Many of the men sought information from staff members when they received a notice to report for an interview. In every known case the staff member explained that the interview was not compulsory but did not discourage the respondent from reporting. At least twice, the executive director asked whether interviewers were getting the cooperation they needed and offered to take action if necessary.

He evidently felt that the camp would be subject to criticism if the research did not go smoothly.

Since there were some questions in the interview schedule about which the camp administration might be sensitive, it was necessary to decide whether to explain and justify the interview schedule to the administration before beginning to interview. The normal procedure is to keep the officers of an organization well informed in order to prevent the spread of rumors and suspicions based on ignorance. In this case, however, it was felt that there was a real danger that the project might be delayed if attempts were made to clear the questions in advance. In order to work at the camp at all, it had been necessary to obtain written approval from the welfare commissioner himself.

Under the circumstances, it was decided to proceed as if the questionnaire were of no interest to the camp administrators. If a staff officer asked to see the interview schedule, it was shown to him, but the staff did not go out of their way to make its contents known. Perhaps because the camp officers did not wish to appear suspicious, or perhaps because they trusted the research staff, no one expressed interest in the interview schedule until the interviewing was more than half-completed. No attempt was being made to evaluate the camp or its staff, and the researchers knew of no requirement that research techniques or instruments be submitted for the approval of the camp or the city.

When the interviews were slightly less than half-completed, the executive director approached the field supervisor and said that a lodger had told him that interviewers were asking questions about the staff. After quoting to him the exact question relating to the staff, the supervisor explained that while interviewers were interested in the attitude of men toward authority, they were not trying to evaluate the camp or its staff, and pointed out that the question could not reasonably be interpreted as an evaluation of the staff. The camp director seemed satisfied with the explanation and declined an offer to examine the entire interview schedule.

A few days later, when the interviewing was about three-fourths completed, one of the social workers asked if she could see the interview schedule. Subsequently the executive director called the field supervisor into his office and said that the head of the staff department was concerned about the questions being asked. The matter was immediately discussed with the department head, who explained at length why the questions were not a fair evaluation of the staff. The researcher agreed and tried to explain the purpose of the questions. The department head asked whether the questionnaire had been cleared with anyone and was amazed that it had not been. Further explanation mollified him somewhat, and throughout the field work he continued to cooperate with the research staff.

Interviewer supervision. Interviewers at the camp had little control over the number of interviews they completed; usually they were able to interview all day as men reported for their appointments. So as not to penalize interviewers whose appointed men did not appear, the pay scale was altered; all interviewers were paid by the day.

Another reason for the relative ease of interviewing at the camp was that the field supervisor was always available nearby. Interviews were turned over to him for checking immediately upon completion. Thus control was considerably tighter than in the Bowery interviews.

SURVEY METHODS IN PARK SLOPE

Universe and sample. The decision to draw a control sample from a neighborhood in Brooklyn was arbitrary. Data from the 1960 U.S. Census were used in selecting a particular census tract as the research site. The following criteria were proposed: the median income of all families and unrelated individuals in 1959 was $4000 or less; the ethnic composition of the population did not differ drastically from that of the Bowery. Of all Brooklyn census tracts only Tract 161 satisfied both criteria. Accordingly it was designated as the universe from which the control sample was drawn.

The universe consisted of all households in Tract 161. During the second week of June 1966, households in the entire tract were enumerated, and thus a list was obtained describing every dwelling unit by address, floor, and apartment number.

Counting households in apartment buildings was easy; the enumerators merely counted mailboxes or doorbells. However, in many brownstone houses it was impossible to ascertain the number of households from the doorbells or mailboxes, and often it was difficult to tell whether stores, garages, or warehouses were inhabited as dwellings. In these circumstances residents or building superintendents were questioned.

The usual approach was to ring any doorbell vigorously; if no one answered, a different bell was tried. When someone responded, the staff member asked the number of apartments in that building. After getting the total, the layout on each floor would be reviewed, thus finding the number on each floor and checking the total as well. Initially, the connection of the project with the Public Health Service was mentioned; but some people thought a check was being made for building code violations, so staff members identified themselves only as people from Columbia University who were taking a census. In Park Slope, as on the Bowery, the university proved to be a rather neutral affiliation.

Children were helpful in providing entry, but their counting was not very reliable. Neighbors could occasionally be relied upon, particularly on streets where buildings were not greatly subdivided; however, most neighbors and even many tenants could not provide the desired information. If an informant was uncertain or inconsistent, the enumerator sought the landlord or superintendent, who often lived in the building or next door.

Errors were likeliest in boarding houses. Many of them are listed with the city building department as one- or two-family houses and are operating in violation of the law. Whenever interviewers were told that a place was a one- or two-family house, they would blandly ask again how many apartments or rooms were on each floor and point out that they were not concerned with violations. Several times additional information was received this way. Also, the number of doorbells and mailboxes would be checked.

Altogether, information about the number of households per building was obtained in all but fifteen of the brownstones. For these fifteen, the number of households was estimated on the basis of information about similar buildings.

The enumeration showed a total of 1863 households in Tract 161, compared with a total of 1578 in 1960. The disparity between the two figures probably reflects underenumeration in 1960 rather than recent subdivision of units. A sample was drawn by numbering the 1863 households serially and then selecting 500 of them with the aid of a table of random numbers.

In an attempt to approximate the age distribution of the skid row population, age 35 was arbitrarily set as the lower age limit for control-group respondents. The control group consisted of all men aged 35 and over residing in the sampled households.

Interviewers were required to describe floor plans on every floor they visited. When a description conflicted with the enumeration, it was rechecked. Sometimes the households on a floor were not enumerated correctly.

In the sample there were 30 cases of overdetermination, that is, enumerated households that proved to be nonexistent. These were treated like vacant households. There were about the same number of cases of underenumeration, where the sample household turned out to be two or more households. There were dealt with by arbitrarily taking the first apartment on the floor or in the building. Thus, if an interviewer found that two or more floors supposedly occupied by one family were really occupied by more, he took the first household on the top floor. Summary statistics on the Park Slope sample are found in Table I-3.

Approaching the men. Interviewers had to gain entry into the building, locate the correct apartment, learn if any men aged 35 or over lived there, and, if so, arrange interviews. The usual approach was to explain to the person who answered the door that a survey of the neighborhood was being conducted and to ask for the ages of the men who lived there; when a positive report was obtained, an attempt was made to get an interview or to make an appointment for one.

In Park Slope, lower-class respondents were interviewed outside of an institutional setting. Neither at Camp LaGuardia nor at the Bowery lodging houses did the staff have institutional sanctions to bring against the men, but the fact that the managers allowed interviews indicated that they were in sympathy with the project to some extent, and this undoubtedly had some influence on the respondents. In Park Slope there was no such institutional support. Rather, project members had to approach people in their homes and to justify the project to each of them individually. Further, in Park Slope there were severe problems of access. Interviewers found it hard to approach many apartments and rooms because they were on the

Table I-3

DISPOSITION OF PARK SLOPE SAMPLE

Sample drawn	504 households
Disqualified	324
Nonexistent households (overenumerations)	30
Vacant households	56
Households with no men aged 35 and over	238
Total effective sample	180 households
Households with more than one respondent	0
Total effective sample	180 men
Refusals	43
by nonrespondents or entry to household denied[a]	19
by potential respondents	24
Not interviewed for other reasons[b]	12
Usable interviews	125

a. These are households where the interviewer never confronted the potential respondent, either because the landlord or other tenants refused to admit him to the building (11 households), wife or other members of households refused on behalf of respondents (5 men), or where respondents refused to answer the door (3 men).

b. Includes potential respondents rarely at home (8 men), mentally retarded (1 man), overlooked due to clerical error (1 man), and unable to speak English (2 men).

upper floors of locked buildings. They often faced a protective landlord or landlady who refused to admit them at all.

Here are some examples of access problems taken directly from interviewer reports.

> "Italian family—woman answered door and refused violently, violently."

> "Old man in basement apartment was belligerent and threatening, would not let interviewer in house."

"Man who lives downstairs is the super, kind of crazy, yelled at interviewer to go away."

"Super, in basement, didn't and/or can't talk but he effectively signalled interviewer away—slammed door in his face—tried to have a tenant let him in, but that didn't work either."

"Lady wouldn't open door—said she was calling police—said people from Columbia were there before."

Man picked up empty garbage can and tried to throw it at two interviewers; he was screaming and carrying on."

"Woman answered basement . . . said we shouldn't bother her roomers; her roomers had asked her not to let anyone bother them."

"Interviewer had trouble with super in basement apartment. Man said if interviewer had no name to ask for [usually the name of a householder was not known] he should get lost. Said, 'Take a walk and don't ever come back.' "

One important difference between interviewing in the control neighborhood and in skid row is that for the skid row samples the interviewers had the men's names, while in Park Slope they merely had designated households. It would probably have been easier to gain access had the respondents names been known in advance.

Interviewing took only about a month on the Bowery, less than a month at Camp LaGuardia, but more than four months in Park Slope. Even excluding enumeration costs, Park Slope interviews were almost twice as expensive as interviews on the Bowery or at Camp LaGuardia.

The interview. Once contacted, Park Slope men were just as willing to be interviewed as skid row respondents; 49 percent of them were classified as frank and cooperative, 31 percent as average, 11 percent as compliant but uncommunicative, and 3 percent as resistant. (Four percent of the respondents were not evaluated by the interviewers.)

The length of interviews in Park Slope ranged from 25 minutes to four hours. The median was one hour. In 37 percent of the interviews, someone besides the respondent was present, usually his wife or children, but sometimes a friend.

In Park Slope about 15 percent of the interviews were interrupted, usually because the respondent had to leave to keep an appointment or to go to work. This figure is about twice as high as for camp interviews, but considerably less than for the Bowery, where more than one-fifth of the interviews were interrupted.

Refusals. In half of the cases where the interview was not obtained, the interviewer never met the respondent; he was refused by the landlady, the respondent's wife, or another tenant. Occasionally, the respondent watched the argument from an upstairs window, ignoring any comments directed at him. One respondent, after observing the interviewer through the window, ignored the ringing of the bell and continued to ignore the interviewer as he rapped on the window.

Park Slope men were more likely to refuse at first contact than were skid row men. About one-eighth of the Bowery men refused the first time interviewers approached them, compared to one-fifth of the Park Slope men. As in the skid row settings, an initial refusal was never taken as final, and the respondent was approached again. Sometimes many weeks elapsed between an initial refusal and the next contact. Often a different interviewer was substituted. Follow-up approaches were about as effective in Park Slope as on the Bowery; in Park Slope about one-third of the refusals subsequently consented to be interviewed, and the proportion of initial refusals later interviewed on the Bowery was only slightly smaller.

Park Slope respondents seemed to fear the confrontation with an interviewer more than skid row men. One Black man refused violently at first. Later, after he had been interviewed, he explained he had been certain that his landlord, who was prejudiced against Blacks, was trying to evict him. He had supposed that the interviewer was there to serve eviction papers. Another respondent insisted that he had a serious heart condition and would die under the strain of an interview. Several interviewers tried to reason with him, but it seemed useless. Later, one interviewer managed to win his confidence and obtain an interview, whereupon it became apparent that his heart condition was a hoax and that he was afraid of losing his welfare entitlement.

One interviewer who was particularly effective at converting refusals into acceptances described the problem and his solution to it in these words:

> In situations such as these it was vital that rapport be established with the respondent. This involved working the interview into a framework of casual conversation and creating an atmosphere with which the respondent was familiar or in which he was at ease. Finding the right conversational gambit was often a hit-or-miss proposition, but if it was successful the interview could often be obtained without further difficulty. In extreme cases it was sometimes necessary to invite the respondent to a nearby bar for a beer, or to bribe him with an offer of cigarettes. The relationship achieved through bribery was never an ultimate goal, but served only to provide an opportunity for more constructive rapport. Maintaining close rapport was also essential to the success of the interview. The informal friendly atmosphere which was often essential was usually very tenuous and fragile. If it was allowed to collapse the respondent often refused to continue the interview, and it was necessary to recreate the rapport before the interview could resume.

Interviewer supervision. The problem of interviewer supervision was more difficult in Park Slope. On the Bowery all of the respondents were concentrated in a few buildings, and supervisors knew where the interviewing was going on and could easily check on interviewers. Interviewers might move from lodging house to lodging house, particularly near the end of the interviewing program when there were only a few men remaining to be interviewed in each house, but supervisors could still locate the interviewers without much trouble. In Park Slope each interviewer had several apartment buildings or houses to visit each day, and there was no lobby or common interviewing location. Interviews took place in the respondents' apartments or rooms, and thus supervision was limited to the beginning and end of the workday. A church in the area allowed use of one of its rooms as an interviewing headquarters, where interviewers checked in and out and were instructed, but even with this office the supervision was more tenuous than in the other settings. Furthermore, interviewers had to travel more in Park Slope than at the camp or on the Bowery, and they perceived the interviewing situation itself to be more difficult. Consequently, when the project moved to the Park Slope area, turnover increased among the interviewing staff.

In summary, it appears that interviewing lower-class respondents is more difficult than interviewing homeless respondents. Despite the stereotype about suspicion, isolation, and the mind-your-own-business ethic of skid row, staff members found it much easier to approach men and gain interviews there than among lower-class respondents in Park Slope.

SURVEY METHODS IN PARK AVENUE

Universe and sample. It was anticipated that the high-income residents of the Park Avenue tract would be more difficult to confront initially than the low-income respondents in Park Slope had been. Not only are the Park Avenue apartment buildings protected by doormen, and the men themselves by secretaries and domestics, but their lives tend to be more scheduled, in the sense that they are unlikely to grant interviews if one does not have an appointment. Consequently, we decided that the procedure of sampling every *n*th household that had been used in Park Slope would not work in Park Avenue. Instead, it was felt that the interviewer always should have the respondent's name when he entered a building, and the potential respondent should be prepared for the interviewer's visit. After considering several alternatives it was decided that a directory of telephone numbers arranged by street address would be used in the drawing of the sample. Then each respondent was notified by mail that an interviewer would be telephoning him for an appointment. Because the interviewers had appointments, they did not have the difficulty entering buildings and getting past gatekeepers that had been experienced in Park Slope.

This sampling procedure had several drawbacks. For one thing, men without telephones or with unlisted telephone numbers were automatically excluded from the sample. It was reasoned that the number of persons in this economic bracket without telephones would be extremely small. As for the men with unlisted telephone numbers, since the purpose was to secure a control sample of wealthy men rather than an accurate description of the male population of tract 0082, the bias associated with missing them seemed preferable to the outlay in time and money necessary to obtain their names and addresses. Additional selective factors were introduced because most of the interviewing was done during the summer, when many Park Avenue residents were on vacation and out of the city. Interviewing began in May 1967 and was completed the following October.

In drawing the sample, the telephone company's serial directory was used; it lists names and telephone numbers by address rather than by alphabetic arrangement of surnames. From this list all names that were obviously female were deleted as were business telephones and listings for office buildings. Some buildings combined business and residential units, however, and for these only those listings were excluded that were clearly only business telephones. For example, if a listing for a physician specified that it was his office telephone, that number was excluded. However, if he was identified as a physician but there was no indication whether the listing was for his home or his office, his name was included in the universe. Many of the men had their professions listed after their names in the directory, for example, "arch" for architect, "art" for artist. If two professional men were found with the same telephone number, it was assumed that the listing was for a business office and it was not included in the sample.

Having deleted the female names and all of the office telephones that could be identified, there remained 1206 listings. These comprised the universe. From this total, 378 names were drawn in several stages, using a table of random numbers. The aim was to obtain about 100 completed interviews. Had the completion rate been higher, fewer names would have been drawn. As in the Park Slope sample, a lower age limit for potential respondents was arbitrarily set at age 35, thus assuring an age distribution fairly close to that of skid row men.

Of the sample of 378 names, 166 later were disqualified for various reasons. For example, some listings represented widows maintaining their husband's telephone listing, men under 35, or men who had moved from the neighborhood. Other disqualified listings were for professional offices that had not been identifiable in the directory and for women whose initials, rather than a complete first name, were listed. A few men were totally inaccessible because of senility or serious illness or because their telephones were never answered over a period of several months. After deleting these names, there were 212 potential respondents, of whom 104 were interviewed for a completion rate of 49 percent. The outcome of interviewer contacts with the remainder of the sample is summarized in Table I-4.

Almost all of the interviewing on Park Avenue was done by two experienced interviewers. Problems of interviewer supervision were minimal. Throughout the summer, letters were sent to potential re-

Table I-4

DISPOSITION OF PARK AVENUE SAMPLE

Sample drawn		378 names
Disqualified		161
Women	53	
Deceased	17	
Too Young	29	
Moved	18	
Offices	40	
Never an answer	4	
Total effective sample		217
Refusals		70
by potential respondents	53	
by nonrespondents	17	
Contacted but unable to interview		43
Busy	17	
Out of town, about to leave, or seldom in town	21	
Too old or too ill	5	
Total usable interviews		104

spondents, and they were then telephoned by the interviewers. Interviewers continued to call by telephone until they made contact with the respondent (or his representative) or until the interviewing was terminated. Refusals were contacted by telephone at least twice. In many cases the project director made a final call to men who had refused to see interviewers, but few changed their minds.

The interview. The average Park Avenue interview (median of an hour and ten minutes) was not as long as the typical Bowery interview (hour and a half), but slightly longer than the usual Park Slope interview (one hour). The range was about the same; on the Bowery the shortest interview was twenty-five minutes and the longest was three and a half hours; on Park Avenue the range was from thirty-five minutes to four hours. The intersample differences in duration of interviews are easily explained. Interviews on skid row were often lengthy because it took considerable time to build and maintain rapport with a respondent, and additional time was needed to explain questions to him or to repeat slowly and distinctly questions that he had not understood. In Park Slope the respondents were in somewhat better condition than the skid row men, and communication was easier. In terms of shared vocabulary and the respondent's alertness, communication was still easier among the high-income men. Other factors operated to reduce the length of the Park Avenue interviews. For one thing, many respondents were interviewed during working hours, and sometimes this limited the length of the interview. Also, both Park Slope and Park Avenue men tended to have less complicated work and migration histories than the skid row men.

On the other hand, rapport and ready communication combined to extend many of the Park Avenue interviews. The interview was more of a social occasion for the Park Avenue respondents than it had been for men in the other samples, and the interviewers were more likely to extend the occasion because they were more comfortable and entertained than they had been in Park Slope, where sometimes an interviewer reported that he couldn't wait to get out at the end of an interview.

Although a smaller proportion of interviews was completed among the Park Avenue men, respondent-interviewer rapport was better there than in the other samples. Perhaps that was because in Park Avenue, potential respondents with negative attitudes were better able to avoid the interviewers; they were approached by telephone and found it easier to refuse than did the Park Slope and skid row men, who were personally confronted by an interviewer. Furthermore, the interviewers, who were middle-class university undergraduates, were more comfortable when meeting with the high-income men than with low-income men. They rated two-thirds of the Park Avenue respondents as very frank and cooperative, one-fourth of them as average in attitude toward the interviewer, and classified less than one in ten respondents as compliant but uncommunicative (5 percent) and resistant (4 percent).

During about one-fourth of the Park Avenue interviews, someone besides the respondent and the interviewer was present. This proportion is somewhat lower than in Park Slope and the Bowery. The proportion of interrupted interviews was slightly higher in Park Avenue than in the other samples.

APPENDIX II

CAN YOU TRUST A HOMELESS MAN? A COMPARISON OF OFFICIAL RECORDS AND INTERVIEW RESPONSES BY BOWERY MEN *

The stereotype of the skid row man does not include the trait of honesty. In fact, one typology of skid row men includes a category of "tour directors" whose function it is to spin tall tales and deceive "outsiders" who visit skid row.[1] Moreover, the alleged desire for anonymity and isolation supposedly characteristic of skid row men makes validation of their responses to survey questions especially advisable.

Empirical studies of the validity and reliability of survey data [2] require sources of relevant information independent of the survey interview. Among such sources are official records,[3] subsequent interviews or other sections of the initial interview schedule,[4] observations of behavior,[5] and statistics on population aggregates.[6]

The tests of reliability and validity considered in this paper consist of comparisons between responses elicited by interview and respondents' records from the files of city agencies. . . . Two-thirds of the Bowery men and all Camp LaGuardia clients had had formal contact with the Municipal Men's Shelter, and hence, it was possible to compare interview data with the client records at the Men's Shelter and Camp LaGuardia.

VALIDITY AND RELIABILITY

A measure is *valid* if it measures what it is supposed to measure; it is reliable if independent but comparable measures of the same phenomenon yield similar results.[7] While the present analysis would usually be placed in the general category of validity studies, in actuality it is concerned with reliability, broadly defined. Some dis-

* By Howard M. Bahr and Kathleen C. Houts. Reprinted by permission of Columbia University Press from *Public Opinion Quarterly,* 35 (Fall 1971) pp. 374-382.

crepancies between official records and interviews may be considered invalidity, while others fall into the category of unreliability—two different measures of the same phenomenon registering different results because of imperfections in the measures rather than variations in the phenomenon being measured. Even when the official record and the interview response are in agreement, it may not be asserted that valid information has been obtained. Instead, it has merely been established that the two sources of data provide *consistent* information; biases in the same direction in both official records and the interviews would yield consistent yet biased information.

One way to avoid the mislabeling involved in calling validity reliability (or the reverse) is to discuss the extent of the *discrepancy* or disagreement between information from interviews and that obtained from other sources without making assumptions about which source is "correct" or which should be used as a standard. Where appropriate, this approach will be followed here.

SOURCES OF INCONSISTENCY

Factors that have been identified as affecting the extent of discrepancy between self-reported interview data and information from official records include the recency of the behavior in question, the social desirability effect, item complexity, and the rapport between interviewer and respondent. Recency is presumed to affect validity and reliability because a respondent is likely to remember current or recent events better than events in the more distant past. Moreover, the increased ambiguity necessarily associated with responses to questions about the past increases the opportunities for selective recall in a manner that enhances the congruity of a response with the respondent's present self-image.[8] As for the effects of item complexity, it is obvious that the greater the number of possible responses, the less valid any one response is likely to be. Social desirability effects refer to distortions related to the impressions the respondent wishes to make on the interviewer or misinterpretations of his own behavior that permit him to maintain or enhance a positive self-image and reduce cognitive dissonance.[9] Finally, the quality of the interaction between interviewer and respondent has been shown to affect response bias. In general, the assumption has been that the more freely information is given, the more valid it is.[10] However, there is some recent evidence that when interviewer and respondent share the same social status, high-rapport interviews may yield more biased results than low-rapport interviews.[11]

PROCEDURES

In the spring of 1966 interviews were conducted with 203 Bowery men and 199 clients at Camp LaGuardia. . . . After the interviews were completed, an attempt was made to evaluate the quality of the interview data by comparing them with records of the Municipal Men's Shelter. The name of each respondent was checked against the Shelter casefiles, and if that did not yield a record, possible alternate spellings were checked. Basic data for positively identifying a matching record were name, birthdate and birthplace, but sometimes even if one or more of these was discrepant, it was possible to match a Shelter record with an interview because of other similarities. Once a record was identified as belonging to a given respondent, his entire Shelter history was reviewed and information relevant to data obtained in the interviews was coded.

The analysis that follows is based only on those cases for which the relevant information is available from both interviews and Shelter records. Items in the interview schedule for which there typically were entries in the casefiles included respondent's name, year and place of birth, marital status, religious preference, education, veteran status, whether he had had contact with the Shelter in the year preceding the interview, whether he had ever been at Camp LaGuardia, and if so, the year he first went, the number of stays there, and the duration of his longest stay at the Camp. The interview schedule also contained an item in which the interviewer evaluated the "cooperativeness" of the respondent on a four-point scale ranging from "very frank and cooperative" to "resistant."

FINDINGS

Discrepancy rates (proportions of cases where interviews and casefiles yielded discrepant information) appear in Table II-1. There is

Table II-1

INTERVIEW-RECORD DISCREPANCY RATES FOR SELECTED VARIABLES, BOWERY AND CAMP LAGUARDIA SAMPLES

Variable	Bowery Discrepancy Rate		Camp LaGuardia Discrepancy Rate	
	%	N	%	N
Name	8	130	2	198
Year of birth	5	130	10	198
Place of birth	6	130	5	198
Ever stayed at Camp La Guardia	7	123	—	—
Ever married	8	121	7	188
Religious preference[a]	12	128	7	188
Veteran status	15	124	11	176
Ever received aid from Men's Shelter	20	123	—	—
Received aid from Men's Shelter during the past year	28	123	—	—
Education[b]	42	100	42	131
Number of separate stays at Camp LaGuardia[c]	49	39	35	197
Duration of longest stay at Camp LaGuardia[d]	59	56	30	197
Year first stayed at Camp LaGuardia[e]	69	36	50	177

a. Six categories: Protestant, Catholic, Greek Orthodox, Jewish, Other, No Preference.

b. Eight categories: 0, 1-2, 3-4, 5-7, 8, 9-11, 12, and over 12 years of schooling.

c. Three categories: 1, 2-4, and 5 or more times.

d. Six categories: 2 weeks or less, 3-7 weeks, 2-5 months, 6-11 months, 12-23 months, 2 years or more.

e. Camp records before 1950 were described as unreliable; accordingly, men who said they came before 1950 are not included in these figures.

considerable variation between items. The highest discrepancy rates (almost 70 percent) are for questions where the respondent had to remember a specific date, such as when he had first stayed at Camp LaGuardia. Lowest discrepancy rates are for "lifetime identity" items such as religious preference (6 to 12 percent) or whether the respondent had ever been married (7 or 8 percent). Comparisons with rates reported in other studies do not indicate that skid row men are more likely than other populations to give discrepant information; discrepancy rates ranging from 20 to 40 percent or more are common.[12]

The effects of recency are apparent in the figures in Table II-1. For example, only 28 percent of the Bowery men gave discrepant responses about whether they had received aid from the Men's Shelter in the past year, but 69 percent were discrepant in identifying the first year they had received such aid. A more definitive test of the recency hypothesis was accomplished by examining the number of discrepancies in respondents' identification of the year they first stayed at Camp LaGuardia as a function of the recency of that event. For the years 1961-66, 38 percent of the Camp residents and 57 percent of the Bowery men who had been at the Camp gave discrepant information about the date of their first stay there; for men who reported that they first stayed at the Camp between 1950 and 1960, the corresponding figures are 68 percent and 87 percent. Thus, the recency hypothesis receives support.

Turning to the item-complexity hypothesis, contrast (Table II-1) the discrepancy rate for whether or not a Bowery respondent had ever stayed at Camp LaGuardia (7 percent) with the discrepancy rates for the duration of longest stay (59 percent) or the number of separate stays at the Camp (49 percent). It is clear that the simpler the item, the greater the consistency between interview responses and official records.

Additional support for the item-complexity hypothesis was obtained by contrasting discrepancy rates on the same variable between men with "simple" histories and those with more complex patterns. For example, consider the variable "number of separate stays at Camp LaGuardia." Ignoring respondents who have never been there, the man with the simplest history is the one who has been to the Camp only one time. Each additional visit increases the complexity of his personal history and, thus, the probabilities of error in recall.

A cross-tabulation of interview responses and information from official records about the number of visits to Camp LaGuardia revealed that the proportion of discrepant responses varied directly with the number of visits to the Camp. Thus, for men who had been there only once (according to the records), the discrepancy rate was 10 percent or below; for those who were recorded as having been there from two to four times the discrepancy rates were 28 percent for the Camp LaGuardia respondents and 43 percent for the Bowery respondents; and for those listed as having been to the Camp five or more times, the discrepancy rate rose to 55 percent for Camp LaGuardia men and 76 percent for Bowery men.

The effects of social desirability were also apparent in the findings. Skid row men reflect the values of the wider society in placing a positive value on education. Often a skid row man will assert that he is "different" or better than the average skid row "bum," offering as evidence the fact that he "went to City University" or has some other educational experience that sets him apart. Skid row men also value personal independence, and those among them who have long histories of total dependence or who become clients of a place like Camp LaGuardia tend to be defensive about their dependence. Finally, skid-row men view military service in a favorable light, so that being a veteran is evidence that one is (or was) "a man." These values on education, independence, and military service are the basis for asserting that the social desirability hypothesis will receive support if interview-official record discrepancies tend to "favor" the respondent, i.e., if the responses in the interview suggest that one is better educated, has been less dependent, or has had more military service than the records indicate.

Record-interview matches on extent of education gave no evidence that skid row men were more likely to exaggerate their education to interviewers than to caseworkers at the Men's Shelter or the Camp. But findings about duration of dependency, as indicated by date of first arrival at Camp LaGuardia, did show evidence of social desirability factors influencing interview responses. Eighty-eight of the 177 respondents who reported to the interviewer that they had first come to the Camp in 1950 or later identified a different year as their first year at Camp than the records showed. Of these 88, 55 told the interviewer they first came to Camp at a later date than the records showed. The same pattern appeared among the Bowery respondents who reported they had been at Camp LaGuardia; out of 25 total discrepancies, 19 were cases where the respondent's statement to the interviewer put him at the Camp later than the Camp records showed.

As for bias in reporting veteran status, it may be recalled that 11 percent of the Camp LaGuardia men and 15 percent of the Bowery men had interview-record discrepancies on this item (see Table II-1). Among Camp respondents this 11 percent represented 19 cases; in 15 of these the discrepancy was in the "social desirability" direction. Among Bowery men the finding was the same: 16 of the 19 discrepancies are cases where the interviewer was told that the man was a veteran but his Shelter record contained contradictory information. It is probable that some respondents answered interviewers honestly but did not report their veteran status to representatives of the Shelter because of fears that if their eligibility for veterans' benefits were known, their chances for receiving assistance from the Shelter would be reduced. This type of bias and the desire to have a "heroic" history both operate in the same direction and combine to produce the apparent "social desirability" effects with respect to veteran status.

Finally, the effects of interview rapport may be assessed. The figures in Table II-2 seem to indicate that the nature of the item was much more important in determining the discrepancy rate than was the degree of rapport as perceived by the interviewer. There are variables where the low-rapport situation seems to produce higher discrepancy rates than the high-rapport situation, but in most cases the differences in discrepancy rates between low- and high-rapport situations are quite small. In contrast, the difference in discrepancy rates between complex and simple questions or between questions referring to recent events and those about more distant situations is very substantial. It is apparent that (1) the direction of discrepancy produced by high-rapport situations is not self-evident; there are times when increasing rapport will *increase* discrepancy; and (2) the amount of variation in response attributable to rapport (provided there is sufficient rapport to produce an interview in the first place) appears to be much less than that which may be attributed to the nature of the question.

Table II-2

INTERVIEW-RECORD DISCREPANCY RATES FOR SELECTED VARIABLES BY INTERVIEW RAPPORT, BOWERY AND CAMP LAGUARDIA SAMPLES

	Bowery				Camp LaGuardia			
	Rapport[a]				Rapport			
	High		Low		High		Low	
Variable	Disc.%	N	Disc.%	N	Disc.%	N	Disc.%	N
Ever stayed at Camp LaGuardia	3	62	9	54	—	—	—	—
Ever married	10	60	6	54	5	64	8	109
Religion[b]	9	64	13	55	6	65	6	110
Veteran status	16	62	15	53	10	63	11	106
Ever received aid from Men's Shelter	19	64	25	55	6	63	21	112
Received aid from Men's Shelter during past year	14	50	29	42	—	—	—	—
Education[c]	47	51	35	43	41	44	57	76
Number of separate stays at Camp LaGuardia[d]	58	19	38	16	36	69	36	119
Duration of longest stay at Camp LaGuardia[e]	59	27	59	29	34	68	29	121

a. Rapport was measured by the interviewer's evaluation of the respondent's attitude, with "high" rapport defined as a "very frank and cooperative" attitude and "low" rapport including the categories "average," "compliant but uncommunicative," and "resistant."

b. Six categories: Protestant, Catholic, Greek Orthodox, Jewish, Other, No Preference.

c. Eight categories: 0, 1-2, 3-4, 5-7, 8, 9-11, 12, and over 12 years of schooling.

d. Three categories: 1, 2-4, and 5 or more times.

e. Six categories: 2 weeks or less, 3-7 weeks, 2-5 months, 6-11 months, 12-23 months, 2 years or more.

DISCUSSION

To return to the question posed in the title of this paper: The evidence assessed here suggests the conclusion that homeless men who consent to be interviewed are no more likely to be consciously untruthful in replying to interviewers' questions than are members of most other disadvantaged populations. However, because they tend to be an aged and somewhat disoriented population, with unusually high rates of both physical and mental illness, their capacity to provide accurate responses seems especially sensitive to variations in the complexity of the information sought and the recency of the situation being recalled. Also, skid row respondents are influenced by social desirability considerations, but there is no reason to conclude that social desirability factors are either more or less influential in biasing their responses than they are among other populations.

The findings about the relative importance of rapport as compared with item complexity deserve comment. Rapport in the interview situation is one of those desirable goals for which the means of attainment are somewhat unclear and often largely beyond the researcher's control. On the other hand, the nature of his instrument is directly under his control, and the present findings suggest that the number of invalid responses can be reduced far more efficiently by greater scrutiny of the kind of question being asked than by lengthy programs aimed at producing "high rapport" interviewers. Sensitivity about respondent capabilities and the validity problems attending certain kinds of items, rather than sensitivity training for staff members, seems the appropriate practical goal.

Finally, some comments about the "recency" variable are in order. Characteristic of many aged persons is a high memory "loss" with respect to things in the recent past, yet clarity of memory about items in the far past. Accordingly, the present findings linking recency to response validity should not be interpreted as support for a disavowal of retrospective research among aged respondents. It may be that retrospective accounts of significant events in the distant past are quite reliable, while memory of fairly recent events is somewhat cloudy. Since information about a respondent's early history often is less readily available via other data sources than are accounts of his more recent years, recognition of the existence of a "memory curve" may operate to increase the researcher's confidence in certain types of "early" recall data while increasing his concern about the validity of reports about more recent behavior. Hopefully this concern will produce many "checks" of personal reports by the use of a variety of unobtrusive measures.

NOTES

1. Samuel E. Wallace, *Skid Row as a Way of Life* (Totowa, N.J.: The Bedminster Press, 1965), pp. 198-199.

2. See, for example, Carol H. Weiss, "Validity of Welfare Mothers' Interview Responses," *Public Opinion Quarterly,* 32 (Winter 1969), pp. 622-633; Aage R. Clausen, "Response Validity: Vote Report," *Public Opinion Quarterly,* 32 (Winter 1969), pp. 588-606; Don Cahalan, "Correlates of Respondent Accuracy in the Denver Validity Survey," *Public Opinion Quarterly,* 32 (Winter 1969), pp. 607-621.

3. Cahalan, *op. cit.;* Clausen, *op. cit.;* Barbara Kirk and Lynn Sereda, "Accuracy of Self-Reported College Grade Averages and Characteristics of Non- and Discrepant Reporters," *Educational and Psychological Measurement,* 29 (Spring 1969), pp. 147-155; C. Weiss, *op. cit.;* David J. Weiss and R. V. Davis, "An Objective Validation of Factual Interview Data," *Journal of Applied Psychology,* 44 (December 1960), pp. 381-385.

4. Examples of studies based on reinterviewing are Margaret B. Bailey, Paul W. Haberman, and Jill Sheinberg, "Identifying Alcoholics in Population Surveys," *Quarterly Journal of Studies on Alcohol,* 27 (March 1966), pp. 300-315; John P. Clark and Larry L. Tifft, "Polygraph and Interview Validation of Self-Reported Deviant Behavior," *American Sociological Review,* 31 (August 1966), pp. 516-523. Those based on intrainterview comparisons include John A. Buehler, "Two Experiments in Psychiatric Interrater Reliability," *Journal of Health and Human Behavior,* 7 (Fall 1966), pp. 192-202; Peter E. Nathan, Marcia M. Andberg, Peter O. Behan, and Vernon D. Patch, "Thirty-Two Observers and One Patient: A Study of Diagnostic Reliability," *Journal of Clinical Psychology,* 25 (January 1969), pp. 9-15.

5. Herbert H. Hyman, "Do They Tell the Truth?" *Public Opinion Quarterly,* 8 (Winter 1944), pp. 557-559; R. T. LaPiere, "Attitudes vs. Actions," *Social Forces,* 13 (December 1934), pp. 230-237.

6. Leonard V. Gordon, "Estimating the Reliability of Peer Ratings,"

Educational and Psychological Measurement, 29 (Summer 1969), pp. 305-313; Allan R. Starry, I. van W. Raubenheimer, and Abraham Tesser, "Stability Ratings as Classifiers of Life History Item Retest Reliability," *Journal of Applied Psychology,* 53 (February 1969), pp. 14-18.

7. Claire Selltiz, Marie Jahoda, Morton Deutsch, and S. W. Cook, *Research Methods in Social Relations* (New York: Holt, Rinehart and Winston, 1964), pp. 155, 166.

8. Cahalan, *op. cit.,* pp. 609-610.

9. Cahalan, *op. cit.;* Kirk and Sereda, *op. cit.;* G. J. S. Wilde and S. Fortuin, "Self-Report and Error Choice: An Application of the Error-Choice Principle to the Construction of Personality Test Items," *British Journal of Psychology,* 60 (February 1969), pp. 101-108.

10. Catherine Bentinck, Byron A. Miller, and Alex D. Pokorny, "Relatives as Informants in Mental Health Research," *Mental Hygiene,* 53 (July 1969), pp. 446-450.

11. C. Weiss, *op. cit.,* pp. 629-633.

12. See C. Weiss, *op. cit.;* Kirk and Sereda, *op. cit.;* Clausen, *op. cit.;* Cahalan, *op. cit.;* W. Bruce Walsh, "Self-Report under Socially Undesirable and Distortion Conditions," *Journal of Counseling Psychology,* 16 (November 1969), pp. 569-574; and W. Bruce Walsh, "Validity of Self-Report," *Journal of Counseling Psychology,* 14 (January 1967), pp. 18-23.

APPENDIX III

THE INTERVIEW SCHEDULE

Note: The interview schedule reproduced here is the basic version used with Bowery respondents. Certain minor changes in wording were necessary in adapting it for use in the other samples.

Columbia University
Bureau of Applied Social Research
Homelessness Project (1024)

INTERVIEW SCHEDULE

Name of Interviewer
Date of Interview
Location of Interview
Time Interview Began

1. How would you evaluate your general health at the present time?
   a. Excellent
   b. Good
   c. Fair
   d. Poor

2. Have you ever had any physical disability?
   a. No *(Skip to question 6.)*
   b. Yes

3. What? *(Describe)*

4. When did you first become disabled? *(Date or age)*

5. Has it interfered with your working at all? How?

6. When did you first spend a night in the Bowery area?

7. Had you ever spent a night on a skid row before that time?
   a. No *(Skip to question 10)*
   b. Yes

8. When was the first time? *(Date or age)*

9. Where?

10. Where were you living before you first came to the Bowery?
    a Manhattan *(Specify section.)*
    b. Brooklyn
    c. Bronx
    d. Queens
    e. Staten Island
    f. Outside New York City (Specify place)

11. Have you ever been away from the Bowery for a month or more since you started living here?
    a. No *(Skip to question 14)*
    b. Yes

12. About how many times?

13. Where did you go? Where else? (*Probe: Where else?)*

14. Are you working now?
    a. No
    b. Yes *(Skip questions 15 and 17; ask question 16.)*

15. When was the last time you worked at all—even if it was only for one day?

16. What did (do) you do? *(Record job title, description of duties, and type of business or industry.)*

17. How long did you work at that place?

18. How often do you read a newspaper?

19. About how often do you go someplace off the Bowery?
    a. Every day
    b. A few times a week
    c. Several times a month
    d. Once a month or less

20. About how many hours a day do you watch television?

21. About how many movies have you seen in the past month?

22. About how many people would you say you had conversations with yesterday?

23. Are there certain men you often hang around with?
    a. No *(Skip to question 31.)*
    b. Yes

24. Do you usually see these men together in a group or do you see them separately?
    a. Separately *(Skip to question 31.)*
    b. Both; sometimes in a group, sometimes separately
    c. In a group

25. Where does the group usually get together?

26. When was the last time you got together with the group? *(If more than one month ago, skip to question 28.)*

27. How many times in the past month have you been with the group?

28. What sorts of things do you usually do together? Anything else?

29. About how long has it been since you first began getting together with this group?

30. About how many regular members does the group have? *(Record the answer verbatim; do not probe for the exact answer.)*

31. Have you ever voted in an election? (Any kind of local, state, or national election.)
    a. No *(Skip to question 33.)*
    b. Yes

32. When was the last time you voted? *(Date)*

33. In regard to politics, do you consider yourself a Republican, a Democrat, an Independent, or do you not have a preference?
    a. Republican
    b. Democrat
    c. Independent
    d. Other *(Specify)*
    e. No preference

34. Have you ever attended church or synagogue services, either as a child or an adult? *(Do not include attendance at mission services.)*
    a. No *(Skip to question 52.)*
    b. Yes

35. What is your religious preference?
    a. Protestant: What denomination?
    b. Catholic
    c. Greek or Russian Orthodox
    d. Jewish
    e. Other *(Specify) (Skip to question 38.)*
    f. No preference *(Skip to question 38.)*

36. *(If Catholic or Greek or Russian Orthodox)* Did you take first communion?
    (If Protestant) Were you ever confirmed, or baptized at any time besides at birth?

(If Jewish) Were you ever Bar Mitzvahed? *(Skip to question 38.)*
a. No *(Skip to question 38.)*
b. Yes

37. At what age?

38. Do you recall how old you were the *first* time you went?

39. When was the *last* time you went? *(Date or age)*

40. Has there ever been a time, from your childhood until now, when you went to church regularly—say, almost every week?
    a. No *(Ask question 41, then skip to question 46.)*
    b. Yes *(Skip to question 42.)*

41. Could you give me a general idea about how much you have attended church throughout your life? *(Probe for changes.)*

42. How old were you when you first began to go that often?

43. How long did that last?

44. Was there another time after that when you went almost every week?
    a. No
    b. Yes *(Ask "when?" and "how long did that last?" for each period.)*

45. Since then, how often have you gone? *(Probe for changes.)*

46. Did you ever have any special duties or positions in the church (such as committee member, elder, choir boy, or altar boy)?
    a. No *(Skip to question 49.)*
    b. Yes

47. What did you do?

48. When was that?

49. As an adult, has your name ever actually been on the membership rolls of any particular church?
    a. No. *(Skip to question 52.)*
    b. Yes

50. When did you join? *(Date or age)*

51. How long were you a member? *(Probe: Any other churches? Ask questions 50 and 51 for each.)*

52. MIGRATION HISTORY. *(Fill out the chart [not shown] by asking the following questions:)*
    A. When were you born?
    B. Where was that? *(Record city and state or country.)*
    C. Who were you living with when you were young?
    D. How long did you live there?
    E. Did you live with the same people the whole time?
    F. Where did you live next?
    G. Who did you live with then?
    (Repeat questions D through G until the chart is filled out to the present time. Draw an arrow through the years for which the place of residence and/or the people lived with remain the same.)

    H. Were you ever in the Army or any other branch of the armed forces?
        a. No
        b. Yes *(Be sure to enter it on the chart.)*
    I. Did you ever live on a farm in any of these places?
        a. No
        b. Yes *(ask "which ones?" and circle those places on the chart.)*
    Notes on recording "Place":
    a. If R lived in more than one place during any year, the place where he spent the greater portion of the year is recorded. If he spent exactly six months in both places, draw a line through the box and record both places.
    b. If R moved at the end of a year and assumed permanent residence in the place to which he moved, draw a line

through the year in which he moved and indicate the month in which he moved.

c. If R worked as a sailor and shipped out from New York City for several years, indicate "shipping out from New York." Do not bother to record where he lived between stints at sea. However, if his home base changes, do indicate that change.

d. The different boroughs of New York City, the Bowery, Camp LaGuardia, the Army or Navy, and prison are each considered one "place."

Notes on recording "Persons Lived With":

a. If R says that he lived with his family, ask specifically which members of the family that includes.

b. The standard abbreviations are: M = mother, F = father, S = sister(s), B = brother(s), W = wife, C = child(ren), E = extended family (all other relatives, e.g., aunts, uncles, cousins, grandparents).

c. IF R lived at a lodging house or hotel, record "O" or ALONE.

53. *(Fill out the chart, a sample of which is given below, by asking the following questions.)*

A. When you were living in (each place mentioned on the MIGRATION HISTORY chart),

B. Did you used to see any of your relatives or family (besides the ones you were living with)? (your wife's relatives or family)?

C. Which ones?

D. About how often?

Place	No	Yes	Who?	About how often?

54. JOB HISTORY. *(Fill out the chart [not shown] by asking the following questions:)*

A. What was your first job? *(Record job title and/or descrip- of duties.)*

B. What type of business was that in?

C. Where were you working? *(Record city and state or country).*
D. When did you start doing that kind of work? *Date or age)*
E. When did you stop doing that kind of work *(Date or age)*
F. About how much of the time were you working?
G. How many hours a day did you work?
H. How many days a week did you work?
I. About how much did it pay?
J. About how many different employers did you have?
K. What did you do next?

(Repeat questions B through K until all jobs have been recorded up to the present one.)

Notes on recording job history:

a. Do not record a job that lasted less than a month unless it was part of a series of short term jobs covering a period of time longer than one month. For example, if he had several jobs as a dishwasher "on and off" for four months, include that; but don't bother to write down that he had one job as a dishwasher for a week before getting a steady job.
b. A series of jobs at the same occupation should be combined in one row. This should always be done when the occupation involves SPORADIC work. The difference between SPORADIC WORK AND STEADY WORK lies in the length of time the employer intends to keep the man. Men who do sporadic work are hired for definite periods of time —a day, a season, until the boat docks again—whereas those with steady jobs are hired for indefinite periods of time. Occupations which usually involve sporadic work include seaman, lumberman, railroad worker, construction worker; all kinds of spot jobs like loading trucks and washing dishes; and seasonal jobs.
c. If R's pay changed while at the same job, record beginning and end pay by drawing a line through the appropriate box.
d. If R mentions that he was unemployed for a period between jobs record that as if it were a job, getting information about location and the dates or ages.
e. Be sure to enter R's current or last job.

55. Between jobs, were you ever unemployed for six months or more?
    a. No
    b. Yes *(Ask "when?" (Dates or ages) and "how long?")*

56. Did you ever have any men under your supervision?
    a. No *(Skip to question 58.)*
    b. Yes

57. Which jobs?

58–65. Let me list a few kinds of organizations, thinking of the time since you left school, I want to know if you have ever been a member or if you've ever had anything to do with them, even if you weren't a member. *(Enter the names of the organizations on the Organization Charts, below.)*

58. Any church groups or clubs?
    a. No
    b. Yes

59. Any fellowship organizations, like the Elks, the Rotary, the Veterans of Foreign Wars, the American Legion, and so on?
    a. No
    b. Yes

60. Any unions?
    a. No
    b. Yes

61. Any recreational groups like a ball team, a poker club, a bowling league, the YMCA?
    a. No
    b. Yes

62. Any political organizations or action groups?
    a. No
    b. Yes

63. Any music groups or other hobby groups?
    a. No
    b. Yes

64. Any community or neighborhood organizations?
    a. No
    b. Yes

65. Any other groups you haven't mentioned yet?
    a. No
    b. Yes

66. ADULT ORGANIZATION CHART. *(Ask the following questions for each organization mentioned in the answers to questions 58 through 65.)*
    A. Name of the organization
    B. Was your name on the membership list?
        a. No *(Ask questions C and D, then skip to question G.)*
        b. Yes *(Skip to question E.)*
    C. When did you start taking part in this organization? *(Date or R's age)*
    D. How long did you take part in it?
    E. When did you join this organization *(Date or R's age)*
    F. How long were you a member?
    G. How often did you take part in the activities?
    H. Did you have any special positions or duties?
        a. No
        b. Yes *(Specify)*

67. Have you ever been married?
    a. No *(Skip to question 90.)*
    b. Yes

68. Have you been married more than once?
    a. No *(Skip to question 70.)*
    b. Yes

69. How many times?
    (Ask questions 70-89 for first marriage and repeat for each subsequent marriage)

70. What year were you married (for the [first, second] time)? *(Year or R's age)*

71. How many grades of school did your (first, second) wife complete?
    a. Some grade school
    b. Completed grade school
    c. Some high school (9-11 grades)
    d. Completed high school
    e. Some college

72. Did your (first, second) wife ever work outside the home while you were living together?
    a. No *(Skip to question 75.)*
    b. Yes

73. How many years did she work? *(Dates)*

74. In general, was that full-time or part-time?
    a. Full-time
    b. Part-time
    c. Other *(Specify)*

75. Did you have any children by this marriage? *(If R reports stepchildren note it but do not count them as "children by this marriage.")*
    a. No *(Skip to question 77.)*
    b. Yes

76. How many?

77. Did you and your (first, second) wife ever go to church together?
    a. No
    b. A few times
    c. Often

78. Did you and your (first, second) wife ever take part together in any organizations such as ....? *(Name the or-*

ganizations R has belonged to; if none, say:) Such as the ones we talked about before?

a. No
b. Yes *(Ask "which ones?")*

79–85. Here are some things husbands and wives often have differences of opinion about. Would you tell me which ones were ever problems in your (first, second) marriage? *(Check appropriate boxes for "rarely a problem" or "often a problem.")*

79. Did your wife think you were away from home too much?

80. Did she nag too much?

81. Did she drink too much?

82. Did you disagree about how much to see her relatives?

83. Did she think you drank too much?

84. Did you disagree about whose friends to see?

85. Were there other important problems in your marriage? What were they? *(Specify)*

86. When did you and your (first, second) wife stop living together? *(Date or R's age)*

87. How did the marriage end? *(Probe if necessary.)*
(If NO to question 75 (". . . any children?"), skip to question 89.)

88. After the marriage ended, did you help with the support of the children?
a. No
b. Yes *(Ask: "for how long?")*

89. When did you last see your wife? *(Year or R's age)*

90. Have you ever lived with a woman as if you were married?
   a. No *(Skip to question 107.)*
   b. Yes *(Ask "When was that?" and "How long?" for each woman lived with. Probe: Any other times?)*

91. What year did you begin living with this woman? *(Year or age)*

92. Did she ever work outside the home while you were living together?
   a. No *(Skip to question 95.)*
   b. Yes

93. How many years did she work? *(Dates)*

94. In general, was that full-time or part-time?
   a. Full-time
   b. Part-time
   c. Other *(Specify)*

95. Did you and this woman have any children?
   a. No *(Skip to question 97.)*
   b. Yes

96. How many?

97–103. Here are some things men and women often have differences of opinion about. Would you tell me which ones were ever problems while you were living with this woman? *(Check appropriate boxes for "rarely a problem" or "often a problem.")*

97. Did she think you were away from home too much?

98. Did she nag too much?

99. Did she drink too much?

100. Did you disagree about how much to see her relatives?

101. Did she think you drank too much?

102. Did you disagree about whose friends to see?

103. Were there any other important problems while you were living together? What were they? *(Specify)*

104. When did you stop living together? *(Date or age)*

105. How did it happen that you stopped living together? *(Probe, if necessary.)*

106. After you stopped living with her, did you help with the support of the children?
   a. No
   b. Yes *(Ask "For how long?")*

107. Do you frequently see any of your relatives or family, other than those you are living with?
   a. No *(Ask question 108, then skip to question 110.)*
   b. Yes *(Skip to question 109.)*

108. When was the last time you saw any relatives or family?

109. Who? and How often? Any others?

110. Do you have any close friends here in the city, other than those you are living with? *(If necessary, add: I mean particular people who know you well, whom you see often, and whom you do lots of things with?*
   a. No *(Skip to question 117.)*
   b. Yes

111. Thinking of the person who you would call your closest friend, when did you last see this person?

112. Where does he live?
   a. On the Bowery
   b. Near the Bowery (within walking distance)
   c. Elsewhere in the city

113. How often do you see this person?

114. How long have you known this person?

115. What sorts of things do you do together? *(Probe: Anything else?)*

116. About how many close friends like this do you have now in New York City?

117. About how many men who live in this neighborhood do you know by name?
   a. None
   b. 1 to 5 men
   c. 6 to 10 men
   d. 11 to 20 men
   e. 21 to 40 men
   f. More than 40 men

118. Would you like to know more? *(Record comments.)*
   a. No
   b. Yes

119. Have you ever been a registered member of any political party?
   a. No *(Skip to question 121.)*
   b. Yes

120. How long were you a registered member? When? *(Probe: "Ever before that? When?")*

121. If a group of people who live in this area got together and formed an organization to petition the city government, trying to get better conditions and services for the people living here, do you think you would join it?
   a. No
   b. Yes *(Skip to question 123.)*

122. Whether you joined or not, would you support such an organization?

a. No
b. Yes

123. Do you think that the activities of such an organization could actually improve the situation of the men who live here? *(Record comments.)*
   a. No
   b. Yes

124. Here are some things that men often talk about. I'm interested in what you usually talk about when you and your acquaintances get into conversations. As I mention each item, try to tell me if it is something you talk about very often, sometimes, or almost never.
   A. Money and financial problems
   B. Drinking
   C. Sports
   D. Politics
   E. Sex
   F. Jobs
   G. Religion
   H. Plans for the future
   I. People you know in common
   J. Your families
   K. Improvements needed in this area

   I'd like to know a little about the experiences you had when you were young.

125. What were your parents' religions?
   A. Mother
      a. None
      b. Protestant denomination
      c. Catholic
      d. Greek or Russian Orthodox
      e. Jewish
      f. Other *(Specify)*
   B. Father
      a. None

b. Protestant denomination
c. Catholic
d. Greek or Russian Orthodox
e. Jewish
f. Other *(Specify)*

126. What countries did your parents' families come from? *(For American Negroes, do not ask; for Whites, do not accept "United States.")*
A. Father's family
B. Mother's family

127. Was your father born in the U.S.?
a. No
b. Yes

128. Was your mother born in the U.S.?
a. No
b. Yes

129. Enter race of respondent
a. Negro
b. White
c. Other *(Specify)*

130. Did your parents always live together until you were 16 years old?
a. No
b. Yes *(Skip to question 133.)*

131. What was the reason?
a. Mother died
b. Father died
c. Other *(Specify)*

132. How old were you then?

133. What was your father's occupation? *(Specify duties and type of business.)*

134. What was your father's main occupation when you took your first full-time job? *(Specify duties and type of business.)*

135. Did your mother work outside the home while you were a boy?
   a. No
   b. Yes

136. Did either of your parents have any special positions in a church?
   a. No
   b. Yes *(Skip to question 138.)*

137. Did they attend church frequently?
   a. No
   b. Yes

138. Were they active in any organizations? *(Record comments.)*
   a. No
   b. Yes

139. Did your parents ever invite their friends over to your house?
   a. No *(Skip to question 141.)*
   b. Yes

140. Would you say at least once a month, or was it less often than that?
   a. Once a month
   b. Less

141. Was your father ever unemployed for as long as a year while you were growing up?
   a. No
   b. Yes

142. How many brothers did you have? *(If NONE, skip to question 144.)*

143. How many older than you?

144. How many sisters did you have? *(If NONE, skip to question 146.)*

145. How many older than you?

146. How old were you when you started school?

147. How old were you when you left school?

148. How many grades did you complete?

149. Have you ever attended classes anywhere since that time (for example, night school)?
   a. No
   b. Yes *(Ask "From when to when?" and "What did you study?" for each period.)*

150. Thinking how well you did in school, would you say you were in the upper part of your class, the lower part, or somewhere in the middle?
   a. Upper
   b. Middle
   c. Lower

151. Why did you leave school when you did?

152. At that time, did you want more schooling?
   a. No
   b. Yes
   c. Didn't care
   d. Other *(Specify)*

153–162. As a boy or a teenager, were you ever a member or did you ever take part in: *(Enter names of organizations in the chart.)*

153. Any clubs or extracurricular activities in school?
   a. No
   b. Yes

154. Any organized athletic teams?
   a. No
   b. Yes

155. The Boy Scouts?
   a. No
   b. Yes

156. The YMCA?
   a. No
   b. Yes

157. A gang *(Specify by name.)*
   a. No
   b. Yes

158. A political club or action group?
   a. No
   b. Yes

159. A 4-H club, or any other outdoor or handicraft groups?
   a. No
   b. Yes

160. Any Boys' Club in the neighborhood?
   a. No
   b. Yes

161. Any church groups or clubs?
   a. No
   b. Yes

162. Any other groups or clubs you haven't mentioned yet?
   a. No
   b. Yes

163. YOUTH ORGANIZATION CHART. *(Ask the following questions for each organization mentioned in the answers to questions 153-162.)*

A. Name of the organization
B. Was your name on the membership list?
  a. No *(Ask questions C and D, then skip to question G.)*
  b. Yes *(Skip to question E.)*
C. When did you start taking part in this organization? *(Date or age.)*
D. How long did you take part in it?
E. When did you join this organization? *(Date or age.)*
F. How long were you a member?
G. How often did you take part in the activities?
H. Did you have any special positions or duties?
  a. No
  b. Yes *(Specify)*

164. When you were a teenager did you hang out with a group of other boys, or mainly by yourself?
  a. Alone
  b. With group
  c. Other *(Specify)*

165. When you were a young man, did you have any ambitions about what you wanted to be in life?
  a. No *(Skip to question 167.)*
  b. Yes

166. What did you want to be?

167. Did you take girls out before you were twenty years old?
  a. No *(Skip to question 169.)*
  b. Yes

168. About how old were you when you first started going out with girls?

169. Do you drink?
  a. No *(Probe, "Not at all?" and if the answer is NO, skip to question 189 and questions for ABSTAINER* [*189-196*]).
  b. Yes

170. Do you drink the same way all the time, or do you ever go on benders or sprees lasting several days or longer?
   a. Same all the time
   (Skip to question 177 and ask questions for STEADY DRINKER (177-188), then skip to question 197.)
   b. Sprees or benders
   (Ask questions for SPREE DRINKER (171-176), then skip to question 197.)

171–176. SPREE DRINKER.

171. About how long do these sprees last, on the average?

172. About how many sprees or benders have you gone on in the past year?

173. When you're not on a bender, how often do you drink?
   a. Daily
   b. Few times a week
   c. Less

174. On the average day when you're not on a bender, about how much do you drink? *(Record the quantity [pints, glasses, etc.] of each kind or liquor [wine, whiskey, beer, etc.])*

175. How old were you when you first began drinking to this extent?

176. Do you consider yourself a heavy drinker, a moderate drinker, or a light drinker?
   a. Heavy drinker
   b. Moderate drinker
   c. Light drinker

177–188. STEADY DRINKER

177. How often do you drink?
   a. Daily

b. Few times a week
c. Less

178. On drinking days, about how much do you drink? *(Record the quantity [pints, glasses, etc.] of each kind of liquor [wine, whiskey, beer, etc.])*

179. How old were you when you first began drinking ____ of ____ per ___?

180. Did you ever drink more heavily than that?
a. No *(Skip to question 188.)*
b. Yes

181. Did you drink about the same amount consistently, or did you go on sprees for several days or more?
a. Same amount (steady) *(Ask questions 182-184, then skip to question 188.)*
b. Sprees or benders *(Skip to question 185.)*

182. How often did you drink?
a. Daily
b. Few times a week
c. Less

183. On drinking days, how much did you used to drink? *(Record the quantity [pints, glasses, etc.] of each kind or liquor [wine, whiskey, beer, etc.])*

184. How old were you when you first began drinking to this extent?

185. How long would these last, on the average?

186. On the average, about how many benders did you used to go on in a year?

187. How old were you when you first began drinking to this extent?

188. Do you consider yourself a heavy drinker, a moderate drinker, or a light drinker?
  a. Heavy drinker
  b. Moderate drinker
  c. Light drinker

189–196. ABSTAINER

189. How long has it been since the last time you had a drink?
  a. Never used to drink *(Skip to question 199.)*
  b. Number of years since last drink.

190. Until that time did you drink about the same amount consistently, or did you go on sprees for several days or more?
  a. Same amount (steady) *(Ask questions 191-193, then skip to question 197.)*
  b. Sprees or benders *(Skip to question 194.)*

191. How often did you drink?
  a. Daily
  b. Few times a week
  c. Less

192. On drinking days, how much did you used to drink? *(Record the quantity* [*pints, glasses, etc.*] *of each kind of liquor* [*wine, whiskey, beer, etc.*]*)*

193. How old were you when you first began drinking to this extent?

194. How long would these last, on the average?

195. On the average, about how many benders did you used to go on in a year?

196. How old were you when you first began going on sprees?

197. Have you ever gone to meetings of Alcoholics Anonymous?
  a. No

b. Yes *(Record this organization on the ADULT ORGANIZATION CHART [question 66.])*

198. Do you usually drink alone or with others?
   a. Alone
   b. With others
   c. Other *(Specify)*

199. About how much is your present monthly income?

200. What are the sources of this income? *(Exclude unemployment.)* *(One probe: Any other sources of income?)*

201. Have you ever received money from the welfare department of any community agencies either here in New York or elsewhere? *(Probe, if necessary: Old age assistance or home relief, for example?)*
   a. No *(Skip to question 204.)*
   b. Yes

202. When was the first time?

203. Have you received any of these payments in the last 12 months?

204. Have you ever gotten a room or meals from the MUNI or from shelter missions anywhere?
   a. No *(Skip to question 206.)*
   b. Yes

205. When was the first time?

206. Have you had any contact with the MUNI or other men's shelters or missions during the past 12 months?
   a. No
   b. Yes

207. Have you ever been arrested for being drunk or disorderly, or on any similar charge?

a. No *(Skip to question 210.)*
b. Yes

208. When was the first time?

209. About how many times in all?

210. Have you ever been arrested for anything else (not counting arrests for being drunk and disorderly)?
a. No *(Skip to question 213.)*
b. Yes

211. About how many times in all?

212. What for?
(Probe anything else?)

213. Have you ever heard of Camp LaGuardia?
a. No *(Skip to question 219.)*
b. Yes

214. What kinds of men usually go there? *(Record comments in order.)*
(If no GOOD points are mentioned: ask "Does it have any good points?")
(If no BAD points are mentioned: ask "Does it have any bad points?")

215. Have you ever been to Camp LaGuardia?
a. No *(Skip to question 219.)*
b. Yes

216. When was the first time you went there?
(Year or R's age)

217. About how many different times have you gone?
a. Once
b. 2 to 4 times
c. 5 or more times

218. What is the longest period of time you have stayed at the camp?

219–245.

Now, this section of the interview concerns a number of questions on which we would would like your opinions. With each statement some people agree and some people disagree. As I read each statement, will you tell me whether you *more* or *less* agree with it, *more* or *less* disagree with it, or if you can't decide one way or another. For example, here is this statement:

219. Most public officials are not really interested in the problems of the average man.

220. Sometimes I get restless because I can't express my real feelings when talking and doing things with others.

221. On the whole, I am satisfied with myself.

222. These days a person doesn't know whom he can count on.

223. At times I think I am no good at all.

224. Nowadays a person has to live pretty much for today and let tomorrow take care of itself.

225. I have found that just being your natural self won't get you very far in this world.

226. I feel that I have a number of good qualities.

227. In spite of what some people say, the lot of the average man is getting worse, not better.

228. I am able to do things as well as most other people.

229. I have found that more often than not, the rules in our world go against human nature.

230. I feel I do not have much to be proud of.

231. When I am around other people, I try to keep in mind that saying what you really feel often gets you into trouble.

232. If you don't watch yourself, people will take advantage of you.

233. I certainly feel useless at times.

234. Most people don't really care what happens to the next fellow.

235. I feel that I am a person of worth, at least on an equal plane with others.

236. We will always have wars, depressions, corruption, and prejudice, and there is no point in trying to do anything about it.

237. No one is going to care much what happens to you, when you get right down to it.

238. I frequently have to do things to please others that I would rather not do.

239. I wish I could have more respect for myself.

240. Human nature is fundamentally cooperative.

241. What others think I should do is usually not what I would really like to do.

242. Men who live on the Bowery are basically honest.

243. All in all, I am inclined to feel that I am a failure.

244. I have found that in order to get along in this world usually you have to put on an act instead of being able to be your real self.

245. I take a positive attitude toward myself.

246. Some people say that most people can be trusted. Others say that you can't be too careful in your dealings with people. How do you feel about it? *(Record comments.)*
    a. Most can be trusted.
    b. You can't be too careful.
    c. Uncertain

247. Which is a greater problem facing the nation: fighting communism or fighting poverty?
    a. Fighting communism
    b. Fighting poverty
    c. Uncertain

248. Would you say that most people are more inclined to help others or more inclined to look out for themselves?
    a. Help others
    b. Look out for themselves
    c. Uncertain

I have just a few questions about your present opinions, and then we'll be finished.

249. Where do you think you will be a year from now? *(If he answers nongeographically, e.g., "dead," record his response and then probe: "If you are living [or whatever else fits his earlier resuonse], do you think you'll be living here in this area, or somewhere else?")*

250. What do you feel are the most important things in life?

251. What kind of person rates highest around here?

252. What was the happiest period in your life? *(Be specific. Probe so that the period can later be identified by dates or ages. However, do not force the respondent to have a "happiest period," and if he reports that his entire life has been happy, record that.)*

253. When was the least happy period in your life? *(Same directions as for question 252.)*

254. Do you have any guiding principle (or principles in life? What is it?

TO BE COMPLETED AFTER THE INTERVIEW IS OVER.

255. Time interview ended.

256. Total length of interview.

257. Were any persons other than the respondent present?
   a. No *(Skip to question 260.)*
   b. Yes

258. Who?

259. What do you think the probable effect of their presence was?

260. Your evaluation of R's attitude
   a. Very frank and cooperative
   b. Average
   c. Compliant, but uncommunicative
   d. Resistant

261. Respondent's name and and address (or room number)

262. General comments

REFERENCES

Altus, William D. "Birth Order and Its Sequelae." *Science,* 151 (January 1966), pp. 44-49.

Anderson, Nels. *The Hobo: The Sociology of the Homeless Man.* Chicago: Univ. of Chicago Press, 1923.

———. *Homeless in New York City.* New York: Board of Charity, 1934.

———. *Men on the Move.* Chicago: Univ. of Chicago Press, 1940.

Angell, Robert C. "Preferences for Moral Norms in Three Problem Areas." *American Journal of Sociology,* 67 (May 1962), pp. 650-660.

Anonymous. "Do Americans go to Church?" *Catholic Digest,* 30 (July 1966), pp. 24-32.

Arnold, Martin. "West Side Asks Aid with Misfits." *New York Times,* March 16, 1965, p. 41.

Babchuck, Nicholas and A. Booth. "Voluntary Association Membership: A Longitudinal Analysis." *American Sociological Review,* 34 (February 1969), pp. 31-45.

Bacon, Selden D. "Inebriety, Social Integration and Marriage." *Quarterly Journal of Studies on Alcohol,* 5 (June and September 1944), pp. 86-125, 303-339.

Bahr, Howard M. "Birth Order and Failure: The Evidence from Skid Row." *Quarterly Journal of Studies on Alcohol,* 32 (September 1971), pp. 669-686.

———, ed. *Disaffiliated Man: Essays and Bibliography on Skid Row, Vagrancy, and Outsiders.* Toronto: Univ. of Toronto Press, 1970.

———. "Drinking, Interaction, and Identification: Notes on Socialization into Skid Row." *Journal of Health and Social Behavior,* 8 (December 1967), pp. 272-285.

———. *Homelessness and Disaffiliation.* New York: Bureau of Applied Social Research, Columbia Univ., 1968.

———. "Institutional Life, Drinking, and Disaffiliation." *Social Problems,* 16 (Winter 1969), pp. 365-375.

———. "Lifetime Affiliation Patterns of Early- and Late-Onset Heavy Drinkers on Skid Row." *Quarterly Journal of Studies on*

Alcohol, 30 (September 1969), pp. 645-656.

——— and Stephen J. Langfur. "Social Attachment and Drinking in Skid-Row Life Histories." *Social Problems,* 14 (Spring 1967), pp. 464-472.

Bailey, Margaret B. "Alcoholism and Marriage." *Quarterly Journal of Studies on Alcohol,* 22 (March 1961), pp. 81-97.

Bailey, Margaret B., Paul W. Haberman and Jill Sheinberg. "Identifying Alcoholics in Population Surveys." *Quarterly Journal of Studies on Alcohol,* 27 (March 1966), pp. 300-315.

Bakan, David. "The Relationship Between Alcoholism and Birth Rank." *Quarterly Journal of Studies on Alcohol,* 10 (December 1949), pp. 434-440.

Baker, F. and G. M. O'Brien. "Birth Order and Fraternity Affiliation." *Journal of Social Psychology,* 78 (June 1969), pp. 41-43.

Baker, Michael A. *An Estimate of the Population of Homeless Men in the Bowery Area, New York City, February 26, 1965.* New York: Bureau of Applied Social Research, Columbia Univ., 1965.

Banton, Michael. "Sociology and Race Relations." *Race,* 1 (November 1959), pp. 3-10.

Barron, Milton L. *The Aging American: An Introduction to Social Gerontology and Geriatrics.* New York: Thomas Y. Crowell, 1961.

Barry, H., Jr., H. Barry, III, and H. T. Blane. "Birth Order of Delinquent Boys with Alcohol Involvement." *Quarterly Journal of Studies on Alcohol,* 30 (June 1969), pp. 408-413.

Bassett, Lucy A. *Transient and Homeless Persons: A Bibliography.* Jacksonville: Florida Emergency Relief Administration, 1934.

Bauer, Catherine and Davis McEntire. *Relocation Study: Single Male Population.* Sacramento: Redevelopment Agency of the City of Sacramento, 1933.

Becker, Howard S. *Outsiders: Studies in the Sociology of Deviance.* New York: The Free Press, 1963.

Bell, Wendell and Maryanne Force. "Urban Neighborhood Types and Participation in Formal Associations." *American Sociological Review,* 21 (February 1956), pp. 25-34.

Bendiner, Elmer. *The Bowery Man.* New York: Thomas Nelson and Sons, 1961.

Bentinck, Catherine, Byron A. Miller and Alex D. Pokorny. "Relatives as Informants in Mental Health Research." *Mental Hygiene,* 53 (July 1969), pp. 446-450.

Berelson, Bernard and Gary A. Steiner, *Human Behavior*. New York: Harcourt Brace Jovanovich, 1964.

Blau, Peter M. "The Flow of Occupational Supply and Recruitment." *American Sociological Review,* 30 (August 1965), pp. 475-490.

———. "Social Mobility and Interpersonal Relations." *American Sociological Review,* 21 (June 1956), pp. 290-295.

Blau, Peter M. and Otis Dudley Duncan. *The American Occupational Structure*. New York: John Wiley and Sons, 1967.

Blumberg, Leonard *et al. The Men on Skid Row*. Philadelphia: Temple Univ. School of Medicine, Department of Psychiatry, 1960.

Bogue, Donald J. *Skid Row in American Cities*. Chicago: Community and Family Study Center, Univ. of Chicago, 1963.

Bonjean, Charles M. and Gary G. Vance. "Port Lavaca Community Survey: A Description and Comparison of Some Characteristics of Businessmen, Managers, and Workers." Austin: Department of Sociology and Hogg Foundation, Univ. of Texas, 1965 (mimeographed).

Bowery Project Staff. *Summary Report of a Study Undertaken Under Contract Approved by the Board of Estimate, Calendar No. 14, December 19, 1963*. New York: Bureau of Applied Social Research, Columbia Univ., 1965.

Breed, Warren. "Occupational Mobility and Suicide Among White Males." *American Sociological Review,* 28 (April 1963), pp. 179-188.

Buehler, John A. "Two Experiments in Psychiatric Interrater Reliability." *Journal of Health and Human Behavior,* 7 (Fall 1966), pp. 192-202.

Burchinal, Lee. "Characteristics of Adolescents from Unbroken, Broken and Reconstituted Families." *Journal of Marriage and the Family,* 26 (February 1964), pp. 44-51.

Button, Alan D. "The Genesis and Development of Alcoholism: An Empirically Based Scheme." *Quarterly Journal of Studies on Alcohol,* 17 (December 1956), pp. 671-675.

Cahalan, Don. "Correlates of Respondent Accuracy in the Denver Validity Survey." *Public Opinion Quarterly,* 32 (Winter 1969), pp. 607-621.

Caplow, Theodore. *Principles of Organization*. New York: Harcourt Brace Jovanovich, 1964.

———. "Transiency as a Cultural Pattern." *American Sociological Review,* 5 (October 1940), pp. 731-739.

———, Howard M. Bahr, and David Sternberg. "Homelessness." *International Encyclopedia of the Social Sciences,* 6 (1968), pp. 494-499.

———, Keith A. Lovald, and Samuel E. Wallace. *A General Report on the Problem of Relocating the Population of the Lower Loop Redevelopment Area.* Minneapolis: Minneapolis Housing and Redevelopment Authority, 1958.

Catholic Charities of St. Louis. *Older People in the Family, the Parish and the Neighborhood.* St. Louis: Catholic Churches of St. Louis, 1955.

Cauter, T. and J. S. Downham. *The Communication of Ideas.* London: Chatto & Windus, 1954.

Cavan, Ruth S., Ernest W. Burgess, R. J. Havighurst, and H. Goldhamer. *Personal Adjustment in Old Age.* Chicago: Science Research Associates, 1949.

Cavan, Sherri. *Liquor License.* Chicago: Aldine Publishing Co., 1966.

Chaves, Aaron D., Arthur B. Robins and Hans Abeles. "Tuberculosis Case Finding Among Homeless Men in New York City." *American Review of Respiratory Diseases,* 74 (December 1961), pp. 900-901.

Clark, John P. and Larry L. Tifft. "Polygraph and Interview Validation of Self-Reported Deviant Behavior." *American Sociological Review,* 31 (August 1966), pp. 516-523.

Clausen, Aage R. "Response Validity: Vote Report." *Public Opinion Quarterly,* 32 (Winter 1969), pp. 588-606.

Clinard, Marshall B., ed. *Anomie and Deviant Behavior.* New York: The Free Press, 1964.

Culver, Benjamin F. "Transient Unemployed Men." *Sociology and Social Research,* 17 (July-August 1933), pp. 519-535.

Cumming, Elaine and W. E. Henry. *Growing Old.* New York: Basic Books, 1961.

Davidson, Percy E. and H. Dewey Anderson. *Occupational Mobility in an American Community.* Stanford, California: Stanford Univ. Press, 1937.

Dumont, Matthew P. "Tavern Culture: The Sustenance of Homeless Men." American Journal of Orthopsychiatry, 37 (October 1967), pp. 938-945.

Duncan, Otis Dudley. "The Trend of Occupational Mobility in the United States." *American Sociological Review,* 30 (August 1965), pp. 491-498.

Dunham, H. Warren. *Homeless Men and Their Habitats: A Research Planning Report.* Detroit: Wayne Univ., 1953.

Eckland, Bruce K. "Academic Ability, Higher Education, and Occupational Mobility." *American Sociological Review,* 30 (October 1965), pp. 735-746.

Eister, Allan W. "Evaluations of Selected Jobs and Occupations by University Students in a Developing Country: Pakistan." *Social Forces,* 44 (September 1965), pp. 66-73.

Erbe, William. "Social Involvement and Political Activity: A Replication and Elaboration." *American Sociological Review,* 29 (April 1964), pp. 198-215.

Fichter, Joseph H. "The Profile of Catholic Religious Life." *American Journal of Sociology,* 58 (September 1953), pp. 145-150.

———. *Social Relations in the Urban Parish.* Chicago: Univ. of Chicago Press, 1954.

Gerard, H. B. and J. M. Rabbie. "Fear and Social Comparison." *Journal of Abnormal and Social Psychology,* 62 (May 1961), pp. 568-592.

Glock, Charles Y., B. B. Ringer, and E. R. Babbie. *To Comfort and Challenge.* Berkeley: Univ. of California Press, 1967, pp. 38-59.

Goffman, Erving. *Behavior in Public Places.* New York: The Free Press, 1963.

———. *Stigma: Notes on the Management of Spoiled Identity.* Englewood Cliffs: Prentice-Hall, 1963.

Gordon, C. Wayne. "Social Characteristics and Life Career Patterns of the Skid Row Alcoholic." *Institute on the Skid Row Alcoholic, Annual Conference.* New York: National Committee on Alcoholism, 1956, pp. 6-9.

Gordon, Leonard V. "Estimating the Reliability of Peer Ratings." *Educational and Psychological Measurement,* 29 (Summer 1969), pp. 305-313.

Greer, Scott and Peter Orleans. "The Mass Society and the Parapolitical Structure." *American Sociological Review,* 27 (August 1962), pp. 634-646.

Gusfield, Joseph R. "Occupational Roles and Forms of Enterprise." *American Journal of Sociology,* 66 (May 1961), pp. 571-580.

Guttman, Louis and Edward O. Laumann. "The Relative Associational Contiguity of Occupations in an Urban Setting." *American Sociological Review,* 31 (April 1966), pp. 169-178.

Harlow, Alvin F. *Old Bowery Days.* New York: Appleton-Century-Crofts, 1931.

Heller Committee for Research in Social Economics. *The Dependent Aged in San Francisco.* Univ. of California Publications in Economics, Vol. 5, No. 1, 1926.

Henshaw, Stanley K. *Camp LaGuardia: A Voluntary Total Institution for Homeless Men.* New York: Bureau of Applied Social Research, Columbia Univ., 1968.

Hodge, Robert W., Paul M. Siegel and Peter H. Rossi. "Occupational Prestige in the United States, 1925-63." *American Journal of Sociology,* 70 (November 1964), pp. 286-302.

Hollingshead, August B. and Frederick C. Redlich. *Social Class and Mental Illness: A Community Study.* New York: John Wiley & Sons, 1958.

Homans, George C. *The Human Group.* New York: Harcourt Brace Jovanovich, 1950.

The Homeless Alcoholic: Report of the First International Institute on the Homeless Alcoholic. Lansing: Michigan State Board of Alcoholism, 1955.

Hopkins, Terence K. *The Exercise of Influence in Small Groups.* Totowa, N.J.: The Bedminster Press, 1964.

Hunter, W. W. and H. Maurice. *Older People Tell Their Story.* Ann Arbor: Institute for Human Adjustment, Division of Gerontology, Univ. of Michigan, 1953.

Hyman, Herbert H. "Do They Tell the Truth?" *Public Opinion Quarterly,* 8 (Winter 1944), pp. 557-559.

Inkeles, Alex and Peter H. Rossi. "National Comparisons of Occupational Prestige." *American Journal of Sociology,* 61 (January 1956), pp. 329-339.

Jackson, Joan K. "Social Adjustment Preceding, During and Following the Onset of Alcoholism." Ph.D dissertation, Univ. of Washington, 1955.

———, and Ralph G. Connor. "The Skid Road Alcoholic." *Quarterly Journal of Studies on Alcohol,* 14 (September 1953), pp. 468-486.

Kammeyer, Kenneth. "Birth Order and the Feminine Sex Role

Among College Women." *American Sociological Review,* 31 (August 1966), pp. 508-515.

Keeping, E. S. "The Problem of Birth Ranks." *Biometrics,* 8 (March 1952), pp. 112-119.

Killian, Lewis M. and Charles M. Grigg. "Urbanism, Race and Anomie." *American Journal of Sociology,* 67 (May 1962), pp. 661-665.

Kirk, Barbara and Lynn Sereda. "Accuracy of Self-Reported College Grade Averages and Characteristics of Non- and Discrepant Reporters." *Educational and Psychological Measurement,* 29 (Spring 1969), pp. 147-155.

Klemmeier, Robert W., ed. *Aging and Leisure.* New York: Oxford Univ. Press, 1961.

LaPiere, R. T. "Attitudes vs. Actions." *Social Forces,* 13 (December 1934), pp. 230-237.

Laubach, Frank Charles. "Why There are Vagrants: A Study Based Upon an Examination of One Hundred Men." Ph.D. dissertation, Columbia Univ., 1916.

Lazerwitz, Bernard. "Some Factors Associated with Variations in Church Attendance." *Social Forces,* 39 (May 1961), pp. 301-309.

Lemert, Edwin M. "The Occurrence and Sequence of Events in the Adjustment of Families to Alcoholism." *Quarterly Journal on Alcohol,* 21 (December 1960), pp. 679-697.

Levinson, Boris M. "The Homeless Man: A Psychological Enigma." *Mental Hygiene,* 47 (October 1963), pp. 590-601.

———. "The Socioeconomic Status, Intelligence, and Psychometric Pattern of Native-Born White Homeless Men." *Journal of Genetic Psychology,* 91 (December 1957), pp. 205-211.

———. "Some Aspects of the Personality of the Native-Born White Homeless Man as Revealed by the Rorschach." *Psychiatric Quarterly Supplement,* 32, (Part 2 1958), pp. 278-286.

———. "Subcultural Studies of Homeless Men." *Transactions of the New York Academy of Sciences,* 29 (December 1966), pp. 165-182.

Lipset, Seymour M. and Reinhard Bendix. "Social Mobility and Occupational Career Patterns." *American Journal of Sociology,* 57 (January, March 1952), pp. 366-374, 494-504.

Lisansky, Edith S. "Alcoholism in Women: Social and Psychological Concomitants." *Quarterly Journal of Studies on Alcohol,* 18 (December 1957), pp. 588-623.

Locke, Harvey J. "Unemployed Men in Chicago Shelters." *Sociology and Social Research,* 19 (May-June 1935), pp. 420-428.

Logan, Thomas L. *Report on the Greater New York Gospel Mission.* New York: Welfare Council of New York City Research Bureau, September, 1931.

Lowell, Jon. "City Faces Skid Row Cluster, Council Told." *Detroit News,* February 24, 1967, p. 4-B.

Maccoby, Herbert. "The Differential Political Activity of Participants in a Volunteer Association." *American Sociological Review,* 23 (October 1958), pp. 524-532.

MacDonald, A. P., Jr. "Birth Order and Religious Affiliation." *Developmental Psychology,* 1 (September 1969), p. 628.

———. "Manifestations of Differential Levels of Socialization by Birth Order." *Developmental Psychology,* 1 (September 1969), pp. 485-492.

MacIver, Robert M. *The Ramparts We Guard.* New York: Crowell Collier and Macmillan, 1950.

Malzberg, Benjamin. "A Study of First Admissions with Alcoholic Psychoses in New York State, 1934-1944." *Quarterly Journal of Studies on Alcohol,* 8 (September 1947), pp. 274-295.

Mauss, Armand, unpublished table from the project "Mormonism and Urbanism." Research Program in Religion and Society, Survey Research Center, Univ. of California, 1970.

McCann, C. W. *Long Beach Senior Citizens' Survey.* Long Beach, California: Community Welfare Council, 1955.

McClosky, Herbert and John H. Schaar. "Psychological Dimensions of Anomy." *American Sociological Review,* 30 (February 1965), pp. 14-40.

McCook, John J. "A Tramp Census and Its Revelations." *Forum,* 15 (August 1893), pp. 753-766.

McCord, William and Joan McCord. *Origins of Crime: A New Evaluation of the Cambridge-Somerville Youth Study.* New York: Columbia Univ. Press, 1959.

McEntire, Davis. "Population and Employment Survey of Sacramento's West End." Sacramento: Redevelopment Agency of the City of Sacramento, California, 1952. Unpublished.

———. *Relocation Plan: Slum Area Labor Market, Sacramento.* Sacramento: Redevelopment Agency of the City of Sacramento, 1959.

McKinsey, John Paul. "Transient Men in Missouri." Ph.D. dissertation, Univ. of Missouri, 1940.

McTavish, Donald G. "A Method for More Reliably Coding Detailed Occupations into Duncan's Socio-Economic Categories." *American Sociological Review,* 29 (June 1964), pp. 402-406.

Merton, Robert K. "The Matthew Effect in Science." *Science,* 159 (January 5, 1968), pp. 56-63.

Merton, Robert K. *Social Theory and Social Structure.* New York: The Free Press, 1957.

Miller, Delbert C. and William H. Form. "Measuring Patterns of Occupational Security." *Sociometry,* 10 (November 1947), pp. 362-375.

Minehan, Thomas. *Boy and Girl Tramps of America.* New York: Farrar, Straus & Giroux, 1934.

Mizruchi, Ephraim Harold. *Success and Opportunity.* New York: The Free Press, 1964.

Moore, Robert A. and Freida Ramseur. "A Study of the Background of 100 Hospitalized Veterans with Alcoholism." *Quarterly Journal of Studies on Alcohol,* 21 (March 1960), pp. 51-67.

Nascher, I. L. *The Wretches of Povertyville: A Sociological Study of the Bowery.* Chicago: Joseph J. Lanzit, 1909.

Nash, George. "Bowery Bars." Project memorandum, Bowery project, Bureau of Applied Social Research, Columbia Univ., 1964.

———. *The Habitats of Homeless Men in Manhattan.* New York: Bureau of Applied Social Research, Columbia Univ., 1964.

——— and Patricia Nash. "The Non-Demanding Society: An Analysis of the Social Structure of a Skid Row." Paper read at the annual meeting of the Eastern Psychological Association in New York City, April 14, 1966.

——— and Patricia Nash. *A Preliminary Estimate of the Population and Housing of the Bowery in New York City.* New York: Bureau of Applied Social Research, Columbia Univ., 1964.

Nash, Patricia. "Homeless Men at Home." An unpublished project memorandum, Bureau of Applied Social Research, Columbia Univ., December, 1965.

———. "The Methodology of the Study of Bowery Lodging Houses." New York: Bureau of Applied Social Research, Columbia Univ., 1964.

Nathan, Peter E., Marcia M. Andberg, Peter O. Behan and Vernon

D. Patch. "Thirty-Two Observers and One Patient: A Study of Diagnostic Reliability." *Journal of Clinical Psychology,* 25 (January 1969), pp. 9-15.

Nisbet, Robert A. *The Quest for Community.* New York: Oxford Univ. Press, 1963.

Nye, F. Ivan. "Child Adjustment in Broken and in Unhappy Homes." *Marriage and Family Living,* 19 (November 1957), pp. 356-361.

Oltman, Jane E. and Samuel Friedman. "A Consideration of Parental Deprivation and Other Factors in Alcohol Addicts." *Quarterly Journal of Studies on Alcohol,* 14 (March 1953), pp. 48-57.

Orbach, H. "Aging and Religion: Church Attendance in the Detroit Metropolitan Area." *Geriatrics,* 16 (October 1961), pp. 530-540.

Palmer, Gladys L. *Labor Mobility in Six Cities.* New York: Social Science Research Council, 1954.

Parnes, Herbert S. *Research on Labor Mobility.* New York: Social Science Research Council, 1954.

Peterson, William Jack. *The Culture of the Skid Row Wino.* M.A. thesis, State College of Washington, 1955.

Peterson, W. J. and M. A. Maxwell. "The Skid-Road 'Wino.'" *Social Problems,* 5 (Spring 1958), pp. 308-316.

Pittman, David J. and T. Wayne Gordon. *Revolving Door: A Study of the Chronic Police Case Inebriate.* New York: The Free Press, 1958.

——— and C. R. Snyder, eds. *Society, Culture, and Drinking Patterns.* New York: John Wiley and Sons, 1962.

Platt, J. J., D. D. Moskalski, and R. Eisenmen. "Sex and Birth Order, and Future Expectations of Occupational Status and Salary." *Journal of Individual Psychology,* 24 (November 1968), pp. 170-173.

Potter, Ellen C. "The Problem of the Transient." *Annals of the American Academy of Political and Social Science,* 176 (November 1934), pp. 66-73.

Reiss, Albert J. Jr., ed. *Occupations and Social Status.* New York: The Free Press, 1961, pp. 263-275.

Reynolds, Lloyd G. *The Structure of Labor Markets.* New York: Harper & Row, 1951.

Rhine, W. R. "Birth Order Differences in Conformity and Level of Achievement Arousal." *Child Development,* 39 (September 1968), pp. 987-996.

Rice, Stuart A. "The Homeless." *Annals of the American Academy of Political Science,* 77 (May 1918), pp. 140-153.

Riis, Jacob A. *How the Other Half Lives.* New York: Hill & Wang, 1957.

Riley, Matilda White and A. Foner. *Aging and Society, Volume 1: An Inventory of Research Findings.* New York: Russell Sage Foundation, 1968.

Robins, Lee N. *Deviant Children Grown Up.* Baltimore: Williams and Williams, 1966.

Rogers, Thomas Wesley. *The Occupational Experience of One Hundred Unemployed Persons in Bloomington, Indiana.* Bloomington: Indiana Univ. Bureau of Business Research, 1931.

Rooney, James F. "Group Processes Among Skid Row Winos." *Quarterly Journal of Studies on Alcohol,* 22 (September 1961), pp. 444-460.

Rose, Arnold M. "Attitudinal Correlates of Social Participation." *Social Forces,* 37 (March 1959), pp. 202-206.

———. *Theory and Method in the Social Sciences.* Minneapolis: Univ. of Minnesota Press, 1954.

Rosen, Bernard C. "Family Structure and Value Transmission." *Merrill-Palmer Quarterly,* 10 (January 1964), pp. 59-76.

Rosenberg, Morris. "Misanthropy and Political Ideology." *American Sociological Review,* 21 (December 1956), pp. 690-695.

———. "Parental Interest and Children's Self-Conceptions." *Sociometry,* 26 (March 1963), pp. 35-49.

Schachter, Stanley. "Birth Order, Eminence and Higher Education." *American Sociological Review,* 28 (October 1963), pp. 757-768.

———. *The Psychology of Affiliation.* Stanford, California: Stanford Univ. Press, 1959.

Schneider, Louis, ed. *Religion, Culture, and Society.* New York: John Wiley & Sons, 1964, pp. 426-439.

Schooler, C. "Birth Order and Hospitalization for Schizophrenia." *Journal of Abnormal and Social Psychology,* 69 (November 1964), pp. 574-579.

Schubert, Herman J. P. *Twenty Thousand Transients: A One*

Year's Sample of Those Who Apply for Aid in a Northern City. Buffalo: Emergency Relief Bureau, 1935.

Scudder, Delton L., ed. *Organized Religion and the Older Person.* Gainseville: Univ. of Florida Press, 1958.

Selltiz, Claire, Marie Jahoda, Morton Deutsch, and S. W. Cook. *Research Methods in Social Relations.* New York: Holt, Rinehart and Winston, 1964.

Shapiro, Joan. "Single-Room Occupancy: Community of the Alone." *Social Work,* 11 (October 1966), pp. 24-33.

Smart, Reginald G. "Alcoholism, Birth Order, and Family Size." *Journal of Abnormal and Social Psychology,* 66 (January 1963), pp. 17-23.

Solenberger, Alice Willard. *One Thousand Homeless Men: A Study of Original Records.* New York: Russell Sage Foundation, 1911.

Spergel, Irving. *Racketville, Slumtown, Haulburg: An Exporatory Study of Delinquent Subcultures.* Chicago: Univ. of Chicago Press, 1964.

Spradley, James P. *You Owe Yourself A Drunk.* Boston: Little, Brown, 1970.

Srole, Leo. "Social Integration and Certain Corollaries: An Exporatory Study." *American Sociological Review,* 21 (December 1956), pp. 709-716.

Starry, Allan R. and I. van W. Raubenheimer. "Stability Ratings as Classifiers of Life History Item Retest Reliability." *Journal of Applied Psychology,* 53 (February 1969), pp. 14-18.

Stearns, A. W., and Albert D. Ullman. "One Thousand Unsuccessful Careers." *The American Journal of Psychiatry,* 105 (1949), pp. 801-810.

Straus, Robert. "Alcohol and the Homeless Man." *Quarterly Journal of Studies on Alcohol,* 7 (December 1946), pp. 360-404.

——— and Raymond G. McCarthy. "Nonaddictive Pathological Drinking Patterns of Homeless Men." *Quarterly Journal of Studies on Alcohol,* 12 (December 1951), pp. 601-611.

Sutherland, Edwin H. and Harvey J. Locke. *Twenty Thousand Homeless Men.* Chicago: J. B. Lippincott, 1936.

Sutton-Smith, B., J. M. Roberts, and B. G. Rosenberg. "Sibling Associations and Role Involvement." *Merrill-Palmer Quarterly,* 10 (January 1964), pp. 25-38.

Tenants' Relocation Bureau. *The Homeless Man on Skid Row.* Chicago: Tenants' Relocation Bureau, 1961.

Terry, Dickson. "Old Skid Row is on the Skids." *St. Louis Post-Dispatch,* March 14, 1965, p. 1-F.

Tibbitts, Clark, ed. *Handbook of Social Gerontology.* Chicago: Univ. of Chicago Press, 1960.

U.S. Department of Commerce, United States Bureau of the Census. *Alphabetical Index of Occupations and Industries.* Washington, D.C.: U.S. Government Printing Office, 1950.

———. "Lifetime Occupational Mobility of Adult Males, March 1962." *Current Population Reports.* Series P-23, No. 11, May 12, 1964, Washington, D.C.: U.S. Government Printing Office, 1964.

———. *1960 Census of Population, Subject Reports, Women by Number of Children Ever Born.* Washington, D.C.: U.S. Government Printing Office, 1964.

———. *U.S. Census of Housing: 1960, Vol. III, City Blocks.* Series HC (3), No. 274. Washington, D.C.: U.S. Government Printing Office, 1961, Table 2.

———. *U.S. Census of Population: 1960. Selected Area Reports. Type of Place.* Final Report PC (3)-1E, Washington, D.C.: U.S. Government Printing Office, 1964.

———. *U.S. Census of Population: 1960. Subject Reports. Marital Status.* Final Report PC(2)-4-E, Washington, D.C.: U.S. Government Printing Office, 1966.

———. *U.S. Censuses of Population and Housing: 1960 Census Tracts.* Final Report PHC (1)-104, Washington, D.C.: U.S. Government Printing Office, 1962.

Wahl, C. W. "Some Antecedent Factors in the Family Histories of 109 Alcoholics." *Quarterly Journal of Studies on Alcohol,* 17 (December 1956), pp. 643-654.

Wallace, Samuel E. "The Road to Skid Row." *Social Problems,* 16 (Summer 1968), pp. 92-105.

———. *Skid Row as a Way of Life.* Totowa, N.J.: The Bedminster Press, 1965.

Walsh, G. E., Deputy Assistant Commissioner of the Bureau of Institutional Services for Adults, City of New York Department of Social Services. Direct Correspondence.

Walsh, W. Bruce. "Self-Report Under Socially Undesirable and Distortion Conditions." *Journal of Counseling Psychology,* 16 (November 1969), pp. 569-574.

———. "Validity of Self-Report." *Journal of Counseling Psychology,* 14 (January 1967), pp. 18-23.

Warren, Jonathan R. "Birth Order and Social Behavior." *Psychological Bulletin,* 65 (January 1966), pp. 38-49.

Weinberg, Samuael Kirson. "A Study of Isolation Among Chicago Shelter-Home Men." M.A. thesis, Univ. of Chicago, 1935.

Weiss, Carol H. "Validity of Welfare Mothers' Interview Responses." *Public Opinion Quarterly,* 32 (Winter 1969), pp. 622-633.

Weiss, David J. and R. V. Davis. "An Objective Validation of Factual Interview Data." *Journal of Applied Psychology,* 44 (December 1960), pp. 381-385.

Welfare Council of New York City. *Homeless Men in New York City.* New York: Welfare Council, 1949.

Western Real Estate Research. *Analysis of the Sacramento Labor Market Area.* Sacramento: Redevelopment Agency of the City of Sacramento, 1957.

What To Do About the Men on Skid Row: Report on the Greater Philadelphia Movement to the Redevelopment Authority of the City of Philadelphia, Philadelphia: Greater Philadelphia Movement, 1961.

Wilde, G. J. S. and S. Fortuin. "Self-Report and Error Choice: An Application of the Error-Choice Principle to the Construction of Personality Test Items." *British Journal of Psychology,* 60 (February 1969), pp. 101-108.

Wilensky, Harold L. "Orderly Careers and Social Participation: The Impact of Work History on Social Integration in the Middle Mass." *American Sociological Review,* 26 (August 1961), pp. 521-539.

———. "Work, Careers, and Social Integration." *International Social Science Journal,* 12, No. 4 (1960), pp. 543-560.

——— and Hugh Edwards. "The Skidder: Ideological Adjustments of Downward Mobile Workers." *American Sociological Review,* 24 (April 1959), pp. 215-231.

Wiseman, Jacqueline P. *Stations of the Lost.* Englewood Cliffs, Prentice-Hall, 1970.

Wood, Margaret Mary. *Paths of Loneliness.* New York: Columbia Univ., 1953.

Young, R. K., D. S. Dustin, and W. H. Holtzman. "Change in Attitude Toward Religion in a Southern University." *Psychological Reports,* 18 (February 1966), pp. 39-46.

———. "How Important Religion is to Americans." *Catholic Digest,* 17 (February 1953), pp. 7-12.

OLD MEN DRUNK AND SOBER reports the results obtained in the first six years of the Columbia Bowery Project, a study of homelessness and disaffiliation conducted at Columbia University's Bureau of Applied Research. Its major theme is, How different is the skid row man? The research reported in this book seems to be the first large-scale survey of a skid row population to include control groups of non-skid row men. The populations studied include samples of lower- and upper-income census tracts in New York City. The major focus has been to compile and quantify the life histories of skid row men and to compare aspects of these life histories with those of other more "normal" populations in an attempt to produce both a systematic description of the Bowery population as a whole and an assessment of the sociological theories of the origins and concomitants of homelessness.

Contrasts among the skid row and control samples repeatedly show that the differences between upper-income and poor men are greater than those between skid row men and other poor men. The findings suggest that many of the supposed characteristics of skid row life are merely attributes of poverty and aging. The Bowery man's life history is less distinctive than formerly supposed with respect, for example, to marginality or undersocialization. There is no doubt that the skid row man is distinctly unhappy, but many of the indicators of unhappiness are linked to his present location on skid row and his identity as a skid row man.